War, Culture and Society, 1750–1850

Series Editors: **Rafe Blaufarb** (Tallahassee, USA), **Alan Forrest** (York, UK), and **Karen Hagemann** (Chapel Hill, USA)

Editorial Board: **Michael Broers** (Oxford, UK), **Christopher Bayly** (Cambridge, UK), **Richard Bessel** (York, UK), **Sarah Chambers** (Minneapolis, USA), **Laurent Dubois** (Durham, USA), **Etienne François** (Berlin, Germany), **Janet Hartley** (London, UK), **Wayne Lee** (Chapel Hill, USA), **Jane Rendall** (York, UK), **Reinhard Stauber** (Klagenfurt, Austria)

Titles include:

Richard Bessel, Nicholas Guyatt and Jane Rendall (*editors*)
WAR, EMPIRE AND SLAVERY, 1770–1830

Michael Broers, Peter Hicks and Agustin Guimerá (*editors*)
THE NAPOLEONIC EMPIRE AND THE NEW EUROPEAN POLITICAL CULTURE

Alan Forrest and Peter H. Wilson (*editors*)
THE BEE AND THE EAGLE
Napoleonic France and the End of the Holy Roman Empire, 1806

Alan Forrest, Karen Hagemann and Jane Rendall (*editors*)
SOLDIERS, CITIZENS AND CIVILIANS
Experiences and Perceptions of the Revolutionary and Napoleonic Wars, 1790–1820

Karen Hagemann, Gisela Mettele and Jane Rendall (*editors*)
GENDER, WAR AND POLITICS
Transatlantic Perspectives, 1755–1830

Ralph Kingston
BUREAUCRATS AND BOURGEOIS SOCIETY
Office Politics and Individual Credit, France 1789–1848

Kevin Linch
BRITAIN AND WELLINGTON'S ARMY
Recruitment, Society and Tradition, 1807–1815

Alan Forrest, Etienne François and Karen Hagemann (*editors*)
WAR MEMORIES
The Revolutionary and Napoleonic Wars in Nineteenth and Twentieth Century Europe

Marie-Cécile Thoral
FROM VALMY TO WATERLOO
France at War, 1792–1815

Forthcoming:

Leighton S. James
WITNESSING WAR
Experience, Narrative and Identity in German Central Europe, 1792–1815

Catriona Kennedy
NARRATIVES OF WAR
Military and Civilian Experience in Britain and Ireland, 1793–1815

War, Culture and Society, 1750–1850
Series Standing Order ISBN 978-0-230-54532-8 hardback 978-0-230-54533-5 paperback
(outside North America only)

You can receive future titles in this series as they are published by placing a standing order. Please contact your bookseller or, in case of difficulty, write to us at the address below with your name and address, the title of the series and one of the ISBNs quoted above.

Customer Services Department, Macmillan Distribution Ltd, Houndmills, Basingstoke, Hampshire RG21 6XS, England

The Napoleonic Empire and the New European Political Culture

Edited by

Michael Broers
Professor of Western European History, University of Oxford, UK

Peter Hicks
Historian, International Affairs Manager, Fondation Napoléon, France, and Visiting Professor, Bath University, UK

and

Agustin Guimerá
Researcher at the Consejo Superior de Investigaciones Cientificas, Madrid, Spain

First published 2012 by
PALGRAVE MACMILLAN

Palgrave Macmillan in the UK is an imprint of Macmillan Publishers Limited, registered in England, company number 785998, of Houndmills, Basingstoke, Hampshire RG21 6XS.

Palgrave Macmillan in the US is a division of St Martin's Press LLC, 175 Fifth Avenue, New York, NY 10010.

Palgrave Macmillan is the global academic imprint of the above companies and has companies and representatives throughout the world.

Palgrave® and Macmillan® are registered trademarks in the United States, the United Kingdom, Europe and other countries

ISBN: 978–0–230–24131–2

This book is printed on paper suitable for recycling and made from fully managed and sustained forest sources. Logging, pulping and manufacturing processes are expected to conform to the environmental regulations of the country of origin.

A catalogue record for this book is available from the British Library.

A catalog record for this book is available from the Library of Congress.

10 9 8 7 6 5 4 3 2 1
21 20 19 18 17 16 15 14 13 12

Printed and bound in the United States of America

Contents

Series Editors' Preface   viii

Acknowledgements   ix

Notes on Contributors   x

Map   xvi

Introduction: Napoleon, His Empire, Our Europe and
the 'New Napoleonic History'   1
Michael Broers

Part I   France, 1799–1814

Introduction   21
Michael Broers

1   Imperial France in 1808 and beyond   24
    Thierry Lentz

2   The Origins of the Napoleonic System of Repression   38
    Howard G. Brown

3   Policing, Rural Revolt and Conscription in Napoleonic France   49
    Alan Forrest

4   Small State, Big Society: The Involvement of Citizens in Local
    Government in Nineteenth-Century France   59
    Marie-Cécile Thoral

5   Napoleon as a Politician   70
    Peter Hicks

Part II   The Low Countries, the Rhineland and Switzerland, 1792–1814

Introduction   85
Michael Broers

6   The Napoleonic Civil Code: The Belgian Case   88
    Michael Rapport

7 The Dutch Case: The Kingdom of Holland and the
   Imperial Departments   100
   Matthijs Lok and Martijn van der Burg

8 Resistance against Napoleon in the Kingdom of Holland   112
   Johan Joor

9 A Tale of Two Cities: Aachen and Cologne in
   Napoleonic Europe   123
   Michael Rowe

10 The Swiss Case in the Napoleonic Empire   132
   Gabriele B. Clemens

   **Part III   Central and Eastern Europe: The Confederation
                of the Rhine, Westphalia and the
                Hanseatic Departments, Prussia**

Introduction   145
Michael Broers

11 Resistance to Napoleonic Reform in the Grand Duchy of Berg,
   the Kingdom of Westphalia and the South German States   148
   Ute Planert

12 Napoleonic Rule in German Central Europe:
   Compliance and Resistance   160
   Katherine Aaslestad

13 The Napoleonic Administrative System in
   the Kingdom of Westphalia   173
   Nicola P. Todorov

14 A Valorous Nation in a Holy War: War Mobilization,
   Religion and Political Culture in Prussia, 1807 to 1815 186
   Karen Hagemann

   Part IV   The Italian Peninsula and the Illyrian Provinces

Introduction   201
Michael Broers

15 The Napoleonic Kingdom of Italy: State Administration   204
   Alexander Grab

16 The Imperial Departments of Napoleonic Italy: Resistance and
   Collaboration   216
   Michael Broers

17 The Feudal Question in the Kingdom of Naples 227
Anna Maria Rao

18 The Illyrian Provinces 241
Reinhard A. Stauber

Part V   Spain and Portugal, 1800–14

Introduction 257
Michael Broers

19 The Monarchy at Bayonne and the Constitution of Cadiz 260
Emilio La Parra López

20 Popular Resistance in Spain 270
Jean-René Aymes

21 Imperial Spain 282
José M. Portillo Valdés

22 The New Spanish Councils 293
Marta Lorente

23 Political Paradoxes in Napoleonic Europe: The Portuguese Case 304
Fernando Dores Costa

24 Conclusion: The Napoleonic Empire in the Age of Revolutions:
The Contrast of Two National Representations 313
Annie Jourdan

Index 327

Series Editors' Preface

The century from 1750 to 1850 was a seminal period of change, not just in Europe but across the globe. The political landscape was transformed by a series of revolutions fought in the name of liberty—most notably in the Americas and France, of course, but elsewhere, too: in Holland and Geneva during the eighteenth century and across much of mainland Europe by 1848. Nor was change confined to the European world. New ideas of freedom, equality and human rights were carried to the furthest outposts of empire, to Egypt, India and the Caribbean, which saw the creation in 1801 of the first black republic in Haiti, the former French colony of Saint-Domingue. And in the early part of the nineteenth century they continued to inspire anticolonial and liberation movements throughout Central and Latin America.

If political and social institutions were transformed by revolution in these years, so, too, was warfare. During the quarter-century of the French Revolutionary Wars, in particular, Europe was faced with the prospect of 'total' war, on a scale unprecedented before the twentieth century. Military hardware, it is true, evolved only gradually, and battles were not necessarily any bloodier than they had been during the Seven Years' War. But in other ways these can legitimately be described as the first modern wars, fought by mass armies mobilized by national and patriotic propaganda, leading to the displacement of millions of people throughout Europe and beyond, as soldiers, prisoners of war, civilians and refugees. For those who lived through the period these wars would be a formative experience that shaped the ambitions and the identities of a generation.

The aims of the series are necessarily ambitious. In its various volumes, whether single-authored monographs or themed collections, it seeks to extend the scope of more traditional historiography. It will study warfare during this formative century not just in Europe, but in the Americas, in colonial societies and across the world. It will analyse the construction of identities and power relations by integrating the principal categories of difference, most notably class and religion, generation and gender, race and ethnicity. It will adopt a multifaceted approach to the period, and turn to methods of political, cultural, social, military and gender history, in order to develop a challenging and multidisciplinary analysis. Finally, it will examine elements of comparison and transfer and so tease out the complexities of regional, national, European and global history.

Rafe Blaufarb, Alan Forrest and Karen Hagemann

Acknowledgements

The editors wish to thank both Palgrave Macmillan and Dr Alexander Grab for their kind permission to reproduce the map on p. xvi. Thanks are also due to Professors Alan Forrest, Rafe Blaufarb and Karen Hagemann, the series editors of 'War, Culture and Society, 1750–1830'. They are also to be thanked for helping us to expand the scope of the book beyond its original incarnation, allowing us to bring in contributors we had originally wished to see included. On the production side, thanks are owed to Michael Strang, Ruth Ireland and, above all, Jenny McCall, who drove it forward when it mattered.

This volume had its origins in a conference held in Madrid in 2008, and without the efforts of all involved in that impressive event, this book may not have come to fruition. It was driven by the efforts of Agustin Guimerá and Albierto Junco of the Centro de Estudios Políticos y Constitucionale in Madrid, and financed through the generosity of Spanish Ministry of Culture, the Sociedada Estatal de Commemoraciones Culturales, and the Universidad de Madrid. The French Embassy in Madrid and the Casa Velazquez also played important roles, as did the Fondation Napoléon and its Director, Thierry Lentz.

The editors wish to thank all the contributors to the volume for their patience and goodwill, and above all for the quality of their scholarship, without which the enterprise would be pointless. Their work, which spans Napoleonic Europe, deserves to reach the wider readership this book is aimed at. It is also the editors' place to regret what we were not able to deliver. A chapter on the Duchy of Warsaw was promised but did not arrive, and there was not time to commission a replacement. Conversely, several contributors stepped into breaches with courage worthy of any Napoleonic veteran.

It has been a long campaign, but we feel it has been worth the effort.

Contributors

Katherine Aaslestad is Professor of Modern European History at the University of West Virginia, USA. Her publications include *Place and Politics: Local Identity, Civic Culture, and German Nationalism in North Germany during the Revolutionary Era* (2005); 'Patriotism in Practice: War and Gender Roles in Republican Hamburg 1750–1815', in *Gender, War and Politics*, ed. Jane Rendall et al. (2010); 'Lost Neutrality and Economic Warfare: Napoleonic Warfare in Northern Europe, 1795–1815', in *War in the Age of Revolution, 1775–1815*, ed. Roger Chickering and Stig Förster (2010).

Jean-René Aymes is Emeritus Professor of Modern History at the Université Paris III, France. His publications include *La Guerra de la Independencia en España (1808–1814)* (6th edn updated, 2008); *La Guerra de la Independencia: héroes, villanos y víctimas (1808–1814)* (2008).

Martijn van der Burg is Lecturer in Modern History at the Universiteit van Amsterdam, the Netherlands. His publications include 'Napoleons Generalgouvernement Holland, 1810–1813. Die Frage von Assimilation und Integration', *Zeitschrift für Weltgeschichte* (2012); 'La police napoléonienne dans les départements néerlandais: entre tradition et modernité (1795–1820)', in *L'Empire : l'échec d'une possible construction européenne?* ed. Jessenne (2012); 'Transforming the Dutch Republic into the Kingdom of Holland: The Netherlands between Republicanism and Monarchy (1795–1815)', *European Review of History* (2010); 'L'école primaire dans le royaume de Hollande et durant l'annexion (1806–1813)', in *Louis Bonaparte, roi de Hollande*, ed. Annie Jourdan (2010).

Michael Broers is Professor of Western European History at Oxford University, UK. His book *The Napoleonic Empire in Italy, 1796–1814: Cultural Imperialism in a European Context?* (2005) won the Prix Napoléon of the Fondation Napoléon. He was a visiting member of the Institute for Advanced Study, Princeton and is now a Major Leverhulme Research Fellow.

Howard G. Brown is Professor of Modern History at Binghamton University, USA. His book *Ending the French Revolution: Violence, Justice, and Repression from the Terror to Napoleon* (2006) won AHA's 2006 Leo Gershoy Award for the best book in seventeenth- and eighteenth-century European History and *Taking Liberties: Problems of a New Order from the French Revolution to Napoleon*, co-edited with Judith A. Miller (2002/2003).

Gabriele B. Clemens is Professor of Modern and Local History at the Universität des Sarrelandes, Germany. Her publications include

'Fürstendiener—Kollaborateure? Die Beamten im Königreich Westphalen', in *Fremdherrschaft und Freiheit. Das Königreich Westphalen als napoleonischer Modellstaat*, ed. Jens Fleming and Dietfrid Krause-Vilmar (2009); 'Integrazione imperiale e progressione di carriera: la politica napoleonica per i funzionari dei territori annessi', in *Gli imperi dopo l'Impero nell'Europa del XIX secolo*, ed. Marco Bellabarba et al. (2008); 'Diener dreier Herren—die Beamtenschaft in den linksrheinischen Gebieten vom Ancien Regime bis zur Restauration', in *Fremde Herrscher—fremdes Volk. Inklusions- und Exklusionsfiguren bei Herrschaftswechseln in Europa*, ed. Helga Schnabel-Schüle und Andreas Gestrich (2006).

Fernando Dores Costa is Professor of History at the Instituto Superior de Ciencias del Trabajo y Empresa, Lisbon, Portugal. His publications include 'Army Size, Military Recruitment and Financing in Portugal in the Period of the Peninsula War—1808–1811', *e-Journal of Portuguese History* (2008); 'An Odd Alliance: William Beresford and D. João VI, Prince and King of Portugal', *Journal of Oxford University Historical Society* (2009); 'A invasão de Masséna em 1810 e as linhas de Torres Vedras: uma paradoxal confluência de objectivos?', *Ler História* (2010).

Alan Forrest is Professor of Modern History at the University of York, UK. His publications include *Napoleon* (2011); *The Legacy of the French Revolutionary Wars: The Nation-in-Arms in French Republican Memory* (2009); *Paris, the Provinces and the French Revolution* (2004); *Napoleon's Men: The Soldiers of the Revolution and Empire* (2002).

Alexander Grab is Adelaide & Alan Bird Professor of History at the University of Maine, USA. His *Napoleon and the Transformation of Europe* (2003) won the first prize of the International Napoleonic Society in 2004. His other publications include 'Conscription and Desertion in Napoleonic Europe', *Wiener Zeitscrift zur Geschichte der Neuzeit* (2008); 'Jewish Education in Napoleonic Italy—The Case of the Ginnasio in Reggio Emilia', *Jahrbuch des Simon-Dubnow-Instituts* (2007); 'The Napoleonic Empire in Italy: The Transfer of Tax Ideas and Political Legitimacy', in *Global Debates about Taxation*, ed. Holger Nehring and Florian Schui (2007); 'Public Education in Napoleonic Italy', in *Napoleon and His Empire Europe, 1804–1814*, ed. Philip Dwyer and Alan Forrest (2007).

Agustin Guimerá is a researcher in International Studies at the Consejo Superior de Investigaciones Científicas in Madrid, Spain. He is co-editor of *Trafalgar y el mundo atlántico* (2004); *El equilibrio de los imperios. De Utrecht a Trafalgar* (2005); *Guerra naval en la Revolución y el Imperio. Bloqueos y operaciones anfibias* (2008).

Karen Hagemann is James G. Kenan Distinguished Professor of History at the University of North Carolina at Chapel Hill, USA. Her books include

'*Mannlicher Muth und Teutsche Ehre*': *Nation, Militär und Geschlecht zur Zeit der Antinapoleonischen Kriege Preußens* (2002); *Gendered Nations: Nationalisms and Gender Order in the Long Nineteenth Century* (ed. with Ida Blom and Catherine Hall) (2000); *Masculinities in Politics and War: Gendering Modern History* (ed. with Stefan Dudink and John Tosh) (2004); *Representing Masculinity: Male Citizenship in Modern Western Culture* (ed. with Stefan Dudink and Anna Clark) (2007); *Soldiers, Citizens and Civilians: Experiences and Perceptions of the Revolutionary and Napoleonic Wars, 1790–1820* (ed. with Alan Forrest and Jane Rendall) (2009); and *Gender, War, and Politics: Transatlantic Perspectives, 1775–1830* (ed. with Gisela Mettele and Jane Rendall) (2010).

Peter Hicks is Historian and International Affairs Manager, Fondation Napoléon, Paris and Visiting Professor at the University of Bath. His book *Clisson et Eugénie* (2007) won the Premio Luciano Bonaparte, Principe di Canino awarded by the Town of Canino, Italy. His publications include 'Napoleon on Elba—An Exile of Consent', in *Monarchy and Exile*, ed. Philip Mansel and Torsten Riotte (2011); 'Late 18th-century and Very Early 19th-century British Writings on Napoleon: Myth and History', *Napoleonica. La Revue* (2010); 'Joseph Bonaparte et la "Réunion de famille" de 1832–1833', in *Catalogue de l'exposition au Musée national des châteaux de Malmaison, 19 octobre 2010–10 janvier 2011, Charlotte Bonaparte 1802–1839: une princesse artiste*, ed. Amaury Lefebure (2010).

Johan Joor is a historian and honorary research fellow at the International Institute of Social History in Amsterdam, the Netherlands. His publications include 'Le système continental et sa signification pour le Royaume de Hollande', in *Louis Bonaparte. Roi de Hollande*, ed. Annie Jourdan (2010); 'History and Myth of Dutch Popular Protest in the Napoleonic Period (1806–1813)', in *Myth in History, History in Myth*, ed. Laura Cruz and Willem Frijhoff (2009); '"A Very Rebellious Disposition." Dutch Experience and Popular Protest under the Napoleonic Regime (1806–1813)', in *Soldiers, Citizens and Civilians: Experiences and Perceptions of the Revolutionary and Napoleonic Wars, 1790–1820*, ed. Alan Forrest et al. (2009); 'De huid die niet mocht zweten. Het Continentaal Stelsel en de betekenis daarvan voor het Koninkrijk Holland', *De Negentiende Eeuw* (2006); 'Tegen koning en keizer. Protest en oproer in de Napoleontische tijd', in *Geschiedenis Magazine* (April 2006).

Annie Jourdan is Associate Professor of European Studies at the Universiteit van Amsterdam, the Netherlands. Her publications include *Louis Bonaparte, roi de Hollande* (2010); *La Révolution, une exception française?* (2004); *Mythes et légendes de Napoléon* (2004); *L'empire de Napoléon* (2000); *Napoléon. Héros, Imperator, Mécène* (1998).

Thierry Lentz is a historian and Director of the Fondation Napoléon, France. His publications include *Nouvelle Histoire du Premier Empire* (4 vols—2002,

2004, 2007 and 2010); *Quand Napoléon inventait la France, Dictionnaire des Institutions administratives et de cour du Consulat et de l'Empire* (ed. with Pierre Branda, François Pinaud and Clémence Zacharie) (2008); *Napoléon, l'esclavage et les colonies* (ed. with Pierre Branda); he is editor of *Mémoires de Napoléon* (3 vols, 2010–2011) and *Napoléon Bonaparte, Correspondance générale* (vols 1–3, 2004, 2005, 2006).

Matthijs Lok is Assistant Professor of Modern History at the Universiteit van Amsterdam, the Netherlands. His publications include *Windvanen: Napoleontische bestuurders in de Nederlandse en Franse Restauratie (1813–1820)* (2009); '"Un simulacre de roi". Les représentations néerlandaises du roi Louis sous la Restauration', in *Louis Bonaparte, Roi de Hollande*, ed. A. Jourdan (2010); 'L'extrême centre est-il exportable? Une comparaison entre la France et les Pays-Bas', in *Radicalités et modérations en révolution. Annales Historiques de la Révolution Française*, ed. P. Serna (2009); '"De schaduwkoning." De beeldvorming van koning Lodewijk tijdens de Restauratie', *De Negentiende Eeuw* (2006).

Emilio La Parra López is Professor of Contemporary History at the Universidad de Alicante, Spain. His publications include *Manuel Godoy. La aventura del poder* (2002); 'Fernando VII: impulso y freno a la sublevación de los españoles contra Napoleón', *Mélanges de la Casa de Velásquez* (2008); 'Les changements politiques en Espagne après Brumaire', *Annales historiques de la Révolution française* (1999); 'Méfiance entre les alliés. Les relations Napoléon-Godoy (1801–1807)', *Annales historiques de la Révolution française* (2004).

Marta Lorente is Professor of History of Law at the Universidad Autónoma de Madrid, Spain. Her publications include *Cádiz 1812. La Constitución juris-diccional* (ed. with C. Garriga) (2007); 'La supresión de los Consejos y la creación del Real de España e Indias' in *Actas del XV Congreso del Instituto Internacional de Historia del Derecho Indiano: Córdoba* (2005); *La Voz del Estado. La publicación de las normas (1810/1889)* (2001).

Ute Planert is Professor of Modern History at the Bergische Universitaet Wuppertal, Germany. Her publications include *Der Mythos vom Befreiungskrieg. Frankreichs Kriege und der deutsche Süden. Alltag, Wahrnehmung, Deutung, 1792–1841* (2007); 'International Conflict, War, and the Making of Modern Germany, 1740–1815', in *The Oxford Handbook of Modern German History*, ed. Helmut Walser Smith (2011).

José M. Portillo Valdés is Professor of Contemporary History at the Universidad del País Vasco, Spain. His publications include *Crisis Atlántica. Autonomía e Independencia en la crisis de la monarquía española* (2006); *Revolución de Nación. Orígenes de la cultura constitucional en España, 1780–1812* (2000); *Cadice 1212. Una Costituzione per la Spagna* (1998).

Anna Maria Rao is Professor of Modern History at the Università degli Studi di Napoli, Federico II, Italy. Her publications include *Lumi riforme rivoluzione. Percorsi storiografici* (2011); *Due francesi a Napoli, Atti del Colloquio internazionale di apertura delle celebrazioni del Bicentenario del Decennio francese (1806–1815)* (ed. with Rosanna Cioffi, Renata de Lorenzo, Aldo Di Biasio, Luigi Mascilli Migliorini) (2008); 'Triennio repubblicano', in *L'Italia napoleonica. Dizionario critico*, ed. Luigi Mascilli Migliorini (2011); 'Dal "letterato faticatore" al lavoro intellettuale', in *Cultura e lavoro intellettuale: istituzioni, saperi e professioni nel Decennio francese*, ed. A.M. Rao (2009).

Michael Rapport is Senior Lecturer in Modern History at the University of Stirling, UK. His publications include *Nineteenth-Century Europe* (2005); *Belgium under French Occupation: Between Collaboration and Resistance, July 1794 to October 1795* (2002); '"The Germans Are Hydrophobes": Germany and the Germans in the Shaping of French Identity', in *The Bee and the Eagle: Napoleonic France and the End of the Holy Roman Empire, 1806*, ed. A. Forrest and P. H. Wilson (2008).

Michael Rowe is Senior Lecturer in Modern European History at King's College, London, UK. His publications include 'Comparing Napoleon's Leadership Style with the Dictators of the 20th Century', in *Rethinking History, Dictatorship and War: New Approaches and Interpretations*, ed. Claus-Christian Szejnmann (2010); 'The Political Culture of the Holy Roman Empire on the Eve of Its Destruction', in *The Bee and the Eagle: Napoleonic France and the End of the Holy Roman Empire, 1806*, ed. A. Forrest and P. H. Wilson (2008); 'France, Prussia or Germany? The Napoleonic Wars and Shifting Allegiances in the Rhineland', *Central European History* (2006); 'Napoleon and the "Modernization" of Germany', in *Napoleon and His Empire. Europe, 1804–1814*, ed. Philip Dwyer and Alan Forrest (2006).

Reinhard A. Stauber is Professor of Modern and Austrian History at the Universität von Klagenfurt, Austria. His publications include *Die Protokolle des Bayerischen Staatsrats 1799 bis 1817, vol 1: 1799 bis 1801* (ed. with Esteban Mauerer) (2006); 'Die Anfänge des bayerischen Staatsrats 1799–1804', *Archivalische Zeitschrift* (2006); 'Zwischen Finanznot, Ideologie und neuer Staatsordnung. Die politischen Entscheidungen der Administration Montgelas auf dem Weg zur Säkularisation 1798 bis 1803' in *Die Säkularisation in Bayern 1803. Kulturbruch oder Modernisierung?* ed. Alois Schmid (2003); 'Empire und Region—Der Alpen-Adria-Raum im Zeitalter Napoleons', *Bericht über den 24. Österreichischen Historikertag in Innsbruck* (2006).

Marie-Cécile Thoral is Senior Lecturer in Modern European History at Sheffield Hallam University, UK. Her publications include *L'émergence du* *pouvoir local: Le département de l'Isère face à la centralisation (1800–1837)* (2010); *From Valmy to Waterloo: France at War (1792–1815)* (2011).

Nicola P. Todorov is History and Geography Teacher at the Lycée Gustave Flaubert and Lecturer in History at the University of Rouen, France. His publications include *L'administration du royaume de Westphalie de 1807 à 1813. Le département de l'Elbe* (2010); 'Ablösung der "preußischen Willkürherrschaft 'durch eine' weise und liberale Verwaltung"? Die Magdeburger und der westfälische Staat', *Parthenopolis* (2007/2008), 'Vaincre la résistance administrative. Le combat pour l'application de la législation française dans un État-satellite : le cas du royaume de Westphalie', in Nathalie Petiteua (coord.) *Journée d'études Poitiers, Cahier no. 9* (2006); 'Finances et fiscalité dans le royaume de Westphalie', *Revue de l'Institut Napoléon* (2004).

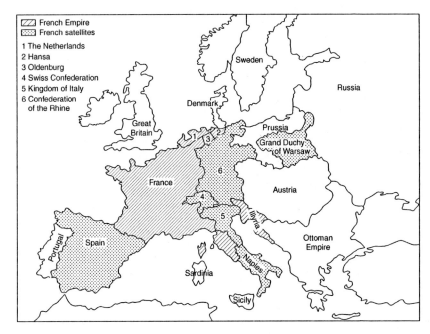

Map 1 Napoleonic Europe

Introduction: Napoleon, His Empire, Our Europe and the 'New Napoleonic History'

Michael Broers

Napoleon was a breaker of worlds. He made and remade most of the European continent almost at will, for well over a decade. Much of our world was forged as a consequence of his actions. Ever since we have taken our revenge—whether as scholars, novelists, politicians or private citizens—by making, unmaking and remaking him. Annie Jourdan, a distinguished contributor to this volume, is perhaps the most recent practitioner of this most necessary historical service.

Napoleon: assassin or saviour of the Revolution? Hero or charlatan? Manager or despot? Warmonger or pacifist? These are the questions French and foreign historians have tried to answer over the last two centuries.[1] With great candour, she declares that these questions are her 'red thread'. The great Dutch historian, Pieter Geyl, put it starkly, for the stark times he wrote in at the end of the Second World War: Napoleon, for or against?[2] The life and deeds are both glittering and black as sin, to return to Annie Jourdan's challenge to every historian of the period.

Behind the man and the life, however, is the legacy of his work. Indeed, the challenge of setting Napoleon in his proper context has become the 'cause' of a whole generation of historians. There is, arguably, the need to push the man if not away, then at least a little aside. The wars swept over Europe and ended in 1814, their diplomatic work undone, and most of their economic ravages were soon repaired. The impact of Napoleon's civil reforms, however subordinate to wars and diplomacy, left more lasting imprints than either, and if there is such a thing as a 'new Napoleonic history', it turns on the examination of these reforms, of what endured, rather than what proved transient. In this, the Napoleonic period is strange territory for the historian, for its true significance lies less in what actually happened, than in what was attempted, outlined and projected. The 'new Napoleonic history' must, of necessity, appear somewhat perverse. The legacy was very unlike the contemporary reality.

The conference that gave rise to this volume generated three themes which encapsulate the major preoccupations of scholars currently active in Napoleonic studies. They stand less as points of consensus than as areas of enquiry, for Napoleonic scholarship remains rich in its diversity of opinion. What has emerged is a growing awareness of the archival richness of the period, but even more, of a very widely perceived need to shift the perspective of research towards the study of civil institutions, ideology and popular history. The first theme is the need to see the Napoleonic empire as a collective enterprise, not just as the capricious work of one man or, indeed, of the French nation, central as both are to the history of the period. Napoleon did not work alone and the empire was not just France. The second strand comes from the realization that Europe was not a *tabula rasa* simply waiting for the men of the *Grande Nation* to arrive and place their imprint upon it; it concerns the interaction—fruitful and collaborative or violent and antagonistic—between Europeans. Out of this comes a third preoccupation, was this an imperialistic, essentially colonial enterprise at its inception? If so, how was it subsequently absorbed into a Europe that found so much of it so alien and repugnant? Yet, this initially alien, aggressive, exploitative presence was absorbed and became the essence of the new common law of Europe, replacing the shards of the world so dear to Burke and so well discerned in its tomb by Tocqueville.

Each of these themes is developed within the five sections of this volume: the first, which examines the Napoleonic constitutions and the Civil Code, turns on the tensions between the desire for a liberal society and the authoritarian tendencies ingrained in the regimes formulated under Napoleonic aegis; secondly, the administrative structures created by the Napoleonic state, balancing precariously between the desire to forge an entirely new regime and that for a partial restoration of the old order; third, the resistance and repression that the twin processes of conquest and reform provoked, which, in turn, forced contemporaries to confront the tensions inherent in order and reform; and finally, there is the irony of an imperial enterprise finding itself so central to the process of nation building. Taken together, the overarching theme— the true *leitmotif* of this volume—is the tension at the heart of the Napoleonic project and the contradictions that tension arose from. It is interesting and revealing to reflect on how many individual contributions touch upon this, in very different ways, across the sections this book is divided into. As Steven Englund has put it recently, the binding force of this volume is the exploration of 'the absurd Napoleonic conception that wished to impose a system on Europe, a system that would subordinate it to an imperial centre...yet at the same time be open, rationalized, modernized, and in many ways progressive'. It goes without saying that the term 'absurd', itself, is a provocation to many, but Englund here sets the tone of what follows.

Englund concludes his survey of the current historiography with the question 'who on earth has the skills (or the languages), the energy, and the will to do such a thing? Who has the intelligence ... ?'[3] The answer may well be no one individual, hence the importance and value of the kind of collective undertaking attempted here. Indeed, this may reflect the emerging view—perhaps the essence of a consensus among scholars—of the empire itself as a collective enterprise, in need of a collective response by those who seek to understand it. There is always a tendency to think in terms of the 'Great Man' school of History when confronted by a great man, and to neglect the wider social and political context that produced *both* the Great Man and the society that produced him. Napoleon rose and ruled because he touched the vital nerves of his own generation; if he inspired those around him, he did not instil them with the new and the unknown—he drew on a common culture, appealed to widespread preoccupations. Napoleon identified with his contemporaries, just as much as they looked up to him.

The anthropologist, Marshal Sahlins reminds us that this probably began with the writing of European History itself, with the Greek historian of the Peloponnesian War, Thucydides, who spoke simply of 'the Athenians' and of their leader, 'Pericles', giving too little thought to the fact that Pericles was also an Athenian.[4] When we speak of Napoleon and the French we are too often inclined to do the same thing, and perhaps this is a fault to be rectified. The American scholar, Isser Woloch, has recently helped us begin to break with this trope in his incisive study *Napoleon's Collaborators*.[5] Woloch's work concerned itself with those politicians who became disillusioned with Bonaparte and who began to distance themselves from him fairly early in his rule. Shifting the historian's gaze from the leader to those around him was a very important breakthrough by Woloch. Nevertheless, perhaps what is needed even more is to hold this perspective when examining those who continued to agree with Napoleon and to drive the imperial machine forward, throughout the period.

By shifting the focus of research from the military and the transient, to the impact of Napoleonic reforms in civil administration, policing, and the law, from the national to the imperial, from the personal to the collective, is to acknowledge Talleyrand's famous quip to Napoleon, *à propos* the plethora of new thrones he had created across Europe: 'You can't sit on bayonets'. Perhaps one result of this volume will be to show the extent to which Napoleon and his collaborators grasped this themselves, as well as its intrinsic wisdom. This may be the essence of what may justly be called 'the new Napoleonic history', the sum of what Englund terms 'nothing less than a scholarly renaissance'.[6]

Having invoked the term 'renaissance', it needs to be emphasized how recent are the preoccupations and lines of enquiry it reflects. The history of the 'new Napoleonic history' is a story in itself. Until roughly a generation ago, Napoleonic studies were all too often the preserve of military historians, hagiographers and demonizers. It was a land of legends, of demons, of warriors; and of poor scholarship and very boring history, and not regarded as academically respectable territory for the aspiring historian. If we, as a cohort of historians from all over the western world, have discovered nothing else we can agree upon, we have discerned how important is the Napoleonic period for an understanding of the history of modern Europe. Stuart Woolf's pioneering study, *Napoleon's Integration of Europe*[7] began this process or, perhaps more accurately, brought this approach to the period into the mainstream in 1991, for Woolf's book was essentially a distillation of existing scholarship. Exactly because of this, its impact was seismic. From this point onwards, Napoleonic studies could no longer remain confined to war, diplomacy and high politics. Woolf's book can boast many great breakthroughs, but among the most vibrant is the emphatic truth that the reforms, and attempted reforms, of the Napoleonic period left an indelible mark on western Europe and, for this reason, they must be analysed in ever-increasing depth.

There was light in the pre-Woolfian darkness, otherwise he could not have written as he did, and much of it was to be found in Spain which was, at the time, the most unlikely of places. In the 1940s, Jesus Pabón published his lucid, penetrating *Las Ideas Napoleonicas*, which was not really rivalled in its theoretical analysis of the regime until the work of Frédéric Bluche forty years later.[8] As early as 1949—who knows how—Joan Mercader Riba produced his study of Barcelona under Napoleon, almost unique in its time as a model of methodology, as well as a monument in its own right, which foreshadowed his later, seminal works on the Napoleonic kingdom and Catalonia, written in easier circumstances.[9] Beside them, was the towering figure of Miguel Artola Gallego, whose 1953 work on the Afrancesados, which confronted directly the complexities of non-French engagement with Napoleonic hegemony, followed by his *Los Origenes de la España Contemporanea*, in 1959.[10] The chosen themes of these scholars—collaboration and its complexities, the institutional and constitutional influence of Napoleonic rule, above all—were taken up by a new generation, but they were there first and their scholarship lives healthily among the flood of new work they pioneered. In the light of the academically excellent, and quite simply courageous, contribution of Spanish scholars of an earlier era to Napoleonic historiography, Madrid was a fitting venue for this work, and the chapters presented here should be seen as, in no small manner, a homage to them.

The doyens of the historiography of Napoleonic Spain dealt in a period, and dealt with it in ways that could have put them in actual danger, which was a genuinely rare set of circumstances in post-war western Europe. Nevertheless, the Napoleonic period was far from popular, if not actually politically volatile, in many other countries. North of the Pyrenees, there was often a long tradition of self-censorship that had roots as far back as 1814. This is made explicit by Gabrielle Clemens on Switzerland, and Mathijs Lok and Marijn van der Burg on the Netherlands. Clemens points to ignored anniversaries, gaps in the chronology of even very recent work on nineteenth century Switzerland, and to the need to fill them. Lok and Burg invoke the long tradition of simply 'forgetting' initiated by William I on his restoration after the fall of Napoleon. Such problems of perception can also be applied to Italian and German history in the period where, particularly after the war, earlier trends were re-enforced in the search for 'useable' national pasts that led historians and statesmen to invoke the pro-French patriots—the native, misnamed 'Jacobins' by the classic literature—as the founts of modern democracy.[11] The corollary of this was to condemn the Napoleonic years as an era not only of shameful collaboration with a foreign invader, but as a period when liberal and democratic hopes were betrayed by many who had championed them in the 1790s. All too often, this found an echo in French historiography as well. For too long the inherent significance of the Napoleonic period, its seminal influence on the institutions of successor states to the Napoleonic empire in the nineteenth century, and its fundamental contribution to the underlying foundations of modern Europe, have been swept aside. This trend is, sadly, only too understandable in the long shadows that hung over the first two generations of scholars to emerge from the debacle of 1945, but the passage of time allows for new perspectives to emerge. It has taken time, most certainly. The contributions of Lok and Burg, and of Clemens, point directly to the fact that the 'new Napoleonic history' has had very recent battles to fight to win recognition and that, in some places, it is still going on. It may be no coincidence that so much of the new scholarship has emerged from the pens of scholars working in Anglo-Saxon academe, who are relatively less constrained by the tides of history. In this volume one can point to the contributions of Alex Grab, Michael Rowe and Michael Rapport in this vein.

The most recent general works to renew Woolf's work is that of Thierry Lentz, who is justly present in this volume. That his monumental study of the Napoleonic empire is so welcome and needed, is a tribute both to his own endeavours—the new edition of the *Correspondence* above all—and to the industry of so many scholars who have opened up the history of Napoleonic Europe—literally, in so many archives in so many places—in the last quarter of a century.[12] Many of them a gratifying blend of the senior and the young, agreed to participate in this volume and the conference it is based upon.

The themes of the volume

1 Constitutions and the civil code

The undeniably authoritarian, militaristic character of the Napoleonic regime and its satellite states has often blinded historians to the central importance of their constitutions—in France and elsewhere—and to the other major reforms that stemmed from the terms of those constitutions.

One of the greatest insights of the 'new Napoleonic history', initiated by scholars like Mercader Riba, Artola Gallego and Jean Tulard,[13] and brought to fruition by Stuart Woolf, was to show just how limiting was the judgement of Georges Lefebvre, in branding it a military dictatorship, pure and simple.[14] This was the fount of the new history. Consequently, the research of the last three decades has been driven by the need to show that it was much more than this and that, even where authoritarian instincts and military priorities prevailed, there was always a tension between the need to rule and exploit on the one hand, and the desire to reform societies and polities torn asunder by the wars of the period on the other. These tensions are revealed very starkly through the Napoleonic constitutions and thus they form a useful starting point for a project concerned with the political and civic heritage of the Napoleonic empire.

In their chapter on Napoleonic rule in the Netherlands, Matthijs Lok and Martijn van der Burg provide a comprehensive narrative of the institutional evolution of the country under successive pro-French regimes, from the 'Batavian' sister republic Napoleon inherited from the Directory, through the satellite Kingdom of Holland under his brother Louis, to the final period of direct rule from Paris. What emerges from their work, in the immediate context of the Napoleonic era, is the experimental nature of each of these regimes and how they differed from each other. Too often, the concept of the 'political laboratory' is seen as ending with Napoleon's seizure of power in 1799, but Lok and van der Burg prove that it was actually under Napoleonic hegemony that change and experiment, as well as the implementation of lasting administrative reforms, took place. These reforms obviously centred on the introduction of the Civil Code and true administrative centralization, but Lok and van der Burg's approach shows how these changes also depended on innovations in the constitution itself. Their approach goes a long way to rectifying the neglect this period has suffered in Dutch historiography, and ends with a thorough appraisal of the fundamental influence the Napoleonic reforms had on the long-term future of the restored Dutch nation after 1814.

Emilio La Parra's insightful contribution on Spanish constitutionalism compliments that of Lok and van der Burg in many important ways, as well as serving as prelude for Marta Lorente's chapter, discussed below. Like Lok and van der Burg, Emilio La Parra examines the pre-history of Napoleonic intervention in his region, outlining a constitutional position that political scientists would term 'state death' in the wake of the crisis of Aranjuez, thus setting the different Spanish reactions to the Napoleonic fiat of Bayonne in an illuminating terms. La Parra next explores the nature of the Constitution of Bayonne in its Napoleonic context, comparing it with the French constitutions of the 1790s and the 'parent' Napoleonic constitutions of 1799 and 1804, as well as its great rival, the 1812 Cadiz Constitution. La Parra's analysis of the often neglected debates of 1810 in Cadiz shows that

Cadiz was a deliberate, calculated, liberal, anti-authoritarian challenge to Bayonne. Finally, he skillfully draws these strands together, to emphasize both the inherently authoritarian nature of Bayonne, but also the possibilities it offered for sweeping enlightened reform. In common with Lok and van der Burg, he takes the examination of this inherent tension to the apex of the state.

The Belgian case, which is the context of Michael Rapport's intensive archival research, explores these issues from the perspective of the workings of the Civil Code. Belgium was that part of Europe longest under not just Napoleonic, but French revolutionary rule. Rapport's work actually shows the system at work and as it was meant to function. In Belgium, the court system and the Civil Code kept the potential for constitutional authoritarianism in check. These judicial institutions survived regime change intact in 1814, when these departments were annexed to the Kingdom of the Netherlands. Rapport's exposition of the effective and comprehensive assimilation of this region to the core Napoleonic institutions enhances Lok and van der Burg's contribution, showing how the acquisition of Belgium made all but impossible any integral return to the Dutch ancien regime.

In all of this, Goethe probably spoke a more tangible and, indeed, a more prosaic truth than he realized when he proclaimed Napoleon 'the spirit of the age'. Napoleon admired Goethe immeasurably, to the point of offering him the post of official poet laureate at the Imperial court, which would have made him the veritable Virgil of his age. Goethe, poignantly, refused but he never ceased to see in Napoleon, the incarnation of the new century. The harbinger of what was to come. In this, he was right, but not in the way either man actually foresaw when they met in the wake of Napoleon's spectacular military triumph over Prussia, in 1806. That he could be so perceived had more to do with his ability to identify with French society than to shape it. Arguably, nothing caught this better than the Civil Code of 1804. Indeed, it was Napoleon himself who predicted the future correctly during his enforced leisure on St. Helena, rather than the intuitive German man of letters. It was in letter, on the printed page, that Napoleon would find his lasting triumph. Even his powerfully influential memoirs are eclipsed in their impact on the future of Europe by the Civil Code of 1804, which Napoleon cited in those memoirs as his single, greatest, achievement. And he did not need those memoirs to justify this assertion. It could be proved by the day-to-day workings of the law in almost every European state that knew his influence, not just his direct rule.

Few official documents have been so effectively, perceptively and lucidly able to reflect the concerns of their society than the Code Napoleon. It is rooted in a profound, at points almost instinctive, anthropological knowledge of its time and place. The Code is a seminal example of the importance of placing Pericles among the Athenians. Stendhal called it the greatest novel he had ever read. Great novelists are usually *of* that of which they write. The story of Napoleon was everywhere the tension between liberty and authority, and the importance of practical reform to both. The Code offered a clear vision of a post-feudal world based on the concept of the individual citizen and his inalienable right to the possession of private property. Nevertheless, even within France, itself, the eventual success of this concept of civil society was hard fought for, not just in the Vendean *bocage*, but in the law courts, where peaceable communities and individuals contested intransigent rearguard actions by the former privileged order to evade the consequences of enlightened reform, be they revolutionary or Napoleonic in origin.

Marie-Cécile Thoral has a very different story to tell, which is set in the heart of provincial France, and she chooses a long time span to do so, ranging from the initial reforms of the Revolution to their refinement and revival under the July Monarchy, in the 1830s. Her subject is not the sound and fury of Howard Brown, for example, but the exploration of how the new regime evolved in the department of the Isère, around the Alpine city of Grenoble. In the course of her careful research, while in search of the 'typical' in post-Revolutionary France, she demolishes many myths in the most effective way, through careful, patient, fresh archival research. Thoral's story gives the lie to the effectiveness, if not to the legal reality, of the centralized, powerful Napoleonic state. Instead, she exposes its practical limitations and its constant, pervasive reliance on the notables, to keep it functioning at local level, even in times of peace. Thoral traces the evolution that followed reform across all the regimes of the early nineteenth century, and so she is also able to show some of the ways its shortcomings were resolved over time. Hers is a work of understated but profound revisionism, all the more powerful for its quiet, provincial setting, far from the heartlands of counter-revolution.

How the whole package of Napoleonic reform worked in practice, in the fraught circumstances that were the usual reality of Napoleonic rule beyond the secure core of the empire, is explored by Fernando Dores Costa, in his lucid, perspective analysis of French rule in Portugal. Costa's contribution to this volume is seminal in three distinct ways. The most obvious is the addition of the Portuguese case to general overviews of the period, for few European societies were as deeply, profoundly and permanently affected by the Napoleonic wars as was Portugal, albeit through British, not French, influence. Costa's contribution has two further striking attributes, however, for it concentrates on the understudied but central instances of French rule in Portugal: Junot's occupation of Lisbon between December 1807 and July 1808, and Soult's occupation of Porto in 1809. These are events worthy of general attention, in themselves evidence that the Portuguese had direct knowledge of Napoleonic rule when radical elements in the army and intelligentsia set up the 'French way' as the radical, reforming alternative to British domination from 1820 onwards. Costa's profound analysis goes further still. He uses Portugal as an example to analyse the inherent tensions and dilemmas the French faced when trying to balance the need to reform the very foundations of a society they perceived as backward but full of potential, with the dangers present on an exposed, remote imperial frontier and the military exigencies such a position entailed. Costa's approach is of significance not only for his own chosen region of study, but it holds important lessons for the Illyrian Provinces, the Kingdom of Naples, and for Josefino Spain.

2   The state and administration

In his almost prophetic book written in 1930, *La rebelión de las masas*, Ortega y Gasset remarked that, although Napoleon led an aggressive force over the Pyrenees, he 'never ruled in Spain for a single day', and made the vital distinction between a process of aggression and a state of rule.[15] The centrality of this distinction stands at the heart of much of the 'new Napoleonic history'; it might be regarded almost as a watchword. Nevertheless, Marta Lorente's chapter on the Spanish Councils throws down both an affirmation and a challenge to this dictum, when she shows that Napoleon did indeed rule in Spain, even though the victory came only in 1845—over twenty years after his death on St Helena—when the first Council of State, fully conceived on his own model, was created. She shows the fundamental importance for the future of Spain of the models shaped at Bayonne and, subsequently, by the embattled, often impotent Josefino regime. Lorente concentrates on the centrality of the concept of 'administrative justice' to the authoritarian nature of the Napoleonic system of government, linking it to its core axiom, the division of powers, but investigates how the regime risked violating its own principles by turning over the administration of justice to bureaucrats. Her story is, in some ways, the opposite side of the coin to Michael Rapport's analysis of Belgium. In common with La Parra, Lorente sets her research in the wider context of the French Revolution, seeing this betrayal as having its origins in the Terror. Under the Committee of Public Safety, she argues, government agents became virtually immune from the courts, a process later consolidated at the apex of the administration, in the Napoleonic Council of State. Again, like La Parra, Lorente draws astutely on the contrasts between the Josefino regime and the blueprint laid out in Cadiz, to make her point: the institution of 'administrative justice' was not only absent in the 1812 Constitution, but virtually unknown in the subsequent Latin American constitutions Cadiz inspired. Nevertheless, it took root in Spain through the Council of State, the resurrection of which, for Lorente, belatedly drew Spain into a 'European club' of which the Netherlands—as shown by Lok and van der Burg—and many German states, to say nothing of Piedmont-Savoy, had long been members by mid-century. Lorente's chapter drives to the heart, as well as to the apex, of the tension between liberal reform and authoritarian centralism, inherent in Napoleonic political culture. In this, as in so much else, Lorente's contribution goes far beyond its initial remit, to become pivotal to the purpose of this volume.

La Parra, Lorente and Costa show how the study of the volatile peripheries of Napoleonic Europe can clarify central issues and concentrate the mind. Like the Netherlands, however, the contributions of Michael Rowe, on the Rhineland, Alex Grab on the Republic/Kingdom of Italy, and of Gabrielle Clemens on Switzerland, are based on generally peaceful regions, where— in common with Michael Rapport's Belgium—institutions and their associated practices had time to establish themselves. Napoleonic hegemony was relative across western Europe and its resultant impact highly variable.

The Republic/Kingdom of Italy was, in many ways, the most prized of Napoleon's imperial possessions. It had been his first powerbase; it was here he served his apprenticeship as a head of state and, indeed, as the creator of polities and founder of regimes. The north Italian plain was also the wealthiest, most useful of his territories in terms of soldiers, revenue and, indeed, of grain, for its rice harvests stemmed off shortages in France in the lean years of 1810–12. The position of the Republic/Kingdom of Italy in the Napoleonic empire might be regarded as comparable to that of Mexico or Peru, in that of Bourbon Spain, just as Lombardy—its core—had been for the Habsburgs before him. In his masterly survey of its life as a state, Alex Grab dissects how Napoleon both exploited the land he called 'the richest fields in the world' when his troops first descended on it in 1796, and how he also took good care of it, in so far as the needs of war permitted. Unlike the Habsburgs, however, Napoleon did not leave the institutional or political structures of this region alone. He smashed its long traditions of local municipal loyalties and the system of urban oligarchies known as *campanilismo*, replacing it all with a polity carved out in accordance with his own ideas. Thus, Grab describes a state very closely modelled on Napoleonic France, to the extent that terming it a 'clone' would not be inappropriate. This was 'the system at work', in conditions as calm as could be hoped for in a war-torn Europe, and bears comparison with Rapport's study of Belgium, that other milch cow of the Habsburg and their Napoleonic successors.

Gabriele Clemens' chapter on Switzerland not only redresses the unjust neglect of this period by Swiss scholars, but by general surveys, as well. Its major contribution to the 'new Napoleonic history' is more profound than this, however. Switzerland stood well within the secure zone of Napoleonic Europe after 1800,[16] although it had been ravaged in the conflicts of the 1790s. This recent legacy made the French hated across a wide spectrum of Swiss society, even as the region was drawn as firmly into the Napoleonic orbit as Belgium or the Italian Republic. Its political and institutional pre-history were not conducive to centralization, as Clemens shows, and attempts at reform too closely modelled on those of France took place in a political culture which found them as alien as Spain or Portugal, if for very different reasons and in very different ways. So much so, that Napoleon saw it himself. The result, as Clemens shows from a deep knowledge of her sources, was a rare set of compromises and devolution within the core of the empire. From the perspective of frustrated Swiss reformers and enlightened absolutists in Paris alike, the result was something more akin to the compromises with feudal orders on the imperial periphery, like Westphalia or the Grand Duchy of Warsaw, than with Italy, literally just over the hill. Key Napoleonic reforms, mainly the abolition of feudalism and freedom of conscience, foundered in communes that chose to reject them. Such advances were traded by Napoleon for their cooperation in supplying his war machine with men and money, much as on his eastern marches. The very process of devolution to the traditional communes and the variety of choices allowed to them was virtually unique in Napoleonic Europe. As Clemens demonstrates, this allowed the Swiss to accept and, above all, to adapt Napoleonic reforms on their own terms. Where Napoleonic policies, practices and institutions were absorbed by the Swiss in their own fashion, they proved durable. Where they did not, the old order of neo-feudal tenures, confessional states and impenetrable local oligarchy continued until the upheavals of the 1840s. Clemens' thoughtful approach to Swiss history in this period has a significance far beyond its chosen borders, not the least because it points directly to the tensions between traditional localism and enlightened reform, authoritarian or not, which Napoleonic reformers inherited. In the Swiss case, they chose retreat as the better part of valour.

These tensions are also present, if in more muted form, in Michael Rowe's elegant, judicious chapter on the Napoleonic Rhineland. Here, as in Switzerland and the Netherlands, the French encountered an older tradition of municipal republicanism—a different concept of liberty rooted in tradition and particularism—that seldom married easily with their new regime. Rowe also reminds his colleagues of the vital importance of local studies, with his concentration on the experience of Napoleonic rule in two Rhenish cities, Aaachen and Cologne. Rowe wisely reminds readers of how the 'new Napoleonic history' can go too far in 'the determination to distance ourselves from a skewered national reading of the past' which, in turn, 'runs the risk of underestimating politics'. Rowe shows how to avoid this, while working resolutely in the context of those same local politics that constituted the focal point of political culture for most people, in most places, in these decades. In common with Clemens, Rowe shows just how great differences could be in a micro-region. He contrasts his two cities cleverly, discerning the limits of real, effective French control even in areas on their border and long under their control. Only where the French were directly present, or were provoked to exert pressure from the centre, could they cut through the webs of local hierarchies and the quasi-clandestine perpetuation of ancien regime practices. As Rowe concludes, 'French administrative uniformity of itself did not overcome local loyalties'. A lesson worth recording.

Rowe's account of the residual loyalty to old ways and local horizons took place in peaceful circumstances, but localism, tradition and the determination to preserve them, however reactionary, from the Napoleonic juggernaut, could take on a very different character in different circumstances. Even at the core of their empire, the new regime and its ways were seldom regarded with affection. More often than not they were hated.

3   Policing and popular resistance

This new regime first had to be fought for, even—and especially—within France itself, and this is where many scholars of the present generation, quite sensibly, began their work. By and large, French imperialism was not meant to be a reciprocal exchange or an integration of different European perspectives or traditions, but the convulsed circumstances in which French occupation usually began ensured that equal cooperation between *occupants* and *occupés* was rare, in any case. Resistance spelled violence; collaboration was fraught with tensions. If this period was the birth of modern Europe, it was not any easy one. Interaction usually meant conflict, that change was imposed from above and from outside, and that even the positive legacy of the 'French epoch' was often grudgingly accepted, and then only by a tiny, if powerful, elite.

Resistance to the Napoleonic state became synonymous with the civil war that had its origins in the 1790s, over the nature and course of the Revolution. Napoleon inherited a nation at odds with itself in 1799, torn apart by every sort of internal antagonism, ideological and purely material, political and economic; local violence hovered at every point on the scale from deep religious conviction to vendettas of the most personal kind. They all fused into a myriad of conflicts, atomized across the towns and villages of the French hinterlands, but reaching their most serious and widespread levels in the highly politicized departments of the west—the *Vendée Militaire*—and the anarchic mixture of banditry, counter-revolution, family feuding and common crime that swept the south. Howard Brown offers this volume a penetrating study of the government offensive begun under the Directory and ended, after considerable effort by Napoleon, around 1804. His recent book, from which this chapter derives, is rapidly becoming seminal.[17] Here, Brown charts the bloody events of the restoration of order, a story crucial in itself for understanding the hard work that Napoleon needed to do in his own powerbase in the years of relative peace between 1800 and 1805, before he could entertain another major war. He does far more than this, however, and his chapter's salient virtue is his emphasis on the political and legal dilemmas the regime faced, and how deeply aware of this it was in creating what he terms 'a security state' in the process of internal pacification. The legal, ideological and philosophical tensions analysed by La Parra and Lorente at the apex of the state, are tackled at their cutting edge—quite literally—by Brown.

Conquest brought havoc and trauma everywhere, but this did not end with the campaigning. After conquest, came conscription, dubbed 'the blood tax' by peasant communities the length and breadth of Europe, whose own local dialects were unintelligible to their neighbours, to say nothing of their occupiers. As Alan Forrest shows in his chapter—the distillation of a lifetime's work on unrest in the French provinces—even within France itself, resistance lingered long, fuelled by the fear of war; where the *triage* functioned, the battle front, even when in Portugal or Poland, was never really far away. Napoleon had another war to fight—that of 'the thousand Vendées' as his gendarmes and magistrates called it—simply to continue his conventional war. The Code and the prefectoral system of administration were one side of Napoleonic hegemony; conscription—and the banditry and insurrection its imposition brought even to once tranquil regions—was a more urgent matter for contemporaries. The campaigns of internal pacification studied by Brown shattered and fragmented resistance, ending it on a widespread, organized level, and giving birth to the instruments of the security state, the Military Commissions and the Gendarmerie chief among them. Forrest shows that the pressures of conscription ensured violent and non-violent resistance continued to the end, even within France, if on a very atomized, parochial level. The security state and its capacity to compromise and pervert reform and liberal institutions, persisted along with conscription.

Jean-René Aymes' eloquent, classic account the Spanish resistance to Napoleon has stood the test of time and is delivered here with erudition, verve, and a sensitivity to evidence, that merit its inclusion in a volume dominated by a younger generation of scholars. Aymes covers every aspect and every region of Spain in this essay, showing the intensity of the anti-Napoleonic struggle. His chapter stresses the popular character of the Spanish resistance, seeing in it a true people's war, driven by patriotism whatever its internal divisions, and demonstrates that the class struggles that threatened to tear it apart are not necessarily incompatible with a national cause. This chapter stands out in its depiction of an aspect of the period that was not dominated by the political and philosophical doubts and tensions which characterized the reactions of the elites, both pro- and anti-Napoleonic, about the inherent contradictions of violence, authoritarianism and reform. For Aymes, the masses resisted and carried the elites with them. His exploration of elite propaganda directed at the people, reveals the extent to which the anti-French ruling classes had, finally, to acknowledge and even embrace, the popular culture that drove and sustained the revolt. Aymes' sweeping survey embraces passive, as well as active, resistance and explores the sources of disunity, as well as those of patriotism. By engaging with the recent revisionism of Chales Esdaile,[18] Aymes points to a field of Napoleonic studies in the grip of an intense scholarly debate.

Katherine Aaslestad examines resistance in the very different regional context of the highly developed, urban environment of the Hanseatic ports of northern Germany, and sets her own work in the comparative context of Germany as a whole. Aaslestad ably demonstrates, as do Costa, La Parra and Lorente for Spain, that the tensions, confusions and doubts aroused by the violent cycle of resistance, repression and its implications for political culture, were a truly European experience for educated elites from Lisbon to Lübeck. She shows the responses of some of the most peaceable, cultivated milieux in Europe, to the devastation and confusion wrought by the Napoleonic wars, particularly in their final stages. In common with Aymes, she explores the roots and character of the 'patriotism'—more local than nationalist—that emerged within these elites, determined to salvage their civilization, especially their enlightened personal sensibilities, from the maelstrom.

4   Imperialism

The similarities between so many of the chapters in the first three parts of this volume, just as much, or even more, than their contrasting regional contexts, underline the imperial nature of the Napoleonic state. As both Annie Jourdan and Thierry Lentz point out in their chapters, conquests beyond the 'natural frontiers' proclaimed by the Legislative Assembly in 1791 had effectively transformed the French Republic into an empire well before Napoleon assumed an imperial title. In this respect, the transition from the Consular Republic into the First Empire was the affirmation of a reality but, as Lentz and Jourdan both go on to argue, the regime change of 1804 was also a genuine shift of emphasis and of political necessity, as well as the culmination of a successful process of external expansion and internal reform.

Jourdan and Lentz both ask themselves the question directly: what kind of regime was this? They have in common a willingness to challenge older orthodoxies directly, and emphatically reject the judgements of Georges Lefebvre and Jacques Godechot that both the Consulate and the Empire were military dictatorships.[19] In this, these two chapters encapsulate the essence of the 'new Napoleonic history', by insisting on the complex nature of the Napoleonic regimes and, indeed, in seeing the Consulate and the Empire as very different entities. If the current generation of Napoleonic scholarship has a point of agreement it is on this complexity, coupled to a rejection of a dismissive, almost simplistic, view of the period that would see the term 'Napoleonic political culture' as little short of ridiculous, and as incongruous, at best. For Jourdan, the creation of the Empire in 1804 marked an institutional revival of the initial phase of the Revolution, 1789–90, stating that 'the First Empire retained more revolutionary achievements than is normally assumed…but in a very special way'. That 'very special way' turned on the Code, which kept the regime 'legal'—a point on which Lentz agrees—and on the use of plebiscites, thus actually re-enforcing the concept of a social contract with the nation, which was in danger of being lost under the Consular constitution, the work of an increasingly elitist and detached Sièyes. Jourdan sees the real model for contemporaries as republican Rome and, in such an intellectual context, there was no contradiction in the concept of a republican empire. That is, Jourdan takes a verchallenging, refreshing line of argument, which sees '1804' as a necessary step, to save the essence of the Revolution. This may be a view with which another contributor, Howard Brown, would take issue, having entitled his last book *Ending the French Revolution*, and ending it in 1804. Where they would agree, however, is in the tensions at work within the regime. In an intriguing comment, Jourdan remarks that 'the empire ought to have been more republican than the Consulate. It was a failure...' yet only a partial failure, thanks to the presence of the Civil Code as its guide. Thierry Lentz warns that 'the (Napoleonic) empire' need not equal 'the (Napoleonic) system'. Lentz shows in detail how the regime was anything but a military dictatorship, and how Napoleon worked actively to prevent just this, but adds that domination marked the actual face of the empire, if institutions encapsulated its system. Lentz, too, gives concrete shape to Napoleonic hegemony, denoting its three circles: the regions annexed directly to France, the satellite kingdoms, and the outer allied states. These two chapters find many points of agreement, but while Jourdan concentrates on the contrasts between the Consulate and the Empire, seeking the essence of each, Lentz builds the case for complexity by systematically showing what they were not.

There were several European empires during this period, as well as Napoleon's, but only that of Spain threatened to fall under his control, however imperfectly. José Maria Portillo's chapter casts the trans-Atlantic repercussions of the Spanish 'state death' of 1808 in a fresh light, by driving to the heart of the contradiction between 'the (Napoleonic) empire' and 'the (Napoleonic) system' discerned by Lentz: the Spanish elites, both in the provinces and in the central government, were all too aware of this distinction in the wake of Bayonne. To side with Joseph in 1808 was to side with enlightened reform, however authoritarian, for Joseph came with a ready-made constitution, at a point when his opponents had not even begun contemplating framing one of their own, a process that started only two years later. That is, in 1808, Lentz' 'system' suited many of them, and thus dynastic change was not the real issue, for this had been accepted in the eighteenth century. The real pivot of Portillo's thesis is the crucial importance of the imperial dimension for the Spanish: to accept Joseph was also to accept the effective loss of national independence, for 'the empire' meant a new kind of domination, subjection to France, if at one remove, that would have meant the loss of the overseas empire. Thus, the imperial dimension prevented Napoleon from effecting the easy regime changes already achieved in Naples, while the American presence in Cadiz helped speed the process of creating a rival, alternative constitution by 1812.

Peter Hicks brings the recurring theme of tensions to the personal level of the Emperor himself in a subtle analysis of the contrasting influences of Rousseau and Machiavelli on Napoleon's political thought. That Napoleon was, as Hicks put it, 'not just a Sunday afternoon political theorist but willing to enter debate with the political greats', marks a seminal contribution to the 'new Napoleonic history'. Through examining Napoleon's reliance on—not just interest in—Rousseau, Hicks shows Napoleon as a politician concerned with the theoretical basis of his regime, whereas his almost instinctive recourse to Machiavelli underpins the tensions at the heart of his thought, not just between enlightenment and authoritarianism, but between the pragmatism demanded by *la force des choses*, and his awareness of the need for solid, philosophical foundations, which alone could legitimize his regime. Hick's chapter reveals the ever-evolving character of Napoleon's politics and helps explain how a regime in such flux could still produce so durable an institutional legacy. That a lasting, pervasive legacy could be the fruit of such tensions and contradictions, represents a fine irony.

Conclusion

The new Napoleonic history is not about creating a subjective consensus. In the face of such complexity and contradiction, this would be as foolish as it would be boring, should it come to pass. Rather, it has been about emphatically shifting the focus of research from the transient events surrounding a whirlwind of conquests and defeats, however enthralling, with their obsession with a dynasty, however colourful, that did not last, to what has proved both permanent and seminal for the character of post-war Europe, be that war 1792–1814 or 1939–45. The last word, like the first, belongs to Annie Jourdan. After over thirty years exploring the richness of the archives, we have said to an older, pre-Woolfian historiography, as Jourdan has put it in this volume, 'it was more complicated than that'.

Notes

1. Annie Jourdan, *L'Empire de Napoléon* (Paris, 2000), 7.
2. Pieter Geyl, *Napoleon. For or Against?* (First English translation, London, 1949).
3. Steven Englund, 'Monstre Sacré: the Question of Cultural Imperialism and the Napoleonic Empire', *The Historical Journal* 51 (2008): 215–250, esp. 249–250.
4. Marshal Sahlins, *Apologies to Thucydides. Understanding History as Culture and Vice Versa* (Chicago, 2004), 122–124.
5. Isser Woloch, *Napoleon and his Collaborators. The Making of a Dictatorship* (New York, 2001).
6. Englund, '*Monstre Sacré*', 216.
7. Stuart J. Woolf, *Napoleon's Integration of Europe* (London, 1991).
8. Jesus Pabón, *Las Ideas Napoleonícas* (Madrid, 1944). Frédéric Bluche, *Le Bonapartisme: aux origines de la droite autoritaire, (1800–1850)* (Paris, 1980).

9. Joan Mercader Riba, *Barcelona durante l'occupación Francesca, 1808–1814* (Madrid, 1946). Idem, *Catalunya i l'Imperi Napoleònic* (Monserrat, 1978). Idem, *José Bonaparte. Rey de España*, 2 vols (Madrid, 1969, 1971).

10. Miguel Artola Gallego, *Los Afrancesados* (Madrid, 1953). Idem, *Los Origenes de la España Contemporanea*, 2 vols (Madrid, 1959). Idem, *Antiguo Regimen y Revolución liberal* (Madrid, 1978).

11. This embraces a vast, and often excellent, corpus of work across all the countries of western Europe. It found something close to a synthesis in Jacques Godechot, *La Grande Nation*, 2 vols (Paris, 1956) and in the conference proceedings published as *Occupants, Occupés* (Brussels, 1969).

12. Thierry Lentz, *Nouvelle Histoire du Premier Empire*, 3 vols (Paris, 2002, 2003, 2007). Nine volumes of the new correspondence have appeared to date.

13. In vast corpus: Jean Tulard, *Napoléon. Le mythe du Sauveur* (Paris, 1977).

14. Georges Lefebvre, *Napoléon*, 2 vols (Paris, 1965).

15. Jose Ortega y Gasset, *The Revolt of the Masses* (English translation, London, 1933), 92.

16. For the empire conceived in this way: Michael Broers, *Europe under Napoleon* (London, 1996). Idem, 'Napoleon, Charlemagne and Lotharingia: Acculturation and the borders of Napoleonic Europe', *Historical Journal* 44 (2001): 135–154.

17. Howard G. Brown, *Ending the French Revolution. Violence, Justice and Repression for the Terror to Napoleon* (Charlottesville and London: University of Virginia Press, 2006).

18. Charles J. Esdaile, *Fighting Napoleon. Guerrillas, Bandits and Adventurers in Spain, 1808–1814* (New Haven and London: Yale University Press, 2004). Idem, 'Heroes or villains? The Spanish guerrillas in the Peninsular War', *History Today*, 38 (1988).

19. Lefebvre, *Napoléon*. Jacques Godechot, *Les Institutions de la France sous la Révolution et l'Empire* (Paris, 1951), which entitles its chapter on the Consulate and the Empire simply 'La Dictature Militaire'.

Part I
France, 1799–1814

Introduction

Michael Broers

Napoleon Bonaparte was brought to power by a coup engineered from within the Directorial government on 9–10 November 1799 (18–19 Brumaire, year VIII, according to the Revolutionary Calendar). Napoleon was one of three Consuls, the others being Ducos and Sieyès. The latter, a veteran of Revolutionary politics, had designed the new constitution to provide a stronger executive than the five man Directory, whose membership rotated frequently; the new constitution reduced the power of the legislative bodies. Ducos and Sieyès were soon replaced by Lebrun, a financial expert, and the jurist, Cambacérès; Talleyrand, an ex-noble, became Foreign Minister; Napoleon's brother, Lucien, was Minister of the Interior; the powerful Ministry of General Police was entrusted to Joseph Fouché. These senior appointments reflected the twin policies of 'amalgamation' and 'rallying' pursued by the regime, designed to reconcile the Royalist and Republican factions to Napoleon and to involve them directly in government. In February 1800 the first plebiscite was held to confirm the new constitution; 1,280,000 voted 'yes', while 1,250 rejected it. Plebiscites were used again by Napoleon to confirm key decisions, notably in 1802 (year X) for the election of Napoleon as Consul for Life, and in 1804 (year XII) for the transition from Republic to Empire, with 2,500,000 'for' to 1,400 opposed.

Fundamental reforms followed quickly on the creation of the Consulate. In February 1800 Lebrun oversaw the creation of the Bank of France, and Lucien that of the prefects, centrally appointed heads of the departments, a key element in the Napoleonic system of government. Lucien accompanied this by a thorough remodelling of the administrative system, with centrally appointed mayors for the communes and departmental councils selected by the prefects. Work started on a comprehensive land register, the *cadastre*; although not completed until the 1820s, it set taxation on a sure footing and bolstered public confidence in its fairness. In March, a new judicial system was set up along the general lines of the civil administration, eliminating elections in favour of appointments made by the Minister of Justice. In August, a new commission for legal reform was created under Napoleon, but usually chaired by Cambacérès, culminating in the Code Napoléon of 1804. The Code still forms the basis of French civil law and consolidated the Revolution's abolition of privilege, if it also curtailed the rights of women. In 1806, the University was created and given authority over the entire French educational system, including the new state secondary schools, the *lycées* (set up in 1802) and offering a secular, modern education to the propertied classes. In November, negotiations began with the Papacy to settle the religious problems begun by the Civil Constitution of 1790 and exacerbated under the Terror and the Directory, which separated Church and state completely; this resulted in the Concordat of 1802, which restored the secular clergy, but affirmed the abolition of the regular clergy and the sales of confiscated Church properties by the Revolutionary governments. The Legion of Honour was established in 1802, which presaged the creation of the Imperial nobility in 1804. One of the first, and most important innovatory reforms was the creation of the Council of State in 1800, an advisory committee composed of ministers and experts from outside the formal government apparatus appointed by Napoleon, which drew up legislative projects for approval and examination by the three legislative organs, the Senate, the Tribunate (which was abolished in 1807, when its original role as critic and interrogator of legislation proved unacceptable to Napoleon) and the *Corps Législatif,* the largest but most junior of the legislatures. Only the executive, working through the Council of State, could initiate legislation.

This early period was also turbulent politically. Royalists attempted to assassinate Napoleon in October 1800—the 'Opera Plot'—although he chose to blame Republicans for it and deported many of them. This was 'balanced' by the execution of the Duc d'Enghien in 1804, after another Royalist attempt on Napoleon's life. Napoleon amnestied many émigré nobles and clergy, but laid down draconian measures against any who did not return within the time limit of the amnesty. For contemporaries, the most important achievement of the Consulate was the series of peaces treaties with the Coalition powers, that culminated in the Peace of Amiens on 25 March 1802. Although hostilities with Britain had resumed within eighteen months, these were confined to colonial and naval actions; the Consulate remained at peace in Europe until December 1805. This allowed the fundamental Napoleonic judicial and administrative reforms to take root, but the regime also initiated a ruthless campaign of internal 'pacification' across France and its newly annexed territories in northern Italy, western Germany and what is now Belgium, spearheaded by its paramilitary police force, the Gendarmerie, which Napoleon had thoroughly reformed and strengthened in the course of 1800–02. These years also saw the systematic, if initially light, imposition of mass conscription under the terms of the Jourdan Law of 1798, a Directorial measure made effective by the Napoleonic reforms of local government and policing. The pattern of Napoleonic rule as it would work in France and throughout the empire and its satellite states was established in the period 1800–05, before the outbreak of the War of the Third Coalition. It inaugurated almost ten unbroken years of conflict.

France suffered indirectly from the wars of the period, mainly through the effects of the Continental Blockade on its ports, mass conscription and the breakdown of relations with the papacy, following Napoleon's separation from Josephine and his second marriage to Marie-Louise of Austria in 1810, which produced his son and heir, Napoleon the King of Rome, in 1811. However, France remained free from the fighting until 1814, when Allied armies invaded from the north and east, and Wellington's Anglo–Portuguese forces from the southwest. Napoleon was deposed by the hitherto subservient Senate on 3 April; he abdicated in favour of his son on 6 May (but this was ignored), and Louis XVIII was restored by the mutual consent of the Senate and the Allies. Napoleon made a final bid for power when he returned from exile on Elba, in March 1815. He assembled an army and mobilized enough support to hold power until defeated at Waterloo on 18 June. He abdicated again, four days later, and was sent into definitive exile on the remote Atlantic island of St Helena, thus ending the episode known as the 'Hundred Days'. Louis XVIII was restored a second time. Napoleon died in exile in 1821 but few of his fundamental reforms were undone by Louis or his successors. France endured a harsh military occupation until 1 December 1818.

1
Imperial France in 1808 and beyond

Thierry Lentz

What was the French Empire?

This initial question may, at first, appear absurd, but it is nevertheless important: what is meant by the 'French Empire', both in 1808 and afterwards? What, in the Napoleonic system, constituted the Empire in its strictest sense?

1 The Napoleonic Empire was not the Napoleonic 'system' but merely its centre.

A number of authors and, more generally, the wider public, confuse the Empire and the system. Indeed the latter's structure is not easily discerned.

'One of my great plans was the rejoining, the concentration of those same geographical nations which have been disunited and parcelled out by revolution and policy...; It was my intention to incorporate these people each into one nation.' That is how Napoleon, on the island of St. Helena, defined what he insisted on calling 'my system.'[1] If he is to be believed, his project aimed at uniting Europe and making France the driving force behind a balanced process of integration. For example, after Tilsit, he announced to the Corps législatif: 'France is united with the peoples of Germany by the laws of the Rhine Confederation, and with those of Spain, Holland, Switzerland and Italy by the laws of our federative system.'[2]

Details of this 'federative system' remain scarce; indeed, the facts all too often contradict Napoleon's generous, visionary claims. Consistency in vocabulary cannot hide Napoleon's pragmatism. Imperial policy emerges as merely 'a series of individual operations, guided by chance, [and dominated] by (1) the wish to profit from an advantage obtained [simply] in order to create new ones, [and] (2) the fear of allowing the enemy, or indeed even a neighbour, to occupy new positions without a compensatory move in retaliation.'[3] If he intended to 'federate' the nations of Europe, Napoleon hid it from both the other continental powers of the day, and their peoples.

2   Napoleon was not looking to create a 'universal empire'.

Napoleon was too realistic to harbour the impossible dream of 'universal empire'. Although he was subject to the 'dictatorship of events', he avoided rigid doctrinal constraints, preferring instead to adhere to a few simple, traditional principles of French diplomacy: Anglophobia and the desire to simplify the maps of Germany and Italy. He was incapable of developing his alliances and, worse still, altered them frequently. He failed to respect treaties. He remained ambivalent towards the problems of the 'nations', be they Poland, Germany or Italy. Moreover, he clouded this issue by creating satellite kingdoms, which combined 'reform and innovation with subordination and exploitation.'[4] He refused to clarify either France's ultimate goals or the ultimate purpose of the 'system'. He thus gave the impression that imperial domination was nothing more than the exploitation of his conquests, despite the fact that the empire introduced profound reforms across the entire continent. This confusion intensified the disquiet felt by his opponents while simultaneously simplifying the task of British diplomats, partisans of the European 'equilibrium', contrary to any continental 'system'. Napoleon's approach eventually proved a liability, for diplomacy requires clarity.

3   The 'system' was organized into three concentric circles.

The first and innermost circle comprised the French Empire in its strictest sense, the second the satellite kingdoms, and the third a system of alliances with various other European powers.

The first circle, Imperial France, covered a good third of Europe, roughly forty-four million inhabitants, the imperial departments proper. Their peoples were all treated as French citizens, subject to French laws and governed by a French centralized administration,[5] with the two outer circles serving simply as support in organizing Europe to the former's advantage.

The second circle comprised what could be called the 'brother kingdoms', successors to the 'sister republics' which had characterized the previous period. Joseph Bonaparte was installed in Naples, then in Spain, Louis in Holland, Jerome in Westphalia and Murat in Berg then in Naples. Eugene de Beauharnais reigned in the Kingdom of Italy on behalf of his step-father. Elisa was Grand-Duchess of Tuscany, Camille Borghese, Pauline's husband, was Governor-General for the French departments in north–western Italy. A mere child, Napoleon-Louis, son of Louis Bonaparte and Hortènse de Beauharnais, was made titular Grand-Duke of Berg after Murat was transferred to the south of Italy.

The third circle was reserved for the various alliances contracted with Spain (until 1808), Prussia, Russia and finally Austria.

To summarize, this Napoleonic 'ensemble' was founded on the two possible meanings of the word 'empire'. It was both 'domination' (the French Empire on the continent) and 'institution' (the French Empire). Indeed the Empire gives an excellent illustration of the definitions developed by theoreticians of the concept of Empire.[6]

It benefited from an enormous territorial expanse and exerted an authority over lands that lay far beyond the borders of 'France'. This space was structured hierarchically in terms of level of dependence on the centre, with the aim of creating a specifically imperial civilization.

Was the regime a military dictatorship?

That the regime introduced by Napoleon was an authoritarian regime can hardly be disputed. That we can characterize it simply as a dictatorship however seems excessive, As we shall see below, the presence of opposing powers, the durability of certain principles limiting the action of the executive, and the circumstances themselves all contrived to reduce the head of state's room to manoeuvre.

According to the celebrated French jurist Maurice Duverger, a regime can only be characterized as dictatorial if it fulfils three conditions:

1. it is installed and maintained by force, notably of a military form;
2. it is arbitrary, that is, it suppresses the elements that safeguard its citizens' liberties;
3. it is not assimilable to a political structure considered legitimate by the majority of its citizens.[7]

Each of these points, when applied to the Napoleonic regime, forces the honest observer to be moderate in his conclusions.

Georges Lefebvre, an historian who had come to Napoleon via study of the French Revolution, wrote that Napoleon's power was 'by its very origins' a 'military dictatorship', an idea also adopted by Jacques Godechot, who called his chapter on the regime 'The Military Dictatorship' without ever explaining why; the most he offers is a brief aside, describing Napoleon's entourage as nothing more than a 'civilian staff council', charged with preparing his decisions.[8] Similarly, Jacques Ellul calls it 'Military dictatorship and the triumph of the State' without even addressing the subject of military dictatorship in the section on the Napoleonic regime.

To argue that the origins of authority are the determining factor in the classification of its 'power-type' is unfair. Such an approach is misleading and serves merely to focus all such thought on the dynamic and the contradictions of the regime. It ignores the Napoleonic state's complex organization, its procedural institutions, its inspiration taken from moderate revolutionaries, indeed the very history of a regime. Brumaire was a coup d'état organized by civilians, executed by civilians and concluded by a return to the laws (the decree creating the Consulate, voted on by the councils);

the seizure of power by Bonaparte and Sieyès is fundamentally different from a *pronunciamiento*. The military intermission which followed, with the forcible expulsion of the deputies from the council, was to have more effect on the final beneficiary of the coup (Bonaparte rather than Sieyès) than the actual nature of the regime. Even if the latter's authoritarian tendencies cannot be denied, the army would only ever play a limited role (which, in any case, was always one of support) in strengthening the executive after this point. It could even be argued that the most troublesome and turbulent generals figured amongst the first 'victims' of Bonaparte's seizure of power.

Once this justification for the definition of the regime as a military dictatorship has been eliminated (that based on the origins of the regime), we can ask whether the First Empire was a military dictatorship. And the answer is no.[9]

'It is unlikely that the army has ever played such a limited role in France, and it certainly did not play a practical role in the maintenance of law and order, a task which was fulfilled by the gendarmerie and the police,'[10] writes Gilbert Bodinier, one of the foremost French historians of the Napoleonic army. This analysis is supported not only by the facts but also by contemporary accounts. Chaptal, not exactly one of Napoleon's admirers, wrote in his memoirs: 'Napoleon was constantly on guard against the generals' ambition and the people's discontent; and he was unceasingly occupied with stifling the one and preventing the other. He was seen throughout to observe the greatest reserve as regards his generals; he always kept them at a great distance from him.'[11]

We often get the impression that the army had a predominant place in Napoleonic society, and this impression is fuelled by the fact that many generals occupied posts of responsibility at the heart of its institutions and administrative bodies. The presence of military pomp and grandeur at the numerous ceremonies and the precedence accorded to superior officers seem like further proof. It is important, however, to put these facts into perspective, even though, during this period of conflict, the army gives the impression of being one of the mainstays—more symbolic, it must be said, than active, at least domestically speaking—of the imperial regime.

Once Napoleon had accepted to serve as Sieyès' 'sword', many were the generals who were tempted to oppose him. Only the Paris garrison enforced the coup of Brumaire, not the army as a whole. Furthermore, while we have no idea of what the ordinary soldier thought about the coup, we do know that the officer corps did not unanimously support Bonaparte's rise to power.[12] In the weeks that followed Brumaire, the new regime had to purge the officer corps to end 'the army's partial autonomy with respect to those in power.'[13] Unreliable generals were relieved of their functions and suspended from duty. Dozens were hounded out of the army or forcibly retired. Nor was a single purge sufficient. After the treaty of Lunéville and even more after Amiens, thousands of officers were suspended on half-pay. The army

was reorganized, which reduced the corps, and there were numerous trans-
fers 'intended to split up supporters'.[14] The last supporters of Jacobinism
bore the brunt of this reorganization. These men were 'let go' and left to
their own devices in Paris and across France at the very moment that several
important military leaders, including General Moreau, openly opposed the
life consulship and the Concordat. In a ceremony held in Notre Dame in
April 1802, a large number of officers blatantly voiced their opposition to
the Concordat. The officer corps was not solidly in favour of the plebiscite
on the life consulship, which was hidden from contemporaries by the vote-
rigging of the Interior Ministry. There were numerous generals in the *non*
camp, including Drouot, Mouton and Masséna. A number of officers close
to Bernadotte circulated pamphlets calling for Bonaparte's removal; they
were punished—although not Bernadotte—while a number of others were
struck off. Those on half-pay were distanced from the capital and the most
unruly superior officers were dispatched to foreign embassies, among them
Macdonald, Lannes, Brune, and Victor.

All this notwithstanding, military opposition continued unabated. The
conspiracy of Year XII however gave Bonaparte the opportunity to punish his
most dangerous 'rival', General Moreau, since the latter had allowed himself
be implicated in it. Arrested, judged, sentenced (albeit leniently) and driven
into exile, Moreau was forced to quit public life. His trial caused considerable unrest in Paris and elsewhere. In the end, however, the army did not
turn against the regime, and Moreau's elimination effectively decapitated
military opposition. From then on, only pockets of resistance remained.
Copies of the satire, *Allons planter nos choux (Let's go plant our cabbages)*, a
text intended to enflame discharged officers, were found and confiscated.[15]
The proclamation of Empire troubled a few military consciences, and there
were some outbursts in taverns, but these rumblings were nothing when
compared to those at the beginning of the Consulate. Dissatisfied generals
had to, for the most part, content themselves with disguised expressions of
their discontent or opposition, such as the Admiral Bruix, who upon discussion of what an effigy of the emperor should wear, declared to the dignitaries
present: 'Make him naked; you will find it easier to kiss his backside'.[16]

Only insignificant plots or isolated outbursts remained, not all, it must
be said, committed by republican generals.[17] One of the biggest plots was,
however, Republican in nature. In 1808, General Malet replaced General
Servan who had died suddenly, at the head of a conspiracy, which was
uncovered by the police and the key conspirators were put behind bars.[18]
The presence of a number of famous generals' names in papers relating to
the affair, which included Masséna, convinced the emperor that he would
have to keep an eye on some of the Revolution's bigger military names.
When the emperor left Paris for the Austrian campaign he made sure to take
Masséna with him, and he was also no doubt pleased to see Jourdan being
kept occupied in Spain, where Augereau would soon join him. When, four

years later, the 'serious' Malet affair broke, it was once again the generals (Malet, Lahorie, Guidal[19]) who led what became known as the 'the attack of 23 October 1812'. Although a couple of units made the mistake of participating, most of the army remained loyal to an Empire increasingly beseiged in Spain and Russia.[20]

Napoleon learnt some valuable lessons from the conspiracies of the Consular period. Henceforth, he kept his officers well away from power, while at the same time, paradoxically, giving them a central role in French society. He made them rich, decorated them, sought to create a personal bond with them through the Legion of Honour, and even guaranteed their retirements with jobs in the police, on stud farms, customs and excise, and in the postal service. He also attempted to draw the more politically 'active' amongst them closer to the regime. New military campaigns were essential in uniting men of all ranks and got troublemakers out of France, a tactic. War brought men together in the spirit of adventure. Finally, military campaigns were also a means of introducing new blood into the officer class.

In arguing that the Napoleonic regimes were not a military dictatorship, it might be countered that a sizeable part of the civilian administration were soldiers. The significance of this ought not, however, to be overemphasized; the number of officers and ex-officers acting in a civilian capacity was no greater than during the old order or even after Napoleon. Almost by tradition, former officers were employed in the administration in so-called 'reserved' positions. This was primarily because the military corps was the only national institution with a proper organization during the Consulate, and the only body to have experience in administrative affairs. Thus, the Consulate relied heavily on this group of men to fulfil certain essential roles within the administration; the training and experience of these ex-soldiers were unique at the time.

Those who benefited were not always battle-scarred warriors lusting after power, far from it. More often than not, they were drawn from the lower ranks on active service and had served in the army administration, or had already retired. Veterans often became mayors or held ceremonial roles in local government. In 1810, 14 per cent of mayors were former soldiers and fifty-eight retired generals were serving as mayors of towns with over five thousand inhabitants, although rarely of larger towns, only seven mayors of the fifty largest cities in France fell into this category. This was intended to compensate for the limited abilities of local notables and/or to introduce government supporters into apolitical administrative posts.

At the apex of the state, of the Empire's ten major dignitaries, only Berthier (Vice-Connétable from 1807) and Murat (Grand Amiral) were generals. Of the thirty-two ministers appointed, twelve had served in the military.[21] Traditionally, the Ministries of War, War Administration and the Navy were held by military men. Only six of the ministers who exercised war-time commands during the Revolution did so under Napoleon. In the Council of State, the first promotion of twenty-nine members included only five generals and two naval officers. Out of a total of one hundred and eighty-four nominations to the Senate, only forty-one were officers, of whom thirty-two could be considered 'career officers'. In the Corps législatif, only 10 per cent of the deputies were officers. There were even fewer in the Tribunat. After a wave of diplomatic postings during the Consulate—18 ambassadors and ministers plenipotentiary from military backgrounds—the Empire saw a reduction in the number of generals posted to embassies; eleven out of the thirty available posts. Fifty-three out of about three-hundred prefects were ex-soldiers, but the pragmatic nomination process ensured that most prefects were civilians. Overall, the military presence in prominent civilian posts should not be exaggerated.

A uniform or formal dress was standard for the majority of State officials, but it was a tradition institutionalized since the Revolution and did not represent a desire to militarize society. However, the influence of the military model was particularly felt in civilian administration. The art of war and the organization of armies had very quickly embraced the rationalism of the Enlightenment, both in terms of recruitment and command. This influence extended to the administration's subordination to the State, a principle that played a far greater role in post-Revolutionary France's 'national' forces than in the mercenary armies of the old order. In this sense, the army was a 'modern' organization ahead of its time, and one that was to have a profound influence, through its very example, on a society that was in the process of restructuring itself.

Despite appearances, the First Empire was not a military dictatorship. We can therefore trust that Napoleon was sincere when he said: 'Military authority has no place or use in civil order'.[22] The emperor appears to have earned the respect of Roederer who, immediately post-Brumaire, stated that he (Napoleon) was 'the most civilian of generals'.[23]

Was the French Empire a 'state based on law'?

The study of the imperial constitutions has often been neglected, because they were regarded as merely window dressing for Napoleon's dictatorship. However, the Empire functioned with a constitution. Moreover, it functioned in the belief—and this applies as much to the Emperor as to those around him—that the constitution was, if not sacred law, at least a restrictive code of behaviour that one ignored at one's peril. It seems excessive to suggest rather abruptly that 'the Napoleonic institutions never truly existed'[24] and even more so to think that the constitutional code was 'rather artificial'.[25] In order to demonstrate that concept of the rule of law had begun to take form at the apex of the state, one simply needs to see how much Napoleon and his advisors took pains to interpret the constitution during the many crises that they faced, even to the point of remoulding it, in order to persuade themselves (and others) that they were acting in respect of it. Indeed, the Senate invoked the fundamental text and the emperor's lack of respect for his constitutional oath when it deposed him in 1814. The constitutions contributed to the regulation of political life, playing the role of a crash-barrier to what Raymond Aron called Napoleon's 'irrational goals'.[26]

Napoleonic power was not exerted arbitrarily but within established judicial norms. The fundamental law of the First Empire was the evolutionary series of reforms begun in 1789, which Godechot called the 'irreversible options': equality before the law, the abolition of feudalism, and a constitutional and representative government.[27] With a few organizational readjustments (the concentration of the executive, the reorganization of national representation, the division of the legislature) there was constitutional activity under Napoleon, which could even be described as lively. Understanding the interpretation, application and evolution of these constitutional principles without being constrained by 'liberal thought'—dominant today but not at the time—allows us better to understand the evolution of the Napoleonic state as it gradually but ineluctably advanced towards the 'legalisation' of the exercise of power in France.

Different forms of government were tried after 1789, so much so that some authors have suggested that the French Revolution was a 'revolution of the executive'.[28] None of them survived the revolutionary storm. Each failure merely confirmed that stability rested only in reducing the absolute control of the legislature over the executive. The directorial constitution was a huge step forward, both on paper and, to a large extent, in hearts and minds, but the supremacy of the legislature was finally discredited by the political realities. Henceforth, the English model of a balance of powers was rejected and considered unsuitable to French circumstances. Bonaparte famously wrote to Talleyrand: 'The English constitution is nothing but a charter of privileges: it is a ceiling all in black though embroidered in gold.' Although in favour of the 'English' regime, Talleyrand sensed that the hour had not yet come to broach the subject and so was not to contradict his correspondent.

The Directorial constitution raised another problem. The executive and the legislature were now both powerful but remained strictly separate entities, with no safety valve to control conflicts between them. Each election led to a coup d'état and, to combat this instability, Sieyès instigated the 'regeneration' project that led to Brumaire.

Bonaparte was already a partisan of strong government, as can be seen in his letter to Talleyrand, itself a sort of first draught for his constitutional project: 'In a government in which every authority emanates from the nation, in which the sovereign is the people, why include in the legislative power such things that are foreign to it? ... The power of the government, in all the breadth I give it, should be considered the true representative of the nation, and it should govern in according to the constitutional charter.... It would comprise the entirety of the administration or the execution, which is by our constitution conferred on the legislative power... [The] legislative power, impassive, without rank in the Republic, without eyes or ears for that which surrounds it, would have no ambition and would no longer inundate us with a thousand circumstantial laws which are self-defeating through their very absurdity, and which make us a lawless nation with three-hundred large tomes of laws.'[29]

Too convoluted, too certain of his own importance and, above all, too theoretical, Sieyès did not long remain the man of providence. One month after Brumaire, he was relegated to presidency of the Senate; though his constitutional ideas still formed the basis of the constitution for Year VIII. Bonaparte had allowed him influence over what he considered secondary matters, the 'legislative plumbing'. However, Napoleon imposed his own views on issues that offered him real power; faced with a divided legislature, the government was concentrated in the hands of the first of the three consuls.

On the day the new constitution came into force, the three consuls proclaimed: 'Citizens, the Revolution has been fastened to the principles that began it. It is finished.'[30] Much ink has been spilled over this last word: some interpret it as meaning that the Revolution was over, for today to the word means finished. However, the 1798 *Dictionnaire de l'Académie française* defines it as: 'When describing paintings, it is said that a work is finished to indicate that it is perfect. It is also used to describe theoretical works.... It is also adjectival, and signifies that which is limited, narrow.... It is also used substantively, particularly in the arts, when speaking of works completed with care.'[31] Thus, in the language of the time, finished meant perfect rather than concluded. It was thus not a denial of the Revolution but rather a recognition of its limits, 'within the principles that began it', that is to say, those of 1789. Those principles were perfect or finished. It is not clear why, unless for practical reasons or, more likely, due to ideological hindsight, a large part of the traditional historiography ends the Revolution in 1799. In a simplified chronological classification the Consulate and at least part of the Empire actually constitute a fourth Revolutionary period.[32]

For fourteen years this text was the foundation on which France's institutions were built, although it underwent serious modifications. The first important reform, on 4 August 1802 (16 Thermidor, Year X), as well as granting Bonaparte the consulship for life and the option to designate his successor, also vastly reorganized the electoral process, the nomination process for members of the legislature and the Senate's powers. The creation of the empire placed an hereditary emperor at the head of the Republic, 'changing the forms of government but not the nature of the regime.'[33] Between then and 1814, there were around thirty *senatus-consultes* that reformed the constitution, both directly and indirectly. Most concerned the revision of a particular detail, but a few modified the fundamental equilibrium at the heart of the constitution, such as the abolition of the Tribunat (19 August 1807) and the modification of the regency (5 February 1813).

This constitutional organization was structured around principles already present in Bonaparte's letter to Talleyrand, and these were subsequently refined. Executive authority was exercised by the emperor, who acted within his own area of expertise, an area enlarged following each reform and subject to no control other than that of the nation, of which he was a representative, with an hierarchical administration below him. The two houses (the Corps législatif and the Tribunat) drafted legislation; they were both elected from lists of approved candidates, followed by an electoral college process, which rarely intervened in affairs of an executive nature: 'The government is no longer a direct product, as it once was, of the Corps législatif; its ties with it are distant', rejoiced Napoleon.[34] The Senate arbitrated in constitutional matters to 'conserve the constitution'. The executive was the crux of, and the driving force behind, the system: 'The great order that governs the entire world must govern each part of the world', declared Napoleon to the Conseil d'Etat. 'Like the sun, the government is at the centre of society: around it the many diverse institutions must trace their orbit, and from it they must never stray. The government must regulate the combinations of each of them in a manner that they ensure the general harmony. In the system of the world, nothing is left to chance; in the system of societies, nothing must depend on the whims of individuals.'[35]

Originally, the power of the executive was tempered by the existence of the legislature and the executive's various councils. Chaptal, who liked neither Napoleon nor what had become of the regime, nevertheless wrote (relatively optimistically): 'Truly it is difficult to conceive of a constitution which offers more guarantees for the rights of the people. It is difficult to leave less to the arbitrary judgement of the head of the government. The limits of power are clear and unconfused.'[36] Others too believed that the text not only gave the chambers great freedom of judgement over legislation, but also, via debate, power to prevent the executive acting at will. The Tribunat long opposed the Code Civil and the creation of the Legion of Honour; budget discussions in the Corps législatif and the Council of State amended several government projects. Nevertheless, without rejecting entirely the separation of powers, the authors of the constitution fashioned a 'state constructed around one power, endowed with a preeminent statute',[37] a concept in place since 1791, both directly and indirectly. By perseverance and immutability over several years in power, Napoleon was able to impose a conception that increasingly worked in the Executive's favour, dominating the executive, legislature and, partially, the judiciary. This was not achieved through brute force, but rather through a pragmatic and sequential approach towards the concentration of legitimacy in the figure of a single sovereign. He also profited from a succession of abdications, often at the very heart of the opposition, whether in the form of the disorderly retreat of the *idéologues*, or the rallying of large swathes of monarchists after the coronation and the marriage to Marie-Louise. He remarked, 'France needs a monarchy that is moderate yet strong'.[38]

In terms of positive law, the successive reforms, extended competences, and expansion of the executive authority beyond its original remit all stemmed from procedures which were, in appearance, juridically correct. The absence of a declaration of rights and the avoidance of a definition of the government's guiding principles made all change possible, provided the formalities were respected. The Napoleonic constitutions were technical, not philosophical, texts. Their authors were modest in their ambitions; abandoning any thoughts of a 'comprehensive endeavour'[39] that would encompass every aspect of State and society. In this context, Napoleon's reign was a progression, uninterrupted and almost without hindrance, towards an 'executive dictatorship'.[40]

Initially, the authors of the constitution of 1799 retained the principle of a collegiate executive, a form retained since 1792. The consular regime, with its three consuls, did not, on the face of it, stray from this revolutionary norm. However, the consular triumvirate was unbalanced; the proclamation of Empire ended this legal fiction. 'Government' was now formally concentrated in the hands of one man.[41] From this point on, no institution other than the emperor could wield this power, not even a group of ministers, or his advisory councils.

Nevertheless, the tripartite separation of powers was not affected, the term government only referred to the executive power. There was nothing shocking for contemporaries about this concentration of power; it was in the French monarchical tradition and the failure of the three-man Consulate encouraged this view. Pragmatically, Bonaparte's personal ability to govern was obvious. The United States, a much-admired Republic, possessed a one-man executive, and still does. Justification was also found in the ancient Roman office of dictator, which entrusted power in times of crisis to one exceptional man, while maintaining republican institutions. Cincinnatus abandoned his plough to become dictator and, having defeated the Aequi, simply returned to his farm as before. Bonaparte was no Cincinnatus, but a Caesar, the dictator who wanted to be, and became, king. In a society awash with references to antiquity, such a comparison could quickly become reality.

Napoleon Bonaparte's personality, successes and actions did the rest. 'I have always commanded…once I had command, I no longer recognized master nor law',[42] he explained in an un-nuanced version of Montesquieu's axiom, 'every man invested with power is apt to abuse it'. Until 1812, he had the support of a large group of political, administrative and economic elites as well as popular approval. As for those who doubted, the strength of the 'government' was enough to instil a certain caution. Napoleon's political traps ensured that individuals could just as easily be ostracized as encouraged to rally, each time with due respect for protocol and without bloodshed. This was impressive progress compared to previous regimes.

Apart from its leader, the State now stood at the centre of French society. One author has even written of a 'Napoleonic Revolution.'[43] Napoleon succeeded where Louis XVI and his ministers had failed in the 1780s. He strengthened and modernized the state, again imbuing it with both unity and authority.

The correlation between the State's authority and the increasing concentration of power in the executive is undeniable. Constitutional and legislative progress was gradually annihilated with the growth of personal rule. Napoleon cunningly profited from the weaknesses and resignation (albeit temporary) of those who could provide checks and balances, so imposing his decisions and views without discussion. Although such moderate 'absolutism' could have degenerated into tyranny or a stifling absolutism in different hands, Bonaparte spared France from a violent, military dictatorship. The Napoleonic regime made its soldiers obedient tools of the government, not a state within a state. Napoleon sent them to fight abroad, their sole legitimate activity after all. The gradual tightening of the Napoleonic regime is of course irrefutable. But to criticize the consular and imperial seizure of power, is to do so in the name of the French Revolution, a revolution which had little respect for the principles it sought to impose on the world.

Notes

1. Las Cases, *Mémorial de Sainte-Hélène*, 11 November 1816, ed. Marcel Dunan (Paris, 1951). Thanks to Hamish Davey-Wright for the translation of this article.
2. Speech given 17 August 1807, reported in *Le Moniteur*, 17 August 1807 (my italics).
3. André Palluel-Guillard, 'Les événements en France', *Histoire et dictionnaire du Consulat et de l'Empire*, ed. Alfred Fierro, André Palluel-Guillard and Jean Tulard (Paris, 1995), 399.
4. Alexander Grab, *Napoleon and the Transformation of Europe* (New York/London, 2003), 19.
5. On Imperial administration: Thierry Lentz (ed.), *Quand Napoléon inventait la France. Dictionnaire des institutions du Premier Empire* (Paris, 2008).
6. See for example Jean Tulard (ed.), *Les empires occidentaux de Rome à Berlin* (Paris, 1997).
7. Maurice Duverger, 'Dictature', *Encyclopaedia Universalis* (Paris, French 1980 edn), V, 551–553. This article resumes the major points of his work on the theme, published by Duverger in the 1960s.
8. *Les institutions de la France sous la Révolution et l'Empire* (Paris, 1968), 553.
9. Jean Tulard, *Napoléon ou le mythe du sauveur* (Paris, 1987 edn), 124. Charles Durand, 'Rome remplace Sparte', in *Napoléon et l'Empire*, ed. Jean Mistler (Paris, 1968), I, 231.
10. Gilbert Bodinier, 'Du soldat républicain à l'officier impérial. Convergences et divergences entre l'armée et la société', in *Histoire militaire de la France. 2/ De 1715 à 1871*, ed. André Corvisier (Paris, 1997 edn), 300.
11. Jean-Antoine Chaptal, *Mes souvenirs sur Napoléon* (Paris, 1893), 247–248.
12. Bernard Gainot, 'L'opposition militaire. Autour des sociétés secrètes dans l'armée', *Annales historiques de la révolution française* 5 (2006): 45–58. Thierry Lentz, *Le 18 Brumaire. Les coups d'État de Napoléon Bonaparte* (Paris, 1995), 380–384.

13. William Serman and Jean-Paul Bertaud, *Nouvelle histoire militaire de la France. I. 1789–1919* (Paris, 1998), 119.
14. Ibid.
15. Bulletin de police, 3 November 1804.
16. Eléonore-Adèle d'Osmond, *Récits d'une tante: Mémoires de la Comtesse de Boigne, née d'Osmond* (Paris 1907), I, 226.
17. The nobles did, to a certain extent, return to the military; their proportion amongst active officers rose from five to ten per cent of the total.
18. For details of this conspiracy, see Henri Gaubert's colourful account, *Conspirateurs au temps de Napoléon Ier* (Paris, 1962), 289–303.
19. These three men were the only generals sentenced to death and executed during the Consulate and Empire, compared to 54 during the Convention and one (Maximilien Jacob) during the Directory (Georges Six, *Les généraux de la Révolution et de l'Empire* [Paris, 1974 edn], 283).
20. For the Malet affair: Thierry Lentz, *Nouvelle histoire du Premier Empire II. L'effondrement du système napoléonien* (Paris, 2004), 334–346. For military plots against Napoleon: Edouard Guillon, *Les complots militaires sous le Consulat et l'Empire* (Paris, 1894).
21. Nine in the army and three in the navy. Nine ministers were division generals (Berthier, Carnot, Caulaincourt, Clarke, Davout, Dejean, Lacuée, Savary) while one was a vice-admiral (Decrès). See Thierry Lentz, *Dictionnaire des ministres de Napoléon* (Paris, 1999).
22. Letter to Junot, 21 May 1806, *Correspondance de Napoléon 1er publiée par ordre de l'Empereur Napoléon III* (Paris, 1858–69), 12, 254.
23. *Oeuvres du comte P. L. Roederer*, ed. Antoine-Marie Rœderer (Paris, 1854), vol. 3.
24. Marcel Prélot and Jean Boulouis, *Institutions politiques et droit constitutionnel* (Paris, 1980 edn), 384.
25. Jean-Jacques Chevallier, *Histoire des institutions et des régimes politiques de la France, de 1789 à nos jours* (Paris, 1977 edn), 107.
26. Raymond Aron, *Introduction à la philosophie de l'histoire* (Paris, 1986 edn), 128.
27. Jacques Godechot, 'Sens et importance de la transformation des institutions révolutionnaires à l'époque napoléonienne', *Revue d'histoire moderne et contemporaine* 17 (1970): 795.
28. See the issue of *Annales historiques de la Révolution française* which discusses this question (332 [2003]).
29. Napoleon Bonaparte, *Correspondance générale publiée par la Fondation Napoléon* (Paris, 2004), 2,065.
30. *Correspondance de Napoléon 1er publiée par ordre de l'Empereur Napoléon III* (Paris, 1858–69), no. 4, 422.
31. *Dictionnaire de l'Académie française* (Paris, 1798 edn), 588. All of the Académie française dictionaries are available online at http://artfl-project.uchicago.edu/node/17.
32. For more on this theme, see Thierry Lentz, 'Les consuls de la République: la Révolution est finie', *Terminer la Révolution* (Paris, 2003), 19–37.
33. Claude Goyard, 'Constitution de l'an XII', *Dictionnaire Napoléon*, ed. Jean Tulard (Paris, 1999 edn), 2 vols, I, 527.
34. At the Conseil d'État, 7 February 1804, Jean Pelet de la Lozère, *Opinions de Napoléon sur divers sujets de politique et d'administration* (Paris, 1833), 150.
35. Adrien Dansette, *Napoléon. Pensées pour l'action* (Paris, 1943), 30.
36. *Mes souvenirs sur Napoléon par le comte Chaptal* (Paris, 1893), 212.

37. Jacques Chevallier, 'La séparation des pouvoirs', *La continuité constitutionnelle en France de 1789 à 1989* (Aix-en-Provence/Paris, 1990), 130.

38. *Mémoires de S* [tanislas de] *Girardin* (Paris, 1834), 2 vols, II, 353.

39. Marcel Morabito and Daniel Bourmaud, *Histoire constitutionnelle et politique de la France* (Paris, 1996 edn), 127.

40. Maurice Hauriou, *Précis de droit constitutionnel* (Paris, 1923), 2 vols, I, 338.

41. The first article of the constitution of Year XII reads: 'The government of the Republic is conferred upon an Emperor, who bears the title Emperor of the French.'

42. Las Cases, *Mémorial de Sainte-Hélène*, 31 October 1816.

43. Michael Broers, *Europe under Napoléon. 1799–1815* (New York, 1996), 50.

2
The Origins of the Napoleonic System of Repression

Howard G. Brown

The upheaval of the French Revolution subtly but profoundly changed the meaning of the word *répression*. By 1802 the long-standing emphasis on containing disorder gave way to a new emphasis on suppressing disorder; in other words, repression as a defensive, prophylactic action was replaced conceptually by repression as an interventionist and transformative action. Repression did not merely defend order, it brought order out of disorder. The timing of this semantic shift indicates that the origins of the Napoleonic system of repression lay mainly in efforts to end the tumult of the French Revolution by imposing a new republican order on France. The great difficulty republicans experienced in achieving their purpose tainted their means and in doing so thwarted their ends. Moreover, Revolutionary and Napoleonic France used similar methods to impose a new form of order in subjugated territories only to find that there too both the methods and outcome could be compromised.

* * *

My previous work has described the form of rule that gradually emerged in France between the Fructidor coup d'état (September 1797) and Bonaparte becoming First Consul for Life (August 1802) as 'liberal authoritarianism.'[1] This phrase means more than strengthening the executive at the expense of democracy and parliamentary governance. It also reflects an increasingly cogent and fixed response to the tension between the liberal democratic polity sought by French revolutionaries and the repeated recourse by successive regimes to exceptional measures that violated these principles in the name of public safety. The resulting form of rule depended on a powerful, yet highly regulated, police and judicial apparatus combined with clearly defined and thoroughly integrated exceptions to liberal constitutional norms in the form of martial law, expedited justice and political policing. This was the essence of the Napoleonic system of repression.

This system was not planned, but resulted from complicated interplay between efforts to restore order and efforts to impose a revolutionary republic. The excesses committed during the Terror tainted any later use of coercive force by the republic. Furthermore, after 1794 the Thermidorian politicians who claimed their authority on the basis of having ended the Terror, nonetheless repeatedly resorted to similar methods—political purges, summary justice, and military repression—always in the name of saving liberty and the republic. Overwhelming hostility to the young republic meant that the constitutional regime that began in 1795 had to be rigorously defended and often simply imposed by force. Thus, in 1795 when it assumed office, the Directory began with a split personality. It was designed as a liberal democratic republic whose legitimacy would rest on representative democracy, constitutionalism, and the rule of law, but it opened with compromised elections, an amnesty for 'terrorists,' renewed persecution of priests and émigrés, and an expansionist war effort. As a result, Directorial politicians found it difficult to separate methods of repression needed to preserve the regime from methods of persecution that favoured a political faction or forced the pace of social change.

The tension between the rule of law as one of the Directory's basic sources of legitimacy and the need to restore order as one of its most pressing problems placed a heavy burden on the new system of criminal justice. Though more effective than often claimed, the criminal courts of the Directory did not perform well when it came to enforcing the laws against 'political crimes'. Jurors tended to sympathize with resistance to the state, especially when it involved refractory priests, reluctant conscripts, or royalist brigands. The anti-republican results of the elections of spring 1797 brought a near collapse in government authority and a commensurate surge in violence. The Directory responded with the Fructidor coup d'état and a battery of exceptional measures. Endemic political violence and rampant brigandage had made it clear that some exceptions to constitutionalism and the rule of law were needed to restore the Republic's authority. However, republican notions about the sources of opposition, which they saw as royalist officials, émigré nobles and refractory priests, shaped the exceptional measures. These ranged from a massive purge of officials, whether elected or appointed, to giving the government exclusive authority to declare individual cities and towns under 'state of siege', thereby transferring all police powers to the local army commander.[2] The application of these measures, however, often made them look less like necessary means to defend the republic and more like opportunities to press the social and cultural revolution, or simply to gain a factional advantage at the local level.

The same mix of defensive measures and social coercion characterized the Directory's response to the crisis of 1799. Witness the discrimination against former nobles added to the law of hostages and the forced loan thereby again combining responses to a security crisis with political persecution. At the same time, the army received ever greater authority to impose the 'state of siege', to command national guardsmen formed up as mobile columns, and to use military justice to prosecute civilians. All of these measures were used in the fight against ordinary crime and open rebellion alike. The Consulate continued the pattern after 1799, including the practice of using exceptional measures adopted in defence of the republic as an opportunity to persecute political opponents. Bonaparte turned the attempt to assassinate him on 24 December 1800 into an opportunity to deport over a hundred radicals, to arrest and imprison scores of royalists without trial, and to cover a brutal repression of brigandage and rural resistance in the west and south. Thus, the repressive measures adopted in 1797, 1799 and 1801 were echoes of the Terror—state violence that trampled on the rule of law in the name of saving the republic and securing liberty; however, the declining scope of the measures ensured that the echo resonated less audibly each time.

In fact, 1801 marked an important turning point in the use of military justice to judge civilians. Lawmakers in the early Consulate decided to let the law that sent brigands before regular military courts lapse on the grounds that it was a travesty of due process. Not surprisingly, the scourge of brigandage continued unabated. Bonaparte responded by creating a more ruthless form of military justice for use against civilians: Extraordinary Military Commissions attached to flying columns (*corps d'éclaireurs*) that combined regular troops, gendarmes and national guardsmen. At least seven of these operated in the spring of 1801, four in the south and three in the west. Those in the south executed more than half—and freed only a fifth—of the 400 hundred 'brigands' and accomplices brought before them over four months. In order to deal with the multifaceted violence of the south-east, the mobile columns and their attendant military commissions moved back and forth between coastal cities (Montpellier, Nîmes, Marseille, Toulon), more remote *chefs lieux* (Rodez, Privas, Digne), and isolated hill towns (Millau, Le Vigan, Alès, Montélimar). Peripatetic justice allowed most executions to be carried out by army firing squads in the towns and villages where the condemned had lived.

Though not without some judicial scruples, the mobile military commissions were insufficiently punctilious to continue for long; thus, the Consulate felt compelled to create a more regulated alternative. Although liberal deputies passionately opposed the government's proposal, the majority of lawmakers still voted to create Special Tribunals, which combined civilian and military judges with a streamlined judicial procedure and no appeals, in order to deal with crimes for which regular juries were deemed inadequate, that is, armed rebellion, highway robbery, vagabondage and counterfeiting. Special Tribunals largely replaced military commissions, though a couple continued to operate in the worst areas (Bouches-du-Rhône, Morbihan). Though ostensibly temporary, Special Tribunals became a permanent feature of the Napoleonic judiciary. Not only were one third of all individuals charged with felonies (*délits criminels*) judged 'spécialement', but, in their early years at least, Special Tribunals were responsible for four-fifths of the death penalties and three-fifths of the lengthy sentences to hard labour (14 to 24 years) meted out by civilian courts in France.[3]

Special Tribunals embodied the Napoleonic solution to the tension between liberal notions of due process and the revolutionary recourse to exceptional justice. Although generally painted as a revival of the hated provostial justice of the ancien régime,[4] Special Tribunals featured considerably more protection for the accused. Furthermore, the alternatives to date—ranging from revolutionary justice in 1793–4 to the Extraordinary Military Commissions of 1801—had all been quicker, harsher, and more prone to error. Thus, the creation of Special Tribunals epitomized the Napoleonic system of repression in France; they constituted a form of exceptionalism made less objectionable by being fully institutionalized and well regulated.

Other features of Napoleon's system of repression followed a similar trajectory. Several deserve mention because they were deemed characteristic of Napoleonic rule. The *gendarmerie nationale* saw its greatest transformation in the years 1797–8 when it was purged, reorganized, and given a professional code. It was then steadily expanded. By 1802, the *gendarmerie* was almost four times the size of the pre-revolutionary *maréchaussée*. Though not usually beloved, the gendarme was certainly respected. Furthermore, the *gendarmerie* had become a truly national police force. The build-up of the *gendarmerie* is especially important because it eliminated the use of the National Guard—that quintessentially local, revolutionary, and often ineffectual institution—as a tool for repressing resistance in the countryside.

Preventive detention too, was rapidly regularized in the early Napoleonic years. During the Directory it had been masked as prolonged incarceration pending further evidence—or the passing of the annual elections—whereas the early Consulate authorized prefects formally to keep criminal defendants who had been acquitted at trial in custody, pending forced enrolment into the army or deportation to the colonies.[5] This evolved into the yet more regulated system of distinguishing between prisoners by '*Haute Police*', the extra-judicial system of arrest and detention and those subjected to 'internal exile'.

Such hallmarks of Napoleonic repression have led some historians to describe the Empire as a 'police state,' though the term 'security state' is preferable.[6] It is here that Napoleon very differed greatly from the Directory. Aware of his violations of due process, and sensitive to the impact this would have on public opinion, he agreed to the formation of a Senatorial Commission on Individual Liberty. Whether this was mere window dressing or whether it served as a conscience for the Ministry of Police,[7] the very existence of the Senatorial Commission represents a continuing effort to square the circle of a fully-fledged rule of law based on constitutionalism and due process, and exceptional measures deemed essential to both public safety and the survival of the regime.

* * *

The origins of the Napoleonic system of repression in France were also the origins of the system used to repress resistance beyond the frontiers. Though calling this latter a system may be an exaggeration, it is possible to discern patterns in the extraordinary tensions between due process and savage slaughter that arose in various areas. There is no doubt that atrocities were committed by both sides, and plenty of them, but there were limits and those limits were usually tied to broader issues of social and political legitimacy.

Revolutionary armies were considerably nastier occupiers than their eighteenth-century precursors. But it needs to be noted that a counter-trend also appeared, one which increasingly defined and refined quasi-judicial methods of dealing with civilians who used force to resist their subjugation. These 'unlawful combatants'—otherwise known as guerillas, partisans, *francs-tireurs* or some other epithet that cast resistors outside the norms of domestic and international law—were generally treated as brigands. But this did not resolve the problem, for even the most heinous of common criminals were thought to merit some form of official justice.

Changes in the methods used to deal with resistors are difficult to discern because they require extensive archival research on a broad comparative basis. Secondary sources that focus on one revolt, one region, or even one country, are essential to establish a sense of context, but they rarely provide details on the nature of the military justice that accompanied occupation or subjugation. In fact, scholars do not usually specify precisely what kind of judicial institution was responsible for the results they cite—often reduced to death sentences—as evidence of extensive repression. In fact, the mere recourse to military justice is itself taken as proof of a general ruthlessness, without any regard for previous practices or the perception of contemporaries. Only by reading the actual military court records themselves does it become possible to gauge the nature of the repression, and thus to assess the part played by law and a formal sense of justice in tailoring responses to resistance. Furthermore, it takes a comparative analysis to identify general trends. Such an analysis must begin by looking more closely at the use of military justice in repressing regional resistance in France itself. This reveals a clear trajectory toward more scruples in the use of military justice during the Directory, at least domestically, but that beyond the borders the pattern is less obvious and was often lacking altogether.

Historians often note the 750 death sentences handed out by the military commissions that followed the Quiberon landings of June–July 1795 in Brittany, but they usually ignore the less draconian aspects of the repression. These include the acquittal of over 1,200 defendants and the sentencing of 200 *Chouans,* the rebels of the Normandy-Brittany border, to four months or less in prison. Above all, most of the 9,000 combatants captured by republican forces were not even put on trial—though as many as 1,000 of these were drafted into the army whereas another 500 died in prison.[8] Nonetheless, General Hoche's eloquent plea against the judicial slaughter of thousands of Frenchmen and the government's focus on making a quick return to order led to genuine leniency. As a result, ordinary *Chouans* were released without trial in exchange for weapons and a fine paid in grain. At least 3,000 *Chouans* took advantage of this arrangement.[9]

The most spectacular use of regular military courts in these years came in response to the so-called 'Peasants War' that erupted in the annexed departments of Belgium in the autumn of 1798. Rather than engaging in massive prisoner releases, almost all the 2,000 Belgian rebels taken prisoner had to face military justice. Six military courts sitting at Brussels and Liège heard cases pertaining to almost 1,800 insurgents. These courts pronounced 280 death sentences and 400 sentences of four months in prison, but they also failed to convict 1,200 other accused rebels.[10] These new figures indicate a truly massive judicial repression pursued systematically through regular military courts rather than the more arbitrary military commissions. All the same, the number of death sentences pronounced at Brussels alone would have meant holding several firing squads a week for months on end.

As significant as this volume of judicial activity was, however, it should be noted that the judicial repression in Belgium did not share important features of earlier repressions. First, apart from a one-day military commission at Malines, rebels were not subjected to the kind of improvised justice that had characterized repression in the Vendée. It is quite clear that the First Republic had a growing conscience. Rather than resurrect military commissions, the Directory used regular military courts (*conseils de guerre*) to judge the insurgents of the Belgian 'Peasants' War.' This meant far more protection for the accused. Unlike the Vendéans, the Belgian rebels were tried for individual actions, automatically received legal council, and had access to an appeal process. These provisions saved many rebels from summary execution. So rigorous was the review of procedures, for example, that verdicts were overturned for anything from failing to hear defence witnesses to not justifying the use of a substitute clerk.[11] As a result, the execution rate for Belgian rebels tried by military courts was a fairly modest 16 per cent.

Evidence of a substantial increase in the legal protections offered rebels can also be found in the Directory's response to the royalist revolt around Toulouse in the summer of 1799. Despite the slaughter of a thousand rebels in two weeks, the subsequent judicial repression combined the most lenient features of the post-Quiberon and Belgian repressions. This led to the administrative release of 2,700 insurgents from the prisons of Toulouse. Even though two military courts sat for over a year, only 15 executions and two deportations resulted. Such leniency resulted from protracted legal wrangling. It was a sign of the times that even military justice got bogged down in legalisms.[12]

The tendency toward more sophisticated forms of military justice in the repression of domestic revolt in the years 1795–1800 was not matched in subjugated territories, whether in the Caribbean colonies or in those parts of Italy under military occupation. The scattered and incomplete nature of the documentation for much of what happened outside France permits only an impressionistic analysis, and yet it is clear that military justice ranged from reasonably consistent to highly improvised.

Repression in the Caribbean colonies had an especially nasty and chaotic quality. General Leclerc's struggle to assert France's power over Saint-Domingue in 1802–03 produced an appalling slaughter on both sides. The extent to which military justice played a part in legitimizing the republic's actions will be forever obscured by such famous atrocities as Rochambeau's importation of dogs trained in Cuba to attack blacks, his use of fumigation ships to exterminate black prisoners en masse, and the notorious arrest, deportation, and imprisonment of Toussaint-Louverture, all without trial and with lethal results. Nonetheless, attitudes to military justice in Saint-Domingue can be discerned from military correspondence. On the one hand, General Arbois, commander of South Province in 1802, reported that a black rebel leader had to be tried a second time because the first trial had been tainted by the gendarmerie's use of torture. On the other hand, Arbois had no hesitation in routinely reporting summary executions of rebels found with powder and balls in their pockets. Therefore, if there were limits to judicial executions, it was more likely to be in terms of efficacy, not of legality or a sense of civilians' rights. Listen to Arbois explain his deport-ation of thirty captured rebels: 'Some deserved to be shot here but, since several executions have already taken place, the excessively frequent repe-tition of such spectacles would destroy their effect, and could... trouble the tranquility which reigns in the region.'[13]

But the experience of Saint-Domingue should not be generalized for all of France's colonies. Matters were far less sanguinary at Guadaloupe, despite also being treated largely as occupied (or subjugated) territory. When the Directory's agent, Victor Hughes, ordered the Constitution of Year III prom-ulgated throughout the island in March 1799, his directive suspended its full application in favour of rule by the army. He did so by exploiting a six-year-old decree which had proclaimed all French colonies under a 'state of siege'. Hughes took advantage of this now fictive state of siege to maintain his four-year-old military commission charged with handling all charges of 'treason, communication with the enemies of the Republic, crime and cowardice, devastation, arson, destruction, stealing and pillaging provisions,' even the terms of which suggest an exceptional discretionary latitude.[14] Regular mili-tary courts, governed by the full panoply of the military code, also played a role. They proved especially useful in Guadaloupe for suppressing conspir-acies against agents of the government because such conspiracies invariably included a handful of soldiers. But political rivals of Hughes' like-minded Jacobin successor, Desfourneaux, accused him of having had twenty men condemned and executed by military courts (which they tellingly called 'military commissions') as a way of controlling the elections of spring 1799 on the island.[15] Clearly, the rules of the game in using military justice to maintain control of the colony had become very complicated.

Though perhaps not quite as messy as in the French colonies, the use of military justice in areas of Europe under French subjugation remained highly confused. This can be illustrated by focusing on occupied Italy. Beginning with the *triennio*, France's occupation and subjugation of various parts of Italy provoked plenty of armed resistance. At first, the French army responded to Italian insurgencies in much the way it had in the Vendée. Nationalist historians inclined to emphasize French atrocities have no difficulty citing examples of summary justice. In 1796, in addition to simply shooting rebels captured with arms in hand, a military commission in southern Piedmont sentenced to death 94 men. The massacre of peasant rebels on the battlefield, which happened with special intensity in 1799, was common currency everywhere in the period. More notable perhaps, was the use of expedited justice following the revolt around Asti which resulted in 86 of the 95 defendants being executed. In fact, military justice did not gain any semblance of regularity in Italy until after 1800. The use of Extraordinary Military Commissions inside France in 1801 is noteworthy as a regression in juridical standards from the late Directory. Furthermore, the Consulate's combination of *corps d'éclaireurs* and extraordinary military commissions figured prominently in France's subjugation and annexation of Piedmont from 1800 onwards. There is still work to be done on the particular forms of military justice deployed in the region at the time. Nonetheless, it is apparent that the French occupation involved a trajectory toward civilian justice complemented by a limited form of expedited justice. Thus, when new military commissions were set up in September 1802 at Turin for the emerging departments of the Po, Doire and Stura, and at Alessandria for the departments of Sesia and Marengo, they were limited to prosecuting armed resistance to the gendarmerie. A later commander, General Menou, failed to have their writ extended to cover more ordinary crimes, but he did manage to prolong them indefinitely.[16] In the meantime, Special Tribunals had also been added to the region. The important difference was made clear by a notary named J-G. Panietti. When ordered to be tried by a military commission at Ivrea, which he described as 'a bloodthirsty, terrifying tribunal, from which there is no appeal' he argued strenuously that he deserved to be tried by the new Special Tribunal at Turin.[17] One did not have to be a notary like Panietti to know that the differences between a military commission and a special tribunal were of critical importance; the peasants of Brittany and Provence were equally attuned to the difference and so routinely discarded their weapons before being arrested so as to avoid the military commissions in operation there during the same years.

Thus, military commissions formed part of the initial armature of annexation throughout Napoleonic Italy. The creation of the 30th Military District in 1809, with its headquarters at Rome, included three military commissions. An expansive interpretation of the concept of brigandage guaranteed a large number of prosecutions, but that did not make these commissions into mere killing machines. True, of the 534 defendants tried between 1809 and 1814, about one quarter were condemned to death; nonetheless, 60 per cent were either freed completely or simply put under police surveillance.[18] The military commission previously created at Milan in 1805 handled a similar number of defendants over two years, but its death toll stood at a mere 10 per cent.[19] The point is not that these commissions served as paragons of due process and judicial rectitude, but that they meted out a more measured form of repression than historians generally acknowledge.

The contrast is especially stark when compared to the brutal repression mounted in Calabria in 1806–10. Here the initial repression was harsh and only grew harsher. In March 1806 the French discovered the bodies of twenty-six soldiers who had been ambushed, tortured, castrated and had their throats slit. Reprisals followed immediately. A nearby village was razed and within a few weeks a military commission established at Cosenza had executed more than two hundred people.[20] And matters only got worse. In August the burning of Lauria and slaughtering most of the civilian population were accompanied by the destruction of twenty-five nearby villages as well as the display of 184 insurgents' heads in iron cages along the roadside. By all accounts, atrocities on one side were matched by atrocities on the other.[21] And yet, what are we to make of the use of regular military courts alongside summary executions without trial, or of quarrelling over the 'right' to be treated as prisoners of war contrasting with heads delivered literally by the basketful to the enemy? Even as some actions displayed the characteristics of 'total war,' others bespoke a heightened sensitivity to the authority earned by using legal means, even if expeditious, to deal with 'unlawful combatants' in zones of organized resistance.

The experience of Calabria, not to mention Spain, shows just how vulnerable any regulated form of repression could be in the face of a brutally intransigent rebellion. If one side believed that it was facing 'total defeat' in social and cultural terms, and the other side was bent on 'total victory' in imperial terms, then the need to legitimize the repression diminished dramatically. Any attempt to win hearts and minds deteriorated into efforts to tip the balance of fear among the populace, thereby making retribution from the occupiers more certain and more significant than the retribution meted out by the resistors. This still left military justice to play a role, but a decidedly secondary one, and one little regulated by the finer points of due process.

*   *   *

There was no linear trajectory towards increasingly sophisticated and better regulated forms of repression, but the process was fraught with backsliding and deviations. In France, however, the compromises between the rule of law and forms of exceptionalism did eventually become more regulated, but at the price of making exceptions to due process an integral part of the Napoleonic system. Once France expanded into new territories, it deployed many of the same instruments of repression developed under the fledgling republic. And yet, as the stakes rose, the scruples fell. As distracting as atrocities are, historians need to pay closer attention to the countervailing efforts to legitimize repression through legal means, even if these appear rather shabby. After all, it is the long history of such efforts that has made 'unlawful combatants' such an uncomfortable phrase even amidst the dangers of the early twenty-first century.

Notes

1. See Howard G. Brown, 'From Organic Society to Security State: the War on Brigandage in France, 1797–1802', *Journal of Modern History* 69 (1997): 661–95, and especially Howard G. Brown, *Ending the French Revolution: Violence, Justice and Repression from the Terror to Napoleon* (Charlottesville, 2006).
2. The most notorious measure was the creation of military commissions to prosecute and execute émigrés caught back in France. These Fructidorian military commissions tried over 1,000 defendants in fifty cities, producing almost 300 executions, most of high standing. However, the Directory repeatedly narrowed the commissions' writ in order to focus on the most dangerous enemies of the regime. Such laws, known collectively as the Fructidorian Terror, were badly designed and managed, and so were easily discredited: Howard G. Brown, 'Mythes et massacres: reconsidérer la 'Terreur directoriale', *Annales historiques de la Révolution française* 325 (2001): 23–52 and Brown, *Ending the French Revolution*, 165–8.
3. Howard G. Brown, 'Special Tribunals and the Napoleonic Security State', in *Napoleon and His Empire: Europe, 1804–1814*, ed. Philip G. Dwyer and Alan Forrest (Basingstoke, 2007), 79–95.
4. E.g. Adhémar Esmein, *Histoire des la procédure criminelle en France* (Paris: Larose & Forcel, 1882), 470–80.
5. E.g. Archives de la Guerre, B¹³ 103, Minister of War to Minister of Police, 10 Thermidor VII.
6. My concept of a security state captures both meanings of repression. More precisely, it combines the mechanisms of coercive force developed to restore public order with the techniques of surveillance and regulatory control developed to maintain it. Furthermore, the phrase security state reflects the social justification, and thus the primary source of political legitimacy, for the more authoritarian administrative and judicial apparatus of rule that replaced the democratic institutions of the French Revolution.
7. For contrasting perspectives, see Isser Woloch, *Napoleon and His Collaborators: The Making of a Dictatorship* (New York, 2001), 192–205. Michael D. Sibalis, 'Arbitrary Detention, Human Rights and the Napoleonic Senate', in *Taking Liberties: Problems of a New Order from the French Revolution to Napoleon*, ed. Howard G. Brown and Judith A. Miller (Manchester, 2002), 166–184.
8. All the numbers here start with Gustave Thomas de Closmadeuc, *Quiberon, 1795: émigrés et chouans, commissions militaires: interrogatoires et jugements* (Paris, 1899). However, Charles-Louis Chassin, *Pacification de l'Ouest, 1794–1801* (Paris, 1896–99), vol. I, 577–8, reveals that the vast majority of the 2,848 Frenchmen acquitted because they had been forcibly enrolled in England were never, in fact, put on trial.

9. The Committee of Public Safety had authorized this *mesure politique* to avoid the staggering cost of applying article 5 of the law of 30 Prairial, III which required rank and file rebels captured in armed gatherings to be tried by a regular criminal court. Chassin, *Pacification*, vol. I, 576.

10. Another 121 did not receive definitive sentences. The basis for these figures is the table on 271 of Xavier Rousseaux, 'Entre droit, état et liberé: la justice pénale dans les départements belges sous le Directoire', in *Du Directoire au Consulat*, ed. Jacques Bernet, Jean-Pierre Jessenne and Hervé Leuwers, vol. 1 (Villeneuve d'Ascq, 1999), 263–87, but the archival source—the J2 series at the Archives de la Guerre—does not distinguish clearly between criminal brigands and rebels involved in the Peasants' War. Nor do they include dozens of Belgian notables transferred to various Parisian prisons on charges of inciting revolt or about 350 Belgian rebels transferred to Lille for trial by regular criminal courts of the 1st Military Division: Archives Nationales, F^7 6176 and 7520, d. 28.

11. E.g. Archives de la Guerre, J2 301, jugements du conseil de révision de la 24e division militaire.

12. Howard G. Brown, 'Revolt and Repression in the Midi Toulousain (1799)', *French History* 19 (2005): 1–28.

13. Archives Nationales 135 AP 1, d. 7, 2 Prairial, IX.

14. Archives Nationales C^{7A} 51, 37, Victor Hugues, 'proclamation pour accompagner la publication de la Constitution de l'an 3, 7 Ventôse, VII.'

15. Laurent Dubois, *A Colony of Citizens: Revolution and Slave Emancipation in the French Caribbean* (Chapel Hill, 2004).

16. Archives Nationales F^7 4309, Minister of War to Minister of Police, 26 Fructidor, X; Michael Broers, *Napoleonic Imperialism and the Savoyard Monarchy, 1773–1821* (Lewiston, N.Y., 1997), 370–72. See also his 'Civilians in the Napoleonic Wars', in *Daily Lives of Civilians in Wartime Europe, 1618–1900*, ed. Linda S. Frey and Marsha L. Frey (Santa Barbara, 2007), 133–174, for a masterful survey of patterns of pacification.

17. Archives Nationales BB^{18} 260, C 1611. Panietti was condemned to death by the Extraordinary Military Commission at Ivrea, 24 Prairial, XII: ibid., C 3129.

18. Paul Bergounioux, 'Brigandage et répression dans les Bouches-du-Tibre: 1810–1813' *Annales Historiques de la Révolution Française* (2006), 93–114.

19. Alexander Grab, 'State Power, Brigandage and Rural Resistance in Napoleonic Italy' *European History Quarterly* 25 (1995): 39–70. Of 518 defendants, 52 were sentenced to death, 239 turned over to civilian courts, 150 put under police surveillance, and 77 freed (53).

20. Milton Finley, *The Most Monstrous of Wars: The Napoleonic Guerrilla War in Southern Italy, 1806–1811* (Columbia, 1994), 26–27.

21. David A. Bell, *The First Total War* (Boston, 2007), 273–274.

3
Policing, Rural Revolt and Conscription in Napoleonic France

Alan Forrest

The system of annual conscription, introduced into France by the Loi Jourdan-Delbrel in 1798[1] and maintained, with minor revisions, across the whole period of the Empire, lay at the heart of Napoleon's military strategy, and was the key to his ability to pursue his wars so relentlessly and on so many fronts. Conscription did not necessarily imply the militarization of society or the sublimation of all other policy to the needs of the army; indeed, when compulsory military service was first introduced, the Revolution had gone out of its way to present it as a duty incumbent on the citizen, part of the contract between the individual and the state which citizenship involved. Under the Empire, of course, the link with rights became increasingly diluted, as the long years of war served to acclimatize the country to the conscription process and to give it legitimacy as a tool of modern statehood. So, with the passage of time, as Napoleon extended conscription across the European mainland it became less associated with citizenship and was increasingly seen as a tribute demanded by the victorious French state.[2] For there was no necessary link between a conscript army and the rights of man; that was only one tradition of statehood, the one advanced by French revolutionary discourse. And when, in response to the mass conscript armies which Napoleon put into the field, Prussia too turned to conscription, it is notable that citizenship and military service were linked in a very different way. Here citizenship was not a right, hence the obligation to serve could not derive from that right. Rather, the King of Prussia demanded military service as a duty from his subjects; and in recognition of that service he was pleased to reward them with citizenship.[3] It was a quite different view of the world, though it is doubtful whether those who were subjected to the ballot in the different states of Europe saw the burden that was placed upon them in such conflicting terms.

Jourdan had weighed up the alternative schemes of recruitment in his report to the Directory in Year VI.[4] He firmly believed that conscription must be, and be perceived to be, an equitable system which shared risk and obligation fairly, and insisted that it was no more than the institutionalization of what the Revolution had already achieved.[5] It should be able to place an impressive force at the disposal of government to defend the public interest, while continuing to maintain the revolutionary fiction that theirs was an army of citizens who were fighting for the common good—in Jourdan's words 'defenders of the fatherland only and not mercenary satellites that are disposed to oppress the people'.[6] On that basis, he argued, conscription could be enforced without alienating the nation and without driving a wedge between soldiers and civilians, especially since in reality only a small proportion of those who were registered as potential conscripts—those who, on reaching their twentieth birthday, were inscribed on the conscription rolls that were to be drawn up in every department in France—would be called upon to serve. Much of the debate in the Convention, indeed, focused on the small print of the law: which groups should leave for the front first; whether substitutions should be allowed; whether key jobs, in agriculture, administration, or the public services should be reserved. In the event, the 1798 law did insist, uniquely among the conscription laws of the Revolution and Empire, that all must serve and that rich and poor should be equally at the service of the state. This, it was assumed, would make the idea of military service more palatable and would reduce the incidence of desertion, draft evasion and public disorder at home.

In the short term Jourdan's optimism appeared well founded. The fact that there was no provision for replacement in the Directory's law reassured the population and made the measure less contested than it might otherwise have been. The sacred principle of equality appeared to have been upheld, an important consideration for men brought up on revolutionary and republican rhetoric. Indeed, it was the case that the proportion of each age group that would be forced into uniform during the Consulate and Empire varied substantially from year to year in accordance with the army's needs: in 1799, in the initial conscription, the numbers were high to take account of army losses since the last major recruitment in 1793; whereas the generation that came of age in 1801 and 1802, around the time of the Peace of Amiens, could afford to breathe more easily. It might appear, therefore, that the politicians' gamble had paid off and that France had become the first European nation to institute conscription successfully on the back of citizenship, as a material consequence of the human and political rights accorded after 1789. The system initiated by the Directory would, after all, provide Napoleon with hundreds of thousands of soldiers, the bedrock that supported his vaulting imperial ambitions and scattered French armies across three continents, to Egypt and Moscow, Iberia and the Caribbean. The achievement of conscription targets would be one of the principal gauges of loyalty and efficiency in the Consulate and Empire, a yardstick by which mayors, sub-prefects and prefects would be judged by the Napoleonic state.[7]

But the law was not imposed without opposition. During the Napoleonic years the atmosphere that accompanied the call to arms to the young, the annual ballots and the cursory medical inspections that followed, was often lowering and heavy with menace; with the intransigence of the war, the increasing weight of the levies and the spiralling death toll as the years passed, there was little of the ritual jollity or the sense that this was a rite of passage that would mark the *fêtes des conscrits* of the Second Empire or Third Republic.[8] In many rural communities, indeed, the moment of the ballot was viewed with fear and loathing, while the recruiting-sergeant continued to be seen as an agent of a distant and hostile state destroying the family economy and dragging their sons off to certain death. In parts of rural Brittany prayers were routinely said for the souls of the departing conscripts as they were accompanied by friends, family and the rest of the community to the boundary of the village to bid them a last poignant farewell.[9] The sense that this was part of what was owed by the individual to the government was far from being widely shared. Nor, after the initial conscription, did Napoleon honour Jourdan's commitment to equality, as administrative jobs were again reserved and the rich were allowed to buy their sons out of personal service. Like his marshals, the Emperor was more interested in having high-quality soldiers, men motivated by the call to arms, than in honouring the Jacobin mantra of equal obligation for all, and he was happy to accept a system of exemptions for those with the money to buy themselves out of personal service.[10] But, as his military ambitions exploded and the numbers conscripted rose inexorably, the existence of such privileged groups within society appeared in the eyes of many as an affront to natural justice, and ordinary people came to resent the fact that they, and not the rich, were being made to shoulder the *impôt du sang*. Inequality could breed contempt and fuel resistance. On occasion it served to unite whole regions against what was seen as an imperial yoke, with full-scale armed rebellions in three areas of the continent, Calabria, the Iberian Peninsula and the Tyrol.[11]

This resentment led to widespread evasion, especially in those areas of the country where the contours of the landscape favoured the fugitive. The patterns of draft dodging during the Empire are instructive, for they do not appear to follow any political or ideological fault lines. Areas which had shown marked anti-revolutionary tendencies do not appear more reluctant to perform military service, though it must have seemed an obvious way for young men and their families to show their defiance of authority. The Vendée and the West, in open revolt as recently as 1800, were admittedly sheltered from the full effects of the early conscriptions, but other areas where there had been a history of defiance of revolutionary decrees showed no consistent pattern of resistance. Rather, the principal difference seems to have lain in topography, and hence in the degree of opportunity which the prospective rebel was offered. Regions with mountain ranges and remote upland pasture, frontier zones where there were borders to cross and smugglers' tracks to follow, areas of marshland and sand dunes offered an ideal terrain for draft dodgers and for the gangs of *passeurs* who hung around the recruiting stations. Such landscape offered cover, of course; it favoured local people who were familiar with the terrain and knew every path and sheep track, and foiled the attempts of gendarmes to hunt them down. It also, frequently, betrayed a country without much tradition of soldiering, a country of peasant farmers or upland graziers whose villages had not been exposed to enemy attack and who had no reason to think of the army as a career.[12]

The contrast with the agricultural plains of the East or the Ile-de-France, long exposed to attack from across the Rhine, could hardly be greater, and it is this contrast that is most clearly reflected in the recruitment figures. Young men from the north and east of France, and those from the larger towns and cities, were most likely to obey the call of the state; while regions with little tradition of soldiering, which had produced few mercenaries and few recruits in past centuries, were slow to respond. In such areas, draft dodging was endemic. Parents protected their children; local peasants gave fugitives jobs on their farms; and village mayors conspired to defend them from the attentions of the authorities. In many areas army deserters could rely on the sympathy and discretion of the villagers through whose communities they passed. Their plight evoked a certain fellow feeling from young and old alike. Soon it was not just those avoiding the draft who defied the orders of the state, but whole communities, inherently suspicious of the motives of state officials and united in their sympathy for the young men hiding in their midst. Much of rural France, it seemed, could no longer be trusted to implement the law. Gendarmes were viewed with suspicion, foreigners in a tightly-knit rural world.[13]

Resentment, in turn, fostered revolt, fanning a spirit of rebellion directed against the recruiting-sergeant and the officials of the state sent into local communities to enforce the law. When gendarmes arrived in a community hunting for conscripts, the effect could be immediately inflammatory as local people closed ranks against them. Friends and relatives of the young men threatened with capture were often the first to get involved, taking up arms and using force in order to ensure their liberty. Women as well as men became implicated in what were often widespread shows of communal solidarity.[14] At Le Taillan in the Gironde an arrested conscript was freed by 'his father, two of his brothers, his sister and a number of other villagers armed with axes'. At Charpey (Drôme), when a gamekeeper arrested a conscript in 1806, he was immediately assailed by three women armed with knives and rocks, among them the victim's illegitimate daughter. At Courlon (Yonne), an arrest was greeted by what the officers described as an explosion of popular rioting. The two unfortunate gendarmes were surrounded by angry villagers, including the mother and brother of the conscript and two other village women, 'who had armed themselves with stones and sticks, struck the gendarmes on the arms and head, and unleashed a huge dog which attacked them and tore their clothing; and this scene took place before a crowd of around 60 people, both men and women'. A number of them, the gendarmes reported, expressed hatred for the police and yelled out that they should 'kill these villains'. It was a matter of honour for the village community to repel those who came to seize fugitives in their midst.

In extreme cases violence to free conscripts turned into full-scale rioting or ended with gendarmes wounded or killed; and there is little evidence that that the villagers felt any sense of remorse. At Saignes (Cantal) in 1808, only the rural bourgeoisie seemed prepared to offer any help to the police; the other members of the local community, and especially the tightly-knit cattle-raising community from the surrounding pasture lands, showed little sympathy for the victim and gave protection to his killers. On occasion, the murder of a gendarme would be met with gratuitous joy and celebration by villagers for whom he had brought nothing but trouble. Take the explosion of violence that rocked Clazay (Deux-Sèvres) in 1806, when three gendarmes were attacked as they led a number of captured deserters back to their base. Two of them were killed by gunfire—according to the police, around forty or fifty shots were discharged—while the third, lying seriously wounded on the ground, was brutally dispatched by one of the rioters with his rifle-butt. For the villagers it was the gendarmes who were the perpetrators of injustice; they, not the deserters, were the enemy, and their deaths evoked little regret.

For a government as obsessively concerned as the Napoleonic regime with law enforcement and public order this represented an unacceptable challenge to the state's administrative control. But Napoleon's intolerance with draft evasion ran deeper. The Empire was becoming increasingly militarized, as *classe* after *classe* was conscripted, and deserters and draft dodgers were seen as undermining the most critical policies of the state. Replenishing and expanding the armies would place a huge strain on France's resources, so much so, that the needs of the military became a major reason for further annexations and Napoleon's wars were increasingly directed at the extraction of vital resources from the rest of the continent. In this context raising conscripts became more than simply one policy among many; and resistance was seen as a deliberate affront to imperial authority. It was also portrayed as immoral and degenerate, the rejection by the peoples France colonized of the social and cultural regeneration which the Empire was offering.[15] Conscription became a litmus test for public compliance with the law and, more than any other single issue, it brought the citizen into direct conflict with agents of the Napoleonic state.

Besides, there was good reason to believe that desertion led to other crimes and to a build-up of lawlessness in rural areas. Deserters and refractory conscripts were young, male and able-bodied, and came from exactly the age group most likely to fall foul of the authorities or to take to a life of crime. They were forced out of their homes, separated from their families and their friends in the village as a result of state legislation, and left with little choice but to lead precarious lives on the margin of civil society. Many were armed, having deserted with their weapons and equipment and, though the government responded by making this a capital offence, few were deterred, since weapons provided them with a vestige of security and the wherewithal to add force to the pathos of their pleas for food and overnight shelter. Almost all were cold and hungry and were cut off from the human company they craved; they were desperate for warmth, companionship and the most basic forms of sustenance, and they were grateful for the support of others, from whatever source it might come. They could not afford to be fastidious about the friendships and associations they made and, like other travellers on the high roads of France, they fell in with what company was available, most often other solitary, desperate men like themselves. The result was predictable. Many turned to crime, using verbal threats or the simple force of numbers of persuade farmers to part with food, priests to be charitable, or passers-by to hand over their possessions. The dividing line between maintaining a basic existence and turning to a life of crime could often be a very fine one indeed.[16]

The most basic weakness of those who found themselves on the run was their daily vulnerability, to footpads and robbers, bullies, informers and, of course, recruiters for the army. They were outlaws, liable to denunciation and arrest, and a prey to every bounty hunter they encountered on their travels. Unlike other people travelling highways or frequenting fairs and markets, they could not turn to the authorities for help when they were robbed or assaulted. Some, it is true, managed to befriend local people, and draft dodgers often blended back into their communities when food ran short or the gendarmes approached. But when they could not—and this was frequently the case for deserters travelling home across hundreds of miles— they could easily be drawn into a life of crime. Desperation forced them to form bands with others trapped in similar conditions, drove them to a life outside the law, where they hid in thickets and woods during daytime and took advantage of the darkness hours to move from village to village, to hunt for food, or to steal from isolated farmyards. Some took to banditry and highway robbery, mingling with others living on the margins of rural life, robbing strangers, travellers, or government mails so as not to antag- onize the local community on whose goodwill they depended. But they did not fail to antagonize the state and its officials. To them they were indis- tinguishable from the other robbers and footpads who infested the high- ways of rural France, especially in the suburbs of the larger towns and along the key routes down the Rhône valley or between the principal cities of southern France.[17] These were the badlands of the Midi, the home to polit- ical opponents as well as common criminals, and one of the repercussions of the policy of mass conscription was to swell their numbers.[18] Many drifted into organized bands through poverty and desperation, others as a result of chance meetings in wayside inns. Most of them were not natural criminals, but they were forced by circumstance to consort with criminals and to take up a life of crime, making them, in the eyes of the state, indistinguishable from the most hardened bandits.[19] They had neither rights nor status; they were men to be feared, to be hunted down with the full repressive power of the state.[20]

If the state could not persuade village France to view desertion as a crime or to share the Empire's respect for the conscription process, it could, and did, resort to fear to implement its policies. The gendarmerie was a unit of the French army and they used whatever force they needed to arrest suspects in the teeth of popular resistance. When the strength of the local gendarmerie proved insufficient, military reinforcements were called in to provide what Howard Brown has described as 'strong-arm policing'.[21] Regular troops were frequently sent to impose order on villages harbouring refractory conscripts, whether to destroy kernels of resistance or to teach the villagers a salutary lesson in obedience and responsibility. The authorities knew that they could not always hunt down draft dodgers or destroy the resistance of bands of deserters; but they knew, too, that the survival of these bands in woods and on lonely farmsteads depended on the protection offered them by kindly villagers or by peasants eager to turn their misfortune to their own financial advantage. Theirs was a resistance that was often much easier to break. The soldiers searched farmyards and outbuildings, scouring the countryside for any sign of clandestine life. They rounded up all the young men they came across, sons and brothers, farmhands and seasonal harvesters, anyone whose appearance suggested that they could be subject to the draft. Where conscripts were known to be missing from their regiments, soldiers would be garrisoned on their families until they were persuaded to hand over their sons or to betray the hiding places of fugitives. After 1806, Napoleon took this tactic one stage further by imposing the garrisons on village mayors and on the richest local families, hoping by this means to divide and rule, to turn rich against poor and so to deprive deserters of work and refuge and drive them back into the open.[22]

When deserters were caught, they could expect little leniency. In wartime theirs was a serious crime, one which Napoleon had every interest in repressing so that others would be deterred from following in their footsteps. But in practice the severity of the punishments imposed varied widely. Those whose offence was limited to desertion or draft evasion could usually count on being returned to their regiment, a fate which, almost by definition, they regarded with distaste, perhaps even with dread. There was little incentive to punish them further; the Emperor needed soldiers, not convicts, in time of war. But those who used violence against agents of the state, who joined armed bands, who fought with the gendarmerie or who took part in riots could expect little mercy. The distinction between deserters and draft dodgers became suddenly more significant, since deserters were subject to military justice and could be sent before a *conseil militaire*, where there was no jury and where summary death sentences were routinely handed down by panels of military judges. From as early as 1795 deserters found bearing arms against the state or who joined armed bands were tried by military courts, as, under the Directory and Consulate, were any other brigands who consorted with them.[23] This policy undoubtedly increased the number of executions, but it did not drive a wedge between deserters and local people, especially in the villages of rural France. It may even have served to increase the levels of sympathy felt by civilians for young men on the run and to dissuade people from handing over conscripts hiding in their midst. It certainly did not end the threat of rioting or guarantee public order as the government intended. At Hazebrouck in 1813 conscription provided the excuse for a mass insurrection of between 1,200 and 1,500 people who attacked, beat and ill-treated the sub-prefect, the official most closely identified with the implementation of the recruitment laws. The government's reaction was immediate and four of the rioters were guillotined. But the message could not have been more clearly spelt out that, even in 1813, after more than twenty years of almost continuous war, and with conscription imposed for nearly a decade and a half on a reluctant country, it had still not been accepted either as a simple duty of citizenship or as a rite of passage into manhood.[24] The anger that it created still led Frenchmen, in their thousands, to defy the authority of the Napoleonic state, putting in jeopardy the most central plank of Napoleon's domestic policy, guaranteeing public order and maintaining a civil society where the law was respected and obeyed.

There was, of course, a serious risk for the government in turning the army against the civilian population. The sight of French soldiers bullying peasants to get them to hand over their sons to the military, of garrisons wrecking the homes and furniture of respectable citizens to get them to break their silence and betray their neighbours, was not the kind of behaviour that helped to unite the French people and their army, or to persuade them—as the Revolution had tried so hard to do—that the cause of the military was also theirs, or the army, the nation in arms united by a burning desire to protect the citizenry against their enemies.[25] Nor did it serve to confirm the revolutionary image of the citizen–soldier as everyone's brother or son, a young man representative of the nation and drawn from all sections of society; that image had evolved, and become professionalized, in the battalions of the Empire, but enough of it remained to suggest a respectability and a decency which the mercenary regiments of the Old Regime had never been able to harness. Plunder and pillaging, threats and physical violence towards civilians did little to enhance the reputation of the soldiery.[26] Rather, they harked back to an uglier image, one which was so widespread in the first half of the eighteenth century[27] or even during the Thirty Years War, when soldiers had been routinely feared as untamed thugs of whom ordinary people lived in fear.[28]

If the robust methods used by the Emperor in France to seize and punish deserters began to alienate civilians and create an unwanted division between the army and civil society, how much more did they damage civil–military relations in the countries which the French occupied, and to which Napoleon increasingly looked to provide him with conscripts for his wars. With the expansion of imperial rule beyond the Rhine and across the Alps the army opened up new recruiting grounds, imposing the same principles of conscription on Germans, Italians and Poles as they did within metropolitan France and encountering, of course, similar levels of resistance. Across the continent, especially in what Michael Broers has identified as the 'outer Empire'—the Tuscan and Roman departments, the Illyrian provinces, or Spain—the imposition of conscription went hand in hand with other administrative and judicial impositions, ranging from the Code to the Concordat and from local government to the Continental System, which were often as deeply unpopular as they were poorly understood.[29] Here resistance assumed a more political form than in France, a resistance that was directed not only at the recruitment process itself—as happened in varying degrees throughout the Empire—but also at a government that was perceived as foreign, as alien and as French. Whereas in France few draft dodgers thought to justify their resistance in political terms—the number who claimed to resist out of royalist or republican principle was insignificant—elsewhere conscription helped to polarize opinion against the invasion of their territory and to fuel a hatred of the French and their army that would find expression in popular uprisings and the Wars of Liberation.[30]

Notes

1. *Réimpression de l'Ancien Moniteur*, 32 vols (Paris, Plon, 1858–63), entry for 5 September 1798 (19 Fructidor, VI).
2. Alexander Grab, *Napoleon and the Transformation of Europe* (Basingstoke, 2003), 26–27.
3. Dierk Walter, 'Conscription in Prussia, 1807–1815', in *Conscription in the Napoleonic Era*, ed. Donald Stoker, Frederick C. Schneid and Harold D. Blanton (London, 2009), 40–42.
4. Jean-Baptiste Jourdan, *Rapport sur le recrutement de l'armée de terre* (Paris, An VI).
5. Annie Crépin, *La conscription en débat, ou le triple apprentissage de la Nation, de la citoyenneté, de la République, 1798–1889* (Arras, 1998), 25.
6. Thomas Hippler, *Citizens, Soldiers and National Armies: Military Service in France and Germany, 1789–1830* (London, 2008), 107.
7. Alan Forrest, *Conscripts and Deserters: The Army and French Society during the Revolution and Empire* (New York, 1989), 34–36.
8. Michel Bozon, 'Conscrits et fêtes de conscrits à Villefranche-sur-Saône', *Ethnologie française* 9 (1979), 29–46.
9. Jean Waquet, 'La société civile devant l'insoumission et la désertion à l'époque de la conscription militaire', *Bibliothèque de l'Ecole des Chartes* 126 (1968): 191.

10. Alain Pigeard, *La conscription au temps de Napoléon, 1798–1814* (Paris, 2003), 133–66.
11. Charles J. Esdaile, 'Popular Resistance to the Napoleonic Empire', in *Napoleon and Europe*, ed. Philip G. Dwyer (London, 2001), 136–141.
12. Forrest, *Conscripts*, 81–84.
13. The example of the South-West is particularly telling. See Louis Bergès, *Résister à la conscription, 1798–1814: Le cas des départements aquitains* (Paris, 2002).
14. The examples of violence against the gendarmerie quoted in these two paragraphs are taken from Forrest, *Conscripts*, 234.
15. Michael Broers, *The Napoleonic Empire in Italy, 1796–1814: Cultural Imperialism in a European Context* (Basingstoke, 2005), 237–239.
16. Alan Forrest, 'Conscription and Crime in Rural France during the Directory and Consulate', in *Beyond the Terror: Essays in French Regional and Social History, 1794–1815*, ed. Gwynne Lewis and Colin Lucas (Cambridge, 1983), 92–120.
17. Bérénice Grissolange, 'Les brigands, le brigandage et les honnêtes gens', in *La Révolution française: la guerre et la frontière*, ed. Monique Cubells (Paris, 2000), 457–66.
18. Colin Lucas, 'Themes in Southern Violence after 9 Thermidor', in *Beyond the Terror*, ed. Lewis and Lucas, 152–194.
19. Richard Maltby, 'Le brigandage dans la Drôme, 1795–1803', *Bulletin d'archéologie et de statistique de la Drôme* 79 (1973), 117–134.
20. Gwynne Lewis, 'Political Brigandage and Popular Disaffection in the South-east of France, 1795–1804', in *Beyond the Terror*, ed. Lewis and Lucas, esp. 212–16.
21. Howard G. Brown, *Ending the Revolution: Violence, Justice and Repression from the Terror to Napoleon* (Charlottesville, 2006), 180.
22. Forrest, *Conscripts*, 208–211.
23. Brown, *Ending the Revolution*, 144–147.
24. Archives Nationales, BB[18]54, Report from the *procureur-général* in Lille to the Minister of Justice, 22 September 1813.
25. The revolutionary ideal is best summed up in the person of Nicolas Chauvin, the *soldat-laboureur* who evolved into an important part of the pedagogy of the nation. See Gérard de Puymège, *Chauvin, le soldat-laboureur. Contribution à l'étude des nationalismes* (Paris, 1993).
26. Martin Boycott-Brown, 'Guerrilla Warfare *avant la lettre*: Northern Italy, 1792–97', in *Popular Resistance in the French Wars: Patriots, Partisans and Land-Pirates*, ed. Charles J. Esdaile (Basingstoke, 2005), 60.
27. E. G Léonard, *L'armée et ses problèmes au dix-huitième siècle* (Paris, 1958), 229–230.
28. Compare, for instance, the accounts of wanton destruction by Swedish soldiers in villages around Freiburg between 1632 and 1634. Geoff Mortimer, *Eyewitness Accounts of the Thirty Years War, 1618–48* (Basingstoke, 2002), 49–57.
29. Michael Broers, *Europe under Napoleon, 1799–1815* (London, 1996), 208–221.
30. Karen Hagemann, 'German Heroes. The Cult of the Death for the Fatherland in Nineteenth-century Germany', in *Masculinities in Politics and War: Gendering Modern History*, ed. Stefan Dudink, Karen Hagemann and John Tosh (Manchester, 2004), 118–120.

4
Small State, Big Society: The Involvement of Citizens in Local Government in Nineteenth-Century France

Marie-Cécile Thoral

Under the Consulate, the law of 28 Pluviôse Year VIII (17 February 1800) set up a new administrative system, which was highly centralized in theory as it revolved around a strict pyramidal structure where the power lay in the hands of only one man at each level of the pyramid: the prefect at the top of the departmental administration, then sub-prefects for the *arrondissements* (the sub-divisions of the *départements*), and, at the last level, the communes, mayors. The 1830 Revolution and the subsequent laws on local government (in 1831, 1833, 1837 and 1838) seemed to introduce relative decentralization but, in fact, the Napoleonic system was but slightly modified. Some contemporaries, such as Stendhal or Madame de Staël, always stressed how radically new the absolute centralization of the Napoleonic local government was. Many historians and legal historians still define it in those terms. However, even though centralization did indeed characterize the law of 28 Pluviôse Year VIII, it was not enforceable in practice because of the flaws and limitations of the state apparatus at that time. The modern bureaucratic state was still in its infancy. The number of civil servants and state employees in the provinces was still far too low. So was the level of public income. An active participation of local citizens was thus essential, either individually or collectively and institutionally (through the intermediate bodies which had been reconstituted in Napoleonic France in spite of the Revolutionary laws which had officially suppressed them, the Allarde decree and the Le Chapelier law).

Was this participation of private citizens in public policy efficient or illusory? Was it the symptom of a small and weak state apparatus? Through the case study of an 'average' French department in the early nineteenth century, the Isère, which was neither one of the biggest *préfectures* of the time nor one of the smallest, poorest or most rural ones, this chapter will analyse the forms and the impact of citizen participation in local government, as well as the reasons for the delegation of a number of public functions of the 'big society', to ordinary citizens.

I   A palliative for the flaws in a weak state

One of the characteristics of the French state in the early nineteenth century, which accounts for the necessity of an active involvement of citizens in local government, was the chronic problem of manpower. The number of state employees was insufficient in all areas of public service, and especially so in the countryside.

The département of the Isère had only 110 *gendarmes* in 1801, 22 brigades of 5 men each.[1] Therefore, there was not a brigade in each of the 45 cantons of the department, as there should have been. Yet the département was rather privileged in this regard compared with others, such as the Manche, which, even though it had a larger population than the Isère (538,000 inhabitants in the Year VIII in the Manche,[2] as opposed to 435,000 inhabitants in the Isère according to the 1801 census) and was on the Channel coast, had but 45 *gendarmes* in total in the Year XII (1803–04).[3] The main rural policeman in France in the early nineteenth century was thus not a (central) state employee, a *gendarme*, but rather a local, municipal employee, the *garde champêtre*. However, there was also a worrying shortage of *gardes champêtres;* in 1817, one third of the villages of the department were unable to employ one.[4] The situation was even worse for forest guards; no more than half the villages close to national or communal forests employed one. Likewise, the number of justices of the peace was insufficient since the law of 8 Pluviôse Year IX had reduced them to one per canton. This chronic shortage of state servants applied to all sectors of local government: police, law, engineering, education, and tax collection.

The involvement of the local population, especially of the wealthiest citizens, was therefore an absolute necessity to compensate for the lack of specialized government agents.

The local elites played a crucial part in construction works tackling the key problem of the poor state of the roads. Because of the economic, strategic, administrative and political issues at stake, transport infrastructure deeply concerned both national and local officials in post-revolutionary France.[5] The supervision of road works was under the authority of mayors for municipal pathways, and of sub-prefects and engineers of the ministry of *Ponts-et-Chaussées* for departmental roads, but small town or village mayors seldom had enough employees to staff their own work, and Ponts-et-Chaussées engineers were too few in the department to be able to cover all the areas where road construction work was undertaken.

As early as 1810 some *Conseillers d'arrondissement* (local councillors) suggested calling on the help of local elites to supervise such field work.

The idea was taken up a few years later, under the Restoration, by prefect Baron d'Haussez. He appointed inspector-commissioners, who were officially in charge of these works within the boundaries of a *canton* or of a section of departmental road. As landowners these men were particularly interested in opening up the area where their properties were located and so they often put a lot of time and zeal into their duties, whether to persuade a landowner to sell the piece of land which was necessary to open a new road or to supervise the works of a subcontracted construction company.[6]

The local elites also contributed financially to local government, which was badly needed at a time when state resources for local government were not yet very large. They thus funded part or all of some public policies at a local level.

This was the case for the funding of the new *Lycée* (secondary school) granted by the government to the town of Grenoble on 16 Floréal Year XI (7 April 1803).[7] The total expense for the works needed inside the existing building amounted to 75,000 francs. As the municipality lacked sufficient to cover this expense, the prefect, Ricard, suggested to the mayor that he resort to raising a public loan. The municipality then issued 250 bonds of 300 francs, and all of them were soon purchased by local inhabitants.[8] The local elites thus covered the entire expense of the establishment of the *Lycée*.[9]

This generosity of the local elites and their important contribution to the funding of local government applied to other areas as well, such as cultural policy (purchase of books for the library or of paintings for the museum). Their contribution was particularly sought after by local officials to fund welfare policies, especially in times of economic crisis. During the serious agricultural crisis of the autumn 1816, the municipal authorities of badly hit villages turned to big landowners to help them provide financial relief for landless agricultural labourers. In the village of Saint Ismier, for example, the deputy mayor drew up a list of all the villagers who were currently unemployed, and some local landowners then offered to hire some of them. By January 1817, 12 landowners had taken part and were employing 81 labourers, in addition to another one Bigillion de la Bathie, who had not hired anyone, but had been providing 60 *livres* of bread per day to the poor. The deputy mayor then communicated to the prefect the names of the most generous landowners, such as General Marchand, who 'has employed 12 labourers for two months and has provided clothes to 13 poor villagers', in order to secure them an official recognition by the government.[10]

II   Specialized expertise at the service of the state, for better quality public services

Private citizens also contributed to local government in a more collective and institutional way, through various associations or 'intermediate bodies' (between the state and individual citizens). In doing so, they were pursuing their own interests by voicing their opinion to the government and trying to influence decision-making in the area. They also contributed to the public interest by putting their professional knowledge and expertise at the service of local development.

The importance of agricultural societies in the improvement of farming techniques in France since the Napoleonic period (well before their heyday under the July Monarchy[11]) is a striking example of the positive impact of the participation of private citizens in local government.

The agricultural society of the Isère, re-established under the Consulate and composed of a majority of landowners (21 out of 38 permanent members) and of other people with a professional interest in agriculture, or connected subjects such as botany, was focused on the practical application of new discoveries in farming practices, new crops and new farm machinery. Thanks to the members' annual fees the society financed several programmes aimed at improving agricultural practices and outputs: books and journals purchased to create a specialized library; writing treatises and guidebooks for local farmers; funding prizes for scientific research in agronomy and agricultural contests. It purchased new crops and cattle breeds to improve local stock; it founded a 'model farm' where new techniques could be tested and where new types of trees could be grown and then distributed to local farmers.

It soon became the main auxillary of local administration for all issues related to agriculture. The society advised local officials on points of rural legislation and communicated journals or treatises of agronomy sent by the government to provincial farmers.[12]

Martine Cocaud observed the lack of interest among landowners in agricultural associations and public action in the western department of Ille-et-Vilaine.[13] The situation was very different in the Isère, where landowners and public officials shared a deep interest in agronomy and agricultural improvement. Moreover, landowners and local farmers were also attracted to the social aspect of the associations and the importance of informal discussions and exchanges of information on farming.[14] Such exchanges were facilitated by the fact that agricultural societies were divided into specialized sub-groups (cattle breeding, forests, rural industry, farming) and their members were divided among those sub-groups according to their knowledge, experience and interests so they met others working in similar areas.

These agricultural societies played an important part in the spread of agricultural innovations through the department, by introducing new machines, new tools, new crops (such as madder), and new farming techniques. In 1836, the society of La Tour du Pin bought a few plowing machines like the 'Hugues' crop sowing machine, which was then loaned to some landowners and led to several of them purchasing one.[15] Thanks to the introduction of new crops and new breeds by the landowners who belonged to the agricultural societies, agricultural practices had significantly improved in the *département* by the end of the 1830s, as the sub-prefect of La Tour du Pin observed in 1837.[16]

Beyond such para-public associations, private citizens took a more active part in local government by being in charge of the management of some public institutions such as prisons, welfare councils and poor houses, schools, museums, libraries, theatres, and hospitals. To date, these specialized committees have as yet caught the attention of very few historians.[17] However, far from being mere 'facades of centralization', as had been argued by Tiphaine le Yoncourt,[18] they played an important part in local government, compensating for the lack of state employees and state resources, and sometimes helping to provide better quality, more humane public services. They were generally composed of lawyers and businessmen, usually the majority; the latter were generally considered more gifted in the economic management of institutions on a tight budget.

In the judicial sphere, the management of prisons by bodies of private citizens helped to alleviate the harsh, punitive character of the new prison regime established by the law of 1808 for criminal prisons, and the severe terms of the Penal Code of 1810.[19] Whereas, in the eighteenth century, prisons were seen as instruments of rehabilitation, during the Napoleonic period they became, first and foremost, instruments of punishment. However, many towns organized, with the support of local elites, a system of prison management which included material, moral and religious welfare. Prison committees were set up in many towns under the Consulate. That of Grenoble, the administrative centre of the Isère, was set up in 1802 and was composed of five members: the mayor, two businessmen and two lawyers.[20] They inspected the town's prisons, made notes of failings or abuses, and wrote reports on the improvements needed.[21] Other committees were set up under the Restoration for prisons established in other towns of the department at Vienne, Saint Marcellin and Bourgoin. Their remits were broadened to include accountants, purchases (of food, linen, medicines and medical instruments), the supervision of building repairs, the drafting of prison regulations, and the provision of religious education for the inmates.[22] The prison committees also took care of providing material relief to the prisoners (additional clothes or food bought thanks to charity donations). They later asked the prefect to delegate this task to existing charities devoted to the relief of prisoners, usually charities generally organized by wealthy local women.[23]

At the beginning of the July Monarchy, the prefect of the Isère, Gasparin, asked each of the sub-prefects of the department about the state and the achievements of their local prison committees in order to compile a report for the Minister of the Interior. This correspondence provides evidence of the activities and positive achievements of these committees. That of Grenoble 'has been very useful for the institution; the supervision of its members is very active. Public health, discipline, food diet, everything that matters for the everyday life of the inmates has been the subject of their constant concern.... In a nutshell, it fully fulfills its requirements'.[24] The prefect then admitted to the Minister of Trade and Public Works, on 14 April 1832, that the prison committees played a central part in local government and that 'the measures that have been taken in accordance with [the Minister's] recommendations to sanitize further those institutions would not have been implemented if the local authorities of the places where they are established [mayors and other civil servants] had not been supported by the zealous members of those committees'.[25]

III   Citizen participation in local government and local democracy

The participation of private citizens, or *administrés* as they were known in official circles, in local government and resorting to the resources of civil society was a way of compensating for the failings of a weak state still in the making. This acquired a political dimension during the July Monarchy, after 1830. By then, it was conceived of as a way of strengthening local democracy, of creating strong links between the state and society, and as the expression of the rights and duties which citizenship entails, as can be shown through the example of the national guards.

Citizen militias, sedentary national guards, were established in all towns and villages of the *département* in the Years VIII and IX (1800–01).[26] The participation of citizens was not voluntary, but imposed by the law of 14 October 1791, according to which all 'active citizens' (those paying taxes, with voting rights and who had lived in the same place for more than a year), aged 18 or older must be enlisted in the national guard of their town or village, with the exception of soldiers, civil servants, mayors and their deputies. Non-attendance incurred a fine equivalent to two days' pay. Those who failed to turn up for their guard duties on three successive occasions had their voting rights suspended for one year.

They were commanded by officers and NCOs (directly elected by their troops under the law of 22 March 1831). Their mission was to police their town or village, to join day or night patrols with their weapons (when they had one). Weapons were provided by the state in case of political or military crisis (as in 1814–15 and again in 1830–32), or in other cases by the municipalities or at the expenses of the guards themselves.

At the end of the Napoleonic Empire, many towns and villages in the department had their own national guard. The two most important ones in the Isère were those of Vienne (753 guards out of a total population of 10,000 in December 1813) and Grenoble (501 guards for a total population of 21,000). However, even though the national guard of Grenoble was the smaller of the two, it was better equipped and were generally more efficient: 424 out of 501 guards in Grenoble had weapons. This figure dropped for the Vienne guards to 101 out of 753.[27]

National guards were reorganized in France at the beginning of the Restoration in 1815–16. The national guard of Grenoble had, by then, risen to 1,327 men (in April 1816).[28] However, in spite of a new organization in 1826–27 (Ordinance of 27 March 1827), the importance of national guards for public order decreased in France during the Restoration.[29] The situation was even more concerning in the Isère where a failed coup (the Didier plot[30]) led to the disarmament of many national guards.

During the days, weeks and months following the July revolution of 1830 the reconstitution of national guards caused great enthusiasm throughout France,[31] but particularly so in the Isère because of its location (then on the border with Piedmont, which stirred up memories of the invasion of the region the last time that there had been a change of political regime in 1814–15) and also because of its Bonapartist political tradition.[32]

The national guards of the early July monarchy were also more socially inclusive. They were no longer confined to the local elites; they now incorporated different social classes, thus becoming genuine 'citizen militias'.[33] Registration was still restricted to those citizens who paid income tax, but in small villages that applied to a great many people, especially small landowning peasants.

After 1830, a great number of Dauphinois (the traditional, pre-revolutionary name for the Isère) belonged to a local national guard, in both town and country. So service in the national guard, as much as schooling or conscription, became an instrument of building both the nation and democracy. A great number of citizens had to devote part of their time to military-style reviews, training, night sentry duty, and patrols. In the small village of Saint Gervais, national guards were to meet once a week, on Sundays, in addition to their duties on public holidays and festival or market days.[34]

The national guard of Grenoble, a 2,500 strong body in August 1830,[35] increased its membership to 3,400 in January 1832.[36] However, the efficiency of all the national guards of the department was weakened by the shortage of weapons; in September 1830 barely half of the 40,000 guards were armed.[37]

In Saint Baudille, the mayor took into account the nature of the professional activity of the majority of the population when deciding the annual duties of the national guards: training every Sundays and public holidays, guard duty and patrols each Sunday and sometimes on other weekdays, except in late summer (20 June–1 September) 'because of the harvest and of other agricultural duties'.[38]

National guards have often been assessed very negatively by historians as local militias without any real training or expertise in keeping public order. However, many local officials were impressed by the level of rigour and professionalism of these units, observing the latest military methods in the care and repair of armaments and other aspects of military service.[39] This may have been because many of their officers were retired army officers or NCOs.[40]

The national guards of the Isère directly contributed to the arrest of several criminals, such as 35 former prisoners who ransacked the *arrondissement* of La Tour du Pin in November 1830[41] or a foreigner walking across the village of Saint Ismier without a passport in December 1830.[42]

The national guards provided the local authorities with additional troops to control big crowd gatherings at markets, fairs and festivals, or to restore public order in the event of a riot. They also assisted local *gendarmes* in the pursuit of military deserters or robbers.[43] They were thus quite useful in making up for the shortage of civil servants in charge of public order. There were indeed more national guards than *gendarmes* or customs officers, and most of them were seen by local authorities as more honest, more skilled and more reliable than *gardes champêtres*.

Conclusion

Following in the footsteps of Tocqueville and Taine, many historians have defined the French political model as highly centralized and anti-liberal, based on an exclusive divide between state and citizens with no intermediate bodies.[44] This vision is not completely inaccurate. It is indeed grounded in a legal reality, in a set of laws that, during the Revolution, abolished all the intermediate bodies that could constitute a screen between the state and French citizens (*Parlements*, lay religious confraternities, guilds), with the exception of the revolutionary 'popular societies'. But this wish for greater administrative and political centralization was difficult to enforce in reality, in a country where associations, guilds, and other intermediate bodies had been reconstituted in the early nineteenth century in spite of the official prohibitions.

At the beginning of the nineteenth century the involvement of citizens in local government did not have the significance it acquired later, in the twentieth century; it was not yet the expression of a conscious form of political action, of a willingness to introduce or reintroduce civil society within the State apparatus and, more broadly, to create a form of reaction against the excesses of a state which had grown too much and had become too democratic. In the early nineteenth century citizen participation was, rather, a practical, makeshift solution to compensate for the failings of a pre-modern state. It was the answer to the shortfalls of a state apparatus still too rudimentary and under-staffed. Was this efficient? The involvement of citizens in the public sphere played a crucial part in local government. The men who put themselves at the service of the state through their supervision of public work, their money, their time, their technical expertise and experience, went beyond the mere role of substitutes for civil servants. Certainly, the initial reason for their involvement was the shortage of public resources and administrators, but their contribution was actually much broader and more significant. They shaped public policy along the lines of their professional expertise and experience, brought a humane dimension to the management of public institutions, and helped to provide better quality public policies and public services. Furthermore, the participation of private citizens in local government enhanced the transparency of the state and increased the links between state and civil society. It was therefore a powerful instrument of local democracy. This political dimension of citizen participation is particularly striking in the case of national guards, which became a kind of 'citizen militia', especially after 1830.

However, this rather positive assessment cannot quite compensate for the original fault that created this citizen participation in early nineteenth century France; it grew out of the failings and limitations of a state apparatus still in the making. It was less a political choice than a practical necessity. It was actually the sign and symbol of a weak state. The lack of weapons and ammunition for national guards, the influence of harvest work on their availability for guard service and, more broadly, the excessive reliance of the state on the zeal and good will of private citizens to implement local policies could be problematic. Their zeal and goodwill varied from one period of time to the other, from one area of public action to another, or even from region to region as is clear in the different attitudes of landowners towards agricultural societies in Ille-et-Vilaine and the Isère. This highlights the limits and the risks of an excessive reliance on extensive delegation of public policy making and control of public services to private citizens, as well as the need for a state sufficiently strong to guarantee equality of services for all citizens, regardless of the enthusiasm or lack of it among local elites and the population as a whole, for active participation in local government.

Notes

1. *Annuaire statistique de l'Isère,* 1801.
2. Francois de Lannoy, *L'administration préfectorale de la Manche sous le Consulat et l'Empire (1800–1815),* thèse d'Histoire, vol. I, (Paris-IV, 1992), 49, 74.
3. de Lannoy, *L'administration,* vol. I, 231.
4. Departmental Archives of the Isère, hereafter ADI: 14M3 and 14M4.
5. Bernard Lepetit, *Chemins de terre et voies d'eau, réseaux de transport et organisation de l'espace en France: 1740–1840,* Editions de l'EHESS, (Paris, 1984). Guy Arbellot, 'Les problèmes de la route française à l'entrée du XIX° siècle', *Histoire, économie et société,* I, (1990), 9–17.
6. Report by the prefect to the Conseil Général, 1821 (ADI: 1N4/1).
7. Letter from the prefect to the mayor of Grenoble, 4 Vendémiaire Year XII (ADI: 181M17).
8. Letter from the prefect to the *Conseiller d'Etat* of Education, 29 Brumaire Year XII (ADI: 181M17).
9. Letter from the prefect to the *Conseiller d'Etat* of Education, 20 Nivôse Year XII (ADI: 181M18).

10. Letter from the mayor adjunct of Saint Ismier to the prefect, 13 January 1817 (ADI: 181M87).
11. R. Hubscher, *L'agriculture et la société rurale dans le Pas de Calais du milieu du XIX° siècle à 1914*, CDMH du Pas-de-Calais, vol. 1 (Arras, 1979), 273.
12. Excerpt from the registers of the society of agriculture of the Isère, 19 Prairial Year X (ADI: 142M1).
13. M. Cocaud, 'Des cadres pour la rénovation agricole : les sociétés d'agriculture en Ille-et-Vilaine en 1757–1880', *Les enjeux de la formation des acteurs de l'agriculture (1760–1945)*, ed. M. Boulet, Educagri éditions, (Dijon, 2000), 199–206 (201–202).
14. Hubscher, *L'agriculture*, vol. 1, 276.
15. Report by the sub-prefect to the members of the *arrondissement* council of la Tour du Pin, 5 August 1837 (ADI: 2N4/1).
16. Ibid.
17. Jean Ferrier, 'L'inspection des écoles primaires entre pouvoir local et pouvoir central', in *L'administration territoriale de la France (1750–1940)*, (Orléans, 1998), 549–562; Tiphaine le Yoncourt, *Le préfet et ses notables en Ille-et-Vilaine au XIX° siècle (1814–1914)*, (Paris, 2001), 68–93.
18. Tiphaine le Yoncourt, *Le préfet*, 68.
19. J.G. Petit, *Ces peines obscures. La prison pénale en France (1780–1875)* (Paris, Fayard, 1990), 91.
20. *Annuaire statistique de l'Isère*, 1803 (ADI: Per 932/4).
21. Letter from the members of the Prisons committee of Grenoble to the prefect, 7 Prairial Year X (ADI: 4Y1).
22. Report by the mayor of Vienne, 8 June 1831 (ADI: 4Y1).
23. Letter from the sub-prefect of Vienne to the prefect, 24 November 1835 (ADI: 4Y1).
24. Report from the prefect to the Minister of Trade, 20 July 1831 (ADI: 4Y1).
25. Letter from the prefect to the Minister of Trade, 24 April 1832 (ADI: 4Y1).
26. Prefectoral *Arrêté*, 26 Prairial Year VIII (ADI: 4K1).
27. National Guard of the *département* of the Isère, no date (December 1813), (National Archives, hereafter AN: F/9/538).
28. State of the national guard of Grenoble on 19 April 1816 (Private Archives of the family Ferrier de Montal).
29. L. Girard, *La Garde nationale : 1814–1871* (Paris, Plon, 1964), 137–138.
30. F. Vermale, *Un conspirateur stendhalien, Paul Didier (1758–1816)*, (Paris, SGAF, 1951).
31. Carrot, Georges, 'La garde nationale, 1789–1871: une formce publique ambigue') Paris: L'Harmattan, 2001).
32. Letter from the prefect to the Minister of Interior, 29 March 1831 (National Archives, hereafter AN: F/9/539).
33. Letter from the prefect to the Minister of Interior, 16 January 1832 (AN: F/9/539).
34. Internal rules of the national guard of Saint Gervais, 25 July 1831 (AN: F/9/539).
35. Letter from the members of the municipal committee (*commission de mairie*) of Grenoble to Lafayette, 17 August 1830 (AN: F/9/539).
36. Letter from the prefect to the Minister of Interior, 16 January 1832 (AN: F/9/539).
37. Letter from Adolphe Périer to General Dumas, 1 September 1830 (AN: F/9/539).
38. Internal rules of the national guard of Saint Baudille, 18 June 1831 (AN: F/9/539).

39. Letter from the prefect to the Minister of Interior, 29 March 1831 (AN: F/9/539).
40. Ibid.
41. Ibid.
42. Letter from the head of the national guard of Saint Ismier to the head of the national guard of Bernin, 6 December 1830 (ADI: 52M26).
43. Letter from the sub-prefect of Vienne to the police superintendent, 1 February 1817 (ADI: 53M13).
44. Pierre Rosanvallon, *Le modèle politique français. La société civile contre le jacobinisme de 1879 à nos jours* (Paris, 2004), 11.

5
Napoleon as a Politician

Peter Hicks

This chapter is a reflection upon some of the manifestations of Napoleon's political makeup. The consensus is that the 'Grand Consulat' (the establishment of consensus around the Consulate itself, the religious pacification of the Concordat, the civil pacification of France's wild outlands in the South West and the Vendée, the creation of the administrative structures of the Consulate, the balancing of the financial books, to name but a few aspects) was a success. That Napoleon could even win hearts and minds when all was against him is clear from the French Campaign of 1814 and the Flight of the Eagle and the Hundred Days. However he is often presented (indeed he presented himself) as without antecedence, emerging on the public stage like political Minerva 'fully armed'. The fact is, he was bathed in the political discourse of his times; indeed his intellectual makeup (I shall argue) was not just history and literature but also political theory. In this chapter I propose to highlight the striking resonances between the works of two political theorists and the words of Napoleon. The first is the profound influence which Rousseau and Rousseauian thinking had upon Napoleon at a young age and, I contend, throughout his career; the traditional view is that his Rousseauism disappears after 1791.[1] The second is Napoleon's exposure to, and interest in, the Renaissance Florentine political thinker and realist, Niccolò Machiavelli. The juxtaposition of these two figures seems to me to be interesting in that it sets into sharp relief two key characteristics of Napoleon's political *modus operandi*: firstly, his manipulation of the systematic thinking of the Enlightenment; and secondly the casuistic, 'realpolitical' nature of Napoleon's statesmanship (obviously typical to his nature but startlingly mirrored in the Italian's *Prince* and *On Livy's Decade*).

Rousseau!

Napoleon was profoundly influenced and impressed by Rousseau.[2] Frédéric Masson noted that Corsican nationalism had brought Rousseau to Napoleon's attention.[3] Not only had Rousseau taken an interest in the polity of Corsica in the 1750s (a subject of particular fascination for Nabulio) and had been friendly with the Corsican politician (and Napoleon's rival) Buttafoco, he was also a literary model for Napoleon the young romantic. In the latter's essay for the Lyons literary prize Napoleon declared that the 'monde sensible' (the world of those who feel) ought to erect a monument in honour of the author of the *Devin du village*. In the same breath, he pined, 'O Rousseau, why did you only live to sixty years old. In the interests of virtue [an interestingly Machiavellian term], you should have been immortal'.[4] It is therefore not surprising that in Napoleon's most developed piece of creative writing, *Clisson and Eugénie*, Rousseauian elements abound.[5] The central character of the novella, Clisson, is a sort of Rousseauian literary construct for Napoleon himself. At the beginning of the novella, Napoleon writes that Clisson 'felt the need to retreat inside himself, [to take] a close look at his life...his physical and emotional state'.[6] Rousseau's *Rêveries du promeneur solitaire* and *Emile ou de l'éducation* were clearly Napoleon's model for this sort of writing.[7]

Rousseau's political theory too, in particular the treatise *On the Social Contract*, clearly found a resonance with the young Corsican. Napoleon opened his *Refutation of Roustan* with the ecstatic envoi, 'Rousseau!' and continued with a paean to that 'profound and penetrating man...who spent his life studying mankind and who so excellently revealed to us the minute causes of great actions'.[8] In the third part of Napoleon's prize essay mentioned above he wrote that *On the Social Contract* (along with Plato's dialogues and Locke's treatise *On Human Reason*) had established truths which perfect society, legislation and modes of conduct.[9] As Arthur Chuquet noted in 1897, 'Just like Rousseau, he declared that for matters which affect all citizens, the law is the acquiescence of individual reason to general reason.'[10]

Anti-Rousseauism?

In the period pre-1800, Napoleon was not however blindly uncritical towards the Genevan theorist. In his 1791 discussion of Rousseau's *Notes sur le discours sur l'origine et les fondements de l'inégalité parmi les homes par J. J. Rousseau*,[11] Napoleon marks the end of each Rousseauian paragraph with an emphatic 'I do not believe this at all'. And F. G. Healey in his fundamental treatment of Napoleon and Rousseau goes on to emphasize (following Frédéric Masson) how Napoleon gradually parted ways with Rousseau, mapping this distancing upon the gradual change from Corsican nationalism to French loyalism.[12] According to Healey, Napoleon's subsequent negativity towards the Genevan theorist derived from his fear that since Rousseauian theory had caused the revolutionaries to overthrow the Bourbons, it could do just the same with his own regime. So (according to Healey) by the time of the Consulate, Napoleon is frankly anti-Rousseau. Hence Napoleon's famous conversation with Stanislas Girardin held over Rousseau's tomb at the end of August 1800.

'It would have been better for the peace of France that this man [Rousseau] had never existed.'

'Why is that, citizen consul?' I asked him.

'It was he who laid the ground for the French Revolution.'

'I would have thought, citizen consul, that you of all people would not be one to complain about the revolution.'

'Well then!' he replied, 'the future will teach us whether it would not have been better for the peace of the earth if neither Rousseau nor I had ever existed.'[13]

Healey goes on to cite later examples pre-dating the Empire which reveal Napoleon's falling out with Rousseau. At a dinner conversation with Roederer, dated 21 Nîvose, Year XI (11 January 1803), the First Consul is said to have remarked: 'The more I read Voltaire, the more I like him. ... Up until I was sixteen, I would have fought for Rousseau against all the supporters of Voltaire. Today it is the opposite. I completely lost my appetite for Rousseau after having visited the Orient. The primitive man is a dog.'[14] And yet Healey's straightforward picture of initial adulation followed by antipathy is not so clear-cut. After dinner on the same evening, Rœderer informs us that Napoleon went on to dictate the bases for a constitution for the aristocratic cantons of Switzerland, making the following particularly Rousseauian remarks: 'There should not be a permanent president [of the Grand Council]: the presidency should change every fifteen days. A president of a democracy would be totally ridiculous. There should be a presidency, not a president.'[15] And other Rousseauian elements in Napoleon's pronouncements can be traced in this supposedly non-Rousseauist period. At a sitting of the Conseil d'état of 28 Thermidor, Year VIII (16 August 1800) the new First Consul, fresh from his victory at Marengo and contemporaneously with his visit to Rousseau's château (noted above), was quite happy to use the language of the Genevan intellectual, famously remarking, 'My policy is to govern men according to the way the majority wish to be governed. That, I think, is the way to recognize the sovereignty of the people'.[16] We can go even further back. A remarkable letter of 1797 shows Napoleon in full 'Rousseau' flight. It is addressed to Foreign Minister Talleyrand dated 21 September 1797, and it reveals the proto-consul's striking sensibility to Rousseau's discussion of government as it appears in Book III of *On the Social Contract*. Written only weeks after the 'regime change' of 18 Fructidor, it shows Napoleon presenting his new political ally with a project constitution. Napoleon criticizes Montesquieu for his analytical but impractical approach, whilst agreeing with the theorist on the question of the separation of the executive, the legislative and the judiciary. On the other hand, he disagrees that the power to make war or raise taxes was the remit of the legislature. Britain had the correct idea, Napoleon opined, in giving one of these (taxation) to Commons (the only possible equivalent of *La Nation*). In his discussion of the polity in France, he happily uses the language of the Social Contract. 'In fifty years, the only thing which we have well defined is the sovereignty of the people.' 'The power of the government...should be considered the true representative of the Nation, and it should govern in accordance with the constitutional charter and the organic laws.'[17]

Here we see Napoleon not just as a Sunday afternoon political theorist but willing to enter into debate with the political greats; and we ought not to be surprised at this is hard core Rousseauian political theory. Napoleon himself noted to his entourage that he was an adept of serious political and legal theory. In a conversation recorded by Rœderer in 1803, the First Consul asks whether the administrator had read Monsieur de Bonald's *Théorie de pouvoir politique* and his *De la Législation primitive*, claiming that he (Napoleon) read everything that was published on such subjects.[18]

As if the plebiscites, constitutions and codes of the Consulate and early empire were not indications enough of Napoleon's indebtedness to Rousseau, there is also a speech made in 1804 which again shows how deeply Napoleon had imbibed Rousseau's theories, long after he had supposedly rejected the theorist.

In chapter VIII of book III of *On the Social Contract*, Rousseau takes up and expounds the 'geographical theory of politics' which had first been enunciated by Bodin in the sixteenth century[19] and then restated by Montesquieu in the *Spirit of Laws*.[20]

Montesquieu wrote a whole chapter on *Laws in Relation to the Nature of the Climate*, noting the general idea that 'If it be true that the temper of the mind and the passions of the heart are extremely different in different climates, the laws ought to be in relation both to the variety of those passions and to the variety of those tempers'. Rousseau reflects upon how environment changes man and so alters the polity.

'We find then, in every climate, natural causes according to which the form of government which it requires can be assigned, and we can even say what sort of inhabitants it should have.

Unfriendly and barren lands, where the product does not repay the labour, should remain desert and uncultivated, or peopled only by savages...: in such places all polity is impossible. Lands where the surplus of product over labour is only middling are suitable for free peoples; those in which the soil is abundant and fertile and gives a great product for a little labour call for monarchical government, in order that the surplus of superfluities among the subjects may be consumed by the luxury of the prince...'

Napoleon takes this theory and makes a comparison of the Englishman and Frenchman and so British and French institutions. This aggressive speech was made by the First Consul to the Conseil d'état in April or May 1804 criticizing the Senate for trying to create itself as a British-style upper house in relation to the Conseil d'état.[21]

'The pretensions of the Senate are reminiscences of the English constitution', opined Bonaparte. 'But nothing could be more different than France and England. A Frenchman lives beneath a fine sky, drinks a strong, heady wine and eats food which excites the activity of his senses. An Englishman, on the other hand, inhabits a humid land, where the sunshine is almost cold, drinks beer or porter and eats a lot of milk and cheese. The blood of the two peoples is not composed of the same elements; their characters could not but be different. The former is vain, frivolous, audacious, and above all a lover of equality; in all periods of history, he has been seen to fight those superior to him in rank and fortune. The latter has more pride than vanity, he is naturally grave and does not mobilize himself against mere distinctions but rather against serious abuses. He is more desirous of keeping his own rights than of usurping those of anyone else. An Englishman is both proud yet humble, independent and yet subordinate. How could one possibly dream of giving the same institutions to two such different peoples?'

This overt Rousseauism in April/May is perhaps not surprising. It was during this period that the Senate was discussing the creation of the hereditary empire for Napoleon. The First Consul wrote a message to the Senate (dated 5 Floréal, Year XIV/25 April 1804), stating 'We/I have been constantly guided by this great truth: that sovereignty resides in the people of France, in the sense that everything, without exception, should be done for its benefit, for its happiness and for its glory. It was for this goal that the supreme magistracy, the Senate, the Conseil d'état, the Corps legislative, the electoral colleges and the diverse branches of the administration are and ought to have been instituted.'[22] In its reply (dated 14 Floréal, Year XIV/4 May 1804), the Senate was even more Rousseauian, referring to 'pacte social' between the First Consul and the people, how it should not be violated, how it 'would last forever', how liberty and equality were both sacred, and how the sovereignty of the people should be always recognized. Although the pact was to be watered down, nevertheless, it was to make its appearance in the form of the coronation oath, establishing what the emperor promised to do for the 'peuple français'.[23]

How can we square this particular circle, one in which Napoleon explicitly damns Rousseau on the one hand and, on the other, is genuinely committed to Rousseauian ideas? The professed youthful fascination and (as I have shown) continuing interest in the Genevan thinker would imply actual commitment and a sharing of belief. But the use of Rousseauian theory might also be the product of political common sense. Despite the single-party state appearances, politics were not dead during the Consulate and Empire.[24] Rœderer's memoirs show us that Napoleon was permanently obliged to 'faire de la politique' in order to keep the regime on track. In the discussion (noted above) of 21 Nîvose Year XI (11 January 1803) in the context of the creation of the life consulship, Napoleon and Rœderer speak explicitly of parties, Cambaceres as the leader of the 'Conventionnel' party. Elsewhere, Rœderer talks of the 'Brumarians' who supported General Bonaparte in November 1799 but who felt concerned at Napoleon's apparent

slip to the right, notably with the organization of the ancien-régime ceremonial of the Sacre. The consul and emperor's adoption of Rousseauian
positions, even when he professed no longer to appreciate the Genevan
theorist's thinking, could be seen as not just a true reflection of his political
beliefs but also as 'good politics', in short, a sort of Rousseauian casuistry.

Nor did the coronation prevent Napoleon from continuing to manipulate
Rousseau's ideas. In 1807, from the château in Finckenstein, he was dictating
how he wished the girl's academy at Ecouen to be arranged, drawing strongly
on the fifth book of Rousseau's *Emile*.[25] In religious matters, the Genevan
theorist can be identified in the emperor's ideas on civil religion. In the
Contrat social, book IV, chapter VIII, Rousseau develops the idea that belief
in the supernatural is an effective instrument of state control and the clergy
could be a sort of 'celestial police force'.[26] Napoleon repackaged this concept
in remarks made in 1806: 'Catholic priests are a great help; they have been
the reason that this year's conscription has gone much better than in
previous years.... No other body of the state speaks about the government as
well as they do'.[27]

Napoleon's Rousseauism was also noted by the men of his time. Sudhir
Hazareesingh singles out Benjamin Constant: 'After his exclusion from the
Tribunate, [Benjamin] Constant wrote a number of works in which he sought
to sketch out a liberal politics as an alternative to Napoleon's authoritarian
rule. In the *Principes de Politique* (1806) he assailed the imperial system, a
mixture of elements drawn from Hobbesian and Rousseauian principles and
absolutist practice.'[28] Nor was Constant incorrect. In the winter and spring
of 1814, when things were falling apart, the struggling emperor tried once
again to reach his 'inner Rousseau', though not long enough to see whether
it would have worked. As the emperor noted to the Corps législatif, 'The
throne without the Nation is only four pieces of wood covered with a bit
of velvet. The Nation is in the throne, the throne is in the Nation; without
this there would be no monarchy.... I do not hold the throne because of my
fathers but rather because of the will of the Nation which gave it to me.'[29]
It is clear that Napoleon saw his Rousseauism as a way of buying himself
popularity with certain political groups and believed that it had the power
to cleanse him from the tarring brush of absolutism.

After the fall of the empire, on St Helena Napoleon was to return to his
first love, Rousseau. He remarked frankly to Las Cases, that he had changed
since Elba, that given time he would have been 'simply the monarch of the
constitution and of peace, just as [he] had been that of the dictatorship
and great enterprises'. Again, to Las Cases, he bathed himself in a liberal
'Rousseauian afterglow': if peace had come, he said, 'my dictatorship would
have ended, my constitutional reign would have begun'.[30] Even forgeries of
Napoleon's writings on Elba attribute Rousseauist sentiments to him.[31] The
ideas of the Genevan theorist abounded in the period and there is no doubt
that Napoleon's contemporaries saw him as an exponent of them.

What I have tried to show here is that Napoleon read (and practised) Rousseau carefully and assiduously at least up to the creation of the Empire and during the difficult times of 1814 and 1815. On accession to the imperial quality, he reached less frequently for Rousseau (though his contemporaries still thought of him as Rousseauist), he became less collegial in his wielding of power, less interested in popular legitimacy and more absolutist. At these moments Napoleon acts as a prince rather than a consul, an autocrat rather than a president.

Machiavelli

Unlike for Rousseau, there is no evidence of Napoleon wanting the 'monde politique' to erect a statue to the author of *The Prince*. However, we do know from the Libri manuscripts in Florence that in his early years he read (and made notes on) Machiavelli's *History of Florence*. According to F. G. Healey, Napoleon first came to the Florentine via Pasquale Paoli, who (it was said) read daily from the works of Machiavelli.[32] We know that Napoleon read Machiavelli later in his career since copies of the *Discourses on the First Ten Books of Titus Livius* were ordered for the emperor's portable library in 1808. Furthermore, the imperial inventories refer to nine and fourteen volume sets of Machiavelli's works respectively held at the libraries of the Trianon and at Malmaison.[33] Metternich, in his famous portrait of Napoleon, noted that it 'was certain that Napoleon deeply admired Machiavelli'.[34] As for Machiavelli's most famous (and controversial) text, *The Prince*, there only remains evidence of direct contact once. The Comte Molé, at the Conseil d'état, heard Napoléon say: 'I am sometimes a fox, sometimes a lion. The whole secret of government consists in knowing when to be one and when to be the other'.[35] This is a direct citation of Machiavelli, *The Prince*, chapter XVIII, 'Since a prince then needs to know how to make good use of the animal kingdom, he should take the example of the fox and the lion. Since a lion cannot defend itself from a trap and a fox cannot defend itself from wolves, the Prince must be a fox then so as to recognize the traps and a lion so as to frighten the wolves.'

Discussion raged during the eighteenth century as to whether *The Prince* was a work encouraging cynicism and 'ends justifies the means' political action or whether it was a work of satire encouraging democratic states to be on the lookout for despots. Rousseau for one had come down on the satirical side[36] but others (particularly Napoleon's enemies) saw the dark side of the cynicism. Madame de Staël, for example, once referred to Napoleon as 'drunk on the bad wine of Machiavellianism'.[37] And this is perhaps one reason why Napoleon was not 'upfront' about his interest in the Florentine theorist; precisely because in certain circles the author's very name was synonymous with cynicism and perfidy. Some of Napoleon's power base, bourgeois Christian circles, would have been aware that *The Prince* was on the Vatican's list of banned books.

Very little has been written about Napoleon and Machiavelli. Thierry Lentz is perhaps the first to have attempted the discussion.[38] He ably shows how Machiavelli's *Prince* could have been written precisely for the Napoleon. We can see the emperor rewarding his close collaborators, putting into practice Machiavelli's chapter 'On liberality and parsimony'. We can see Napoleon highlighting his own clemency during the famous Madame Hatzfeld incident (did he not sometimes model himself on Trajan?), following to the letter Machiavelli's chapter 'On Cruelty and Clemency'. Lentz also adduces Napoleon's fascinating early-empire-period confession to Chaptal of his 'princely' Machiavellianism: 'Five or six families share the thrones of Europe and they see with pain that a Corsican has come to sit on one of them. I can only keep myself here by force. ... My empire is destroyed if I cease to be terrifying.[39] ... Internally, my position is nothing like that of the old sovereigns. They can live in indolence in their chateaux. ... For everything is very different: there is not a single general who does not think that they have the same rights to the throne as I have. There is not a man of influence who does not think that he paved the road to 18 Brumaire for me. I am obliged to be very severe with these men. ... They do not like me at all, but they fear me, and that is enough. ... Both externally and internally, I only reign by the fear I impose. ... This is my position and these are the motives for my actions.'[40] This is an astonishingly Princian credo.

But Machiavelli was not just the coldly calculating promoter of the amoral Cesare Borgia. He was also passionately convinced that we can learn how to become more virtuous from the past. It was in this strain that he composed his *Discourse on the first ten books of Livy*, a three-book treatise on statecraft in a commentary on the first ten books of Livy's history of the Romans. This work is generally positive towards democracy and Machiavelli hoped that his work would encourage people to do good. In the prologue to Book II he notes: 'I shall boldly and openly say what I think of former times and of the present, so as to excite in the minds of the young men who read my writings the desire to avoid the evils of the latter and to prepare themselves to imitate the virtues of the former ... .' In this politician's *vademecum*, he gives examples from antiquity to reveal what it takes 'to found a republic, maintain states, to govern a kingdom, organize an army, conduct a war, dispense justice, and extend empires ... .' Antiquity did not make the politics of the past inopportune in the present, argued the Florentine. The planet and its inhabitants have not changed in intervening times, he went on; there is no reason why politics should have done so. One can imagine this speaking very clearly to the young Corsican. And the chapter headings alone read as if Machiavelli were discussing the problems faced by Napoleon.

Chapter VI: Whether it was possible to establish in Rome a government capable of putting an end to the enmities existing between the Nobles and the People.

Chapter IX: To found a new republic, or to reform entirely the old institutions of an existing one, must be the work of one man only.

Chapter XII: The importance of giving religion a prominent influence in a state, and how Italy was ruined because she failed in this respect through the conduct of the Church of Rome.

Chapter XXI: Princes and republics who fail to have national armies are much to be blamed.

Chapter XXIV: Well-ordered republics establish punishments and rewards for their citizens, but never set off one against the other.

Chapter XXXIV: The authority of the dictatorship has always proved beneficial to Rome, and never injurious; it is the authority which men usurp, and not that which is given them by the free suffrages of their fellow-citizens, that is dangerous to civil liberty.

One English contemporary of Napoleon's was in no doubt that Napoleon 'invariably pursued the doctrines of Machiavelli'. He was the loyalist Sir John Scott Byerley, who received the Russian order of St Vladimir from emperor Alexander in Paris in 1814 and an annual stipend of £200 from the Prince Regent.[41] In 1810, Byerley published a translation of *The Prince* which was prefaced with a long introduction 'shewing the close analogy between the principles of Machiavelli and the actions of Buonaparte'.[42] And although Sir John's comparison aims at denigrating the French leader, there is also admiration. His argument is that Britain can only defeat Napoleon by out-Machiavelliing him. The introduction to the translation then goes on to highlight just where the Emperor sticks close to his sixteenth-century Florentine model. The chapter 12 of the text on Livy (title given above) is notable (says Byerley): 'we here perceive, that three hundred years after this denunciation of the mischiefs arising from the temporal power of the Popes, Buonaparte not only performs what Machiavelli prompted Lorenzo de Medici to undertake, but even assigns *the very reasons* (Byerley's emphasis) alleged by Machiavelli ... '.[43] Sir John then goes on to list further similarities. The French emperor's position as mediator of Switzerland, King of Italy and Protector of the Confederation of the Rhine (the Yorkshireman contends) corresponds to the chapter 2 of Machiavelli's *Prince* where the Florentine observes that by creating such a composite power he is able to create jealousy amongst the weaker princes, making it very difficult for them to unite against him. It also allows the prince to have more troops to hand at no further cost (such as, as Byerley points out, the Bavarians defeating the Austrians in the 1809 campaign).[44] Machiavelli notes in his Livian text chapter 25, that 'Whoever wishes to change the constitution of a free state, in such a manner as that the change will be accepted with the consent and approbation of the people, should necessarily retain some vestiges of the ancient form'.[45] So Napoleon was an Arab to the Arabs in Egypt, he was careful to bring back religion via the Concordat, and in his arrangements with 'petty princes and vassal kings, [he] consult[ed] the genius and manners of each state … settl[ing] his sovereignty on a firm and stable basis, leaving them the semblance at least of what they cherished most, whether it was forms of religion or government'.[46]

In the end, however, Sir John need not have gone to such trouble to unpick the Machiavellian strains in Napoleon's actions. As the empire ages, Napoleon himself (as was noted by his entourage) adopts more and more the autocracy of a Cesare Borgia. Thierry Lentz cites Marmont's remarkable conversation with French navy minister Decrès: 'Napoleon is mad, completely mad', remarked the naval man. 'He will throw us all, just as we are, "arse over tit" (cul par dessus tête), and it will end in a terrible catastrophe'.[47] Napoleon's extreme Princian Machiavellianism had led to his obsession with the position of the prince, to the complete alienation of his entourage.

I have tried here to highlight two significantly different strands in Napoleon's statesmanship. One resolutely theoretical, following the Moderns, grounded in Rousseau and his theories expounded in the treatise *On the Social Contract*. The other is 'ends-oriented', arguably following the Ancients, and Machiavellian in style, in both autocratic and democratic guises. These strands stem perhaps from the same urge within the man; to do things his way, sometimes as a fox, sometimes as a lion.

Notes

1. See F. G. Healey, *The Literary Culture of Napoleon* (Geneva, 1959), 37 and ed. Adrien Dansette, *Napoléon. Vues politiques* (Paris, 1939). See however Luigi Mascilli Migliorini for the identification of Napoleon's hidden Rousseauism beyond his youthful years in *Napoleone* (Rome, 2002), 34 'Il rousseauianesimo romantico, che segna profondamente la giovinezza di Napoleone e rimane impronta nascosta nel maturo protagonista della storia europea …'.
2. See F. G. Healey, *Rousseau et Napoleon* (Geneva, 1957).
3. Frédéric Masson and Guido Biagi, *Napoléon inconnu*, vol. I (Paris, 1895), 138–140.
4. Frédéric Masson and Guido Biagi, *Napoléon*, vol. II, 314.
5. See Napoleon Bonaparte, *Clisson et Eugénie*, ed. Peter Hicks and Emilie Barthet (Paris, 2007).
6. Ibid., 8.
7. Cf. Jean-Jacques Rousseau, *Les Confessions de J.-J. Rousseau, suivies des Rêveries du promeneur solitaire* (Genève, 1782) t. II. 'second promenade': 'Having chosen the project to describe my usual emotional state … I found no simpler … method … than to keep a faithful account of my solitary walks and the reveries which filled them … These hours of solitude and meditation are the only ones when I am fully me.' As Napoleon says of Clisson later on: 'reverie had replaced reflection', *Clisson et Eugénie*, 11.
8. Frédéric Masson and Guido Biagi, *Napoléon. Manuscrits inédits. 1786–1791* (Paris, [1927?]) esp. 7–10.
9. Frédéric Masson and Guido Biagi, *Napoléon*, vol. II, 316.

10. Arthur Chuquet, *La jeunesse de Napoléon: La Révolution* (Paris, 1897–99), 219.
11. Frédéric Masson and Guido Biagi, *Napoléon*, vol. II, 285–286.
12. F. G. Healey, *Rousseau et Napoléon*, 47 on.
13. Pierre-Louis Rœderer gives a different version of this conversation (*Œuvres du comte P. L. Rœderer*, vol. 3 [Paris, 1853–1859], 336): on a visit to the room in which Rousseau died, Napoleon supposedly said 'He's a lunatic, your Rousseau; he's the one who has brought us to where we are today'. To which Girardin replied, 'But here's not bad'.
14. Ibid., 461.
15. Ibid. Cf. Jean-Jacques Rousseau, *Du Contrat social*, ed. Gérard Mairet (Paris, 1996) Livre II, 61: 'Le souverain... n'est qu'un être collectif'.
16. Rœderer, *Œuvres*, vol. 3, 334.
17. *Napoléon Bonaparte: Correspondance générale*, tome 1, letter 2,065 (Paris, 2004), 1,197.
18. Rœderer, *Œuvres*, vol. 3, 461.
19. *Les six livres de la République* (Paris, 1576).
20. (Geneva, 1748), chapter XIV.
21. B[ar]on Pelet (de la Lozère), *Opinions de Napoléon sur divers sujets de politique et d'administration* (Paris, 1833), 63–64.
22. *Napoléon Bonaparte: Correspondance générale* tome 4, letter number 8, (Paris, 2007) 834, 687.
23. As Thierry Lentz (in *Le sacre de Napoléon* [Paris, 2003], 170) has noted, 'Napoleon continued to invoke to invoke a pact which bound him to the French people.... In 1813, in an address to the Corps législatif, he specified however that only he had the power to break that pact...'.
24. Cf. Isser Woloch, *Napoleon and his collaborators* (2001) and Thierry Lentz, *Le Grand Consulat* (Paris, 1999).
25. See *La Correspondance de Napoléon Ier* (Paris, 1858-) letter 12,585, Finkenstein, 15 May 1807, to Lacépède, 'Note sur l'établissement d'Ecouen'. For Napoleon on female education, see J. Balde, 'Napoléon et l'éducation des filles', *La Revue hébdomadaire* (20 August 1921), 333–351. See also Antonietta Angelica Zucconi, 'L'educazione delle principessine Bonaparte', *Napoleone, le donne, Protagoniste, Alleate, Nemiche.* ed. Massimo Colesanti with Giampaolo Buontempo and Peter Hicks (Rome, 2009), 165–187.
26. Will and Ariel Durant, *Histoire de la civilisation: Rousseau et la Révolution* (Paris, 1969), 329.
27. Quoted in Bernardine Melchior-Bonnet, *Napoléon et le Pape* (Paris, 1958), 87. See also Matthieu Molé, *Le comte Molé : 1781–1855: sa vie, ses mémoires,* vol. 1 (Paris, 1922–1930), 65.
28. *Legend of Napoleon* (London, 2004), 159.
29. Spoken to the Corps législatif, recorded by Matthieu Molé, 1 January 1814, *Le comte Molé*, vol. 1, 198.
30. Emmanuel Las Cases, *Le mémorial de Sainte-Hélène*, ed. Marcel Dunan vol. 1, 10–12 March and vol. 2, 24 August 1816 (Paris, 1951).
31. See Anonymous (attributed to Victorien-Donatien Mussay), *Suite au Mémorial de Sainte-Hélène, ou Observations critiques, anecdotes inédites pour servir de supplément et de correctif à cet ouvrage* tome 2 (Paris, 1824), 310.
32. F. G. Healey, *The Literary Culture of Napoleon*, 32. See also Arthur Chuquet, *La jeunesse*, vol. 2, 62.
33. See Annie Jourdan, *Napoléon, héros, imperator, mécène* (Paris, 1998), 130.

34. Clemens Metternich, *Mémoires: documents et écrits divers / laissés par le prince de Metternich*, vol. 1 (Paris, 1881–1884), 282.
35. Matthieu Molé, *Le comte Molé*, tome I, 86.
36. Jean-Jacques Rousseau, *Du contrat social*, book III, chapter VI, 'On Monarchy', 100. Rousseau notes that Machiavelli's *Prince* was a book for Republicans and that Machiavelli was an honest and a good citizen.
37. *Considérations sur la Révolution française*, 1983 edition, 422. Quoted in Thierry Lentz, *Nouvelle Histoire du Premier Empire*, vol. III (Paris, 2007), 14.
38. Ibid., 9–21.
39. Cf. Napoleon's advice to Joseph on the latter's accession to the Kingdom of Naples, dated Paris, 8 March 1806 (*Correspondance générale*, letter 11, 610, 191): 'It is only by a salutary terror that you will impose yourself upon the Italian people.'
40. Adrien Dansette, *Napoléon*, 56–57.
41. See R. V. Taylor, *Anecdotae Eborancenses. Yorkshire Anecdotes; Or Remarkable Incidents in the Lives of Celebrated Yorkshire Men and Women* (London, 1883), 74.
42. Sir John Scott Byerley, *The Prince...by Machiavelli, to which is prefixed an introduction shewing the close analogy between the principles of Machiavelli and the action of Buonaparte* vii (London, 1810), xv–xxvi.
43. Ibid., xxiii.
44. Ibid., xli.
45. Quoted in ibid., xlvi.
46. Ibid., xlvi.
47. A. F. G. Marmont, *Mémoires du maréchal Marmont, duc de Raguse, de 1792 à 1841: imprimés sur le manuscrit original de l'auteur*, tome III (Paris, 1857), 336–340, cited in Thierry Lentz, *Nouvelle Histoire*, vol. III, 18.

Part II

The Low Countries, the Rhineland and Switzerland, 1792–1814

Introduction

Michael Broers

The small states along France's eastern border were a power vacuum in the eighteenth century. They comprised the small polities of: the Austrian Netherlands (present-day Belgium), under the Habsburg Monarchy; the patchwork of small states of the Holy Roman Empire between the French border and the left (western) bank of the Rhine; the Dutch Republic (effectively a confederation of provinces); and the loose confederation of cantons that constitute modern-day Switzerland.

The War of the First Coalition in 1792 turned these regions into the frontline between the Coalition and France. When the French Republic declared as one of its war aims the achievement of France's 'natural frontiers'—an unheralded concept of claiming territorial rights—they designated the Rhine as France's 'natural frontier' on the east. These claims were realized first with the annexation of the Austrian Netherlands in 1795 as eight departments, plus the department of Forêts, which was the Grand Duchy of Luxembourg. These departments remained part of France until 1814. As for the left bank of the Rhine, French occupation became permanent by 1797, when this mass of tiny states and some Prussian provinces became four French departments, again until 1814.

There had been serious unrest in the Austrian Netherlands just before the outbreak of the French Revolution in 1789, when a diverse coalition of interests rebelled unsuccessfully against the reforms of the Habsburg Emperor, Joseph II. It was known as the Vonckist Revolt, after one of its radical leaders, Vonck, who promised the French revolutionaries solid support in the region when they first invaded in 1793. This was not forthcoming and the early phases of French rule were turbulent. After a widespread revolt in 1798–99 (the Peasants' War) which arose from resentment of conscription and the French religious reforms, the Belgian departments settled down to a period of stability under Napoleonic rule, as did the Rhenish departments. Unlike all the other regions later annexed to France, the Belgian and Rhenish departments were integrated fully into the French zone of economic preference created by the Continental System after 1806. They were among the most urbanized and industrialized parts of Europe in this period; Belgian textiles and mining and Rhenish commerce fared relatively well since, as a result of their full inclusion into the French economy proper, they received preferential status vis-à-vis the rest of Napoleonic Europe. These regions, annexed before the coup of Brumaire in 1799, received all the fundamental Napoleonic legal, administrative, religious and educational reforms at the same time as France.

The Dutch Republic—or the United Provinces—was also brought under French hegemony early on, but its subsequent history was very different from that of the Rhineland and Belgium. Although a loose union of seven, technically independent provinces, the Dutch Republic was, nonetheless, one of the best-established states in Europe. It had seen unrest in 1787–88, broadly similar to that of the Vonckist Revolt, in opposition to the centralist reforms of its nominal head of state, William V, the Stadholder, head of the House of Orange. In 1795, driven by the French, the old Republic and the House of Orange were overthrown and replaced by a 'sister republic', the Batavian Republic, with a constitution modelled on the French Directory. Napoleon refashioned the constitution in 1800, bringing it into line with the Consulate, but the Batavian Republic continued until 1806, although French control progressively tightened. With the decree of the Europe-wide blockade against Britain in 1806 and the Continental System, this region became vital for Napoleon's strategy of economic warfare. Napoleon abolished the Batavian Republic in 1806, turning it into the Kingdom of Holland under his brother, Louis. By 1810, Napoleon considered Louis useless; the blockade was impotent and the unsuccessful British attempt to destroy French shipbuilding capacity in Antwerp (via Walcheren) concentrated his mind. He annexed Holland directly to France, each of the former provinces becoming a French department and Lebrun, the former Consul, became its Governor-General. Even after annexation, however, the Dutch departments remained outside the French economic zone. The region remained under French rule until liberated by the Allied armies in December 1813.

Switzerland, too, was an old, if very decentralized union, of nineteen virtually independent cantons. Its territories were much fought-over in the 1790s and, by 1798, it was securely occupied by the French who, that year, turned it into a 'sister republic', the Helvetic, with a constitution modelled on the French Directory. The city state of Geneva was annexed to France as the department of Léman. As with the Batavian Republic, Napoleon imposed a new constitution on it in 1800, which proved untenable. In 1802, he decreed the Act of Mediation, devolving more power to the cantons. This remained the basis of the regime henceforth. After 1802, Napoleon seldom interfered in Swiss internal affairs, but the Helvetic Republic reliably supplied him with troops and money.

In 1814, the House of Orange was restored, but the territories of the old Republic were now renamed the Kingdom of the Netherlands, and the son of the last Stadholder became King William I; the Belgian departments were annexed to it by the Congress of Vienna but broke away in 1831, becoming the Kingdom of Belgium. The neutrality of the Helvetic Republic was recognized by the Congress of Vienna in 1814 and Geneva was reunited to it. Now consisting of twenty-two cantons, the Helvetic Republic remains the last state in Europe still to call itself by the name given it as a 'sister republic'. It did not undergo large-scale constitutional change until 1848.

6
The Napoleonic Civil Code: The Belgian Case

Michael Rapport

When the armies of the French republic poured into Belgium in the summer of 1794, they stampeded across a landscape which had been ravaged successively by civil strife, repeated invasion and economic disaster. Only two years prior to the first French conquest of 1792, the Austrian Netherlands had been struggling in its fight for independence from the Habsburgs and the internecine battle for power between the conservative Statists and the more progressive Vonckists. The French Revolution, therefore, struck a country which was already at war with itself over breaking with the past. By the time the Civil Code was promulgated in 1804, therefore, Belgium had undergone the shock of *its own* revolution, followed by successive military occupations and the annexation to the French Republic, all of which was a transformative experience for Belgian society. Consequently, the Napoleonic order was a break with both Belgium's ancien régime past and its more recent and traumatic history. It is in this context that one can consider whether or not Napoleonic law represented a new form of liberal order, or merely the instrument of French domination.

There is no doubt that the impact of the French Revolution in the 1790s was both dramatic and traumatic. Historians were once strongly divided as to how far this problematic decade left Belgium with any constructive legacy. For some, the French occupation in 1792–93 and again in 1794, followed by the annexation from 1795, represented an insidious assault on Belgian nationhood.[1] For others, the very foundations of the modern, independent and liberal Belgian state were laid precisely in the French republican years.[2] This is not the place to engage with this debate in any great detail—for what it is worth, the truth probably lies somewhere in between these two positions—but it is probably fair to say that, more recently, historians have focused in a less ideologically-charged way on the difficulties the republicans had in transplanting revolutionary institutions into Belgium. Among these problems was, of course, resistance in its multifaceted ways, culminating in the great peasant insurrection of 1798. The uprising represented the failure of the Directory to ensure the rule of law in the Belgian departments.

By contrast, then, how far did the Napoleonic regime represent its restoration? This chapter shall firstly discuss how the Napoleonic legal system was a break with the ancien régime. Secondly, it will examine to what extent it represented the re-establishment of the rule of law after the trauma of the Directory—in other words, how far it was also a rupture with the more recent, republican past. Thirdly, it will explore how far the Napoleonic Codes may have been an instrument of conquest, seeking to turn 'Belgians into Frenchmen'.

I

Republican efforts to introduce a workable network of law courts—and indeed the law itself—had floundered on the mass resignations of unwilling jurists and on the social dislocation of the late 1790s, which left large areas of the country in states of emergency. The result was that under the relative stability of the Napoleonic regime, the introduction of French law was still something of a novelty. This is well-illustrated in the introduction of juries and of pleading in open court. In Mons at the end of 1804, an unemployed lawyer, Philippe Vigneron, successfully petitioned for a position in the new French courts in the department of Jemappes. He cited as one of his qualifications the fact that, having been a representative on the Estates of Hainault and having been a member of the town council prior to the revolution, he was used to public speaking. Other Belgian lawyers, he implied, were not. Prior to the initial introduction of the first French law courts into Belgium during the period of the annexation, 'in this country we did not have any orator at the bar; everyone pleaded before our old courts either in chambers or in writing—nothing verbally—...I was the first to undertake pleading with my own, live voice, which was new for us, and this will serve as an example for ...my colleagues to follow'.[3]

Yet the Napoleonic regime did not want to rely too heavily on jurists who had served the old system. The introduction of French law was an opportunity to break with the past by introducing a new generation of lawyers who were untainted by the received ideas from the old order. When in March 1808, the ministry of justice told the court of appeal in Brussels to appoint *juges auditeurs*, the three chambers of that court took the opportunity 'to appoint young men, educated and from good families, and not *very old lawyers*' (underlined in the original). This was partly a response to the original decree itself, which made it clear that these appointments were meant to be for lawyers in the early stages of their careers. The problem in Belgium, however, was that the law school in Brussels, which had two hundred students, was still ten months away from producing its first graduates. The court's prosecutor Beyts, pointedly explained that this was because of 'the interruption of public instruction in this country, and because the study of law and of jurisprudence was only re-established two years ago'.

The French process also insisted that law graduates then practise for two years at the bar before qualifying as magistrates, so that it would now be close to three years before the students would be ready to take up their appointments at the *cour d'appel*. Yet for Beyts and the other existing magistrates, it was better to appoint only three *juges auditeurs* now (half the contingent required) and to wait for another three years in order the fill the vacant posts with young lawyers, than to fill all the positions immediately with older colleagues: 'if three of those places remain open for two or three years, the students will compete much more with others in their zeal and their work, and the result will benefit the *chose publique*, by an expansion in the education of almost 200 students, and at the same time it will be to the advantage of the Court of Appeal, whose *auditeurs* will later on be better chosen on all accounts and be much better trained.'[4]

Beyts may well have been wearing his other hat, as inspector-general of the law schools, and be thinking only of the training and education of his young charges. Yet it is also telling that he regarded the still green lawyers as potentially better trained and, certainly, as superior candidates for the appeal court than their older colleagues. The implication here is that the experience of the latter counted for little, because they belonged to the now defunct world of the old regime system. When recommending jurists for positions in the criminal tribunal of the department of Jemappes, Latteur, who had been a Vonckist, a democrat in the struggle against Austria, and who was now the president of the Brussels appeal court, was impressed less by ancien régime credentials than by more recent service. Legal qualifications from the Austrian regime were fine, but Latteur emphasized service in the French system imposed on Belgium from 1795.[5] The younger generation represented the future of the new legal order.

Reliance on jurists who had some experience from the ancien régime was virtually inevitable, however, particularly when they had more than adequately demonstrated their loyalty to the new order. These continuities proved to be especially true at a local level, where a precise knowledge of particular communities was important. Pierre Abrassart, President of the lower court at Mons under the Consulate, had served on the sovereign court of Hainault from 1782 until the second French conquest in 1794. Thereafter, he had worked as an administrator—on the municipality of Mons, then on the departmental administration and, under the Consulate, as a member of the departmental electoral college—all this in addition to being a magistrate in the new legal system.[6] Service under the Austrian regime was not necessarily a black mark against a jurist. In February 1811, the Prefect of Jemappes was explicit on this point, writing to the minister of justice, describing the former Hainault's former sovereign court, commending the judges for their 'talents and their probity'. The court 'enjoyed a wide respect in this region to the very last'.[7]

The employment of experienced lawyers seems to have represented an effort by the Napoleonic order to fuse the old elites with the new, it was the *amalgame* at work. In fact, so fragmented had Belgian politics been prior to Napoleon's seizure of power that the choice of magistrates, from the justices of the peace to the appeal courts, was, as the nationalist historian, Paul Verhaegen, grumbled, 'eclectic'[8] and included Jacobins, Vonckists and Statists alongside servants of the former Austrian regime, as well as jurists imported from France. Ultimately, the regime saw this in a positive light, provided that the talents and experience were used in the service of the new legal system. As late as 1811, the authorities were still paying tribute to the talents and commitment of old regime jurists. In the department of Jemappes, the president of the court of first instance at Mons, Charles Gobort, was commended on the grounds that under the ancien régime he had found distinction 'by his talents, by his constant love for the work, the purity of his morals and his attachment to the government. This is how he carries out his duties, surrounded by the greatest public confidence and esteem.'[9] Several points emerge from this. Gobort is considered a fine judge not just because of his experience under the old regime, but also because he transferred his skills and loyalty to the new order. He has public confidence, which was essential for the imperial regime. The co-option of the judicial elites is the policy of *amalgame* in action. This is borne out in the same document where another judge is recommended because, among other things, he was 'born into a distinguished family of the high magistracy'.[10] When Charles Brouckere was recommended for the presidency of the appeal court in Brussels, amongst his sterling qualities was the fact that he was well-connected in local society; he was wealthy and enjoyed status thanks to a good marriage—'une alliance distinguée'.[11] Effectively, the legal system was a means of absorbing the local elites, using their knowledge, talents and connections to give the system credibility. The regime wanted to work through the local elites as a means of ensuring the good workings of the justice system, but this could only work if, firstly, Napoleonic officials worked with moderation and sensitivity towards the old elites, and secondly, if the latter were willing to use their authority to work for the new order rather than against it.[12]

II

As historians like Colin Lucas and Howard Brown have shown, one of the great failures of the Directory was to ensure the rule of law; there was a collapse of law and order and the regime failed to bury the bitter political factionalism of the past.[13] To what extent, then, did the Napoleonic system represent a return both to normal legal process and the protection of life and property? In other words, how far did the Napoleonic Codes represent, as Henri Pirenne argued about the regime as a whole, a break with the turbulence of the Republic and the beginnings of the truly constructive work of the French Revolution in Belgium?[14]

With memories of the peasant insurrection still raw, the officials of the early Consulate insisted on republican credentials in their jurists. When Lambrechts, one-time minister of justice under the Directory but a Senator in Brumaire Year 9, proposed to the then minister of justice, Abrial, candidates for the law courts in the department of the Ourthe (which had Liège as its chef-lieu), he insisted on the good qualities of the department itself ('full of well-informed patriots') and also of a judge named Spiroux, then president of the tribunal at Huy, but now being proposed for the Court of Appeal in Liège. Among his excellent credentials, Spiroux had 'languished for eighteen months in prison during the tyrannical reign of the Bishop of Liège'.[15] The Prefect of the Ourthe agreed that political orthodoxy was essential; when writing to the minister at the end of Year 8, he admonished him not to forget that 'a sure entire devotion to the republic' was essential for the public good.[16]

This changed over time as the Napoleonic regime found its feet. It came to value stability, efficiency and good conduct above political commitment in its choice of judges. The regime did not want to alienate an influential section of the elites and it wanted the law to work effectively and impartially. Still, if a solidly revolutionary past became less urgent, jurists still had to be loyal to the Napoleonic order, or at least not obstructive. In June 1811, E. J. Regnier, the prosecutor at the court in Liège, criticized the choice of a certain Deponthière as a substitute judge because of his formerly anti-French opinions and conduct and his relations with the clergy. Yet Regnier also passionately criticized the intrusiveness of the police on the workings of justice:

> The police! The police! I confess to believing that their evidence has too often influenced the reform of the legal system which has just finished: the police sees a lot, it has a hundred eyes, but it is not always just.[17]

The regime's repressive impulses was the heavy price paid for the restoration of law and order after the turbulence of the 1790s. In stamping out the last remnants of brigandage around Brussels in March 1805, Everaerts, acting as a juge d'instruction for the Criminal Court, ordered the arrest of no less that 600 suspects, who were held in prison in appalling conditions, which alone accounted for seventy deaths. Yet the civil authorities felt confident enough to protest vigorously—and the public prosecutor in the Lys, Van de Walle, successfully prevented the arbitrary arrests from spreading into his own jurisdiction. The affair ended a year later when Everaerts was removed and, in co-operation with one of Napoleon's Conseillers d'État, who had been sent to investigate, his replacement ordered the release of the survivors.[18]

The system responded to complaints by following its own rules. The well-publicized abuses aside, it was generally transparent and predictable. One interesting case, in the canton of Diest (department of the Dyle) in 1810 illustrates this well. Pierre Claude Malingré had been the justice of the peace since the Year 12. His appointment, it was later claimed, was only reluctantly accepted, since he had little legal experience and was known for his rather erratic behaviour. The locals gave him a chance to settle in, but by 1810 they had had enough. According to the petition demanding Malingré's removal, the initial fears proved all-too-correct:

> …he surrounded himself with vile and tainted men, of whom he was successively their friend, their protector, their enemy and their denouncer; discussing the affairs of his tribunal in cabarets; only judgements notable for their ignorance and the most revolting partiality drop from his pen. A swarm of men, calling themselves *défenseurs officieux*, appeared in order to open cases for alleged verbal injury—often his court room was the arena of the most scandalous discussions for truly miserable people.[19]

The signatories of this petition included all the mayors of the canton, plus a list of local worthies—landowners, clockmakers, brewers and rentiers. Clearly, Malingré did not have the confidence of the local elites. The judge's Achilles heel, however, was that he had been declared bankrupt, which offered the minister of justice an easy way of responding positively to the public outcry, while also acting within the law. The imperial constitution stated that no bankrupt could hold public office, so the matter was closed within weeks, from the petition in October to the ruling against Malingré in December.[20]

The affair is an important illustration of the legal system at work, for three reasons. Firstly, it operated, apparently, for the benefit of the citizens, who managed to rid themselves of an incompetent, troublesome judge by laying out their case to the authorities. Secondly, the fact that officials and jurists got involved at almost every level—the mayors of the communes, the departmental prefect, the president of the tribunal of the second arrondissement, the procureur-général at the court of appeal and the minister of justice, and above all the prompt response of the minister in Paris—suggests that both local people and the regime wanted the system to operate well, free of corruption and caprice. This was, arguably, especially important when it came to the *juges de paix*, for this cheap and accessible source of justice represented the kind of civic order the French revolutionaries had hoped to create. Thirdly, when the regime did rid itself of a turbulent judge, it did so by using the letter of the law; at this localized level (and in a stable, peaceful area of the Empire like Belgium), it cost the regime nothing to follow its own rules. When it did not, there were plenty of Belgian lawyers willing to protest. When, in 1811, the government attacked the jury system and abolished the criminal courts, Henri Senbrant, one of the judges on the Bruges court, though faced with redundancy, turned down the offer of a position in the civil tribunal, pointedly explaining to the minister of justice that this was partly due to 'the uncertainty faced by the entire judicial order over its existence, particularly those of the criminal courts whose suppression is striking'.[21]

III

If the system worked, more or less, then to what extent was the French legal system a means of converting Belgians into French citizens (or after 1809, 'subjects') and of binding them into the French Empire? Almendingen, a leading German jurist from Hesse-Nassau and long-term opponent of the regime, warned that, in imposing the Civil Code in Germany, Napoleon was seeking to forge 'a single law in all the confederated States submitted to the French dictatorship and have them bend beneath the pressure of foreign legislation'.[22] Yet, unlike much of the Rhenish Confederation, which was the product of a specifically *Napoleonic*—and therefore recent—surge of French power, Belgium, like the Rhineland, had been part of the French conquests for longer and was rapidly becoming part of the Napoleonic heartland and these regions stood to benefit economically. The Continental System temporarily blocked British competition with Belgian and Rhenish manufacturing, but such protectionism proved to be only a short-term benefit which carried mixed blessings.[23] More importantly, Napoleonic rule gave these regions, which had been ravaged by war in the 1790s, the social stability they needed to resume the economic development which had been in evidence prior to 1789.[24] With the economy firmly rooted in the Napoleonic core, the legal system was potentially a means of completing the assimilation of these European regions.

As Mike Broers has argued, this Napoleonic heartland was a cultural and political space more than a geographical area. Those parts of Europe, such as the Rhineland, Piedmont and Lombardy, where French institutions and practices were allowed to settle in, were 'more integrated into the imperial centre than the *Vendée militaire* or much of the Midi'.[25] The Napoleonic regime established itself best in a society that was settled and urban. Generally speaking, both Belgium and the Rhineland fit this description, so they too were potentially more readily absorbed into the Napoleonic core than the more inaccessible parts of France. Yet, even in Belgium one could still find pockets where old social practices made assimilation into the new civic order fraught with difficulties. In August 1804, when asked to nominate justices of the peace for the department of Mons, Abrassart explained that it was very difficult to make a decent choice for the canton of Paturage, because the population was:

> ...composed of charcoal-burners, who have made their dwellings on a large commons, so that they can be close to their place of work; and all that which has not been successively exploited is used for the common

grazing of their livestock and those of their neighbouring communities. There is very little land which can be used for agriculture, so that there are no eligible electors and the inhabitants are limited to learning to read and to write, so that it is very difficult to find among them any who are capable of fulfilling the functions of justice of the peace.[26]

This was not active resistance, but rather it was the difficulty faced by any regime trying to impose its own vision of order on a society where traditional practices do not lend themselves to a regular system of law and administration. This was, in short, one of those marginal communities within the inner empire identified by Broers as 'hostile to—and relatively remote from—the pre- and post-conquest centres of power, but too weak and dispersed to resist the new regime'. With time, these could be absorbed, sometimes with the help of heavy policing.[27]

Even where the reach of the Napoleonic state was unambiguously firm, the evidence for the codes and the courts as a tool of assimilation is still ambiguous, particularly over the linguistic issue. When the French legal system was being introduced for the first time in 1795–96, it did represent a complete rupture with the ancien régime practice of employing the local language in the courts. From the annexation in 1795, the language to be used was French, even in Flemish-speaking Belgium. Yet this seems to have been driven less by a formal policy than by the circumstances in which Belgium was absorbed into the French Republic: the invasion and military occupation had sent many of the old regime jurists into flight; or bilingual lawyers switched to French to ensure the survival of their own careers. Moreover, the very fact of the introduction of new tribunals encouraged the *francisation* of the Belgian legal profession. By contrast, it is significant that Flemish persisted in pre-existing institutions, such as that venerable ancien régime profession, the notaries. Yet, until 1803 there was no law explicitly ordering that all hearings had to be in French, so it was left to the officials on the ground to decide whether or not to impose French across the country and, while they generally insisted on French in civil cases, they were very reluctant to follow this through in criminal courts, where there was so much more at stake for the defendants. This changed with the order of 13 June 1803, whereby all public acts had to be in French, although local officials could attach a translation of the document in the local language. Private acts, such as those drawn up by a notary, could remain in the original language, provided that a French translation was provided by an official translator. Nonetheless, despite the actions of some zealous prefects who saw their mission as one of extirpating Flemish, the language persisted, particularly amongst those notaries who had trained under the old regime.[28]

There was a pragmatic recognition that, for justice to be done—and for it to be *seen* to be done—Flemish had to be admitted where it was necessary to do so. When the court of appeal in Brussels—whose jurisdiction included the five western of the nine Belgian departments—came to appoint the president of the criminal justice section in November 1809, Beyts warmly recommended Charles Brouckere, who was at the time the president of the criminal court of the department of the Lys, sitting at Bruges. Brouckere was the best candidate not only because of his *lumières*, but also because he spoke, wrote and understood Flemish, which gave him a distinct advantage over his rival candidates. This was crucial, for Flemish 'is the only language of habitual use in four departments of this jurisdiction'.[29] By this date, it was assumed that any lawyer appointed to serve in the new courts could speak and read French. Yet it also seems to have been a matter of unwritten policy to appoint bilingual magistrats, many of whom appeared to have studied at the University of Louvain. Of those who appear in correspondence regarding the Flemish-speaking department of the Lys, for instance, the majority seem to have Flemish names, but they all write in excellent French.[30] This makes perfect sense, the state had to have jurists who could read, understand and interpret French laws, but at the same time dispense justice fairly to local people who could not do so on their own.

In this sense, the law codes were not to be tools for the aggressive cultural assimilation of Belgians into the French state: for one, *francisation* had already occurred less out of any consistent policy than from the circumstances of the conquest and annexation. For another, Napoleonic officials understood that some pragmatism was required if the regime was to get at least the acquiescence of the Flemish population. By 1812, there were grumblings in Paris that the law of 13 June 1803 was placing an intolerable financial burden on those who had to pay for a French translation for private legal acts which had no bearing on the state. Moreover, it was reported to the Emperor, many translators proved to be either unequal to the task of rendering legal documents into French, or, with a deliberate slip of the pen, might mistranslate key phrases of fiscal documents in order to mislead tax collectors.[31] For imperial officials, it seemed to suffice that the peoples of the annexed territories were assimilated in an administrative, institutional sense, but also that the citizens at least understood what was expected of them and that they, in turn, could be confident that they would be heard and understood by the courts.

IV

The Civil Code and other aspects of the French legal system were retained by the Belgians after independence from the Netherlands in the 1830s, so they had gained widespread acceptance.[32] The legal system represented a break with the past in legal terms; even the nationalist historian Verhaegen admits that this was a positive legacy, at least when finally shorn of both its revolutionary and authoritarian plumage by the Belgian Constitution of 1831: 'civil and criminal justice worked for all, easily, rapidly and cheaply. This is one of the most precious benefits of the conquest...one can give homage to the French legislation which markedly improved our ancient institutions'.[33] That being said, the new system also represented the *amalgame* at work; the Napoleonic regime was willing to use old regime jurists because they helped to implant the new order, to help it to function effectively and to ensure that it gained the wider acceptance of the elites, if not of the entire population. It helped that Belgium was in the heartland of the French imperium, well removed from the war for close to a decade between 1804 and 1814. After the social upheaval and military exploitation of the 1790s, the rule of law could work at last and was welcomed by the weary Belgians. Moreover, while the circumstances of the conquest in the 1790s brought with it a *francisation* of Belgian courts, there was no concerted effort to expunge Flemish altogether. Regardless of what the government in Paris wanted, jurists unsurprisingly found that being bilingual remained an asset, which was quite openly a positive factor in making judicial appointments. Auguste Orts, the patriotic nineteenth-century Belgian jurist and historian, claimed that the French had sought to 'confiscate our nationality',[34] but while it was certainly hoped that Belgians would be assimilated administratively into the French Empire, there was never any concerted effort to use the legal system do so linguistically. Belgian legal professionals were willing to work with and through the Napoleonic system, provided that its guarantees were respected by the government. Belgian jurists protested when the regime broke its own rules. This is telling, for it suggests that the Belgians themselves had accepted many of the legal precepts and assumptions of the French Revolution. In this respect, the legal system could be seen as a surrogate, if vulnerable, constitution in the face of the Napoleonic dictatorship.

Notes

I would like to thank Águstin Guimera for his invitation to this conference and for his many kindnesses. I also thank Mike Broers for bravely reading this chapter on my behalf during my absence.

1. See, for example, Paul Verhaegen, *La Belgique sous la domination française*, 5 vols (Brussels, 1922–9) and Auguste Orts, *La Guerre des Paysans 1798–1799: épisode de l'histoire belge* (Brussels, 1863).
2. R Devleeshouwer, *L'arrondissement de Brabant sous l'occupation française 1794–1795: aspects administratifs et économiques* (Brussels, 1964). For the middle ground between the old nationalist view and the more optimistic perspective, see Michael Rapport, 'Belgium under French Occupation: between Collaboration and Resistance, July 1794 to October 1795', *French History* 16 (2002), 53–82.
3. Archives Nationales, Paris [hereafter AN], BB/5/278 (Vigneron to minister of justice, 3 Nivôse, Year 12).
4. AN, BB/5/271 (Cour de Bruxelles: Présentation des Candidats par la Cour d'Appel de Bruxelles).

5. AN, BB/5/278 (Latteur, President of tribunal d'appel de Bruxelles to the minister of justice, 19 Frimaire, Year 12). Verhaegen, *La Belgique*, vol. 4, 56.
6. AN, BB/5/278 (Abrassart to the Minister of Justice, 2 Fructidor, Year 12).
7. AN, BB/5/278 (Dossier: 1811, prefect of Jemappes to the minister of justice, 26 February 1811).
8. Verhaegen, *La Belgique*, vol. 4, 56.
9. AN, BB/8/278 (Dossier: 1811: Tribunal de première instance, 15 February 1811).
10. AN, BB/8/278 (Dossier: 1811).
11. AN, BB/5/271 (Cour de Bruxelles: Beyts to the Duc de Massa, 14 November 1809).
12. See, by way of contrast, Michael Broers, *The Napoleonic Empire in Italy, 1796–1814: Cultural Imperialism in a European Context?* (Basingstoke, 2005), 189–93. An experienced judge in Parma was denied a position in the Napoleonic courts, despite his undisputed skills and probity, because he was suspected less of counter-revolution than of a desire to obstruct the introduction of French legal practices.
13. Colin Lucas, 'The First Directory and the Rule of Law', *French Historical Studies* 10 (1977), 231–60. Howard G. Brown, *Ending the Revolution: Violence, Justice, and Repression from the Terror to Napoleon* (Charlottesville, 2006).
14. Henri Pirenne, *Histoire de Belgique*, vol. 6 (Brussels, 1926, 6 vols), 123.
15. AN, BB/5/283 (Lambrechts to Abrial, 12 Brumaire, Year 12).
16. AN, BB/5/283 (Prefect of the Ourthe to the Minister of Justice, 5e jour complémentaire, Year 8).
17. AN, BB/8/283 (Regnier to Minister of Justice, Duc de Massa, 12 June 1811).
18. Verhaegen, *La Belgique*, vol. 4, 259–61.
19. AN, BB/8/51 (juges de paix: petition).
20. AN, BB/8/51 (letter of minister of justice, 18 December 1810).
21. AN, BB/5/279 (letter of Senbrant to the minister of justice, 18 May 1811).
22. Paul-L. Weinacht, 'Les États de la Confédération du Rhin face au Code Napoléon', in *Napoléon et l'Europe: Colloque de la Roche-sur-Yon*, ed. Jean-Clément Martin (Rennes, 2002), 93.
23. Michael Rowe, *From Reich to State: the Rhineland in the Revolutionary Age, 1780–1830* (Cambridge, 2003), 205–209.
24. Jan Craeybeckx, 'The Brabant Revolution: a Conservative Revolt in a Backward Country?', *Acta Historiae Neerlandica* 4 (1970), 64–6.
25. Broers, *Napoleonic Empire in Italy*, 15–16.
26. AN, BB/5/278 (Jemappes, Year 12: Abrassart to the Minister of the Interior, 20 August 1804).
27. Broers, *Napoleonic Empire in Italy*, 20–21. See also Michael Broers, 'Napoleon, Charlemagne and Lotharingia: Acculturation and the Borders of Napoleonic Europe', *Historical Journal* 44 (2001), 135–54.
28. Herman van Goethem, 'La francisation révolutionnaire, résultat d'initiatives locales: le cas de tribunaux en Flandre et en Alsace', *Études sur le Dix-Huitième Siècle* 16 (1989), 39–52.
29. AN, BB/5/271 (Cour de Bruxelles: Beyts to the Duc de Massa, 14 November 1809).
30. AN, BB/5/279, passim.
31. Fondation Napoleon, 'Rapports et Projet de Décret concernant la Traduction des actes et l'impression des journaux en français dans les départemens réunis où l'usage des deux langues est conserve (1812)', www.Napoléonica.org (10 March 2008).

32. Jean Limpens, 'Territorial Expansion of the Code', in *The Code Napoléon and the Common Law World: the sesquicentennial lectures delivered at the Law Center of New York University, December 13–15 1954*, ed. Bernard Schwarz (New York, 1956), 93.
33. Verhaegen, *La Belgique*, vol. 5, 286.
34. Orts, *Guerre des Paysans*, 5.

7

The Dutch Case: The Kingdom of Holland and the Imperial Departments

Matthijs Lok and Martijn van der Burg

A forgotten period

The Napoleonic era is traditionally not a very popular epoch in Dutch historiography. Most older studies have treated the period of Incorporation into the Empire in 1810 as only a prelude to the establishment of the Orange Monarchy in 1813. Indeed, there is still no general monograph on the Incorporation (*Inlijving*) of the Dutch provinces. The reasons for this neglect are twofold. Firstly, the Napoleonic period has been perceived as one of national decline; political independence was under threat and finally lost entirely in 1810. Instead of returning to the glories of the Golden Age of the Dutch Republic, the economy shrank, cities depopulated and young men were conscripted for the Napoleonic army. Indeed, immediately after the collapse of the Empire in the Dutch departments in October 1813, many pamphlets were published describing the atrocities committed by the French. Secondly, and probably more damaging for the Dutch remembrance of Napoleonic rule, was the official policy of forgetting by King William I (r. 1813–40). According to this policy of *oubli*, the Napoleonic period was simply not to be mentioned, whether positively or negatively. Thus, the years 1795–1813 were draped in silence during the Restoration.[1]

Dutch historians are not solely to blame for this lack of interest. The Dutch case is also often neglected in general surveys. Even Simon Schama has placed most emphasis on the revolutionary years and sees the Napoleonic period only as the aftermath of conflicts of the Revolutionary period.[2] Dutch researchers have only now begun to show interest in the Napoleonic period. As a result new insights are emerging, partly from fresh archival research, partly under the influence of new concepts being applied to Napoleonic studies. We think that the Napoleonic Netherlands should no longer be studied from an exclusively national point of view, but from a European perspective, as Michael Broers suggested in his introduction to this volume, and that new insights will be gained from making comparisons with other European countries and regions under Napoleonic rule. It has become clear that Napoleonic control was not as absolute as has been portrayed, and in many subject states the French took a pragmatic approach to incorporating annexed lands into the Empire.[3]

In this chapter we will examine the extent to which pre-Revolutionary Dutch institutions and elites survived or re-emerged as a result of Napoleonic rule. The years 1799–1814 are marked by a series of regime changes and each of these regimes had their own characters and specific problems. The question of whether Napoleonic rule represented a revived old order or a new regime will be examined for each regime, in turn, but it is not easily answered.

The Regency of State (1801–05): the politics of *fusion*

In 1795 French troops overthrew the old federal Dutch Republic and Orange Stadholderate and engineered the Batavian Revolution. With French support, a coup d'état was staged in 1798 by radical Batavian revolutionaries, resulting in the Constitution of 1798, which turned the Netherlands into a unitary state for the first time. This first Dutch constitution closely resembled its French counterpart of 1795, which ushered in the Directory, although in many respects it also drew on earlier Batavian drafts, as well as the American Constitution.[4] By 1801, however, the French Consulate sought an end to the revolution it had helped to create six years before. The French envoy, Sémonville, and his master Talleyrand, the Foreign Minister, now saw the constitution of 1798 as a disreputable relic of radical republicanism. In accordance with Napoleon's policy of *fusion* within France itself, Sémonville supported the rapprochement between moderate revolutionaries and supporters of the House of Orange, who had been excluded from office after the 1795 Revolution.[5] French calls to reform the Batavian constitution coincided with a general climate of disillusionment with the Revolution in the Netherlands. Eminent revolutionaries were disappointed with the results of the 1798 constitution and felt that reform was needed in order to implement a truly revolutionary programme. According to some radical revolutionaries, the Constitution had been too quick to discard the old provinces, the pillars of the pre-Revolutionary Dutch Republic, while the growing popularity of the ideas of Montesquieu gave the old provinces a renewed role as intermediate bodies that formed barriers against state despotism.[6]

However, the attempts by the Directors in September 1801 to replace the radical constitution with a new one modelled on the Napoleonic constitution of the Year VIII/1799 met with resistance in the representative assembly, which, in turn, provoked a Caesarian solution to the problem of reform. On 18 September, French troops sealed the doors of the legislative assembly and its proceedings were terminated. A new constitution, establishing the *Staatsbewind* (Regency of State) was proclaimed. It was not nearly as groundbreaking as the first Dutch constitution of 1798, but it promised the stable administration that a large part of the population hoped for. The 1801 Constitution was indeed more moderate than its predecessor and aimed at political reconciliation. In this new constitutional order, political participation by large sections of the population diminished, just as in the French Napoleonic constitution of 1799.

The constitution of 1801 also implied a partial return to pre-revolutionary institutions. The pre-revolutionary frontiers of the old provinces were restored and the eight ancien regime provinces, as well as the great cities, received more powers at the expense of the central government. Importantly, instead of concentrating all executive powers in the hands of one figure, as in France, the French and Dutch agreed that the Netherlands needed a collegiate administration. Thus, collegial government, the hallmark of the administration of the old Republic, was restored. In this spirit, the Batavian Republic was renamed the Batavian Commonwealth, to give it a less revolutionary flavour, and the symbolism of the old regime gradually reappeared.

Along with the symbolism and the institutions, the old regime elites also started to re-emerge. Henceforth, the vacancies in the legislative assembly were filled according to provincial quotas just as under the ancien régime. Moderate patriots like the Amsterdam regent, Jan Bicker, were appointed in this way, as well as staunch Orangists, who had been excluded after the Revolution. Thus, old enemies who had fought during the ancien regime, now formed a united front against a new common enemy, radical revolutionary republicanism and, in this way, Napoleonic rule ended centuries-old conflicts within the Dutch elite. The reconciliation of moderate patriots and Orangists was facilitated by the fact that the last Stadholder, William V, had given up his claims to the Netherlands in exchange for a financial indemnity. For his cooperative attitude, Napoleon awarded William's son, the future King William I, the government of Fulda and Corvey, in Germany. Just as in Napoleonic France, the Dutch governing elite was no longer selected for its ideological purity, but according to social standing and wealth.

Despite appearances, the Regency of State was not a real return to the past, but the start of something new. First, it meant another step in the process of Dutch state formation. While the regime was supposed to be less centralist than the previous administrations, in reality the government managed to get a firm grip on local and provincial administration. It initiated important new policies hitherto considered impossible to implement. Above all, provincial finances, primary education and the creation of new cultural institutions could at last be dealt with on a national level. As a result, the bureaucracy in The Hague grew considerably, whereas one would have expected a decreasing civil service in the process of federalization.[7] Second, the Regency of State was the first attempt to find a middle way between the old regime and the revolution. A new policy of national unity was proclaimed from which only radicals of the extreme left and right were excluded. What resulted was the Dutch corollary of the Napoleonic policy of *fusion*, the dominant presence of moderate revolutionaries and Orangists within the new government. Successor regimes continued this striving for national reconciliation and the search for a compromise between the old order and new regime. From 1801 onwards the middle way would form a central theme in Dutch political culture.

Schimmelpenninck (1805–06): a presidential government

The moderate Staatsbewind did not prove the stable ally Napoleon hoped for. Although the need for a national figurehead had been questioned by the Dutch, discussions on the necessity of a stronger executive authority kept resurfacing in the years following 1801. Napoleon criticized this lack of a strong executive authority, and wanted to impose a head of state on the Batavian Republic. Consequently, Talleyrand and Napoleon asked Rutger Jan Schimmelpenninck, the Batavian ambassador in Paris, to draw up a new constitutional framework for the Netherlands. A plebiscite was then staged, and the Staatsbewind was pushed aside. Schimmelpenninck's new constitution restored the unitary state without its radical revolutionary ideology. The new constitution was considerably shorter than its predecessor of 1801, notably curbing the civic and political rights of citizens. Schimmelpenninck became *Raadpensionaris*, Grand Pensionary, of the Batavian Republic, a term that used to designate the highest post within the province of Holland. This archaic title was insisted on by the French, whereas Schimmelpenninck, an admirer of the American model, actually preferred the title President of the Batavian Republic.[8] Most surprisingly, Schimmelpenninck, who in his youth had been an advocate of popular sovereignty, reduced the power of the legislature to a minimum.[9] During his one-year presidency, Schimmelpenninck was reasonably successful. He appointed a number of excellent men who managed to complete the initiatives of the Staatsbewind. In place of provincial excise taxes, the Minister of Finance, Isaac Gogel, introduced a progressive income tax, while Adriaan van den Ende completed the new legislation on primary education, which was far ahead of its time.[10]

However, Napoleon continued to be troubled by the instability of the Batavian regime, which he attributed to its political organization and the weakness of the Grand Pensionary. He felt that only a monarchy could prevent either the country succumbing to British pressure, or the Dutch continuing to long for a return to the old regime.[11] The conversion of the country into a kingdom was unconstitutional and undemocratic, and therefore impossible, according to the well-known jurist Joan Melchior Kemper. He stressed the need to hold a referendum, but at the same time feared the 'apathetic' Dutch would stay at home.[12] When Rutger Jan Schimmelpenninck sent his diplomatic delegation to Paris for talks with Napoleon in spring 1806, he also impressed upon the diplomats that a hereditary head of state was incompatible with the Batavian national character.[13]

The Kingdom of Holland (1806–10): a monarchical experiment

On 5 June 1806 the Batavian Republic and the French Empire signed the Treaty of Paris and Louis Bonaparte was created King of Holland. Napoleon gave his brother an ambiguous job description, which placed Louis in an unfavourable position from the outset; the Emperor had simply placed Louis at the head of the Batavian Republic without working out this dramatic constitutional change in detail. This produced half-hearted results. Seemingly, the Kingdom of Holland was a fait accompli, but the Batavian Republic remained hidden under the surface as its political reality. Unhappy with this situation, Louis began to give real shape to his kingship. He considered constitutional monarchy the form of government best suited to coping with the political difficulties that had plagued the country for decades. Louis's words made reference to the general desire of the Dutch for harmony and unity, a desire of which he could make use. Louis hoped to fuse his personal interests, that is those of the new Dutch monarchy, with the general interests of his subjects. He therefore consistently presented himself as the *Majesté nationale*, a title he regarded as 'the most beautiful and the most appropriate'.[14]

Because the Kingdom of Holland found itself in a constitutional vacuum—the old constitution was not geared to the monarchy and the new constitution was still in the making—royal power knew relatively few bounds. During the rewriting of the constitution, Louis himself took over executive power, in piecemeal fashion.[15] In a short period of time, the Netherlands received a new set of constitutional laws that promised a very authoritarian monarchy. Louis had control over the administration, made the legislature dependent upon him, juggled ministerial positions and created new royal administrative bodies at will.

Among his first acts as King of Holland, Louis opened an inquiry into the codification of Dutch law. He instructed the legal expert, Joannes van der Linden, to formulate a civil code. Van der Linden's approach was original; he was the first to compose a civil code designed explicitly for the new centralized Dutch state, which was also partly based upon customary law. Napoleon intervened, however, for an original Dutch civil code could undermine the allegiance of his brother's people to the French Empire. 'A nation of 1,800,000 souls cannot have a separate legal system', Napoleon claimed.[16] Instead, Louis appointed a commission to arrange a Dutch translation of the Code Napoléon. Rather than just translating the Code Napoléon from French, however, it came up with a number of significant changes. The commission felt that the Code Napoléon did not meet Dutch requirements as it was written in a foreign language, was not grounded in local circumstances and it conflicted with Dutch conventions.[17] The outcome was a civil code that was a fusion of the French and Dutch legislation which repealed all local regulations and customs. It would remain in force until the French Incorporation in 1810. Under Louis, Holland also received an original Dutch penal code, very close to earlier Batavian projects, which came into force early in 1809.[18]

The rewriting of the Code Napoléon is typical of the reign of Louis Bonaparte. He wanted to modernize the Dutch state in a French style, but without neglecting tradition. His administration was modelled on the Napoleonic state, but retained many Dutch features.[19] Similarly, the administrators of the Kingdom of Holland worked on their own versions of the Institute and the Imperial University. Just like the previous regimes, the Kingdom of Holland offered a middle way between new reforms on the model of the Napoleonic Empire and older Dutch traditions.[20]

Incorporation (1810–13): the incomplete police state

Dissatisfied with his brother's obstinate stance against his demands, Napoleon used the British invasion of the southern island of Walcheren in 1809 as a pretext to incorporate the Kingdom of Holland into the Empire in 1810. Napoleon presented the Incorporation as something inevitable; the Netherlands were simply too small to survive in the world of great power politics. The 'adoption', as Napoleon euphemistically called the Incorporation, was essentially a compassionate act in his eyes. There was surprisingly little Dutch resistance to the loss of independence and a large part of the elite supported the Incorporation, or at least thought it inevitable. The diplomat Anton Reinhardt Falck felt an immediate incorporation by France would 'be better for most of the nation than another temporary or intermediary administration'.[21] The Incorporation was seen by Dutch administrators, such as the lawyer Cornelis van Maanen, as a chance finally to establish the uniform legal system he had been striving for since the outbreak of the Batavian Revolution in 1795.

The period of the Incorporation presents a break with the norms of the earlier Napoleonic regimes, all of which sought to find a *juste milieu* (the right balance) between historic tradition and revolutionary reform. In civil administration, the legal system and policing, Napoleonic institutions were ruthlessly introduced. Napoleon ignored suggestions made by the Conseil pour les affaires de Hollande, a committee of thirty Dutch notables that was sent to Paris to facilitate the Incorporation of the Dutch provinces into the Empire.[22] In the organic decree of 18 October 1810, the general contours of administration in the Dutch departments were laid down. At the top stood the Governor-General, who was to be the eyes and the ears of the Emperor in the Netherlands; Charles-François Lebrun, an administrative veteran who had also overseen the incorporation of the Ligurian Republic into the Empire in 1806. Together with six senior civil servants, the Governor-General formed the General Administration which was to function as an intermediary between the Dutch departments and the central government in Paris.

At the departmental and local levels, a system of civil administration was established consisting of prefects, sub-prefects and mayors. A uniform system of administration, controlled by the Parisian Ministry of the Interior and the General Government, was now in place, reaching into the smallest and most peripheral towns of the Dutch departments. Although its implementation was far from perfect, this new administrative hierarchy greatly enlarged the control of the central government over its subjects. The traditional administrative culture of collegial government, which had to a certain extent survived under the previous regimes, was now replaced by the French system of centralized government at every level of the administration.

A wholly new legal system was also installed. On 1 March 1811, the hybrid Wetboek Napoleon was replaced by the Code Napoléon, since Napoleon wanted a uniform legal system throughout the Empire.[23] Following the introduction of the Code Napoléon, the public registration of births, deaths, and marriages was introduced. Its purpose was to facilitate taxation and conscription. In general, all this represented an attempt by the Napoleonic state to increase its control over the subject population. The power of the state was also enlarged by the systematic collection of information and the gathering of statistics on the Dutch population by the imperial administrators.

Importantly, the Incorporation ended the long debate in the Netherlands on the establishment of a uniform organization of legal institutions. Just as with the civil administration, a hierarchical and uniform court system was introduced. At the lowest level, justices of the peace were established in each canton. A law court was established for each arrondissement, the subdivision of the department. At the top of the legal pyramid in the Dutch departments was the Imperial Court in The Hague, chaired by its president, Cornelis Felix van Maanen. The legal officials of the old Dutch republic, such as the aldermen and the sheriffs, were abolished and replaced by new administrators on the Napoleonic model. Judges were usually chosen by Van Maanen from among the old Dutch legal elite. The public prosecutors, however, were selected by a Belgian, Beyts, and were often Belgian or French. The particularistic and multiform legal tradition of the old republic, was now replaced by a uniform system on the imperial model. Legally, the ancien régime had ended.[24]

Another aspect of the new regime of the Incorporation period was the creation of a modern police force, replacing the traditional urban model. The new police organization was also much larger than before. In this way the Ministry of Police in Paris had direct access to every Dutch town, greatly increasing the control of the central government over law and order—something unprecedented in history.[25] Typical ancien régime institutions were replaced by professional gendarmes and *agents de police*. The wholly new figure of the *commissaire* entered Dutch policing. This official was the core of a political police, concerned with political crimes. Besides the ordinary police force, Holland counted 127 Gendarmerie brigades scattered over the country, each consisting of five to ten soldiers. In times of need, the military Gendarmerie was called upon by the authorities, making it a swift, loyal and feared apparatus of repression.[26] One pamphleteer would later describe the general climate of suspicion and fear in the period 1810–13 as follows: 'the sister would denounce her brother, the son his father and friends suspected each other of being a traitor'.[27]

Although the Incorporation presented a radical breach with the age old particularistic republican tradition of administration, the legal system and the police, in many other ways state formation in the period 1810–13 was a failure. To a large extent, the cultural and educational institutions of the old Dutch regime survived under the Incorporation, and even the implementation of the Napoleonic legal and police apparatus was not flawless. Many French institutions that were introduced suffered from a constant lack of resources.[28] A total failure, furthermore, was Napoleon's policy of nation building. Napoleon's attempt to fuse the Dutch with 'the Great Nation', for instance through marriages between French officers and the daughters of the Dutch elite, was not successful. Quite the reverse, for the experience of the Incorporation actually reinforced Dutch national consciousness.[29]

The failure of Napoleon's reforms must to a large extent be explained by the short duration and the timing of incorporation into the Empire. From 1812 the overstretched Empire came under increasing pressure from the armies of the Fourth Coalition. Some Napoleonic officials like Lebrun and the Intendant for the interior, François, Baron d'Alphonse, genuinely tried to establish an enlightened administration in the interests of the local Dutch population, as well as serving their imperial master. Other French officials regarded the Netherlands merely as a conquered country, whose only purpose was to provide as many men and materials for the Grande Armée as could possibly be squeezed out of the impoverished population.

The first and foremost task of the Napoleonic prefect was enforcing conscription. The oppressive character of the regime met with increasing opposition from the Dutch population, which had initially remained quiescent over the loss of independence. The protest started among the lower social strata of the population against the increased taxes, the regulations against smuggling and conscription. When on 1 April 1813, the sons of the Dutch notables were forced to become *gardes des honneurs* in France to guarantee the loyalty of their fathers, the compliant Dutch political elite became increasingly hostile to the Napoleonic regime. As a result of the demands of war and the short period of the Incorporation, the process of creating a new and uniform regime was not completed when imperial rule collapsed in November in 1813. Paradoxically, the Napoleonic project would, in many ways, only be achieved after Napoleon's fall.

Restoration (1813–30): the nationalization of the Napoleonic heritage

Joseph Fouché famously said of the restored French monarch, Louis XVIII, that he slept in the bed of Napoleon, implying that he took over the institutions of the Napoleonic state instead of restoring the ancien régime as the term Restoration might suggest. This is equally true of King William I, the son of the last Stadtholder, who had no intention of going back to the old regime. The powerful instruments of the Napoleonic state were far too useful for him to dismantle. In many ways, the incomplete police state of the Incorporation years was brought to completion during the Restoration. Not only were the institutions of the Napoleonic state retained and further developed by the Restoration, as was most of its personnel.[30]

This does not imply that the regime change of 1813–15 had no effect on the administration. The Council of State, the pinnacle of the Napoleonic administrative system, for instance, diminished in importance under the Restoration. By contrast, the role of the Secretary of State grew enormously after 1813, as it was the ideal, obedient vehicle for the authoritarian objectives of King William. The Napoleonic legacy was nationalized under the Restoration, and the institutions of the newly centralized state were given traditional names suggesting continuity with Dutch tradition. The legislative assembly of the restored monarchy, for instance, was called Estates-General, although this institution had hardly anything in common with its ancien regime namesake. The Council of State, a Napoleonic institutional innovation, was given the historic medieval name of *Raad van State*.

Although William's monarchy was in many respects the heir of the Napoleonic regimes, he far from acknowledged this debt. The recent past was not mentioned by the officials of the Restoration, whether in a negative or a positive sense. Those few reactionaries who demanded retribution for the behaviour of Dutch officials during the Incorporation, were derided as mischief-makers who endangered the stability of the new state.[31] The postrevolutionary centralized state presented a breach with the federalist and particularistic traditions of the old Dutch republic. After 1813, however, it was increasingly viewed as a system of government that was typically Dutch.

Conclusions: a new regime or a revived order?

In *Napoleon's Integration of Europe*, Stuart Woolf describes 'the gradual emergence of a class of civilian professionals, convinced of the potential of modern administration and expert in its application' as the most important legacy of the Napoleonic empire.[32] The Napoleonic era, according to Woolf, marked the beginning of modern administration, while Isser Woloch sees an increased pervasion of the state in many aspects of society. French civic order in the years 1789–1820, according to Woloch, was transformed into a 'new regime' that was radically different from its pre-revolutionary predecessor.[33] However, Michael Rowe, studying the case of the Rhineland, offers a different interpretation. The importance of the Napoleonic age for the Rhineland, according to Rowe, lies not in political modernization and renewal, but in the way the imperial system allowed older political forms to survive and reinforce themselves.[34]

Rowe's thesis is also true for the Dutch Regency of State of 1801–05. Napoleonic rule ended centuries' old conflicts within the Dutch elite. In a classic case of *fusion* or *ralliement*, Napoleon tried to blend moderate revolutionaries and the moderate Orangists who stood aside from the anti-Orangist Batavian Republic. The fusion of elites is a theme in all regimes before the Restoration of 1814. At the level of institutions, the so-called Staatsbewind meant a partial return to the ancien régime, which had been abolished by the founding of the unitary state by radical revolutionaries in 1798. In other ways, however, the process of state building was continued. The regime change of 1805 reinforced the executive power and consolidated the unitary state, although during Schimmelpenninck's rule, classic republican symbolism had a brief revival. Subsequently, Napoleon placed his brother Louis on the Dutch throne. Louis' reign ended more than two hundred years of republican tradition in the Netherlands.

During the Incorporation, after 1810, Napoleon imposed his centralized model of administration on the Dutch provinces without much ado, establishing an authoritarian police state. The administrative innovations were facilitated by the collaboration of many Dutch administrators at all levels of the imperial administration, who regarded the incorporation as a unique chance to implement institutional reform and break the resilience of the old institutions. The Napoleonic period, however, was too short and the Empire was already under too much stress, to complete all these reforms. In many ways, the Napoleonic project was fulfilled after his fall. The restored Prince of Orange, the new King William I, retained most elements of the centralized state and many Napoleonic administrators. The Napoleonic origins of the new state were, however, officially forgotten. In short, the new Dutch state resembled a modern new regime, along the lines outlined by Woolf and Woloch but, just as in the Rhineland, the Napoleonic era also consolidated and revitalized many political and social structures of the old regime. Therefore, we can conclude that the Napoleonic legacy in the Netherlands, was in fact a new regime disguised as a revived order.

Notes

1. N. C. F. van Sas, *De metamorfose van Nederland. Van oude orde naar moderniteit, 1750–1900* (Amsterdam, 2004), 345.
2. Simon Schama, *Patriots and Liberators. Revolution in the Netherlands 1780–1813* (London, 1977).
3. E.g. Michael Broers, *Europe Under Napoleon, 1799–1815* (London, 1996). Michael Rowe, *From Reich to State. The Rhineland in the Revolutionary Age, 1780–1830* (Cambridge, 2003). Stuart Woolf, *Napoleon's integration of Europe* (London, 1991).
4. Annie Jourdan, 'Le rôle des agents français dans la constitution batave de 1798', *Annales historiques de la Révolution française* 351 (2008), 99–119.
5. See for literature on the Regency of State in English: Schama, *Patriots and Liberators*, 410–465.
6. W. R. E. Velema, 'Revolutie, republiek en revolutie. De ideologische context van de eerste Nederlandse grondwet', in *De eeuw van de grondwet. Grondwet en politiek in Nederland, 1798–1917*, ed. N.C.F. van Sas and H. te Velde (Deventer 1998), 20–44.
7. Hendrik Boels, *Binnenlandse Zaken. Ontstaan en ontwikkeling van een département in de Bataafse tijd, 1795–1806: een reconstructie* (Den Haag, 1993), 349.
8. L. de Gou, *De Staatsregeling van 1805 en de Constitutie van 1806* (Den Haag, 1997), XIX.
9. Renger de Bruin, 'De opbouw van een nieuwe staat. Bestuurlijk-politieke veranderingen tussen 1780 en 1815', in *Het ontstaan van het moderne Nederland: staats- en natievorming tussen 1780 en 1830*, ed. Wantje Fritschy and Joop Toebes (Nijmegen, 1996), 123–156, 149. H.T. Colenbrander, *Schimmelpenninck en Koning Lodewijk* (Amsterdam, 1911), 30–37.
10. Martijn van der Burg, 'L'école primaire dans le royaume de Hollande et durant l'annexion à la France', in *Louis Bonaparte, roi de Hollande*, ed. Annie Jourdan (Paris, 2010), 185–197.
11. Archives nationales Paris, AFIV 1820, 5. Louis Bonaparte, *Documents historiques et réflexions sur le gouvernement de la Hollande*, vol. I (Bruxelles, 1820), 68–69.
12. J. M. Kemper, *Brieven over de tegenwoordig in omloop zijnde geruchten* (Amsterdam 1806), 13.
13. Martijn van der Burg, 'Transforming the Dutch Republic into the Kingdom of Holland', *European Review of History* (2010) forthcoming.
14. Louis Bonaparte, *Documents historiques*, vol. I, 141–142.
15. De Gou, *De Staatsregeling*, 309.
16. Schama, *Patriots and Liberators*, 700.
17. A.H. Huussen, *Huwelijks- en huwelijksgoederenrecht tot 1820* (Bussum, 1975), 313–314.
18. Schama, *Patriots and Liberators*, 543.
19. J. Roelevink, 'Cette grande inertie qu'on rencontre sans cesse dans la marche des affaires. Lodewijk als wetgever en uitvoerder', *De Negentiende eeuw*, 30 (2006), 177–191.
20. Martijn van der Burg, *Nederland onder Franse invloed. Culturele overdracht en staatsvorming in de napoleontische tijd, 1799–1813* (Amsterdam, 2009). See also: Martijn van der Burg, 'Transferts culturels franco-bataves à l'époque napoléonienne', http://geschichte-transnational.clio-online.net/forum/id=1009&type=artikel.
21. J. Naber, *Overheersing en vrijwording. Geschiedenis van Nederland tijdens de Inlijving bij Frankrijk* (Haarlem, 1913), 23–24.

22. Marie Elisabeth Kluit, *Cornelis Felix van Maanen. Tot het herstel der onafhankelijkheid* (Groningen, 1953), chapter 7.
23. Van der Burg, *Nederland onder Franse invloed*, 94.
24. Johan Joor, *De Adelaar en het Lam. Onrust, opruiing en onwilligheid in Nederland ten tijde van het Koninkrijk Holland en de Inlijving bij het Franse Keizerrijk (1806–1813)*, (Amsterdam, 2000), 582–586.
25. Martijn van der Burg, 'Law Enforcement in Amsterdam: between Tradition and Modernization', in *Serving the Urban Community. The Rise of Public Facilities in the Low Countries*, ed. Manon van der Heijden et al. (Amsterdam, 2009), 217–241, 235.
26. Joor, *De Adelaar en het Lam*, 639–641.
27. *Schets der gevolgen van den invloed der Franschen op Nederland sedert het jaar 1795* (Amsterdam, 1814), 18.
28. This goes especially for the French *Université impériale*. See Van der Burg, *Nederland onder Franse invloed*, chapter 6 and 'Transferts culturels franco-bataves'. See also Chapter 8 in this volume Johan Joor, 'Resistance against Napoleon in the kingdom of Holland'.
29. Van Sas, *Metamorfose*, 87–89.
30. Matthijs Lok, *Windvanen. Napoleontische bestuurders in de Nederlandse en Franse Restauratie, 1813–1820* (Amsterdam, 2009). Idem, 'L'extrême centre est-il exportable? Une comparaison entre la France et les Pays-Bas, 1814–1820', *Annales historiques de la Révolution française* 3 (2009): 147–163.
31. Jeroen van Zanten, *Schielijk, Winzucht, Zwaarhoofd en Bedaard. politieke discussie en oppositievorming 1813–1840* (Amsterdam, 2004).
32. Woolf, *Napoleon's integration of Europe*, 69.
33. Isser Woloch, *The New Regime. Transformations of the French Civic Order, 1789–1820s* (New York, 1994), 429.
34. Rowe, *From Reich to State*, 8.

8
Resistance against Napoleon in the Kingdom of Holland

Johan Joor

The police apparatus in Louis' Kingdom

The Napoleonic period, as the years of the Kingdom of Holland (1806–10) and the French Occupation (1810–13) were known, was of fundamental importance for the police in Holland. Before 1806 no separate police corps existed and the word police was commonly used in the traditional meaning of policy and regulation and not associated with police work, as we know it today.

The term police was certainly used by Louis in a modern sense when, soon after he was proclaimed king, he founded a Ministry of Justice and Police in July 1806. Louis was reluctant to create a separate Minister of Police on the French model, as the Dutch would find it controversial.[1] The main duties of the new Minister of Justice and Police were vigilance over state security, maintaining public order, observation of foreign nationals, press control and suppression of contraband and other illegal international trafficking, especially regarding navigation of waterways.[2] The Minister was largely dependent on the existing local administrative and judicial authorities such as the officers of justice in the towns (*hoofdofficier*) and the public prosecutors in the departments (*procureurs*). The King created new police officials only for the specific control of navigation.

The first true police force was set up in Holland by autumn 1806 under these terms. The Dutch coast was divided into three districts, with Amsterdam, Rotterdam and Harlingen as their centres. In each of these places a chief police commissioner was appointed. The joint police commissioners supervised a total of six police officers, who were assigned to control coastal navigation from six small harbours and seaside villages scattered along the coast.[3] Thus, the first Dutch police force was small in number and limited in its competence to the control of navigation. Although the instruction for police offiers issued in November 1806 ordered them to inform the Minister of Justice and Police about public opinion in their areas, this was only added because of the war.[4]

Louis' police and the continental blockade

After the proclamation of the Berlin Decrees of November 1806, Louis' police force became deeply entangled with the enforcement of the Continental Blockade. From the outset, a new and strict division was made between the police officials and the employees of the Ministry of Finance. Henceforth, the former were restricted to controlling illegal correspondence and passengers. The latter became exclusively responsible for the ships' cargoes. Louis' decree of February 1808, which closed all Dutch ports with immediate effect, led to a further reorganization of the police. The office of chief commissioner disappeared and his subordinates were renamed inspectors. Their number was increased to fourteen, but as the legal shipping trade was almost completely non-existent, their role henceforth appeared to be confined to the inspection of fishing boats for the presence of illegal passengers.[5]

Contrary to the common historiographical image, Louis seriously tried to enforce the Continental System. A series of decrees and regulations were issued, whose enforcement fell to a wide range of military and civilian authorities. His efforts notwithstanding, Louis failed. The Dutch estuaries in the southwest and the north made a total closure of coast and harbours practically impossible and Louis tried desperately to convince his brother that maintaining a blockade in Holland was like 'trying to stop skin sweating'.[6]

Moreover, an effective enforcement of the blockade was seriously hindered by the overlapping competences among the different departments and offices charged with the control of navigation. A clear-cut division between the control of illegal passengers and mail on coasts, ships and fishing boats on the one hand and commodities on the other, soon appeared very difficult, if not virtually impossible, to achieve. This operational overlap resulted in many disputes between police officials and employees of the Ministry of Finance, both when they were on missions or simply doing their daily, routine work.[7]

The reorganization of the police in February 1808 and the realization of Louis' long cherished wish to make Amsterdam his capital, prompted him to create a new branch of the police for his kingdom in April 1808. Louis was very suspicious of both British and French secret agents and therefore he created one police inspector and three assistant police inspectors for specific service in the capital, charged with high security surveillance. In Louis' initial plans the police officials of Amsterdam were also intended to deal with the public order. However, in the final instruction of July 1808, issued by the Minister of Justice and Police, the majority of the articles concerned the surveillance of foreigners; a separate additional instruction was drawn up to cover this aspect of the police.[8]

Louis was constantly overpowered in his attempts to enforce the blockade by his brother Napoleon, who operated according his own hidden agenda. From the end of 1808 tension mounted between them over the enforcement of the Continental System. To reconcile Dutch interests and the Emperor's demands more satisfactorily Louis changed his policy and on 31 March 1809 he proclaimed a double decree in which the harbours were partly reopened and a customs system was announced on the French model. Paradoxically, Louis' final measures regarding the enforcement of the blockade effectively completed his reform of the Dutch police. The King explicitly stated that the Minister of Justice and Police was no longer authorized to interfere in affairs dealing with the Continental System and consequently he had to abolish his inspection officers as a service. As custom officials of the Ministry of Finance, they were now transferred to the new Directory of Customs, which was under the direct supervision of the King. This reorganization was seen by Cornelis Felix van Maanen, Louis' Minister of Justice and Police at the time, as an attack on his personal authority and as a result, he resigned.[9]

The police force during the Occupation

During the Occupation important changes were made to the police in Holland. As early as October 1810 a Director-General of Police, Paul-Etienne Devilliers Duterrage, was appointed to the General Government, the central French administration in the new Dutch Departments. In practice, nothing changed until the beginning of 1811 when, in the wake of the administrative reforms, the French police system was introduced at local level. The French police system originated under the Revolution but was only completed during the Consulate with the law of 17 February 1800. In October 1795 a police commissioner was established for every town with a population over 5,000. The new legislation confirmed this but now an extra commissioner had to be appointed for each additional 10,000 inhabitants. Moreover, in very large towns a General Commissioner of Police could be installed as head of the police. Unlike the ordinary commissioner, who got his orders mainly from the mayor and prefect, this General Commissioner was in direct contact with the officials of the *Ministère de la Police-Général*.[10]

In March 1811 special measures were taken in Holland to organize the police in Amsterdam. The city was divided into twelve police districts under their own police commissioners, each with his own inspector, two sergeants and four police agents. The appointment of the commissioners of police in Amsterdam had just begun when, on the 25 March 1811, an imperial decree issued a new *Réglement général à l'organisation de la police de l'Empire*. Four classes of police official were distinguished within an hierarchical framework: Directors-General, an office introduced in 1808; general commissioners; special commissioners, charged exclusively with the enforcement of the Continental System; and the ordinary commissioners of police in the towns. The appointments of all the police officers had to be made by the central government and, ultimately, by the Emperor. However, the towns in which the officer served were obliged to pay their salaries, or at least a substantial part of them.[11]

With the exception of the special commissioners, these offices were already established, as were the police duties attached to them. However, under the new regulations, the local police commissioners were now thoroughly integrated into the central police machinery. Henceforth, the state had eyes and ears everywhere.

The first police commissioners appointed were the twelve commissioners of Amsterdam in March 1811. Almost all the other police commissioners in Holland were appointed in two successive waves of April and June 1811.

Regarding the appointment of the higher police officers in Holland, it is striking that only French officials were eligible, another clear instance of how important police organization was to the key interests of the central government. Devilliers was a protégé of the head of the first police district, Pierre-François Réal. Before his appointment in Holland he had served as general commissioner of Boulogne-sur-Mer. Little is known about the personal history of De Marivault who was appointed as general commissioner of Rotterdam in January 1811. However, he was certainly an experienced French police officer as were the special commissioners: Malleval (Island of Texel), Babut (Den Helder), Pondeville (Petten), Eymard (The Hague) and Mariandier (Island of Goeree). They had worked at the office of the general police commissioners of Livorno, Bordeaux, Marseille, Boulogne-sur-Mer and Genoa respectively before coming to Holland. The other four special commissioners had all been members of the State Council before they started their police work.[12]

Unlike the higher police officers, the ordinary commissioners of police were almost all Dutch, although some strategic exceptions were made, again for the most populated cities: Amsterdam, Rotterdam, Utrecht and The Hague.[13]

The role and impact of the police during the Occupation

As a result of the appointment of commissioners of police in the towns, the police force during the Occupation was greater than under Louis. There was also a significant change in its range of duties.

A police instruction drawn up by Devilliers in July 1811 probably best represents what the police was meant to do under the Occupation. In fact Devilliers captures in a nutshell the development of the police in the last two decades in France. In this circular the Director-General distinguishes three main fields of police activity: the supreme police, the municipal police and the judicial police. The first field covers everything involving state security, the regime and society in general. Devilliers typifies the task of the supreme police as the control of public opinion, the surveillance of religious and political gatherings, the control of internal order and the enforcement of the Continental System. Second, as a municipal police officer, the commissioner of police was especially responsible for maintaining public order in his town. More specifically, he was to keep an eye on church services, markets and road safety, as well as on beggars, quack doctors and prostitutes. Third, the judicial police was concerned with guaranteeing the administration of justice, through arresting criminals and gathering evidence.[14]

Devilliers' instruction clearly demonstrates the difference between the police force under the Occupation and that of the Kingdom of Holland. While Louis' police force was mainly concerned with controlling suspicious foreigners, the force during the Occupation was basically designed to control the nation itself.

The permanent control of society was put into practice through strict press control, day and night street patrols, and the secret observation of public and private places such as societies, shops, inns and churches. Large sums were set aside for this kind of police work. In Devilliers' budget for 1811 this sum was already 10,000 francs, one fifth of the total amount his service was officially allowed to spend. In 1812 Devilliers' total budget was raised by an annual income of 20,000 francs, including a proportional raise for secret police work.[15] At police headquarters in Amsterdam a special *Bureau de la Police Secrète* was also set up. According to a list, which is kept in the Archives Nationales in Paris, it employed at least 35 secret agents in 1812.[16]

This secret police work made a great impact on the daily lives of ordinary people. Fear of secret police activity coloured private life; as memoirs show, people often went on reading illegal anti-Napoleonic writings among family and friends in their private homes, but only after taking intensive precautions.[17] Jokes about the Emperor, which were made in tow barges, shops or just on the street could get someone into very serious trouble. In June 1811 a man in Amsterdam was even sentenced to death by a Military Commission, which accused him of taking part in an uprising in the city in April 1811. He had not been on the scene but was nevertheless arrested that day because he had insulted Napoleon in a private conversation on his doorstep, which unfortunately was overheard by a police spy.[18] In this respect, it is significant that the police could arrest citizens considered to be suspect, without the knowledge of the judiciary. These suspects could be held for unlimited periods in special police prisons, the *prisons d'Etat* in Amsterdam, Rotterdam and Groningen, which were established under the decree of 3 March 1810.[19]

The significance of the police in Holland and Dutch protest during the Napoleonic period

It is important to remember that the police were not the only repressive force at the disposal of the Napoleonic regime in Holland.[20] In brief, two major observations about Napoleonic repression in Holland can be made.

Firstly, there were general and special forces of control. The general forces included the regular administrative and judicial institutions and, after 1806, the new police authorities. Under Louis, the local administrative authorities, especially the burgomasters of the big cities, were primarily responsible for maintaining public order in the towns, although in case of riots there was often a conflict over competence with the judicial authorities, especially with the *hoofdofficier*. During the Occupation the number of special corps increased rapidly. Besides *gardes champêtres* and the different corps of customs officials, who could also act as a fierce instrument of repression, were paramilitary units like the National Guard, or truly military forces, such as the Departmental Guards and, of course, the Gendarmerie. Under both the Kingdom of Holland and the Occupation military forces were used regularly in times of trouble to restore civil order.[21]

Secondly, repression under Louis differed significantly from that under the Occupation. Louis was reluctant to use violence and preferred a policy of civil reconciliation, whereas, from the outset of the annexation Napoleon initiated a policy of harsh military repression and coercion, including the use of arbitrary Military Commissions.[22]

In contrast to the long-standing image of peace and passivity presented by Dutch historiography, the Napoleonic period should really be considered as a time of turmoil rather than one of peace. Literally hundreds of protests are recorded for the Napoleonic years, when a wide variety of acts of unrest, incitement and protest are taken into consideration. These actions included more than eighty revolts, which we can define under the terms of the *Code Pénal* as breaches of the peace in which twenty or more people, collectively and violently, challenged the authorities in public. Even though Louis' government had already had to deal with considerable unrest, protests intensified enormously after June 1810. Fifty-nine revolts, or 67 per cent of the total revolts in the Napoleonic years, took place under the Occupation.[23]

The difference between the police in the two periods of the Kingdom and the Occupation is reflected in the way people protested. During the Kingdom of Holland, opposition to police officials was minimal; occasionally a skirmish occurred between the locals and a police officer in the coastal villages, as in April 1808 in Egmond on Sea, where a police inspector was attacked with stones and his daughter threatened by local seamen with a vicious dog, but the connection between the police and the state was never made.[24]

However, during the Occupation such a connection was certainly present, and various major conflicts between the people and police did occur. The riots in Arnhem, Rotterdam, Scheveningen and The Hague in 1812 and the great Amsterdam conscription revolt in April 1811 are all examples of this.[25]

Yet the most violent protest against the police was the November rising in 1813 in Amsterdam. This revolt started on the evening of 15 November 1813 with a march on the town centre by some women, agitated by anti-French and pro-Orangist rumours. Soon they were joined by a wide cross-section of the working classes, and within an hour the city was in total revolt. Terrified by the angry masses, Lebrun, the French Governor-General, fled to Utrecht in the early morning of 16 November and went on almost immediately thereafter to France. In his wake, all the French high officials fled Amsterdam, including Devilliers. On the second day of the uprising, the masses surrounded the police prison in the town and liberated between 130 and 180 prisoners.[26] After freeing political prisoners in other jails, the crowd marched from one police post to the next and assaulted the police headquarters, which was thoroughly ransacked and finally set alight. By then, Devilliers' flight was already known, so it seems this collective action was less of a practical and more of a symbolic significance. By attacking the police, the crowd was attacking the regime itself!

After the proclamation of a provisional administration at the city hall, the riots were all but over by the night of 16–17 November 1813. Nevertheless, the impact of the revolt was enormous, the instantaneous flight of Lebrun virtually terminated French rule in Holland.

State Police and Police State and the limits of Napoleonic repressive police power

By concentrating our attention on the relationship between the origins of the police and the development of the modern state, it is clear that the police in Napoleonic Holland was certainly an instrument of the state. It was the central government which took the initiative of setting up a police force and later it was that same government which exercised control over it. However, again it is essential to stress the great differences between the organization of the police force during the Kingdom of Holland and under the Occupation. In the first period, the police was literally a marginal phenomenon. The true police force was very small and competent only in the specific field of navigation. At most, one can speak of only a State Police at this time.

In the latter period, however, the police was a multi-faceted organization, which was thoroughly integrated into public and private life. Notwithstanding the validity of the debate on the use of alternative terms, the extensiveness and intensity of the impact of the new police, as expressed in its hierarchy, the wide variety of public and secret activities it undertook, and its broad powers in the field of the supreme police, justify calling the Occupation a Police State.[27]

Moreover, the rebellion of 15 and 16 November 1813 in Amsterdam underlines an intensive use of police prisons, typical of a police state. As we have seen, at least 130 political prisoners were liberated. In this respect, it is important to observe that the masses were acting very purposefully and that they deliberately did not intend to free common criminals. The large number of police prisoners in Amsterdam is surprising and seems to show us that, if studied at a local level, the view of the Napoleonic police as relatively less repressive needs some modification, at least towards the end of Napoleon's reign.[28]

Nevertheless, a reservation must be made regarding the significance of the police force, even during the time of the Occupation. The police certainly operated as a fearsome instrument of state in the Dutch departments of the Empire in the years 1810–13, but the practical constraints it faced meant that its repressive power should not be exaggerated. In the first place, there were few cities with a population of 5,000 in the north and east of the Netherlands and so there were fewer police officials in those parts of the country than in the west.

Also, police finances were often strained. Besides budgetary miscalculations, which were widespread, purposefully or not, police officials were underpaid. Their salaries were related to French prices, which were significantly below those in the Dutch departments. Many policemen were paid irregularly and, even if regularly, they were still confronted with a salary that was barely a subsistence wage.[29] This caused amusing as well as harrowing scenes. One such example is the case of the special commissioner of Hellevoetsluis, who had to run an office in a pub for a long while, because the local administration of his jurisdiction could not pay the rent for a more appropriate location.

By contrast, a harrowing example is the situation of the commissioner of police of Veendam, who, because he was constantly forgotten in the budget, fell into such terrible poverty that his wife died from hardship in the spring of 1812.[30]

Predictably, these financial troubles had their implications for police work. Certain duties could not be carried out properly, partly because no money was available and partly because the underpaid policemen were not really committed to their jobs.

A final, telling, example of the distressed state of police officials in Dutch departments can be found in Lebrun's letter to the Minister of General Police, Savary, of 22 January 1813, in which the Governor-General recommends a special commissioner, Eymard, for a vacancy in France, because the general lot of a police officer in Holland was devoid of prospects and *bien misérable*.[31]

Epilogue

The police force was introduced into the Netherlands for the first time in the Napoleonic period. In both sub-periods, the Kingdom of Holland (1806–10) and the Occupation (1810–13), the police operated as an instrument of state. However there were fundamental differences between the two regimes. During the Kingdom of Holland, the police remit of the Minister of Justice and Police was, indeed, extensive but the true police force was very small and competent only in the specific field of navigation. Because of their organization and operational capabilities, most certainly one can speak of a State Police during this time.

During the Occupation, however, the police force was much larger than during the Kingdom of Holland and the intensity and impact of its actions also changed substantially. The local police commissioners were thoroughly integrated in the central police machinery and the police officials were now competent in a broad field of activities, above all overseeing public safety and public order. The permanent control of society, the spying of secret agents and the broad powers in the field of the supreme police justify the conclusion that there was a Police State in the last phase of the Napoleonic period in Holland.

After the Napoleonic period the police remained one of the instruments of the further evolution of the modern nation state. Nevertheless, the fearsome deployment of the police during the Occupation was not completely erased from the Dutch collective consciousness. The police became the subject of complex and intense political discussion during the decades after 1813, until the municipal police and the central police, both branches of the former Napoleonic police system, were moulded as separate police organs in 1851, in the wake of important legal and administrative reforms.[32]

Notes

1. Louis Bonaparte, *Documents historiques et réflexions sur le gouvernement de la Hollande*, vol 3 (Amsterdam, 1820), 80.
2. Stadsarchief, Amsterdam (SAA) 5053, Nieuw Stedelijk Bestuur (NstB) 231, Wethouders, Bijlagen Notulen, 5 August 1806 (instruction).
3. For more detail see Johan Joor, *De Adelaar en het Lam. Onrust, opruiing en onwilligheid in Nederland ten tijde van het Konininkrijk Holland en de Inlijving bij het Franse Keizerrijk (1806–1813)* (Amsterdam, 2000), 418–20.
4. Ibid. and Nationaal Archief, Den Haag (NADH), Rijksarchief Zuid-Holland (RAZH), Hof van Justitie, 5636, Criminele Zaken, 1 (Van der Hoven) ([concept] instruction).
5. On the Continental System, see Joor, *De Adelaar en het Lam*, 413–444 and Simon Schama, *Patriots and Liberators. Revolution in the Netherlands 1780–1813* (New York, 1977), 561–577.
6. 'Empêchez donc le peau de transpirer!', Bonaparte, *Documents historiques*, vol. 1, 273.
7. See NADH, 2.01.10.04, Ministerie van Justitie en Politie (MvJP), 353, Index Verbaal, 'Commisen van Toezigt', 14 January 1809.
8. NADH, MvJP, 353, 'Maatregelen tot Zekerheid des Rijks', 6 June and 20 July 1808, and SAA, 5053, Burgemeester, 247, Bijlagen Verbaal, 23 July 1808.
9. M. Elisabeth Kluit, *Cornelis Felix van Maanen. Tot het herstel der onafhankelijkheid* (Groningen, 1954), 264–267. See also Matthijs Lok, *Windvanen. Napoleontische bestuurders in de Nederlandse en Franse Restauratie (1813–1820)* (Amsterdam, 2009), 247–292 and references to Van Maanen's vital role during early Dutch Restoration, 1813–1820.
10. Cyrille Fijnaut, *Opdat de macht een toevlucht zij? Een historische studie van het politieapparaat als een politieke instelling* (Antwerpen, 1979), 757–758.
11. *Règlement général à l'organisation de la police de L'Empire... 25 Mars 1811*, in NADH, 2.01.12, Binnenlandse Zaken (BiZa), Intendance van Binnenlandse Zaken

(IvBiZa), 1811–1813, Ingekomen Stukken, 986, Politie. See also Fijnaut, *Opdat de macht een toevlucht zij?*, 758 and 784–786. For more on police salaries, expenses etc. in Holland, see Archives Nationales, Paris (AN), F7, Police générale, 3224, 3225, comptabilité des commissaires généraux de police, An XII-1814, d'Amsterdam, 1811–1812; 1813. Idem, 3228, idem, ... 1813, Rotterdam and idem, 3232, idem, 1808–1814, Hardenberg, (le) Helder, Hellevoetsluis. In October 1811 a new regulation regarding the special commissioners in Holland was issued. Their salaries had to be financed out of the so-called '20ᵉ du revenue des communes' which until then were used to finance the 'compagnie de réserve', see NADH, BiZa, IvBiZa, 986, *Décret Impérial*, 23 October 1811.

12. *Réglement général*, 25 March 1811, art. 3 (selection higher police officials). Johanna W.A. Naber, *Overheersching en Vrijwording. Geschiedenis van Nederland tijdens de Inlijving bij Frankrijk, juli 1810—november 1813* (Haarlem, 1913), 36 (Devilliers). BiZa, IvBiZa, 986, Decree of 23 January 1812 (personal information special commissioners). The other four special commissioners were stationed at Jever, Delfzijl, Dokkum and Hellevoetsluis.
13. NADH, BiZa, IvBiZa, 986, *Etat Général des Commissaires de Police dans les Départements de la Hollande ...*, 16 July 1812.
14. AN, F7, 4217, [miscellaneous], *Instructiën voor den Dienst der Commissarissen van Policie*, 11 July 1811.
15. AN, F7, 3224, *rapport Martignet à l'Empereur*, 1811 and idem, *Compte d'emploi des fonds mis à la disposition du Directeur General de la police en hollande*, 1er–4me trimestre, *fonds à la charge du Trésor Public* and *fonds à la charge de la ville d'Amsterdam*, 1811–1812.
16. Idem, *Etat des agents secrets employés par le Directeur Général de la police en hollande pendant le courant de l'année 1812.*
17. NADH, Collectie 077, Jorissen, 1777–1884, 89, Van der Chijs, *Mijne herinneringen uit de jaren 1810–1813.*
18. Johan Joor, '"A very Rebellious Disposition": Dutch Experience and Popular Protest under the Napoleonic Regime (1806–1813)' in *Soldiers, Citizens and Civilians: Experiences and Perceptions of the Revolutionary and Napoleonic Wars 1790–1820*, ed. Alan Forrest, Karen Hagemann and Jane Rendall (Basingstoke, New York, 2009), 190. Spies in tow barges: Stads Archief Dordrecht, Dordrecht (SAD), Stadsarchieven, 1795–1813, Secretarie, II, Raad, Politie, 199c, Registers en dagrapporten, II, brieven commissaris van politie, (1811–1813), 23 April 1812.
19. NADH, BiZa, IvBiZa, 986, *Arrêté SAS* [=Lebrun], 14 January 1811 (Amsterdam and Rotterdam). See also: AN, F7, 3308, [miscellaneous], [Zuiderzee], *Etat des individus de l'un et de l'autre sexe détenus par mesure de police administrative ou de sûreté dans les sept départements de la ci-devant hollande*, 15 March 1813.) (Amsterdam, Rotterdam, Groningen and Emden, then part of the Dutch Departments).
20. Joor, *De Adelaar en het Lam*, 571–674. See also Martijn van der Burg, 'Law Enforcement in Amsterdam: between Tradition and Modernization', in Manon van der Heijden et al., *Serving the Urban Community. The Rise of Public Services in the Low Countries* (Amsterdam, 2009), 217–241, www.lowcountries.nl/papers2009/papers2009_vanderburg.pdf ,(June 2009).
21. Joor, *De Adelaar en het Lam*, 641–649.
22. Joor, 'A very Rebellious Disposition', 187, 189–190.
23. Joor, *De Adelaar en het Lam*, 620–622.
24. NADH, 2.01.14.02, Ministerie van Oorlog (MvO), 1042, Verbaal, 23 August 1808 and idem, 1048, Relatieven Verbaal, 23 August 1808 and NADH, MvJP, 353, Index Verbaal, 160, 20 August 1808, 149.

25. Joor, *De Adelaar en het Lam*, 620–621. Idem, 'A very Rebellious Disposition', 189–90.
26. H. T. Colenbrander (ed.) 'Inlijving en Opstand', 1810–1813, in *Gedenkstukken der Algemeene Geschiedenis van Nederland van 1795 tot 1840* ('s-Gravenhage, 1912), vol. VI, 1851, Letter from Provo Kluit to Van Maanen, 17 November 1813, 1,704–5. See for the November 1813 Revolt of Amsterdam also Joor, *De Adelaar en het Lam*, 211–212, 522–525.
27. Howard G. Brown, *Ending the French Revolution. Violence, Justice and Repression from the Terror to Napoleon* (Charlottesville and London, 2006), 343 ('Security State') and Michael Sibalis, 'The Napoleonic State', in *Napoleon and Europe*, ed. Philip G. Dwyer (Harlow, 2001), 79–80 ('Police State'). See also Jacques Godechot, *Les institutions de la France sous la Révolution et l'Empire* (Paris, 1985, 3rd edn), 624 and Thierry Lentz, 'La France et l'Europe de Napoléon 1804–1814', in idem, *Nouvelle histoire du Premier Empire* (Fayard, 2007), 313–31.
28. Michael Sibalis, 'Political Prisoners and State Prisons in Napoleonic France', in *Napoleon and His Empire. Europe 1804–1814*, ed. Philip G. Dwyer and Alan Forrest (Basingstoke, New York, 2007), 96–113 and idem, 'The Napoleonic State', 93–94. Fijnaut gives a figure of 2,400 prisoners in all state prisons in France in 1814 in Fijnaut, *Opdat de macht een toevlucht zij?*, 788.
29. NADH, BiZa, IvBiZa, 986, *Copie d'une lettre écrite par le Ministre de l'intèrieur à Mr. le Duc de Rovigo, Ministre de la police Générale*, Paris, 2 September 1813, attached to a note of Devilliers addressed to Lebrun, 14 September 1813 and idem, *Etat Général des Commissaires de Police dans les Departemens de la Hollande...*, 16 July 1812. Some examples of 'miscalculations' in the budget: idem, 6 July 1811 (Den Helder), 18 December 1811 (Monden van de Maas, Special Commissioner), 22 February 1812 (Amsterdam), 27 February 1812 (general note of Devilliers: the situation is alarming in many towns), 8 April 1812 (Hoorn).
30. NADH, BiZa, IvBiZa, 986, 8 April 1812 (Hellevoetsluis) and 31 March 1812 (Veendam).
31. AN, F7, 4291, Correspondance des ministres et des grand dignitaires, 1810–1814, Letter from Lebrun to Savary, Minister of General Police, 22 January 1813.
32. Cyrille Fijnaut, *De Geschiedenis van de Nederlandse Politie. Een staatsinstelling in de maalstroom van de geschiedenis* (Amsterdam, 2007), 55.

9

A Tale of Two Cities: Aachen and Cologne in Napoleonic Europe

Michael Rowe

Memories of the Napoleonic episode—the ceaseless wars in particular—helped shape identities in the nineteenth century. National historiographies naturally identified moments like Trafalgar, the Dos de Mayo, 1812 and Leipzig as key in the evolution respectively of the British, Spanish, Russian and German nations. Historians today have moved on from acting as drum beaters of nationalism, but nonetheless remain interested in whether or not Napoleonic hegemony was accepted by those on whom it was imposed. The terms of the debate have shifted, though; the focus is now less on national factors or differences—race, language, the writings of prominent politicians and philosophers—and more on phenomena that belong to geography and sociology—terrain, population density, the degree of urbanization, the relationship between town and country, between different social strata and so forth. These lines of enquiry have been fruitful in creating new maps of Napoleonic Europe.[1] However, determination to distance ourselves from a skewed national reading of the past runs the risk of underestimating the importance of politics in shaping responses to Napoleonic rule. Politics in this period means, of course, primarily local politics—politics that took place on a level too small to illustrate neatly on a map of Europe. This chapter is in large part concerned with local politics, including both the structures within which it was practised and the individuals who practised it. The aim is to show how, even within a relatively small region, experiences of Napoleonic rule could vary significantly.

* * *

This chapter examines Aachen and Cologne. They lie within approximately 65 kilometres of each other in the region of the Lower Rhine. Today, this is part of Germany, but in the centuries before the Napoleonic period it was part of the Holy Roman Empire. By most measures, Aachen and Cologne were relatively well integrated into Napoleon's empire; they paid their taxes and supplied their conscripts without the need for much coercion.[2] Both cities fought hard after Napoleon's defeat in 1815 to see important aspects of his legacy preserved. So, in some respects, this was a positive example of empire building and an example of Napoleonic rule founded on a degree of public consent. However this is not the whole story, though in order to see why it is necessary to extend our gaze back to before French rule. Aachen and Cologne were a type of polity that Napoleon was to drive close to extinction, the independent city state. Aachen and Cologne were *Reichsunmittelbar*, which meant they owed allegiance to no one but the Holy Roman Emperor. The Emperor enjoyed certain rights, and his Aulic Council (*Reichshofrat*) in Vienna acted as a kind of supreme constitutional court for the cities.[3] However, in every other sense they were self-governing, a fact of which they were immensely proud. All this looks remarkably out of date in the Europe of 1789. The imperial cities were a throwback to a time when the Empire had universalistic pretensions that were taken seriously, but this era had been superseded in most of Europe by the rise of the large territorial state. Yet, in a strip of territory stretching from the North Sea to Northern Italy alternative forms proved remarkably resilient; not only city states, but also church states, independent lordships and sovereign abbeys. Historiography has been unkind to these alternatives. This observation applies especially to the imperial cities and home towns, entities that had, according to most scholarly accounts, rotted into decay by the eighteenth century. They no longer justified the saying, *Städteluft macht Frei* (city-air makes free), but rather acted as breaks to reform and stifled innovation.[4]

This picture of decay and stagnation is misleading and obscures a vibrant politics that distinguished the old Empire's imperial cities—not just Aachen and Cologne—in the final decades of their existence. This period witnessed an upsurge in urban political conflict in the Holy Roman Empire.[5] This generally followed a similar pattern; the protagonists were relatively exclusive governing elites on the one side and a wider group, the *Bürgerschaft* (those enjoying civic rights within the framework of the trade guilds), on the other. However, the fault lines were in practice more fluid than that with competing factions within the governing elites generally appealing in turn to the wider *Bürgerschaft*, which for its own part was not usually without division. These urban conflicts proliferated in part because of Germany's impressive economic recovery in the eighteenth century. This was a century that witnessed improvements in agricultural productivity and an upsurge in trade as Central Europe became integrated into the wider Atlantic economy. Paradoxically, the extreme territorial fragmentation of the Empire assisted this in that it bred competition between individual territories to offer the best environment for businessmen. Increasingly, the imperial cities lost out to this competition as they suffered from what modern German political pundits refer to as *Reformstau*—an inability to reform, caused by political structures that enabled vested interest groups to block change. Entrepreneurs—that group Mack Walker refers to as the Movers and Doers—responded to *Reformstau* in the same way they do today, they re-located elsewhere. In the fragmented Empire this was easy and often involved simply moving beyond the city gates.[6] A more aggressive response was to penetrate the institutions of the imperial cities. This could be done, for example, by purchasing membership of a guild and using it as an institutional Trojan horse to counteract forces hostile to innovation.[7]

From today's perspective one might well sympathize with the Movers and Doers in their struggle to overcome incorrigibly conservative forces. This is especially so when we consider some other characteristics of the *Bürgerschaft:* their religious bigotry, philistine culture, and suspicion of new technology. However, this damning shortlist is only one part of the picture. In the conflicts of the 1770s and 1780s the *Bürgerschaft* also fought for principles we might regard as progressive. These typically included: socially more inclusive government, greater transparency in decision-making processes, independent scrutiny of public finances, and a separation of administration from the judiciary. These were the demands a nineteenth-century liberal would have happily supported.[8] Nor were the protagonists in these conflicts ignorant of developments beyond the city walls. Cologne, despite its ultra-Catholic reputation, remained a significant centre of trade that bound it to the outside world. The same was true of Aachen, a popular destination for visitors on account of its spas. Both cities contained those institutions historians associate with the expanding public sphere: coffee houses, Masonic lodges, lending libraries, and so forth.[9]

* * *

The well developed public sphere meant that the outbreak of the French Revolution was well reported in both cities.[10] Protagonists in the ongoing political conflicts quickly adapted the new political vocabulary developing in France. The *Bürgerschaft* initially associated itself with the Third Estate in France and pointed to its triumph as indicating that a similar victory, based on the restoration of ancient civic charters to their pristine form, would follow in the imperial cities. Travellers passing through Aachen and Cologne on their way to witness events in Paris at first hand reached the opposite conclusion, namely that the French Revolution highlighted just how obsolete the constitutions of the old imperial cities had become.[11] The magistracies, for their part, exploited the growing violence in France to point to the dangers of attacking established authority.

The war which started in 1792 brought the French Revolution to the region.[12] French victory over the Austrians at Jemappes resulted in the occupation of Aachen, though Cologne remained free for the time being. The French in Aachen posed as liberators and a minority of radicals supported them. The majority, whose civic patriotism remained closely bound up with Catholicism and a vaguer allegiance to the Emperor—entities to which the French were openly hostile—became alienated within the initial weeks of the occupation, something that military exactions—requisitioning, forced billeting, and so forth—further hastened. Not that there was any large-scale popular physical resistance, either in Aachen or elsewhere in the region. The sheer scale of the French military occupation in relation to the size of the native population, which far exceeded for example the ratio of troops to civilians in Spain after 1808, made this obviously suicidal. Nonetheless, popular hostility manifested itself openly in Aachen when the French army suffered defeat in early 1793; indeed, civilians assisted in the expulsion of the occupation forces, an act of defiance that provoked Robespierre into declaring, before the National Convention, that Aachen would be razed to the ground when the French returned.[13] Robespierre was ultimately denied his vengeance. Thermidor preceded by a few months the onset of the second occupation of Aachen (in autumn 1794) which on this occasion extended to the entire left bank of the Rhine including Cologne. This phase of occupation—from 1794 to 1798—was characterized less by political idealism and more by exploitation.

These were hard times for Aachen and Cologne, but as imperial cities they enjoyed certain advantages over other occupied areas. One was that their elites remained in place, something that was not the case in the neighbouring territories whose rulers fled to the right bank, taking their movable assets with them. Elites remaining in place helped the French who relied upon collaborators. To an extent it helped mitigate the effects of the occupation, and encouraged a sense of continuity in a period otherwise characterized by upheaval. This degree of continuity was especially pronounced in Cologne, whose inhabitants—magistrates and burghers—consistently spoke as if they were representatives of an authentic, ancient, republican tradition.[14] This republican rhetoric was so consistently applied that one is forced to the conclusion that it reflected deeply-held convictions; it was no simple negotiating ploy. It was a sentiment that, despite some fractures, bound together the political ruling class and the burghers in the face of a common challenge.

In Aachen there was less unity. In part, this was a legacy of the political divisions within the imperial city in the years immediately prior to the French occupation.[15] These divisions had been more profound and the conflict more severe than in Cologne. Furthermore, Cologne's elite had been more successful in integrating new elements, including wealthy Movers and Doers and professionals, than was the case in Aachen.[16] Here, the legacy of confessional division meant that a sizeable business elite of Protestants resided in the vicinity of Aachen but not within it; the French occupation gave them the opportunity to set aside their status as outsiders and join instead the new elite of notables governing the city.

* * *

Brumaire ushered in a new phase of French rule, though this was not immediately apparent; it was, after all, simply the latest in a long line of coups that distinguished the Directory. Nonetheless, the new regime quickly introduced important administrative innovations, not least of which was the introduction of prefectures, sub-prefectures and *mairies* that replaced the previous hierarchy of administrative councils.[17] In many respects, Aachen emerged the winner from this process of administrative integration into France. The city became the seat of the prefecture of the Roer department, which was one of the wealthiest in France. It also became the regional centre of other branches of the French state, including those dedicated to financial, judicial and police affairs. Following Napoleon's Concordat, it even became a bishopric. Cologne in contrast did badly, very badly given its status as the most populous city in the four Rhenish *départements réunis*. All it attracted was a sub-prefecture, plus some subordinate law courts and fiscal administrations. Indeed, the presence amongst the latter of the customs service—an organization that provided few openings to locals—was viewed as a curse rather than a blessing. However, even worse was that Cologne lost its status as an archdiocese; it was no longer even a diocese (for the first time since the fourth century), but simply a collection of parishes. Nor did it subsequently enjoy any success in attracting any educational institutions of note, such as a *lycée* or a special school of law or medicine, as did Koblenz and Bonn to the south. This spectacular failure, despite some fierce lobbying, must be in large measure ascribed to Cologne's not entirely unfounded reputation as a centre of clericalism and opposition to the Enlightenment.

The contrasting denseness of French administration in Aachen and Cologne had some bearing on the relationship between the native population and the Napoleonic state. At this point attention must be drawn to the lack of any regional Rhenish solidarity when confronting the French. Loyalties remained focused on locality, which meant on the town/city or on the *Land,* the latter defined by similar traditions, ways of speech, legal customs and landholding patterns rather than political or dynastic boundaries. Competition between localities went deep and, within the wider region, was reinforced by confessional divisions.[18] Economic rivalry between the imperial city of Cologne and the Duchy of Berg ran especially deep. Berg had done well in the eighteenth century, persuading Movers and Doers from Cologne to settle in the duchy. The resentment this bred manifested itself in the Napoleonic period in *Schadenfreude* at Berg's economic ruination caused by its exclusion from traditional markets by the French tariff barrier along the Rhine.[19] An even older rivalry existed between Cologne and Bonn. This went back to the Battle of Worringen in 1288 when the burghers of Cologne wrested independence from the archbishop. The archbishops subsequently made Bonn their main residence, and from there asserted their remaining rights in the imperial city. By the 1780s this was reinforced by a new layer of ideological conflict: Bonn, with its newly-founded university and under a progressive Archbishop-Elector became a centre of the catholic enlightenment; Cologne, with its much older university and with its papal nuncio, a centre of orthodoxy. The first phase of the French occupation in the 1790s deepened this existing fissure, as Bonn was favoured by the occupiers as an administrative centre for the surrounding region, including Cologne. Conflict between occupier and occupied thus was grafted on to a much older struggle. Nor did this stop following Napoleon's takeover for, if anything, he played on local rivalries.[20] Through the consultative institutions he created—the *arrondissement,* and departmental assemblies and prefectoral councils—he merely established new structures through which old conflicts could be played out. French administrative uniformity of itself did not overcome local loyalties.

Aachen, as noted, successfully lobbied Paris and became a centre of French administration. This brought tangible benefits to the local economy, including an ambitious public works programme and a large number of well-paid French officials who were also consumers.[21] Cologne did not receive this. However, one advantage of its loss of status was that central government scrutiny of the workings of its public affairs were not as great as they would have been had a French prefect been physically present. The most senior Napoleonic officials in the city were not natives of old France, as was the case in Aachen, but rather insiders; the long-serving sub-prefect, Klespé, and the equally long-serving *maire,* Wittgenstein, both of whom had been *Bürgermeister* prior to French rule. In Cologne, unlike in Aachen, there was a tendency for things to proceed as they had done previously. For example, Cologne's municipal council enjoyed a higher status than the French system strictly allowed: its members continued to be addressed as senators and convened quite regularly; the mayor continued to receive a substantial salary as had previously been the case, though again this was not really legal.[22] Overall, one gains the impression that the French never really penetrated Cologne and that instances of malpractice or anti-government sentiment were effectively hushed-up. In the final years, the centre sought to tighten its grip through the appointment of special police commissioners to strategic points along the French Empire's periphery, including Cologne. This created trouble, with the police commissioner losing no opportunity to expose hostile sentiment in the city. The municipal administration reciprocated, going out of its way to make the commissioner's life difficult by employing administrative and legalistic tools to obstruct him. In this, Cologne was assisted by the prefect's rivalry with the special police commissioner. These two representatives of the central government effectively cancelled each other out.[23] In Aachen, in contrast, not only was the prefect firmly in charge but, in the last years, he was assisted by a newly appointed sub-prefect—a native of old France and auditor of the Council of State no less—who very much represented the interests of the centre in the periphery.

There were further fundamental divergences in the experience of Aachen and Cologne under Napoleonic rule, but space limitations prevent further exploration at this juncture. Suffice it to note that the impact of Napoleon's economic policies was felt very differently in each city: Cologne, which traditionally depended on trade, suffered a significant downturn; whilst Aachen, a centre of manufacturing, benefited, in the short term at least.[24]

* * *

In conclusion, it might appear that superficially the similarities between Aachen and Cologne overshadowed the differences. They had much in common: both were relatively stable parts of the Napoleonic Empire; they paid their taxes and supplied their conscripts without much bother; this despite the fact that neither had been broken in by a prior phase of absolutism. That said, there were significant differences between them that resulted in distinctive experiences of French rule, two of which demand attention:

First, the extent to which elites had successfully opened themselves to new aspiring social groups before the French period. Cologne's ruling class had been more successful in this respect, opening itself to entrepreneurs and also to professionals. In Aachen, in contrast, a significant group of mainly Protestant businessmen remained outsiders until the French occupation gave them the opportunity to integrate with the established elite; whereas in Cologne, political and economic power amalgamated successfully before French rule, in Aachen it took the occupation to bring about this modernizing change. In terms of the composition of elites French rule made a difference in Aachen but not in Cologne, which was distinguished by greater continuity.

The second difference is the respective position of the two cities within the administrative structure of Napoleon's empire. Centres and peripheries existed at the level of the French Empire as a whole; they also existed within the individual departments. Cologne was something of a periphery in the Roer: it was marginalized to an extent, whereas Aachen, not least because of the association with Charlemagne, was favoured. The result of this was that Cologne's elite enjoyed greater scope for running things as they had done previously, so long as the city supplied its fair share of taxes and conscripts. In Aachen, in contrast, the municipal administration operated under the eyes of the resident prefect, and the scope for independent action was very much diminished in these circumstances. The long-term irony is that Cologne rather than Aachen became the centre of resistance against Prussian attempts to abolish French institutions after 1815. In part this was because in Cologne the well-established elite had successfully operated these institutions in such a way that they conformed to local interests. The city thus had a stake in their preservation.

Notes

1. In this context see especially Broers's identification of inner and outer empires whose frontiers did not correspond with the traditional borders dividing states. Michael Broers, *Europe under Napoleon 1799*–1815 (London and New York, 1996).

2. Not surprisingly, a rather glowing account of the department of the Roer, in which Aachen and Cologne were located, is provided by the last Napoleonic prefect, Jean Charles François de Ladoucette, *Voyage fait en 1813 et 1814 dans le pays entre Meuse et Rhin, suivi de notes, avec une carte géographique* (Paris, 1818). For more recent (and balanced) surveys of Aachen and Cologne in the French period, see respectively: Thomas R. Kraus, *Auf dem Weg in die Moderne. Aachen in französische Zeit 1792/93, 1794–1814* (Aachen, 1994) and Klaus Müller, *Köln von der französischen zur preußischen Herrschaft 1794–1815* (Cologne, Köln, 2005).

3. The best survey of the Holy Roman Empire in the late eighteenth century remains Karl Otmar Freiherr von Aretin, *Heiliges Römisches Reich 1776–1806*, 2 vols (Wiesbaden, 1967). For the Aulic Council and the Imperial Cities, Christopher R. Friedrichs, 'Urban Conflicts and the Imperial Constitution in Seventeenth-Century Germany', *Journal of Modern History* 58 (supplement) (1986): 98–123.

4. Mack Walter, *German Home Towns: Community, State, and General Estate, 1648–1871* (Ithaca and London, 1971).

5. Klaus Müller, 'Städtische Unruhen im Rheinland des späten 18. Jahrhunderts. Ein Beitrag zur rheinischen Reaktion auf die Französische Revolution', *Rheinische Vierteljahrsblätter* 54 (1990): 164–187.

6. Max Barkhausen, 'Government Control and Free Enterprise in Western Germany and the Low Countries in the Eighteenth Century', in *Essays in European Economic History 1500–1800*, ed. Peter Earle (Oxford, 1974), 212–273.

7. For Aachen's guilds, Michael Sobania, 'Das Aachener Bürgertum am Vorabend der Industrialisierung', in *Vom alten zum neuen Bürgertum. Die mitteleuropäische Stadt im Umbruch 1780–1820 Historische Zeitschrift*, ed. Lothar Gall (Munich, 1991—Beiheft 14), 183–228, here 187–188.

8. Thomas Theuringer, *Liberalismus im Rheinland. Voraussetzungen und Ursprünge im Zeitalter der Aufklärung* (Frankfurt a. M., 1998).

9. Winfried Dotzauer, *Freimaurergesellschaften am Rhein. Aufgeklärte Sozietäten auf dem linken Rheinufer vom Ausgang des Ancien Régime bis zum Ende der Napoleonischen Herrschaft* (Wiesbaden, 1973).

10. Joseph Hansen (ed.), *Quellen zur Geschichte des Rheinlandes im Zeitalter der französischen Revolution 1780–1801*, 4 vols (Bonn, 1931–8). Reactions to the outbreak of the French Revolution in the regional press are in volume 1.

11. Uwe Hentschel, 'Revolutionserlebnis und Deutschlandbild', *Zeitschrift für historische Forschung* 20 (1993): 321–344.

12. T. C. W. Blanning, *The French Revolution in Germany. Occupation and Resistance in the Rhineland 1792–1802* (Oxford, 1983).

13. Hansen, *Quellen*, vol. 2, 775–777.

14. Justus Hashagen, *Das Rheinland und die französische Herrschaft. Beiträge zur Charakteristik ihres Gegensatzes* (Bonn, 1908), 9–24, 29–45.

15. Carl Horst, 'Die Aachener Mäkelei 1786–1792. Konfliktregelungsmechanismen im altern Reich', *Zeitschrift des Aachener Geschichtsvereins* 92 (Sonderdruck, 1985),103–188.

16. Joachim Deeters, 'Das Bürgerrecht der Stadt Köln seit 1396', *Zeitschrift der Savigny-Stiftung für Rechtsgeschichte* 104 (1987):,1–83; Dietrich Ebeling, *Bürgertum und Pöbel. Wirtschaft und Gesellschaft Kölns im 18. Jahrhundert* (Cologne and Vienna, 1987). Wolfgang Herborn, 'Der Graduierte Ratsherr. Zur Entwicklung einer neuen Elite im Kölner Rat der frühen Neuzeit', in *Bürgerliche Eliten in den Niederlanden und in Nordwestdeutschland. Studien zur Sozialgeschichte des europäischen Bürgertums*

im Mittelalter und in der Neuzeit, eds Heinz Schilling and Hermann Diederiks (Cologne, 1985), 337–400.

17. Roger Dufraisse, 'L'Installation de l'institution départementale sur la rive gauche du Rhin (4 novembre 1797–23 septembre 1802)', in *L'Allemagne à l'époque napoléonienne. Questions d'histoire politique, économique et sociale,* ed. idem (Bonn and Berlin, 1992), 77–103.

18. Michael Rowe, *From Reich to State. The Rhineland in the Revolutionary Age, 1780–1830* (Cambridge, 2003), 112–113.

19. Eli F. Heckscher, *The Continental System. An Economic Interpretation* (Oxford, 1922), 314.

20. Hashagen, *Rheinland,* 47–50, 72.

21. Kraus, *Auf dem Weg in die Moderne,* 265–285.

22. Rowe, *Reich,* 99–100.

23. Ibid. 105–6, 172–3.

24. For the economic impact of Napoleonic rule on the region, Roger Dufraisse, 'De quelques conséquences économiques et sociales de la domination française sur les régions du Rhin inférieur 1794–1814' in *Franzosen und Deutsche am Rhein 1789–1918–1945,* ed. Peter Hüttenberger and Hansgeorg Molitor (Essen, 1989), 129–41. Also, Marie-Luise Schultheis-Friebe, 'Die französische Wirtschaftspolitik im Roër-Département 1792–1814' (Bonn D. Phil, 1969).

10
The Swiss Case in the Napoleonic Empire

Gabriele B. Clemens

Of France's neighbours it was not only Italian, German and Belgian territories that were drawn into the maelstrom of political and military turbulence and radical change that followed the outbreak of the French revolution. Switzerland, too, was pulled in. Yet, while the Rhenish, Italian and Belgian territories had been annexed to France in the 1790s, first provisionally and later on a permanent basis, most of Switzerland did not share this fate. Only the cantons of Neuchâtel (Neuenburg), the bishopric of Bâle and Valais, and the city of Geneva and its surroundings, became French territory.[1] Even during the Napoleonic era, the remaining cantons largely retained their independence, as least as far as domestic policy was concerned. It goes without saying that the different degrees to which Switzerland was subject to French domination had far-reaching effects on its political, economic and social structures during the Napoleonic era.

Historians, journalists and politicians are apt to use anniversaries as a reason for conferences and exhibitions. The anniversaries of 1789 (in France), 1848 (throughout the whole of Europe) and even the outbreak of the First World War produced a plethora of publications. Two Swiss anniversaries attracted particular attention. The first was the founding of the Helvetic Republic, which existed from 1798 to 1803, and the second was the Act of Mediation via which, in February 1803, Napoleon created the modern structures of present-day Switzerland. On the one hand Swiss historians view the political experiment of the Helvetic Republic with a certain degree of sympathy, as demonstrated by a considerable number of publications on the topic, on the other, scarcely anyone in the Alpine republic was interested in the Napoleon's epoch-making refashioning of the confederation in 1803. Up to the present day, it is the legendary oath of the *Rütlischwur* of 1291 that forms the basis of the narrative of national origin.[2]

On the occasion of the 200th anniversary of the passing of the Act of Mediation only three historical conferences marked the event. The first, held in Paris, was organized mainly by historians from the French-speaking canton of Fribourg,[3] where a further conference took place.[4] The third was held in Geneva, a city that, as a French department at the time, was never actually affected by the Act of Mediation.[5] In the German-speaking part of Switzerland there were no noteworthy activities on the part of historians relating to the anniversary. Moreover, up to the present day, no comprehensive study of the period has been published.

Recent and, on the whole, innovative studies completely ignore the French period, both the Helvetic Republic and the later constitution imposed by the Act of Mediation. One example is a doctoral thesis by Barbara Weinmann on republicanism and communalism in the canton of Zurich in the late eighteenth and nineteenth centuries. Her account is interrupted in the year 1798 and is not taken up again until the period of *Restauration* or restoration of the ancien regime in the 1820s,[6] although it would have been intriguing had she examined how the political elite actually behaved during this phase of radical change and, in particular, how they succeeded in retaining their dominant position, what manner of political discussions they engaged in, which old cliques and coteries they continued to nurture to their own advantage, or whether they managed to construct new political networks. Of such issues, alas, the author makes no mention.[7] A similar approach is adopted by Oliver Zimmer in his study of the genesis of Swiss nationalism from the waning of the ancien regime onwards. He, too, leaps from the end of the Helvetic Republic to the pre-revolutionary 1840s.[8] This quotation from Pierre Louis Chantre and Thierry Sartoretti is equally revealing: 'Vichy and the German occupation are to France, what the Helvetic Republic and the French occupation are to Switzerland'.

What follows is an attempt to elucidate the reasons why the Swiss have so many problems with their French historical heritage. To that end, I shall outline Switzerland's place in international affairs up to the beginning of Napoleonic rule in 1802. The second section examines the effects of Napoleonic rule on the peasantry, the economy and the political elite and, within this context, on public administration. In the final section, I will examine how the Swiss themselves judged the Napoleonic era retrospectively.

The Swiss political intelligentsia in the late eighteenth century were no exception in paying great attention to the revolutionary upheavals in North America and in France.[9] All over Europe, intellectuals influenced and inspired by the spirit of the Enlightenment never ceased to criticize the antiquated political structures, their main target being oligarchic domination. However, every plan to give the new political elite access to the traditional models of political representation failed dismally in Switzerland, just as they had done in Cologne or Venice.[10] Nowhere did the old European republic succeed, on its own, in breaching the unbreakable wall of privilege.

Ever since the Thirty Years War, the thirteen old communes or cantons of Switzerland had developed a principle of neutrality that was respected in all the European wars of the seventeenth and eighteenth centuries.

However, the imperialist policy of the French Directory was undeterred by Swiss neutrality. After the Treaty of Campo Formio (1797), Switzerland was overrun by France, since the Directory considered it on the side of the Coalition. After some resistance, mostly around Berne, and in some pockets in the canton of Schwyz, Switzerland capitulated in March 1798. Unlike the annexed territories of Belgium, the left bank of the Rhine or Italy, Switzerland remained independent in a formal sense, but was compelled to adopt a constitution which turned it into a French sister republic. The next five years, the lifespan of the Helvetic Republic, provided time enough for political experiments that shook the very foundations of Switzerland. Helvetica, as it was called, was transformed into a sort of New Age laboratory. The man of the hour was one Peter Ochs, a progressive patrician of Bâle, who made a radical break with Swiss federative structures when the Directory commissioned him to draft the Helvetic Constitution.

Faithful to the precepts and models of the French Revolution, Ochs created a modern national state organized on strictly centralist principles. One of the basic tenets of the old confederation, namely local self-government (the principles of which could differ from place to place), was largely abolished. For the first time in Swiss history, the principles of equality before the law, the division of powers, sovereignty of the people and representative democracy came into effect. In addition, a number of individual rights were guaranteed, including freedom of conscience, of religion, freedom of the press, and the protection of private property.[11] The traditionally powerful city cantons (and the traditional patrician elites with them) lost their surrounding lands and with them power and wealth. All men obtained equal political rights, as the distinctions between patricians, common citizens, new citizens and subjects were removed.[12] Henceforth, the legislature was to consist of two chambers, as in Paris, with each of the cantons electing four delegates to the Senate (upper house) and eight to the Grand Council (lower house). Executive powers were given to a five man Directorate. The new corridors of power were now primarily occupied by liberal republicans; one of the most prominent was the Director Frédéric-César de la Harpe. Although a convinced proponent of the new order, he is depicted in one older Swiss textbook in a less than flattering light as a 'violent, tyrannical Jacobin'.[13]

Nor was it only in the field of personal rights that comprehensive innovations and far-reaching reforms were introduced during the Helvetic period.[14] The question of the freedom of the peasantry also became an urgent issue. Initially, this centred on economic reform with the aim of granting the peasantry full rights of use of the land they cultivated, but it developed into a significant process of increasing political awareness within the rural population. Long discussions ensued over whether encumbered land (land burdened with feudal dues) should be relieved with or without compensation, with the initial result that very moderate disencumberment payments were agreed on, but these were replaced in the following years by disproportionately higher payments. Nonetheless, by May 1798 the removal of personal feudal rights and the abolition of serfdom, which still existed in some parts of Switzerland, was achieved, as well as the strict division of Church and State on the French model. The properties of monasteries, abbeys and convents were sequestered and declared the property of the nation. The issue of Jewish suffrage was, however, treated differently, there being no enthusiasm for radical solutions. While the Jewish population was freed from personal levies, Jews were still denied civil rights. Much of what was planned and discussed at the time and that even became valid in the short term—issues such as freedom of commerce—could not ultimately be brought to fruition until the 1848 revolution.

The new system of government did not meet with universal approval throughout Switzerland, but a sharp distinction must be drawn here among the individual cantons.[15] That which was viewed as emancipation in the former subject *lands* (lands that were subordinated to cities along feudal lines, as serfs to knights, such as Waadt and Aargau) was deemed to be an imposition in the traditional cantons of inner Switzerland, where the people felt that they had been deprived of their ancient confederative freedom.[16] The federalists, as powerful supporters of the old regime, reacted vehemently against the new republic and a massive pamphleteering campaign ensued between republican unitarians and federalists regarding the correct form of government for Switzerland. This at a time when the Republic suffered considerable economic burdens due to the presence of foreign troops throughout the country.

It was in this altogether complex and thorny situation that Napoleon intervened personally in Swiss internal affairs for the first time. First Consul for barely a year, he handed over his draft constitution to a Swiss delegation at his country residence at Malmaison on 29 April 1801, a draft that bears witness to his excellent knowledge of circumstances in the Alpine republic. With no room for manoeuvre, the Swiss Legislative Council had no choice but endorse it at the end of May. Known by the name of the place where it was conceived, the Malmaison Constitution may, in principle, be held to be a wise compromise between unitarism and federalism, the latter being decisively upgraded. Through it, Napoleon recreated Switzerland as a federal state in which the seventeen cantons were to recover important competencies, particularly in the fields of finance and education. Yet ultimately the relationship between the legislature, known as the *Tagsatzung* and consisting of 102 members, and the 25 senators composing the executive, led by two alternating high officials or *Landammänner*, was not clearly defined so there was still sufficient room for power struggles. The *Landammann* presiding at any given time was, together with four senators, to form the core of the executive, as a sort of Privy Council.

The time was not ripe for such a compromise, however, and there was soon discontent on all sides: the federalists were disgruntled because a strong centralized power continued to exist; the unitarians were disaffected because their ambitious project of a unified republican state had failed. Four coups d'etat were to take place resulting in chaotic changes in government. In addition, the withdrawal of French troops led to a situation tantamount to civil war. The events of these years demonstrate how far Swiss politicians were from any ability to compromise, and how adamantly each faction pursued its own aims.[17] Taken as a whole, the Helvetian experiment ended in tumult.

But did Helvetica mean liberation or a curtailment of traditional freedom? Even in 1998 in the many papers on the Helvetic Republic published for the bicentenary, historians responded to this question in very different ways.[18] The fact that Helvetica had been created by the grace of France was a heavy load for the Republic to bear. The fiscal pressures exerted by the Directory, coupled with other economic burdens,[19] led nineteenth-century commentators to give a negative account of the Helvetic republic, describing it as an exercise in trial and tribulation.[20] Furthermore, the republic's existence led to a civil war, a civil war quashed only by the intervention of a foreign power, France. Helvetica did not fit into the traditional proud narrative of Swiss federalism and independence. In any case, the majority of the population at the time, no doubt suffering from the shock of modernization, rejected the new regime altogether.[21] Nonetheless, it cannot be denied that the positive and forward-looking reforms initiated in, and designed to be enacted during, the Helvetic Republic period did not come into full force immediately; they finally took effect in the course of the nineteenth century. Indeed, historians now interpret the Helvetic Republic as a significant step in the development of a modern national state and the gradual emergence of a liberal Swiss national identity.[22]

For Napoleon it was obvious that the Helvetic political experiment had proved a failure. He therefore intervened in Swiss internal affairs a second time, with the aim of pacifying the Alpine region. To this end, he invited delegates from each canton to Paris for talks on the political future of Switzerland. There were many important figures of the Helvetic Republic among the approximately seventy delegates, such as Pestalozzi and Ochs, who were to make each other's acquaintance for the first time on the journey to Paris. The federalists were represented, *inter alia*, by Hans von Reinhard from Zurich and Ludwig von Affry from Fribourg, both of whom were to become influential politicians in the years that followed. Although the unitarians held the majority in this assembly, known as *Consulta,* Napoleon declared that Switzerland was, by its very nature, a federative state, and it was for this reason that the cantons would be restored to their former importance. Each canton was to create its own constitution and this was the task of the *Consulta.* The national constitution as a whole, however, can largely be attributed to Napoleon.[23]

These consultations culminated in the Act of Mediation of 1803. The intervention of a mediator might have been viewed as politically promising

in view of the fact that the Unitarists and the Federalists held totally irre-
concilable views and were ready to stop at nothing to defend them. Yet, for
Napoleon, it was not merely a question of exporting his political maxims
on domestic policy. His aim was, rather, to isolate Switzerland from both
a military and a diplomatic point of view. Henceforth, Switzerland was to
place troops at his disposal and, in the case of political insubordination,
the Swiss would have to reckon with a new occupation.[24] To achieve these
aims, Napoleon largely complied with the political wishes of the traditional
ruling classes, so as to ensure their loyalty—as he had done elsewhere in
Europe—or at least their passive support.[25] Against this background, the
tremendous achievement that Napoleon and his advisors had engineered
with the Act of Mediation found little acclaim among the Swiss. Their attention was first and foremost focused on foreign interference in their domestic
affairs.

The Act of Mediation brought forth fruit that was both sweet and bitter.
It marked the birth of the present federative structure of Switzerland and in
the ten years following the Act of Mediation there was stability in the Swiss
Confederation. This has been underlined again and again as Napoleon's
lasting achievement, for without his *diktat* unity would scarcely have been
possible. The cantonal status of the thirteen old communes or cantons was
for the most part restored and six new ones were added (St. Gallen, Aargau,
Graubünden, Thurgau, Waadt and Tessin). Forthwith, the cantons were to
enjoy equality of status; feudal condominiums and dependencies ceased
to exist. The entire state—henceforth the Helvetic Confederation—was
endowed with a constitution acknowledging a central authority in the form
of a legislative council or diet known as the *Tagsatzung*.

It is true that the granting of unlimited rights to communities and individual cantons in the regulation of their internal affairs (thus allowing
them to develop in quite different ways) caused certain complications. The
six new cantons opted for forms of government significantly different from
that of the thirteen older ones.[26] The former hastened to reform the School
and Poor Laws, as well as the legislation for medical services and forestry
regulations. Road-building programmes were intensified and governance
was carried out on the basis of modern representative constitutions. Only
the canton of Glarus could lay any claim to fame for its pursuit of reforms,
notably with its adoption of stricter measures in the fight against nepotism
and in its development of one of the most glorious projects of the Mediation
era, namely an ambitious plan to build a canal between the River Linth and
Lake Wal, which was finally completed in May 1811. Five years later, the
course of the River Linth between Lakes Wal and Zurich was corrected in
such a way as to prevent the flooding and swamping of the Glarus region
that had posed a major problem in the past. As for the remainder of the traditional cantons, the Act of Mediation had rendered it impossible for them
to revert to the conditions prevailing under the ancien regime. The act had

nullified the status quo and thenceforth representative constitutions were to remain in force, which would in turn generate further reforms over the course of time.

In this light, Napoleon's absolute refusal to re-establish the subjected dominions that had been in existence until 1798 becomes a significant achievement. It made possible the reduction of the dominance of the townships over their surrounding rural areas. Claims like those of Berne on the newly-founded cantons of Aargau and Vaud could now be dismissed. Commentators may disagree as to whether it was thanks to the French alone that Swiss subjects were emancipated from traditional forms of oppression, but one fact is undeniable, the principle of civic and civil equality was upheld in every single case. Article 3 of the Act of Mediation is unambiguous: 'There are no subject territories in Switzerland, nor do any townships, persons or families enjoy any privileges [in relation to others].' These words not only terminated the rule of municipalities over subject territories; they also put an end to the special position enjoyed by patricians.[27]

As for the bitterness, this came from the restoration of aristocratic structures in the city cantons and the domination of the aristocracy in the rural cantons. The civil law that had been in force throughout the whole of the Helvetic Republic ceased to exist and discrimination on confessional grounds became the rule. Even penal law was altered in such a way as to give grounds for concern. The sole exception was the canton of Lucerne, where the Helvetic Penal Code and a Habeas Corpus Act retained their validity; elsewhere, penal law adopted reactionary features, notably permitting medieval methods of torture as a means of interrogation.

This then—albeit too briefly sketched—was the political and legislative framework of the Helvetic Republic and the 1803 Confederation. Against this background it is easier to analyse the specific social conditions, beginning with the rural situation. At the beginning of the nineteenth century, large parts of Europe were dominated by and dependent on agriculture. About 80 per cent of the population lived in rural areas and drew their income from the cultivation of the land. A comparison of the peasantry in Switzerland with that in France reveals that little changed for the Swiss peasant. The French revolutionary government had abolished feudal burdens in France in one fell swoop, but in the Swiss cantons the ruling patricians were able to prevent such far-reaching reforms during the Napoleonic era. As beneficiaries of the agricultural status quo, they were little interested in diminishing their own privileges or incomes. It was the pressure for reform from without that led to the first half-hearted efforts, such as when laws were enacted in the individual cantons enabling peasants to buy their freedom from tithes and land tax; the price was so high however that it was out of reach for most of the rural population.[28]

This was why the proclamation of a Tithe and Property Tax Law in the canton of Zurich in 1804 led to the so-called Bocken Rebellion, which the ruling nobility suppressed by force of arms.[29] When the ringleaders of the uprising were tried in court the patricians made use of their power and influence to exact political revenge. Even Talleyrand criticized their actions. However, Napoleon was dependent on the support of the ruling elite so Paris did not intervene in favour of the peasants.

Indeed, external pressure ought to have compelled the cantons to accept free trade, but the aristocratic families were adamantly opposed to such new laws and did their best to evade them. Some cantons prevented unwelcome competition by re-imposing immigration restrictions. Another example of patrician skulduggery can be seen in the canton of Appenzell. Opinion there held that freedom of commerce (regulated by the Act of Mediation and therefore binding in all the cantons) was not binding in Appenzell since the Appenzell Inner-Rhode delegate had rejected the proposal in the course of the debate leading to its acceptance in Paris.

The effects of the trade embargo imposed by Napoleon's Continental System are also much discussed.[30] Prior to the French Revolution, an export-oriented cottage industry producing cotton textiles had developed in Switzerland. The Continental System cut Switzerland off from its most important import and export markets, although much smuggling took place in the years after 1807. However, the Continental System was also a motor of technical innovation for textiles (now free from British competition), which proved profitable in the middle term. As far as the annexed city of Geneva, the capital of the *département du Léman,* is concerned the picture presented by current research oscillates between economic stagnation on the one hand, and technical innovation on the other.

Napoleon did not interfere with the cantonal bureaucracies, with their majorities of patricians, and they enjoyed great freedom of action. In Zurich, for example, Hans von Reinhard, an influential citizen who had been at the head of the Minor Council during the Mediation era, held the post of *Landamann* or chief magistrate of the canton hosting the diet (confederal parliament) in 1807 and again between 1813 and 1814. At each investiture, he stage-managed the ceremony with such pomp that the event resembled the crowning of a baroque potentate; indeed, it was no surprise that he took the time to travel to Paris in 1804 to witness the spectacle of Napoleon crowning himself emperor. Possibly the most influential Swiss politician of the Mediation era, von Reinhard, was revered as head of the aristocracy almost like a prince. With one exception, all the other chief magistrates derived from the ancien regime aristocracy.[31] Typical of them were the Bernese Niklaus Rudolf von Wattenwyl,[32] who held the post in1804 and 1810, and Ludwig August Philipp von Affry, mayor of Fribourg in 1803 and 1809 and said to be on the best of terms with Napoleon.[33]

The political elite of the cantons declined to fraternize or amalgamate with the new elites created by Napoleon, even though the individual cantonal constitutions by and large complied with the French pattern. In each case, the cantonal parliament consisted of two chambers or councils, the Grand and Minor Council respectively, with some variance in the composition of the electoral guilds, the numbers of members and voting procedures. Regardless, the old aristocracy succeeded in asserting itself, dominating each Minor Council and therefore keeping a tight rein on the executive. The prerequisite for election to this chamber was wealth. Both in Zurich and Berne representatives of the old aristocracy held twenty of the twenty-five seats. In theory, the electoral guilds could replace council members every two years, but in fact this never occurred. Those wealthy pre-eminent burghers who were elected to a post on the council in 1803 retained the sinecure for life. This was, once again, very much in accordance with Napoleon's intentions, seeking as he did to establish an elite of notables in Europe based on the old aristocracy and the new aristo-meritocracy, with the aim of gaining support for his own self-defined system of government. Yet it was in the Empire proper that new aristocracies were created; in Switzerland the old elites managed for the most part to retain their footing.

What remained of all the Napoleonic reforms in Switzerland after the downfall of the Emperor? At first sight it would appear nothing; in 1813 the Act of Mediation was revoked in every canton. However, the revolutionary and Napoleonic inheritance continued to exert a powerful influence. In the years between 1813 and 1815 it became clear that the earlier political changes were irreversible and complete restoration was impossible.Furthermore, the Napoleonic years between 1803 and 1813 had not been entirely devoid of positive qualities: the nineteen Swiss cantons could not but acknowledge that they had managed to exist without undue conflict and in relative peace amidst a Europe at war. Many cantons therefore took the opportunity to absorb one or two aspects of the sudden and precipitous revolutionary reforms and renewals that the Helvetic Republic had brought forth, though adapting them to their own requirements. The demands of extreme conservatives to restore the subordinate status to certain dominions were to be rejected and, above all in the new and more forward-looking cantons, rationalist ideals of freedom and equality were perceived as so firmly established that in the years following 1815 those in favour of restoration could no longer subdue them.

Notes

1. Liliane Mottu Weber and Joëlle Droux (eds) *Gèneve française 1798–1813. Nouvelles approches. Actes du colloque tenu du 12 novembre au 14 novembre 1998* (Geneva, 2004).
2. Manfred Hettling, 'Einleitung. Nation und Nationalisierung in der Schweiz', in *Die Konstruktion einer Nation. Nation und Nationalisierung in der Schweiz*, ed. Urs Alttermatt, Catherine Bosshart-Pfluger, and Albert Tanner (Zurich, 2008), 19–33. Georg Kreis, *Mythos Rütli. Geschichte eines Erinnerungsortes* (Zurich, 2004). Guy P. Marschal, *Schweizer Gebrauchsgeschichte, Geschichtsbilder, Mythenbildung und Nationale Identität* (Basel, 2006).

3. Alain-Jacques Czouz-Tornare, 'Introduction', in *Quand Napoléon recréa la Suissse. La genèse et la mise en œuvre de l'acte de mediation: aspects des relations franco-suisses autour de 1803*, ed. ibid. (Paris, 2005), 12.

4. Francis Python (ed.) *Pouvoirs et société à Fribourg (1803–1814). Actes du colloque de Fribourg (journée du 11 octobre 2003)* (Fribourg, 2005).

5. Alfred Dufour, Till Hanisch, and Victoir Monnier (eds), *Bonaparte, la Suisse et l'Europe* (Brussels, 2003).

6. Barbara Weinmann, *Eine andere Bürgergesellschaft. Klassischer Republikanismus und Kommunalismus im Kanton Zürich im späten 18. und 19. Jahrhundert* (Göttingen, 2002).

7. In contrast, on the political developments in Geneva see Anja Victorine Hartmann, *Reflexive Politik im sozialen Raum. Politische Eliten in Geld zwischen 1760 und 1841* (Mainz, 2003).

8. Oliver Zimmer, *A Contested Nation. History, Memory and Nationalism in Switzerland, 1761–1891* (Cambridge, 2003).

9. Simon Netzle, 'Helvetisiertes Amerika: Der Blick der eidgenössischen Spätaufklärung auf die erste modernen Republik', in *Republikanische Tugend. Ausbildung eines Schweizer Nationalbewußtseins und Erziehung eines neuen Bürgers*, ed. Michael Böhler and Etienne Hoffmann (Geneva, 2000), 503–529. Volker Reinhardt, *Geschichte der Schweiz* (Munich, 2006), 81.

10. For an account of the political dispute in the free *Reichsstädte* of the Rhineland before the upheaval of the revolution, see Michael Rowe, *From Reich to State. The Rhineland in the Revolutionary Age 1780–1830* (2nd edn, Cambridge, 2007).

11. Regarding the preparation of the laws, see Pascal Delvaux, *La République en papier*, 2 vols (Geneva, 2004).

12. On the issue of civil rights, see Silvia Arlettaz, *Citoyens et étrangers sous la Republique helvétique (1798–1803)* (Geneva, 2005).

13. Andreas Staehelin, 'Helvetik', in *Handbuch der Schweizer Geschichte*, vol. 2 (Zurich, 1980), 785–837, esp. 797. Laharpe has left a significant body of source material relating to the history of Helvetica: Jean Charles Biaudet and Marie-Claude Jequier, *Correspondance de Frédéric-César de la Harpe sous la République Helvétique*, 3 vols (Neuchâtel, 1978–1980).

14. Kurt Jenny, 'Die Helvetik—Meilenstein auf dem schweizerischen Weg vom Ancien Régime zum modernen Bundesstaat', in *Blicke auf die Helvetik*, ed. Christian Simon (Basel, 2000), 95–129.

15. Christian Simon (ed.), *Widerstand und Proteste zur Zeit der Helvetik* (Basel, 1998).

16. Holger Bönnig, *Der Traum von Freiheit und Gerechtigkeit: Helvetische Revolution und Republik (1798–1803). Die Schweiz auf dem Weg zur bürgerlichen Demokratie* (Zurich, 1998).

17. Tobias Kästli, *Die Schweiz. Eine Republik in Europa. Geschichte des Nationalstaats seit 1798* (Zurich, 1998), 152.

18. Simon (ed.) *Blicke auf die Helvetik.*

19. Hence, Zurich's upper classes could certainly be classified as losers as a result of the new fiscal laws: Nicola Berens, *Zürich in der Helvetik. Die Anfänge der lokalen Verwaltung* (Zurich, 1998), 398.

20. Benjamin Adler, *Die Entstehung der direkten Demokratie. Das Beispiel der Landgemeinde Schwyz 1780–1866* (Zurich, 2006).

21. Charles Simon notes that new mainstream historiography is running the risk of interpreting Helvetica as a simple success story, and he highlights the manifold forms of resistance and protest; Charles Simon, 'Introduction' in *Widerstand und Proteste zur Zeit der Helvetik*, ed. Idem (Basel, 1998), 1–37, esp. 2.

22. Daniel Frei, *Die Förderung des Schweizer Nationalbewusstseins nach dem Zusammenbruch der Alten Eidgenossenschaft 1798* (Zurich, 1964), 201–204.

23. Kästli, *Die Schweiz*, 158.

24. Carlo Moos, 'Zur Schweizer Truppenstellung an Napoleon', in *Souveräntitätsfragen—Militärgeschichte*, ed. Christian Simon and André Schluchter (Basel, 1995), 125–145. Michael Broers, *Europe under Napoleon* (London, Arnold, 1996), 63. Kurt Münger, *Militär, Staat und Nation in der Schweiz* (Münster, 2000).

25. Stuart Woolf, *Napoleon's Integration of Europe* (London, 1991).

26. Alexander Grab, *Napoleon and the transformation of Europe* (New York, 2003), 119.

27. Ulrich Im Hof, *Mythos Schweiz. Identität—Nation—Geschichte 1291–1991* (Zurich, 1991), 127.

28. On the question of buying freedom from feudal burdens, see Christian Pfister, *Im Strom der Modernisierung. Bevölkerung, Wirtschaft und Umwelt im Kanton Bern 1700–1914* (Bern, 1995), 180–184.

29. Rolf Graber, 'Jezt seye es einmal Zeit, die Freiheit und Gleichheut zu erfechten und den letzte Blutstropfen für dieselbe sprüzen zu lassen. Zur sozialen Logik des Volksaufstandes von 1804 auf der Züricher Landschaft', *Schweizerische Zeitschrift für Geschichte* 54.1 (2004): 1–19.

30. Katherine Aaselstad, 'Revisiting the Continental System: Exploitation to Self-Destruction in the Napoleonic Empire', in *Napoleon and his Empire, 1904–1814*, ed. Philip G. Dwyer and Alan Forrest (New York, 2007), 114–133.

31. Vinzenz Rüttimann alone, a mayor of Lucerne, was a commoner.

32. S. Hans Braun, *Die Familie von Wattenwyl* (Bern, 2004).

33. For details see Georges Andrey, *Louis d'Affry 1743–1810, premier landamman de la Suisse. La Confédération suisse à l'heure napoléonienne* (Geneva, 2003).

Part III

Central and Eastern Europe: The Confederation of the Rhine, Westphalia and the Hanseatic Departments, Prussia

Introduction

Michael Broers

From the outset, Napoleon sought good relations with the rulers of the middle-sized states of the Holy Roman Empire. Between 1801 and 1805 he detached Bavaria, Baden, Württemberg, Nassau and Hesse-Darmstadt from Habsburg control and helped them to expand their territories at the expense of the smallest states of the Empire, the tiny fiefs of the Imperial Knights and the Imperial Free Cities whose only effective protection had been the courts of the Holy Roman Emperor. These middle-sized states proved useful allies against the Habsburgs in the war of 1805 and were further rewarded at the Peace of Pressburg. Napoleon then grouped them together in the Confederation of the Rhine in July 1806 with himself as Protector, although he did not interfere directly in their internal affairs. One month later Emperor Francis I dissolved the Holy Roman Empire, allowing the rulers of the Confederation states to assume royal titles and claim full sovereignty over their territories. Most of them remained loyal allies of France until 1814.

The defeat of Prussia in 1806 expanded Napoleonic hegemony further into Germany. That year the Grand Duchy of Berg was created from territories confiscated from Prussia; Napoleon first gave it to his brother-in-law and cavalry commander, Murat, and then, nominally, to his infant nephew, Napoleon-Louis, with himself as regent. The whole of the Electorate of Hesse-Kassel, whose ruler had fought with Prussia, parts of Hannover and Brunswick and other Prussian territory, became the Kingdom of Westphalia at the Treaty of Tilsit in 1807, under Napoleon's youngest brother, Jerome. Napoleon's ally, Saxony, gained Prussian Posen at this time and its ruler, Elector Frederick-Augustus, became a king and also the ruler of the newly-created Grand Duchy of Warsaw, a partial resurrection of the Kingdom of Poland consisting of ex-Prussian Poland (Grand Duchy territory was expanded in 1809 when Austrian Poland—Galicia—was annexed after the Wagram campaign). The last Napoleonic expansion in Germany came in 1810 when the Hanseatic cities of the North Sea coast—Bremen, Hamburg and Lübeck—became three French departments, although they had been under military occupation for some time.

The character of Napoleonic hegemony in Germany—including the Grand Duchy of Warsaw, which was essentially ex-Prussian territory—varied enormously, as did its impact on the individual German states. The Confederation states were heavily influenced by the Napoleonic system and increasingly copied Napoleonic administrative and judicial reforms: several of their chief ministers—principally Montgelas in Bavaria, von Reitzenstein in Baden—had served the Habsburg Emperor Joseph II in the 1780s and so were sympathetic to the Napoleonic model of government; the larger, more heterogeneous nature of their expanded states made centralization imperative and efficient administration essential to meet the heavy conscription quotas Napoleon sought as the price of his support. Berg was effectively ruled by two of Napoleon's most trusted administrators, Beugnot and Rœderer, but suffered economically as its light industries based on metallurgy were run down through the Continental System, which sought to eradicate competition to French industry; many of Berg's enterprises transferred across the Rhine to the French departments of the left bank to avoid this. The Hansa ports suffered from the blockade, which ruined their maritime commerce. In contrast, most states of the Confederation benefitted from the higher levels of commercial integration its terms permitted them. Saxony, too, profited from Napoleonic hegemony since its textile industries were protected from British imports. Westphalia was meant to be a model kingdom for the Napoleonic state system, but Jerome had to compromise over the abolition of feudalism to enforce conscription effectively, as did Frederick-Augustus in the Grand Duchy of Warsaw. In both states, where serfdom was widespread, reform proved difficult. The former Hessian and Prussian aristocracies of Westphalia remained aloof from Jerome, whereas the Polish nobility proved very loyal to Napoleon as the restorer of a semblance of their former independence, even if they paid only lip service to Napoleonic reforms.

When war broke out with Austria in 1809, the reactions of the various German states reflected these varied experiences. The governments of the Confederation served Napoleon loyally, but a serious revolt broke out against Bavarian rule in the Tyrol, an Austrian province awarded to King Maximilian in 1806 which resented Montgelas' reforms. There were several small revolts across northern and central Germany led by those worst affected by the Napoleonic reordering of Germany, namely former imperial knights and former Prussian officers, like Schill.

Most of the restructuring of central and eastern Germany, and Poland, came via the reduction of Prussian territory after its crushing defeat in 1806. The rump of the Prussian state, barely one third of its original size, was forced into an alliance with France and subjected to financial reparations, whilst its army was severely restricted. However, after 1806, a reforming group of soldiers and civil administrators emerged who quietly rebuilt the state and the army. In 1813, Prussia re-emerged as a formidable force in the War of Liberation that accompanied the Russian advance west in 1812.

In 1814, the princes of the Confederation only agreed to join the Allies provided the gains made under Napoleon were guaranteed, thus leaving the Napoleonic territorial settlement intact in these states; however, the Tyrol was returned to Austria. The territories of Berg and Westphalia were restored to Prussia and Hesse-Kassel. The Hansa ports regained their independence; Hannover and Brunswick were returned to the British royal family. Prussia regained little territory from the Grand Duchy of Warsaw; most of it, together with Russian Poland, became the Congress Kingdom, with significant autonomy within Russia, which was lost after the revolt of 1830. A new body, under Austro–Prussian supervision, the German Confederation, was created in 1814. Overall, the Napoleonic territorial restructuring of Germany survived Napoleon's fall in 1814. The more than 2,000 polities of the Holy Roman Empire had been reduced to forty between 1800 and 1810, and this settlement endured.

11
Resistance to Napoleonic Reform in the Grand Duchy of Berg, the Kingdom of Westphalia and the South German States

Ute Planert

1 Central Europe after the end of the ancien regime

The convulsions that followed the French Revolution split the former Holy Roman Empire of the German Nation into four different zones of influence after 1806: Prussia, Austria, the French Rhineland and the Confederation of the Rhine. To a greater or lesser extent, all states underwent considerable modernizing reforms, whether in sustaining or opposing Napoleon's rule. In Prussia and Austria, reforming policies were moderated by dynastic continuity and, with respect to recruitment, general habituation to earlier forms of military service through the canton system introduced in the eighteenth century.[1]

In the Rhineland, advantages arising from a direct incorporation into the French Empire—above all political stability, legal reforms and economic improvements—proved sources of integration while desertion rates were lower than in France itself. Moreover, supporters of the old order had few political alternatives, as the numerous ecclesiastical states and principalities which had dominated the political landscape on the left bank of the Rhine had been dissolved.[2]

2 The Confederation states before 1809

The situation in the Confederation states was somewhat different. Here the territorial revolution of 1803–06 had merged different dynastic and religious traditions. In the south, former ecclesiastical and princely states and the Imperial free cities were incorporated into the Confederation states of Baden, Württemberg and Bavaria, with Austrian territories added after the defeats of the Habsburg Monarchy in 1805 and 1809. Further north,

Napoleon merged the ex-ecclesiastical states and conquered regions of, among others, Prussia, Hessia, Hannover and Brunswick to form the satellite states of Westphalia and Berg. In order to cope with the need for higher efficiency, the Confederation states introduced a set of administrative reforms, thereby continuing the attempts of enlightened absolutist rulers to disperse intermediate powers and to foster bureaucratic control by the central government. Territories were divided up, with no respect for historical borders, into specific administrative units governed by a hierarchical prefectoral system that was meant to abolish the traditional influence of church and nobility even at the parish level. New metric units of measurement and currency were introduced, the taxation and judical systems were reformed, and Jews were partially emancipated. Guilds, Cathedral chapters and provincial representatives (*Landstände*) were abolished, as well as the majority of feudal privileges and religious customs. In order to establish the *Bürgergesellschaft*, a new class of francophile civil servants concentrated on the transformation of the state, law, economy, religion, and political culture through an administrative revolution.[3]

The case of Westphalia was particularly striking. Since there was no need to compromise with old authorities (unlike in the southern kingdoms), Napoleon took great pains to follow territorial acquisition with moral conquest. The implementation of the *Code civil* and the decree of Germany's first constitution were meant to provide the basis for a modern, bourgeois society. This would, Napoleon believed, win him the hearts of the public and set an example for other, more reluctant Confederation states.[4]

Yet, despite all his declarations, liberalization and modernization policies were in fact to serve the interests of Imperial France. The Continental System prohibited trade with Great Britain, while high tariffs favouring French products caused additional economic disruption. In Westphalia, large areas were donated to Napoleon's followers, augmenting the financial deficit of the state and violating the principles of the *Code Napoléon* by creating a new feudal class of landowners. All over the Confederation states, fiscal duties reached new peaks as Napoleon's German allies had to contribute to the ever-growing armies of the Emperor. A whole generation of young men was sent off to war, imposing the burden of conscription essentially on the lower social strata, while in most states the well-off were allowed to buy their sons out of conscription.[5] Little wonder Westphalia and the newly incorporated territories in the south became centres of rebellion during the war against Austria in 1809.

The initial integration of the territories into the Confederation states had taken place with little friction. Displeasure with the new regime was usually limited to symbolic actions, such as the removal of the coats of arms of the new rulers. Conflict first occurred when reforms directly impacted upon the lives of subjects, such as the imposition of new taxes, the abolition of privileges, the prohibition of traditional forms of religious devotion, or the introduction of conscription. These reforms were more likely to provoke protest in newly incorporated or created territories (where traditional loyalties were absent), than in regions enjoying dynastic continuity. This was particularly the case where both old and new provinces of a given region were confessionally distinct from the core of the new ruler's domains as in Baden or Württemberg or where, as in Bavaria, the state engaged in a vigorous policy of modernization and secularization. In Catholic and rural regions, the inhabitants persistently clung to their religious traditions and only grudgingly bent to pressure from the authorities. However, despite the dissent, open conflict centred upon religion remained limited and while religiosity tended to expand rather than contract in these years of crisis, it had lost the power to move believers to revolt.[6]

The introduction of conscription, on the other hand, provoked much wider resistance. Whereas in the core regions of the Confederation states young unwilling recruits tended to desert, levies in newly conquered or incorporated territories provoked open revolt. In southern Germany, revolts remained limited to former Austrian provinces, Imperial cities, small principalities, and secularized ecclesiastical possessions—areas in which conscription was virtually unknown prior to the Napoleonic reorganization of Central Europe. In many cases, unwilling conscripts resorted to traditional ways of protest, revealing the persistence of early modern forms of conflict resolution. There were armed processions to the new regime's nearest seat of authority, loud and public defamations, heavy collective drinking bouts, and the arrest of conscription officials. In general, rural communities with their higher social homogeneity proved much more capable of collective action than the more social and politically fragmented towns. Yet the rebellions remained geographically isolated and were easily suppressed.[7] Socially, the protests were limited to those among the lower social orders who were liable for conscription. The nobility and middle classes initially enjoyed exemption from conscription or could send a substitute, while later reforms made them only partially liable to it.[8] Consequently, local elites remained aloof from rebellions provoked by the introduction of conscription, or even participated in their suppression.

A similar pattern of rebellion and social differentiation was observable in Westphalia. Here, the levy organized under Jerome's government turned into an uprising when about 15,000 rebels gathered in the former Prussian Mark and the former Electorate of Hesse-Kassel in December 1806. Both regions had been repeatedly occupied by the French during the Seven Years War, the memory of which provoked an enduring animosity.[9] Acting alongside the peasantry were many former soldiers and officers left unemployed by the dissolution of the Electorate of Hesse. The rebels succeeded in seizing several garrisons, but lacked organization, concrete goals, or—similar to the situation in the south—support from the local middle classes, who violently opposed the crowds converging on Kassel. This lack of solidarity significantly facilitated the military suppression of the revolt.[10] Indeed, the actions of the rich and educated *Besitz-* and *Bildungsbügertum* in 1806 established a pattern of behaviour that was to become symptomatic of other rebellions during the Napoleonic era in German Central Europe.

As in France, the reforms adopted by the Confederation states were primarily directed at winning the allegiance of the middle classes for the new regimes. Bavaria, in particular, exemplified the extent to which the reforms in these states were a continuation of pre-Revolutionary enlightened absolutism. As a result, most of the bureaucracy willingly provided their new rulers with practical support. Initially, the new states also succeeded in eliciting sympathy among the educated elite. This was particularly the case in Westphalia, where the introduction of the *Code Napoléon*, a constitution, and the first parliament on German soil evinced widespread enthusiasm among the *Bildungsbürgertum* and reform-minded nobility. However, this policy was progressively undermined by the demands of war such as rising taxes, conscription, and limitations to trade by the Continental System which had an increasing impact on everyday life. While the southern princes could, at the very least, rely on the dynastic loyalty of a portion of their subjects, in Westphalia neither the ambitious reforms nor the economic and cultural impact of the royal court were enough to compensate for the growing burdens Napoleonic rule placed on the inhabitants.[11]

3   The year 1809

When Napoleon invaded Spain in 1808 and was met by fierce resistance,[12] Berlin and Vienna observed these events with great interest and the war parties in both states thought about imitating the resistance. In Prussia, Gneisenau fused the concept of small war (as used during the Seven Years War) with elements of a people's war, developing plans for a *Volkskrieg* (people's war) in Westphalia. However, he stood as little chance of realizing his plans as the officers who clamoured for an alliance with Austria in 1809, since the Prussian monarch would not countenance a war without Russian support.[13] In contrast, the forced abdication of the Spanish Bourbons led the Austrian Emperor to endorse the war plans of his foreign minister, Johann Philipp von Stadion. Stadion and his colleagues circulated pamphlets attacking Napoleon's policies in Spain and Italy and distributed patriotic propaganda such as militia songs (*Landwehrlieder*) and poetry emphasizing the commonality of German and Austrian interests. Long before the so-called German uprising in Prussia, Vienna had employed the full panoply of propaganda in support of a patriotic-nationalist mobilization against France, expecting the inhabitants of the Confederation states to take up arms and side with the Austrian forces.[14]

Despite all these efforts, the propagated *Volkskrieg* never materialized. In Bavaria, neither the behaviour of the Austrian troops in past campaigns nor

Habsburg expansionist ambitions had been forgotten. Only in Tyrol and in Vorarlberg—both former Habsburg territories which had been given to Bavaria in 1805—did true revolts erupt. They quickly spread to neighbouring Alpine regions and parts of Upper Austria. In Westphalia, in contrast, the rebellions did not involve peasant uprisings, but instead took the form of incursions into Westphalian territory by Prussian *Freikorps* and attempts at a military *putsch*.

3.1   Westphalia

Westphalia differed from the Confederation states in southern Germany in that it did not consist of a core territory with a long dynastic tradition onto which newly conquered regions had been grafted. Instead, the model state incorporated several Upper Saxon provinces and former bishoprics, with three large territories with strong regional and dynastic traditions: Prussia west of the Elbe, the Principality of Brunswick, and the Electorate of Hesse whose rulers never gave up their claim to power. The state had also inherited a large group of unemployed soldiers and officers who had previously served in the Prussian and Hessian armies. These groups, especially Hessian veterans of the American War of Independence, formed an enduring source of unrest.[15] Furthermore, to the east, Prussian patriots concocted plans for insurrection, while military reformers and part of the Prussian officer corps argued in favour of a new war against Napoleon. Given these factors it is not surprising that the Kingdom of Westphalia was shaken by rebellion more than any other state, especially in the former Prussian and Hessian provinces. For the most part, the revolts took the form of military incursions by active or former Prussian officers like the dispossessed Duke of Brunswick, who circumvented Prussian neutrality by trying to recruit troops in his former territories.

The level of cooperation by the population in the various uprisings in the old Hessian provinces varied greatly. The ex-Hessian Colonel Emmerich hoped to resurrect the Electorate via an attack on Marburg and had recruited former Hessian soldiers along with peasants from several villages in Upper Hesse to his cause. The revolt was suppressed in a matter of hours, however, as his goal of restoration proved unattractive to townspeople and students alike. More effective was the cooperation between the former Prussian, later Westphalian, officer Wilhelm von Dörnberg and the Homberg lawyer, Siegmund Peter Martin, an early National Liberal who had participated in the unrest of 1806. In an attempt to restore the old regime, Dörnberg tried to launch a military *putsch;* he gathered Hessian nobles and officers around him and sought Martin's support in forming the peasant rebels from Homberg and Wolfhagen into a traditional military formation *(Landsturm).* Martin, however, did not want a return to the ancien regime. Instead, he favoured the establishment of a constitutional, liberal state. Inadequate coordination between the two movements and the loyalty to Jerome of the

Westphalian military (on whose defection Dörnberg's plan had depended) rendered the rebellion easy to suppress.[16]

As in 1806, the peasantry and former soldiers provided the social basis of the rebellions. They were motivated by a desire to return to the conditions of the ancien regime and an amelioration of immediate burdens. Moreover, the goals of restoration and dynastic loyalty strengthened their bond with the rebellions' military leaders. Only Martin's political circle went beyond this conservative framework, but it did not ultimately exert a discernable influence. The overwhelming majority of the urban middle classes distanced themselves from these events. Lacking military support from Prussia, the insurrections did not seriously endanger the Napoleonic regime.

3.2   The Austrian influence: Tyrol, Vorarlberg, southern Germany

In contrast, Austrian military support played a crucial role in underpinning the rebellions in the south. During its centuries-old affiliation to the Habsburg Monarchy, Tyrol had enjoyed extensive autonomy from Vienna. Its privileges included its own military system, exemption from conscription and limited taxation. Following its incorporation into Bavaria in 1805, this privileged county became the dependent province of a centralized, absolutist state, bent on reform and guided by radical Enlightenment principles. It was Munich's rigid religious policy as much as the abolition of privileges, increasing taxation and conscription that provoked widespread hatred of the Bavarian regime. Austrian emissaries and Viennese propaganda made every effort to enflame this discontent. Pamphlets on the Vendée revolt and the war in Spain were designed to propagate the problems guerrilla war posed for Napoleonic rule. When the rebellion finally occurred, its timing was coordinated with the invasion of Habsburg troops, while Vienna also provided the rebels with arms and money.[17]

Thus, the Tyrolese rebellion was not a spontaneous people's uprising, but a deliberate action planned with the knowledge and support of Vienna. Its organizational backbone was provided by a still-functioning militia system. The rebels aimed at restoring regional privileges and the traditional role of the Church. As such, their rebellion represented resistance to modernizing tendencies and a demand for a return to the status quo *ante*, while, as traditional legitimists, they fought against both Bavaria and France in order to return Tyrol to Austrian rule.

Although a conception of German identity played a certain role in their rhetoric, the Tyrolese rebels did not regard their revolt as a declaration for a German nation state. Instead, their allegiance belonged to the Habsburg Monarchy and the traditional political system of the ancien regime. It was therefore not a German uprising, but a traditional, anti-centralist and religiously motivated revolt against the anti-clerical, modernizing policies of Bavaria that, within the context of international politics, became a component in the wider conflict between France and the Habsburg Monarchy.[18]

Only in the outlying districts of Tyrol, which shared an homogenous social structure and where Catholic influence was strong, was there widespread participation by the population, akin to similar events in isolated, outlying provinces in France, Switzerland and southern Europe.[19] By contrast, the townspeople of Tyrol's capital, Innsbruck, remained passive, reflecting the same general picture that had occurred in Westphalia in 1806 and 1809. This also was discernable in Vorarlberg, Tyrol's neighbouring province which had enjoyed similar privileges under Habsburg rule. Here too, there was discontent over the modernizing policies which followed incorporation into Bavaria, not least because the new borders and tollgates cut off existing markets. However, the decision to cooperate with the Tyrolese rebels was far from unanimous. Support was strongest amongst the so-called highland estates based in Feldkirch, which included the outlying mountainous regions. Here, society was not only strongly influenced by the Catholic Church, but the region was also particularly badly affected by the new Bavarian policies. The majority of the poverty-stricken populace depended on seasonal work in neighbouring countries and were virtually deprived of their most important source of income when passports for travel outside the area were banned to enforce conscription. It was only in the highlands that volunteer sharpshooter companies were formed before the official decision to join the Tyrolese rebellion was made, and it was only here that the struggle continued even after Austria's defeat at Wagram.

In Vorarlberg's more urbanized Alpenrhein valley and in the Lake Constance region around Bregenz, the estates representing the lowland regions only hesitantly joined the military levy. The Bregenz Civil Guard, for example, steadfastly refused to participate in the fighting. Similarly, lowlanders were a minority among the military leaders of the Vorarlberg revolt. Representatives from this region, whose economy and society were based on trade, early industrialization and a strong central government, at length pleaded for an armistice. Meanwhile, the peasant troops from the highlands took prisoner the General Commissar and Bregenz lawyer, Anton Schneider, after he advocated peace and attempted to hinder the retreat of the beaten Austrian troops.[20]

The extent to which socio-economic conditions and political action were linked is most clearly illustrated by the anti-conscription unrest in Mergentheim, a territory previously controlled by the Teutonic Order of Knights. Here unrest flared into a veritable and widespread revolt as Austrian troops drew near in 1809. During the war against Austria, Napoleon had dissolved the Teutonic Order and deposed its Grand Master, Anton Viktor, brother of the Austrian Emperor. Without waiting for the official realloca-tion of the region by Napoleon, Württemberg dispatched troops to occupy the principalities of Hoch- and Deutschmeister. While the town's represent-atives and magistrates welcomed the new ruler, the peasantry did not attend the official ceremony of homage. Consequently, they did not feel bound by an oath of loyalty to the new lord[21] and so considered themselves exempt from direct obedience. Consequently, they violently resisted any attempts to remove young men from their midst to supply the Württemberg army. In this situation, rumours made politics. As the Austrian army was said to be approaching, the number of rebels swelled into the hundreds. They seized the town, imprisoned the Württemberg officials, removed the new ruler's symbols of authority and, in hopes of an Austrian victory, demanded the suspension of recruitment until the war was over. The Mergentheim military contingent, a force the city had been obliged to raise under the Holy Roman Empire during times of war, along with the Civil Guard resisted the rebels and defended the Württemberg officials. Meanwhile, the urban middle classes not only avoided the rebel villages and parishes, but actively helped to hold off the peasants until reinforcements from Württemberg arrived.[22]

Clearly, the townspeople of the Confederation states feared that the spread of unrest would lead to a rebellion by the lower orders, a social group that the enlightened sections of the *Bürgertum* regarded as hopelessly backward. In the towns, unrest was therefore not only suppressed by the military, but also by the local Civil Guard.

4   Conclusion

Contrary to older historical interpretations, there was no sustained national movement or even a rebellion capable of uniting social groups against the Napoleonic regime in Central Europe in 1809. In fact, the corresponding events were primarily inspired by rather specific regional motives. Wherever rebellion did occur, it was predominantly aimed at restoring traditional rule.

Succoured by strong support from both the Court in Vienna and the Austrian military, a popular peasant movement did develop in the less socially stratified Alpine regions. The movement in the south was to defend Tyrol and Vorarlberg's traditional privileges from the Bavarian state's modernizing and anti-clerical policies. The war, Austria's pretensions to reclaim the region, and the leading role played by the clergy lent this royalist rebellion moral legitimacy and wide appeal. The rebellion was essentially driven by the rural population, including the farming elite. The middle and enlightened classes, on the other hand, maintained their distance. In the more urban areas, the enthusiasm for rebellion was weak and soon declined. Nevertheless, the support of Austrian troops enabled Tyrolese rebels to operate for over six months, posing serious difficulties to the Bavarian and French military.

In northern Westphalia, revolt took the form of military incursions or attempted coups led by serving or former Prussian officers in contact with patriotic circles or the Austrian military. The participation of the population did not go beyond basic declarations of sympathy and the only true rebellions occurred in the old Hessian territories. Here too officers played a leading role. The main goal was the restoration of previous rulers. Political and constitutional concepts remained an exception, while religious motives were wholly absent. The uprisings were sustained by peasants and former soldiers, while the middle classes remained either indifferent or actively hostile. The individual incidents soon collapsed without endangering the Westphalian government.

Despite these differences, there were some structural commonalities between the two regions which allow for conclusions regarding the character of the Napoleonic regime. As in previous years, such as 1806, the uprisings of 1809 occurred only where the demands of modernization were accompanied by a crisis of legitimacy and, in the Catholic south, by a disruption of religious traditions. Thus, it is no coincidence that rebellions were geographically centred on Bavaria and Westphalia, since both states vigorously pursued reform. For the rebels, the enemy was not primarily France, but the newly-created states of the Confederation of the Rhine. The military suppression of earlier revolts meant that the 1809 rebellions could only take place under the influence of the dominant German powers and could only develop within the context of renewed warfare.

As in other European regions, the magnitude of unrest and potential for rebellion depended on the existence of several factors: the presence of the French military and its allies, the behaviour of the native elites, the existence of traditional forms of militia organization, the geographical position of a given area, and the expectation of military aid from the anti-Napoleonic powers.[23] Finally, perceptions of dynastic legitimacy and the social structure of the regions affected, played crucial roles in transforming latent unrest into open revolt. Successful insurrections only occurred in German Central Europe where the Napoleonic regime had a weak military presence, where outside military aid was expected, where militia traditions could provide organization, and where the elite provided unambiguous support—factors that were only present in Tyrol.[24]

Events in Westphalia and Tyrol might be described as a military insurrection from above and a rural-clerical people's movement respectively. However, despite the sporadic German national rhetoric that accompanied both cases, the importance of dynastic elements must not be underestimated. The aim of the uprisings was the restoration of the ancien regime. At their core, they were traditional revolts led by coalitions of noble officers, soldiers, the clergy (in the case of Tyrol) and the peasantry, groups that had formed the pillars of the pre-Napoleonic regimes and governments. The only exception was the Westphalian lawyer, Martin, whose early liberal and constitutional concepts had little influence. Apart from Martin and his personal circle, the *Bürgertum* and reformist nobility did not join the rebels. They were separated from the rebels by both political goals and social worlds.

In contemporary perceptions, the insurgents were in no sense the heroes that later epochs would make of them. Irregular warfare and Catholic religious fanaticism were abhorred by the educated public. Far from regarding them as heroes, the educated elites saw both the Tyrolese and Spanish rebels as backward mountain men manipulated by the Catholic Church.[25] The educated middle classes had nothing in common with these forces of the ancien regime. Instead, they were committed to political renewal. In 1809 their interests in a transformation of the social order, their demands for political participation, and their hopes for personal and social advancement still seemed best served by the reformist states of the Confederation of the Rhine.

Notes

1. See also E. Zehetbauer, *Landwehr gegen Napoleon. Österreichs erste Miliz und der Nationalkrieg von 1809* (Vienna, 1999). M. Rauchensteiner, *Kaiser Franz und Erzherzog Carl. Dynastie und Heerwesen in Österreich 1796–1809* (Vienna, 1976). O. Heinl, *Heereswesen und Volksbewaffnung in Vorderösterreich im Zeitalter Josefs II. und der Revolutionskriege* (Freiburg, 1941) and R. Lenz, *Volksbewaffnung und Staatsidee in Österreich 1792–1797* (Vienna, 1926). For Prussia, see O. Büsch, *Militärsystem und Sozialleben im alten Preußen, 1713–1807* (Berlin, 1962) and C. Clark, *Preußen. Aufstieg und Niedergang, 1600–1947* (Munich, 2007).
2. See H. Molitor, *Vom Untertan zum Administré. Studien zur französischen Herrschaft und zum Verhalten der Bevölkerung im Rhein-Mosel-Raum von den Revolutionskriegen bis zum Ende der napoleonischen Zeit* (Wiesbaden, 1980). J. Smets, *Les Pays Rhénans 1794–1814. Le comportement des Rhénans face à l'occupation française* (Bern, 1997). Idem, 'Von der Dorfidylle zur preußischen Nation. Sozialdisziplinierung der linksrheinischen Bevölkerung durch die Franzosen am Beispiel der allgemeinen Wehrpflicht, 1802–1814', *Historische Zeitschrift*, 262 (1996), 695–738. M. Rowe, *From Reich to State. The Rhineland in the Revolutionary Age, 1780–1830* (Cambridge, 2003). Idem, 'Resistance, Collaboration or Third Way? Responses to Napoleonic Rule in Germany', in *Popular Resistance in the French Wars*, ed. C. J. Esdaile (Basingstoke, 2004), 67–90. C. Hudemann-Simon, 'Réfractaires et déserteurs de la Grande Armée en Sarre (1802–1813)', *Revue Historique* 277 (1987): 11–45. R. Dufraisse, 'Une rébellion en pays annexé: Le "soulèvement" des gardes nationales de la Sarre en 1809', *Bulletin de la Société d'histoire moderne* 14/10 (1969): 2–6.
3. For further references, see E. Fehrenbach, *Vom Ancien Régime zum Wiener Kongress* (Munich, [4]2001). Ch. Dipper (ed.) *Napoleonische Herrschaft in Deutschland und Italien—Verwaltung und Justiz* (Berlin, 1995).
4. See J. Flemming and D. Krause-Vilmar (eds), *Fremdherrschaft und Freiheit. Das Koenigreich Westphalen als napoleonischer Modellstaat* (Kassel, 2009). A. Owzar, 'Frankreich in Westfalen. Konstitutionalisierung und Parlamentarisierung unter Napoleon (1806–1813)', *Westfalen* 79 (2001): 97–117. M. Hecker, *Napoleonischer Konstitutionalismus in Deutschland* (Berlin, 2005). H. Brandt and E. Grothe (eds), *Rheinbündischer Konstitutionalismus* (Frankfurt/Main, 2007).
5. See H. Berding, *Napoleonische Herrschafts- und Gesellschaftspolitik im Königreich Westfalen 1807–1813* (Göttingen, 1973).

6. For more detail and further references, see U. Planert, *Der Mythos vom Befreiungskrieg. Frankreichs Kriege und der deutsche Süden 1792–1841* (Paderborn, 2007).

7. See Planert, *Mythos*, 424–37. Idem, 'Militär, Krieg und zivile Gesellschaft. Rekrutierungsverweigerung im Süden des Alten Reiches', in *Krieg und Umbruch in Mitteleuropa um 1800. Erfahrungsgeschichte(n) auf dem Weg in eine neue Zeit*, ed. Idem (Paderborn, 2009), 111–136. T. Kies, 'Rosenkranzrevolution und Rekrutierungsverweigerung: Reaktionen auf den Umbruch ländlicher Lebenswelten 1800–1815', in ibid. 137–156.

8. See Planert, *Mythos*.

9. See H. Carl, *Okkupation und Regionalismus. Die preußischen Westprovinzen im Siebenjährigen Krieg* (Mainz, 1993).

10. See W. Speitkamp, 'Unruhe, Protest, Aufstand. Widerstand und Widersetzlichkeit gegen die napoleonische "Fremdherrschaft"', in Flemming and Krause-Vilmar, *Fremdherrschaft*, 135–152. Idem, 'Sozialer und politischer Protest im napoleonischen Deutschland', in *Hundert Jahre Historische Kommission für Hessen 1897–1997*, ed. W. Heinemeyer (Marburg, 1997), 713–730.

11. Cf. A. Owzar, 'Eine Nation auf Widerruf. Zum politischen Bewußtseinswandel im Königreich Westphalen', in *Fremde Herrscher—fremdes Volk. Inklusions- und Exklusionsfiguren bei Herrschaftswechseln in Europa*, ed. H. Schnabel-Schüle and A. Gestrich (Frankfurt/Main, 2006), 43–72, esp. 50. G. B. Clemens, 'Fürstendiener— Kollaborateure? Die Beamten im Königreich Westphalen', in Flemming/ Krause-Vilmar, *Fremdherrschaft und Freiheit*, 119–134. M. Lahrkamp, *Münster in napoleonischer Zeit 1800–1815* (Münster, 1976). D. S. Puhle, *Das Herzogtum Braunschweig-Wolfenbüttel im Königreich Westphalen und seine Restitution 1806–1815* (Braunschweig, 1989). S. Brakensiek, *Fürstendiener—Staatsbeamte—Bürger. Amtsführung und Lebenswelt der Ortsbeamten in niederhesseischen Kleinstädten, 1750–1830* (Göttingen, 1999). B. Severin-Barboutie, *Französische Herrschaftspolitik und Modernisierung. Verwaltungs- und Verfassungsreform im Großherzogtum Berg, 1806–1813* (Munich, 2008). B. Wunder, *Die badische Beamtenschaft zwischen Rheinbund und Reichsgründung, 1806–1871* (Stuttgart, 1998). W. Demel, *Der bayerische Staatsabsolutismus, 1806/08–1817* (Munich, 1983). G. Dethlefs, A. Owzar, G. Weiß (eds) *Modell und Wirklichkeit. Politik, Kultur und Gesellschaft im Großherzogtum Berg und im Königreich Westphalen 1806–1813* (Paderborn, 2008). M. Bartsch (ed.) *'König Lustik!?' Jérôme Bonaparte und der Modellstaat Königreich Westphalen* (Munich, 2008).

12. See M. Broers, *Europe under Napoleon, 1799–1815* (London/New York, 1996).

13. Regarding the Spanish factor in Austrian politics in 1808/09, see R. Wohlfeil, *Spanien und die deutsche Erhebung* (Wiesbaden, 1965). for Prussia, see Clark, *Preußen*, 400–409.

14. See Wohlfeil, *Spanien*. Zehetbauer, *Landwehr*. H. Rössler, *Graf Johann Philipp Stadion. Napoleons deutscher Gegenspieler*, vol. 2 (Vienna, 1966), 20.

15. See I. Auerbach, *Die Hessen in Amerika, 1776–1783* (Darmstadt/Marburg, 1996).

16. See Speitkamp, *Unruhe*. K. Lynker, *Geschichte der Insurrektionen wider das westphälische Gouvernement* (Kassel, 1857).

17. For further references, see M. Hamm, *Die bayerische Integrationspolitik in Tirol 1806–1814* (München, 1996), 314–320. L. C. Türkel, *Das publizistische Wirken des Joseph Freiherrn von Hormayr* (Vienna, PhD thesis, 1980). J. Fontana, *Geschichte des Landes Tirol, vol. 2, Von der Restauration bis zur Revolution, 1814–1848* (Bozen, 1986).

18. See F. G. Eyck, *Loyal Rebels. Andreas Hofer and the Tyrolean uprising of 1809* (Lanham, 1986). L. Cole, 'Religion und patriotische Aktion in Deutsch-Tirol, 1790–1814', in *Patriotismus und Nationsbildung am Ende des Heiligen Römischen Reichs*, ed. O. Dann, M. Hroch and J. Kroll (Cologne, 2003), 345–378. M. P. Schennach, *Revolte in der Region. Zur Tiroler Erhebung von 1809* (Innsbruck, 2009). A. Oberhofer, *Der andere Hofer. Der Mensch hinter dem Mythos* (Innsbruck, 2009). B. Mazohl and B. Mertelseder (eds), *Abschied vom Freiheitskampf. Tirol und 1809 zwischen politischer Realität und Verklärung* (Innsbruck, 2009). B. Mazohl and B. Mertelseder (eds), *Tirol 1809: Geschichte und Erinnerung* (Innsbruck, 2010).

19. S. G. Heeb, 'Logik des traditionalistischen Aufstandes. Revolten gegen die Helvetische Republik 1798–1803', *Historische Anthropologie* 9/2 (2001), 233–253. Broers, *Europe*

20. M. Tiefenthaler and A. Benzer, *Vorarlberg 1809. Ein Kampf um Freiheit und Selbständigkeit* (Bregenz, 1959). H. Weitensfelder, *Industrie-Provinz. Vorarlberg in der Frühindustrialisierung, 1740–1870* (Frankfurt/Main, 2001).

21. In an age of rational rule, the oath of loyalty had long lost its importance as a constitutive of lordship, but its sense was easily resurrected in the conditions of 1809.

22. See M. Gindele, 'Der Aufstand der Bauern des Oberamts Tauber im Jahre 1809', *Zeitschrift für württembergische Landesgeschichte*, 46 (1987): 163–203.

23. See C. J. Esdaile (ed.) *Popular Resistance in the French Wars* (Basingstoke, 2004).

24. See Esdaile, *Popular Resistance*.

25. See Planert, *Mythos*, 568–571. Wohlfeil, *Spanien*.

12

Napoleonic Rule in German Central Europe: Compliance and Resistance

Katherine Aaslestad

On 21 November 1808, Hamburger Ferdinand Beneke thought of Spain: 'The war between Napoleon and Spain has begun; it must destroy Satan's Empire, or God has surely abandoned us. At the Town Hall the excitement on the news from Bayonne is general and widespread; it is our last spark of hope.'[1] One year later, news of Major Schill's stand against the French captured Beneke's interest.[2] As revealed in his diary, letters and public papers, Beneke openly grieved for the loss of his republic's autonomy and constitution, lamented the decline of commerce, sympathized with smugglers arrested by the *douaniers* at the city gates, and viewed both Spanish fighters and Schill as heroes battling against a corrupt Empire. In practice, however, he offered no resistance to French authorities in Hamburg until spring 1813. Following the dramatic events of a local uprising, the departure of French forces and the arrival of Russian Cossacks, Beneke volunteered for a local militia and spent the next year in military camps across northern Germany working within the Hanseatic Directory to liberate the Hanseatic cities. Beneke's experiences illustrate the relationship between militarization, compliance and resistance in Napoleon's Empire.

Despite geographical and political differences, and varied forms of imperial subjugation, intense militarization characterized life in the Empire for German states from both the inner and outer Empire, or to draw on Imperial terms *pays réunis, pays conquis* and *pays alliés*.[3] The territories and states in northern Germany—occupied in 1806 and annexed to the Empire in 1811—experienced the combined burdens of occupation and economic warfare. For citizens throughout German Central Europe, with Imperial rule came the militarization of civil society, since military occupation and conscription (and concomitant administrative reforms) were essential to the functioning of the Empire. Soldiers were omnipresent, regardless of their nationality, and they represented Napoleon's new order. In private homes and in public spaces they symbolized a new authority as well as cultural, economic and political systems imposed by the armed power of the Empire.

The historiography

In the past, civilians' experience of Imperial occupation and conscription received marginal attention from German historiography. The subject found no place in the older literature which concentrated on the nationalist narrative of the Wars of Liberation,[4] and newer research has centred on state building and the reform movement associated with Napoleon's new order. Other scholars, following Stuart Woolf's seminal work in 1991,[5] consider the mechanics of occupation and conscription but only in terms of them as the tools of Napoleonic conquest.

Recently, the subject of popular responses against the Napoleonic Empire has come to prominence. Some scholars downplay the ideological motivations for resistance and highlight the material basis of popular hostility. Such works underscore how day-to-day problems caused by military rule—namely, declining economies, requisitioning, billeting and conscription—led to popular resentment and in some cases to violent upheaval. Other works attribute pockets of anti-French sentiment primarily to social elites, in direct contrast to Marxist approaches that emphasize class struggle as the basis of social conflict.[6] Yet others interpret popular resistance as traditional peasant uprisings and social protest, and as indicators of a crisis of modernization or transition to a bureaucratic state.[7] This chapter emphasizes the shared experiences of imperial rule and the militarization of civil society as seen in military occupation and conscription, underscoring these as the common origin of growing anti-Napoleon sentiment in the regionally and politically varied German-speaking territories.

The terminological problem: collaboration and resistance

Discussion of non-French experience of Napoleonic rule usually passes via the dichotomy of collaboration and resistance. Yet such an approach is problematic since these ambiguous and relative terms do not render the essential complexity of the issue.[8] Civilian response, as we will see, could range from ideological alliances, through functional collaboration, to acquiescence, not to mention passive, symbolic, and armed resistance. Moreover, acts of resistance did not necessarily indicate efforts at liberation from oppression. Resistance could signify popular discontent related to the problems of daily life under military occupation: hunger, plunder, unemployment or poor working conditions, increasing levels of violence, and a decline in standards of living. Generally, the closer soldiers came to civilians in everyday life, the greater the likelihood of some form of popular response, often understood by both parties as resistance. Occupation and conscription provided the prominent framework for both civil/military contact and confrontations in German Central Europe. In fact, civilian difficulties with occupation and conscription ultimately stripped the Empire of legitimacy and generated widespread popular hostility.

I   Accommodation and compliance

The earliest reactions in German central Europe to Napoleonic rule began with accommodation and compliance. Prior to 1806, most German states preferred not to take sides in the ongoing international warfare. Austria seemed too weak to offer them protection and Prussia too unreliable and even dangerous. Armed opposition to French rule would be counter-productive and self-destructive. On the one hand the northern Hanseatic city states lobbied for their traditional neutrality, on the other many German states favoured a Third Germany guaranteed by France and Russia.[9] Peace and stability clearly remained the central concern of the population at large.[10]

In the Rhineland, for example, with the years of lawlessness and violence caused by the Revolutionary Armies and their enemies still fresh in mind, most desired accommodation with the French by 1806, especially if the government could return order and stability. In fact, personal and institutional patterns of collaboration or *ralliement* often ensured the short-term success of French centralization and modernization policies within the Confederation of the Rhine. Michael Rowe's work on pragmatic compliance in the Rhineland demonstrates that 'hard-nosed self-interest, not broader ideological considerations' motivated Rhinelanders to comply with French occupiers.[11] As for the south Germans, Ute Planert details how, after a decade of warfare, numerous figures of varied political backgrounds celebrated Bonaparte as a 'Prince of Peace,' a bulwark of bourgeois progress, restorer of the church, and implementer of law and order.[12] On paper, military alliances with Napoleon seemed a clear improvement on potential Revolutionary violence and disorder. Napoleonic administration in the Rhineland and other regions sought pragmatically to win over popular loyalties with the restoration order via centralized power.[13]

Far from attempting any kind of futile idealistic resistance to the Napoleonic regime, local elites throughout the Empire prepared to cooperate with the Imperial establishment in order to temper the new structural changes and to further their own interests. As in other German states, members of Hamburg's government continued to serve under the French administration following the city's annexation into the Empire in 1811. They sought to neutralize the impact of the French and salvage what they could of the city's former prosperity and political culture.[14] Likewise, Germans elsewhere generally sought to accommodate Napoleon's Imperial Order, assuming it would lead to stability and in some cases authentic reform and prosperity. The brutal disappointment of these hopes is the key to understanding the varied forms of resistance to, and popular mobilization against, the Empire by 1813.

Conscription and occupation

Stability was to remain illusive because of the emperor's policy that the war should pay for itself. Thus, the burdens of conscription and military occupation—billeting, requisitions, contributions, tribute and, in dire cases, plunder, rape, and violence—were ever present in civilian life. Military service, expanded under Napoleon to an unprecedented extent, penetrated and disrupted civil society on a variety of levels. Its intrusion into private and social lives destroyed family life, local economies and social equilibrium, and it emerged as the most unpopular demand of Imperial rule. Many Germans, traditionally exempt from military service, found conscription intolerable, in particular in areas where soldiering had been a fate reserved for the poorest of the poor.

In the Rhineland, where conscription remained low until 1805 and rose steadily until it exceeded that of France by 1810, 80,000 men were drafted into the *Grande Armée,* and more than half did not survive the wars.[15] Nor was conscription merely an Imperial imposition. Allied states and *Royaumes frères* too adopted the French recruitment system and enlisted growing numbers of men to meet their quotas. In the 1809 campaign against Austria, the Rhine confederation provided 120,680 soldiers, over 47,000 of which came from Bavaria.[16] Between 1809 and 1813 over 70,000 Westphalians were conscripted, and of the 22,000 who marched into Russia only 1,500 survived.[17] For Württemberg it was even worse; of the 15,800 strong initial contingent only 500 survived the Russian snows.[18] Thus, not only did the militarization of society through conscription lead to death for very many through disease, wounds, the elements and combat, it also placed hardships on the societies left behind, depriving rural economies of subsistence labour, generating social asymmetry, sparing those with privileges and assets and consuming the poor and rural populations. These inequalities were the source of great social tensions.

As for occupation, this could come in many ways. It could originate from a military campaign, as in the case of Lübeck in 1806, when approximately 53,000 Imperial troops drove 21,000 Prussian soldiers from the neutral city. Following brutal street combat and house to house fighting, Imperial soldiers molested residents and plundered the city for three days until Bernadotte interceded to halt the violence. The hundreds of wounded soldiers that had to be housed in private and public buildings and the requisitions to be fulfilled in support of the occupying troops drove city officials to appeal directly to Bonaparte for relief. The emperor did reduce the number of occupying troops to 3,000, but he insisted that Lübeck assume all costs for them.[19] In contrast, Hamburg and Bremen surrendered peacefully to Imperial forces. But their fate was as severe as Lübeck's. In November 1806 6,000 imperial troops arrived in Hamburg and this was to grow to 12,000 soldiers and 600 officers and remain on average at that level until 1810.[20] The arrival of toll officers and other imperial administrators added to the number. The small city of Harburg, just across the Elbe from Hamburg, was to become a French garrison town, providing quarters for 3,524 officers, 77,730 soldiers and 3,999 horses over the course of six months in 1807.[21] In December 1807 Ferdinand Beneke reflected in his diary on the variety of foreign soldiers: 'We have seen French, Italian, Dutch, and Spanish [soldiers] celebrate as we lost our peace, trade, prosperity, and freedom. We have been plundered one and all, we are slaves to foreign occupation, and cut off from all sources of acquisition....'[22]

In the Hanseatic cities, as elsewhere, residents had to provide the occupying troops with daily rations of food and drink and monetary allowances for officers. The French military requisitioned private and public buildings and obliged the cities to procure coats, boots, shirts and medical supplies for the Imperial armies. By September 1807 the French military had requisitioned stalls, cellars and attics to house new troops and inns and boarding homes for officers.[23] Cities, towns and villages alike were required to sustain and nourish Napoleon's soldiers, regardless of their capacity to meet these obligations. In Prussia between 1806 and 1808, Berlin's population of 145,900 supported 15,000 French soldiers and officers, whereas in the rural Kurmark region outside the city, 22,700 soldiers were billeted in farming villages creating serious grain shortages and deprivation.[24] The quartering of Imperial soldiers placed a severe burden on small towns; Krempe, near Glückstadt in Holstein, with a population of 1,000 inhabitants and 200 homes, had to house and feed over 2,000 soldiers in 1813.[25]

In times of peace, only select cities or garrison towns supported military occupation, however during military campaigns both urban and rural populations had to feed, clothe and house thousands of soldiers, officers and their horses on the move. The south German states experienced waves of thousands of soldiers marching through their villages, towns and cities. The numbers grew with each conflict, as 450,000 in 1805 became 600,000 by 1809. Civilian populations supplied them with food and lodging.[26] Though an example from Upper Austria shows what could happen. The relatively small city of Linz, occupied several times in a row during the war of the Second Coalition, quartered over 50,000 men between December 1800 and February 1801; the War of the Third Coalition brought an increase in soldiers between November 1805 and February 1806; finally, in the war of 1809 more than 224,163 men and 198,385 horses resided in the city between May 1809 and January 1810. Along with daily requirements, occupying armies requisitioned thousands of coats, boots, shoes, pants, horseshoes, saddle-belts, as well as hay, straw and livestock.[27] As the number of soldiers increased, so did the support demanded from the civilian population in a time of near constant warfare.

Enemies and allies alike paid the staggering expenses of conscription and occupation. The two-year occupation of Prussia cost nearly 217 million taler; Berlin spent 51.1 million taler in billeting and contributions.[28] Following the Franco-Saxon peace treaty in 1806, Saxony assumed the burdens of military occupation and paid France 25 million francs as war indemnity.[29] In Linz, requisitions and contributions during the third French occupation in 1809 ruined city finances and led to bankruptcy in 1811. The city did not resolve its financial losses until the 1840s.[30] In October 1807 Bonaparte demanded that the Hanseatic cities pay 400,000 francs monthly in salary for his troops at a time when occupation costs alone had risen to over 10 million francs.[31] By 1811, Hamburg directed one third of its finances to outfitting and arming Napoleon's army.[32] Even partner states from the Confederation of the Rhine paid heavily. The French alliance cost the state for Bavaria 55.7 million gulden, and financing troops for the Russian campaign alone totalled 600,000 gulden for Baden.[33] By 1809, Bavarian state authorities had come to recognize that it was impossible for civilians to continue to pay the combination of French taxes, requisitions, and tariffs.[34] Military expenses generated huge community expenditures. To prepare for the invasion of Russia, France turned Prussia into a deployment zone for the invasion troops in 1812; this renewed occupation cost the Kingdom 85 million taler for flour, drink, horses, oxen, munitions, fieldhospital supplies, as well as an outfitted auxiliary corps of 30,000 men for the *Grand Armée*. The Prussian Monarchy faced bankruptcy.[35]

Conscription, occupation and billeting cost communities more than money. Epidemic disease among both humans and livestock accompanied soldiers to cities, towns and villages. Outbreaks of typhus followed troop movements in south German states in 1813, where Stuttgart lost 3,000 residents, and Freiburg's death rate tripled with the loss of civilians and soldiers estimated at 17,000.[36] Sexually transmitted diseases and unwanted pregnancies also followed the soldiers, and the coupling of deteriorating economic conditions with military occupation led to a drastic rise in prostitution and illegitimate births. For example, prior to 1790, 1 child in 57 was illegitimate in Baden's town of Villingen, yet between 1800 and 1810, that number rose to 1 in 18, and between 1810 and 1820 to 1 in 6.[37] Difficulties associated with the fair distribution of the burdens of conscription and quartering divided occupied societies and generated great social tensions, despite the establishment of Quartering and Requisitions Deputations in cities like Hamburg and Bremen. The combination of quartering and requisitions, declining economies, and the abandonment of poor relief programs by the French led to growing criminality among the lower classes. Respectable citizens viewed rising crime with worry and suspicion, as it revealed a fundamental decline in the public authority that lay beneath traditional public order and stability.[38]

Economic warfare between France and Britain compounded the hardships imposed on civilians. If scholars still debate the long-term structural consequences of Napoleon's economic strategies, it is clear that the

Continental System's disruption of traditional trade routes and markets, the rapid decline in colonial goods and raw materials, the shortage of liquid assets and the rising number of insolvencies—in short the subjugation of continental economies to serve France—led to wide-scale economic dislocation for most Europeans.[39] Although economic dislocation took place unevenly across German Central Europe, commercial and industrial decline detrimentally influenced the livelihood of the majority of civilians as they underwrote Napoleon's wars. Following the arrival of more French troops in Hamburg in August 1810, Beneke articulated the combined burdens of the Continental Blockade and military occupation: 'Quartering is oppressive. Only well-fed and fine-clothed soldiers strut around the market places that once engaged in commerce'.[40]

Imperial tariffs also contributed to economic hardship. Imperial tolls on imports and exports, including basic foodstuffs, combined with taxes increased the price of daily groceries.[41] Throughout German Central Europe Napoleonic economic exploitation combined with ongoing military campaigns caused rapid inflation; in Hamburg bread sold for 1 mark in 1798 and rose to 16 marks by 1813.[42] In Linz, wheat more than doubled in price between 1800 and 1806, and by 1817, it had increased tenfold from original costs in 1800.[43] Likewise, in southern Germany food prices increased by one third between 1800 and 1806, and an additional 20 to 30 per cent between 1811 and 1815.[44] The decline of the economy and rising unemployment, in combination with ongoing requisitioning and billeting, generated a general breakdown in law and order throughout German Central Europe. Declining livelihoods and destitution provoked the majority of the population to circumvent and defy Imperial policies. Confrontations between smugglers and imperial customs agents—*douaniers*—grew increasingly hostile, especially after 1810. Beneke described the *douaniers* as 'the vampires of our trampled freedom.'[45] The practices of Imperial governance ultimately defined Napoleonic rule as illegitimate.

II   Resistance

It was largely the intrusion of conscription, military occupation and material and social hardships that eventually stoked popular hostility to Napoleon's Empire and not political conspiracy; at least so the French police reported. In Hamburg, for example, public dissatisfaction with Imperial rule concentrated (they noted) on concrete economic grievances not politics.[46] Likewise in Berg, the French police reported great social need as the source of illegal activities.[47] Furthermore, a range of localized uprisings in 1809 in Marburg, the Saar and in the Rhineland revealed popular frustration with French policies.[48] There were, in addition, three openly political rebellions against French rule in 1809, all of which called for the restoration of traditional rights or dynasties. However the Tyrol insurgency, Schill's campaign in northern Germany and Dörnberg's revolt in Westphalia were not coordinated and had no chance of success.[49] All these rebellions taken together demonstrate the growing sense that Imperial rule in German central Europe was losing its legitimacy.

Civilians began to seek to evade conscription, whether through legal exemptions and marriage, bribery, falsification of documents, purchasing replacements, self-mutilation, and flight. Indeed, along with smuggling, dodging the draft remained the most common form of protest against French rule. Prevalent in regions near border frontiers, with rough or isolated geography and a supportive population, draft dodging provoked increased Imperial intervention in civil society as authorities endeavoured to harness manpower for the armies. In the Rhineland the French restricted freedom of movement, demanded internal passports, deployed mobile columns and gendarmes, and imposed collective punishments to reduce the number of draft dodgers and deserters.[50] Resistance to conscription could also manifest itself in riots, especially in rural areas. Armed with pitchforks and scythes, peasants in Württemberg rallied to demonstrate their opposition to conscription. In fact, in order to subdue these revolts, Württemberg's armed forces were forced to move in to occupy towns and villages in order to restore order.[51] The growing presence of local gendarmes and state authorities, necessary for the enforcement of conscription, fed the hostility against the tightening and progressively invasive Imperial system. As Alan Forrest has demonstrated in France, conscription aggravated relations with civil society and jeopardized the governability of the Empire.[52]

Popular unrest against the Empire was also very symbolic. Protesters attacked tollhouses, administrative buildings and imperial ensigns as representations of French authority. Targeting officials like toll inspectors and tax collectors illustrated the source of local grievances and popular hostility. Locals despised those Imperial authorities who brought war, occupation, poverty and misery. For example, during the 1813 revolt in Hamburg, angry crowds sang the popular civic anthem *Auf Hamburgs Wohlergehn* as they vented their frustration on French authorities.[53] They equated French rule with the destruction of their city's previous stability, constitution and affluence. Rowe pointed out that even in the Rhineland in 1813 *douaniers* and tax collectors became objects of public retribution as desertions multiplied.[54] Singing civic anthems, wearing patriotic cockades and traditional ensigns or colours, publicly toasting the King of Prussia, or marking foreheads with an R for rebel and for Russia, expressed popular outrage at French policies that destroyed local stability and basic livelihoods.[55] Popular protest and anti-French sentiment expressed across German Central Europe remained uncoordinated and local in origin, but originated from the common experiences of conscription, occupation and exploitation.

The failure to generate a general popular uprising against the French until 1813 provides important insights into the nature of both French rule and the subjugated populations. Research indicates that most civilians did not participate in armed revolts. When frustrated with excessive French policies, they chose to circumvent rather than confront the power of the Empire. Deserters and smugglers vastly outnumbered rebel leaders like Dornberg and von Schill. When local and Imperial authorities called for order and peace the general population often responded appropriately because they too sought stability. For instance, an uprising of farmers and soldiers against the French in Marburg in 1806 failed to generate any support from the urban population; in fact, locals demanded peace and order.[56] Nor did the Duke of Braunschweig, von Schill, von Katt, Dornberg or the Tyrolean revolts foster common or copycat uprisings in 1809. Indeed, popular outbursts against the French were rarely tolerated by local communities. In Hamburg, the Senate appealed to all inhabitants to behave peacefully towards the French; those who defied such warnings would have to answer to the French, as the Senate would not put the community in jeopardy to protect rebellious individuals.[57] Such compliance demonstrated that, despite the ongoing militarization of society, most Germans hoped Napoleon's reforms would return stability and prosperity to a continent marred by war since 1792.[58] Even in 1811, most Hanseatics felt that annexation, at its worst, would be an improvement on the economic hardships endured under military occupation.[59] Yet the long hoped for restoration of order and stability in Napoleon's Empire proved impossible, and this problem ultimately led to its delegitimatization and steady dissolution in 1813. As Winfried Speitkamp has emphasized, political disappointment, material impoverishment and social destabilization proved a dangerous mixture[60] for by 1813 many civilians had transformed themselves from a resigned and compliant populace into a hostile, desperate, and in some cases, a militant one.

Unlike similar earlier revolts, popular protest against the French in January and February 1813 resonated widely. News of the Imperial catastrophe in Russia travelled fast across the continent, even to areas under strict censorship. French military power seemed vulnerable. Short-lived popular revolts in Berg and later Hamburg triggered subsequent insurrections in the neighbouring cities of Harburg, Lübeck, Stade and Lüneburg, as well as in towns along the Elbe, and contributed to a mass desertion of north Germans from the *Grande Armée*. By March 1813, Hamburgers established a Citizens' Militia and united with the liberated citizens of Lübeck to form a voluntary militia, the Hanseatic Legion, to protect their cities. Up to this point, most Hanseatics were content to let other Europeans fight and simply await liberation from French rule. The formation of local militias during the spring of 1813 represented a fundamental break in Hanseatic political culture. The cities' residents, men and women alike, underwent intense militarization and mobilization for war in 1813.[61] In northern Germany in particular, material distress and economic decline, combined with imperial occupation and conscription, alienated the local population from Napoleon's Empire and fostered a new militarized ethos. As Karen Hagemann has noted, in Prussia most military volunteers and recruits hailed from regions formerly occupied by the French. Military mobilization in East and West Prussia, exploited by the French in 1812, was exceptionally high.[62]

III Militarization of society

The militarization of society through conscription and military occupation represented the shared experience of most Germans in the Napoleonic era. If the popular uprisings and anti-French sentiment across German Europe were local in origin and far from coordinated, they shared a common context. Popular hardship related to the militarization and exploitation of German society provided authentic fodder for a long-term process of civilian mobilization against French. By 1813, average German livelihoods had deteriorated under the dual impact of military occupation and economic decline. The emergence of a politicized popular press in northern Germany at the same time drew on authentic examples of oppressive Imperial occupation to condemn the French as illegitimate rulers. By 1813, exploitative occupation experiences, heightened calls for new recruits, shattered economies and livelihoods delegitimated the Empire and generated a new and dynamic patriotic rhetoric that required action and engagement from ordinary civilians to drive out their former occupiers.

In the long run the consequences of Imperial conscription and military occupation undermined Napoleon's Empire by militarizing society, intruding into private lives, provoking hostility and generating daily hardships. If traditional scholarship tacitly accepted the dichotomy between the civilian and the military, collaboration and resistance, as well as the contrast between the home front and the field of battle, the experience of conscription, military occupation, and economic warfare broke down these dualisms for Germans between 1806 and 1813. Imperial policies brought the consequences of war into private homes, churches, businesses and shops and dramatically contributed to mobilizing once compliant civilians to provoke, abandon or fight the Empire they initially hoped would bring peace and stability.

Notes

* Thanks to Gabriele Clemens, Ute Planert, and John Lambertson for insightful and helpful comments as well to the *Hamburger Stiftung zur Förderung von Wissenschaft und Kultur—Beneke-Edition* for access to the Beneke diaries.

1. Staatsarchiv Hamburg (hereafter cited as Sta Hbg) Familienarchiv Beneke C 2, Mappe 11: Tagbücher 21 November 1808.
2. Sta Hbg Familienarchiv Beneke C 2, Mappe 12: Uebersicht des Jahres 1809.
3. Michael Broers, *Europe under Napoleon, 1799–1815* (London, 1996).

4. Whilst traditional assessments of Napoleonic rule in German lands underscore German resistance to the French citing it as evidence of nationalist aspirations and the mythic regeneration of Prussian Germany, the research of the past three decades, on the other hand, indicates that nationalist ideas seldom motivated insurrection in German Central Europe; for example, Schill led his insurgents to support a revival of traditional Prussia, and Hofer's insurrection was directed against the Bavarians more than the French.

5. Stuart Woolf, *Napoleon's Integration of Europe* (London, 1992).

6. Heinz Heitzer, Insurrection zwischen Weser und Elbe: Volksbewegungen gegen die französische Fremdherrschaft im Königreich Westfalen (1806–1813) (Berlin, 1959). Woolf, Integration, 237. Matthew Levinger, Enlightened Nationalism: The Transformation of Prussian Political Culture, 1806–1848 (Oxford, 2000).

7. F. G. Eyck, Loyal Rebels: Andreas Hofer and the Tyrolean Uprising of 1809 (Lanham, 1986), 224–228, Mahmoud Kandil, Sozialer Protest gegen das napoleonische Herrschaftssystem: Äußerungen der Bevölkerung des Großherzogtums Berg 1808–1813 aus dem Blickwinkel der Obrigkeit (Aachen, 1995) and Burghart Schmidt, Norddeutsche Unterschichten im Spannungsfeld von Krieg, Okkupation und Fremdherrschaft (Hamburg, 2004). Winfried Speitkamp, 'Sozialer und politischer Protest im napoleonischen Deutschland', in Hundert Jahre Historische Kommission für Hessen, 1897–199, ed. Walter Heinemeyer (Marburg, 1997), 713–730 and Lothar Gall, Von der ständischen zur bürgerlicher Gesellschaften (Munich, 1993).

8. Michael Rowe, 'Resistance, Collaboration or Third Way? Responses to Napoleonic Rule in Germany', in *Popular Resistance in the French Wars: Patriots, Partisans and Land Pirates*, ed. Charles Esdaile (London, 2005), 67–90, Broers, *Europe*, 99–141.

9. Paul W. Schroeder, The Transformation of European Politics 1763–1848 (Oxford, 1994),, 252, Katherine Aaslestad, Place and Politics: Local Identity, Civic Culture, and German Nationalism in North Germany during the Revolutionary Era (Leiden, 2005), 203–225.

10. Ute Planert, Der Mythos vom Befreiungskrieg: Frankreichs Kriege und der deutsche Süden: Alltag-Wahrnehmung-Deutung, 1792–1841 (Paderborn, 2007).

11. Michael Rowe, 'Resistance, Collaboration or Third Way? Responses to Napoleonic Rule in Germany', in *Popular Resistance*, 67–90, especially 86, and idem 'Between Empire and Hometown: Napoleonic Rule on the Rhine, 1799–1814', *The Historical Journal*, 42,3 (1999), 643–674.

12. Ute Planert, 'From Collaboration to Resistance: Politics, Experience, and Memory of the Revolutionary and Napoleonic Wars in Southern Germany', *Central European History*, 39, 4 (2006),681–684.

13. Michael Rowe, From Reich to State: The Rhineland in the Revolutionary Age, 1780–1830 (Cambridge, 2003), 87–93.

14. Burghart Schmidt, Hamburg im Zeitalter der Französischen Revolution und Napoleons (1789–1813) (Hamburg, 1998), 473, 477–485. Schroeder, Transformation, 378. and Woolf, Integration, 187–196.

15. Rowe, 'Between Empire', 643–74.

16. John H. Gill, With Eagles to Glory, Napoleon and his German Allies in the 1809 Campaign (London, 1992) 23.

17. Alexander Grab, *Napoleon and the Transformation of Europe* (Basingstoke, 2003), 102.

18. Planert, Befreiungskrieg, 414–415.

19. Gerhard Ahrens, 'Von der Franzosenzeit bis zum Ersten Weltkrieg 1806–1914', in *Lübeckische Geschichte*, ed. Antjekatrin Graßmann (Lübeck, 1989), 536–537.

20. Schmidt, Hamburg, 336.

21. Schmidt, Hamburg, 341.
22. Sta Hbg Familienarchiv Beneke C 2, Mappe 9: Ueberblick des Jahres 1807, fo. 2306.
23. Katherine Aaslestad, 'Paying for War: Experiences of Napoleonic Rule in the Hanseatic Cities', *Central European History*, 39/4 (2006), 641–675.
24. Karen Hagemann, 'Occupation, Mobilization, and Politics: The Anti-Napoleonic Wars in Prussian Experience, Memory, and Historiography,' *Central European History*, 39/4 (2006), 580–610, esp., 591.
25. Dieter Kienitz, Der Kosakenwinter in Schleswig-Holstein 1813–1814 (Heide, 2000), 99.
26. Planert, Befreiungskrieg, 265–269.
27. Anneliese Schweiger, 'Die Stadt Linz in den Napoleonischen Kriegen,'*Historisches Jahrbuch der Stadt Linz*, 1990, 109–198, esp. 186–189.
28. Christopher Clark, *Iron Kingdom, The Rise and Downfall of Prussia* (Cambridge MA, 2006), 313, Hagemann, 'Occupation', 591.
29. Robert Beachy, The Soul of Commerce: Credit, Property, and Politics in Leipzig, 1750–1840 (Leiden, 2005), 139–140.
30. Schweiger, 'Die Stadt Linz', 193–195
31. Schmidt, *Hamburg,,*362–364, 366–367. Gerhard Ahrens, 'Staatsschuld und Anleihepolitik der hanseatischen Stadtrepubliken im frühen 19. Jahrhundert, '*Blätter für deutsche Landesgeschichte*, 1998, 361–406.
32. Frank Hatje, Repräsentationen der Staatsgewalt: Herrschaftsstrukturen und Selbstdarstellung in Hamburg, 1700–1900 (Basel, 1997), 257.
33. Planert, Befreiungskrieg, 224–225.
34. Hans-Peter Ullmann, Staatscchulden und Reformspolitik. Die Entstehung moderner öffentlicher Schulden in Bayern und Baden 1780–1820, vol. 1 (Göttingen, 1987), 181.
35. Hagemann, 'Occupation', 539.
36. Planert, *Befreiungskrieg,,* 281–302, esp. 298–299. Hagemann, 'Occupation', 591
37. Planert, Befreiungskrieg,, 314.
38. Aaslestad, *Place,,* 236–240.
39. Katherine Aaslestad, 'The Continental System Revisited: Imperial Exploitation to Self Destruction,' in *Napoleon and the Empire*, ed. Philip Dwyer and Alan Forrest (London, 2007), 114–132.
40. Sta Hbg, Familienarchive Beneke C 2, Mappe 11, TB 15 August 1810.
41. Schmidt, *Hamburg*, 594–595. Planert, *Befreiungskrieg*, 222–227.
42. Mary Lindeman, *Patriots and Paupers: Hamburg 1712–1839* (Oxford, 1990), 179 and Schmidt, *Hamburg*, 662.
43. Schweiger, 'Stadt Linz', 197.
44. Ute Planert, 'Conscription, Economic Exploitation, and Religion in Napoleonic Germany,' in Dwyer and Forrest (eds) *Napoleon*, 133–148, esp. 138.
45. Sta Hbg, Familienarchiv Beneke C2, Mappe 9, TB 30 January 1807.
46. Archives Nationales, Paris France (hereafter cited as AN) dossier F⁷6348, Report, 26 March 1811. Burghart Schmidt, 'Die französischen Polizei in Norddeutschland: Die Berichte des Generalpolizeidirektors d'Aubignosc aus den Jahren 1811–1814,' *Francia* 26 (1999), 99–114, esp. 103.
47. Kandil, Sozialer Protest, 31–34.
48. Speitkamp, 'Sozialer und politischer Protest', 718–719. Rowe, 'Shifting Allegiances', 620–621. Roger Dufraisse, 'L'opposition anti-napoléonienne en Allemagne 1805–1809', in idem *L'Allemagne à l'époque napoléonienne* (Bonn, 1992), 449–469.

49. Planert, 'Collaboration', 686. Speitkamp, 'Sozialer und politischer Protest', 726.
50. Rowe, *Reich to State*, 180–183.
51. Planert, Befreiungskrieg, 424–437.
52. Alan Forrest, Conscripts and Deserters. The Army and French Society during the Revolution and Empire (Oxford, 1989).
53. See AN dossier F⁷6348, letter dated 14 March 1813. Rigsarkivet, Copenhagen, Dpt. f.u. A. 1771–1848, Hamburg II, Depecher 1813, 24 February 1814.
54. Rowe, Reich to State, 220.
55. Speitkamp, 'Sozialer und politischer Protest', 716–719. Kandil, *Sozialer Protest*, 99. Aaslestad, *Place*, 252.
56. Speitkamp, 'Sozialer und politischer Protest', 716–719. Compare Planert, *Befreiungskrieg*, 422–442.
57. See 'Publicandum,' *Wöchentliche gemeinnützige Nachrichten von und für Hamburg*, 10 December 1806, 22 April 1807, 10 October 1807, and especially 28 September 1808 and 16 August 1809.
58. Planert, 'Collaboration', 681–684. Grab, *Napoleon*, 20–24.
59. Aaslestad, *Place*, 246–250.
60. Speitkamp, 'Sozialer und politischer Protest', 724.
61. Karen Hagemann, *Mannlicher Muth und Teutsche Ehre, Nation, Militär und Geschlecht in der Zeit der antinapoleonischen Kriege Preussens* (Paderborn, 2002), 271–393. Katherine Aaslestad, 'Republican Traditions: Patriotism and Gender in Republican Hamburg 1750–1815,' *European History Quarterly*, 37/4 (December 2007), 582–602.
62. Hagemann, 'Occupation', 604–607,

13
The Napoleonic Administrative System in the Kingdom of Westphalia

Nicola P. Todorov

'What people would seek to return to life under an arbitrary Prussian government having enjoyed the benefits of a wise and liberal administration?' Napoleon to Jerome, 15 November 1807, *Correspondance de Napoléon*, no. 13,361.

'In informing me that your administration is terrible, you are informing me of nothing new.' Napoleon to Jerome, 10 December 1811, quoted by H. A. L. Fisher, *Studies in Napoleonic Statesmanship*, Oxford, 1903, republished 1969, 288.

A strand of recent German historiography on the kingdom of Westphalia emphasizes the discrepancy between Napoleon's reformist ambitions and the actual results of his rule,[1] a discrepancy explained by: first, the prioritization of French military requirements over the reform project; and second, the lack of competent, willing local administrators to implement the new Napoleonic legislation. This school of thought argues that Napoleon's continued fiscal and military exploitation of the territory discredited the newly-created state, provoking a widespread rejection of the regime and its administration. Moreover, the argument goes, only a small section of the population was ever prepared to cooperate with the French.[2] One of the first to criticize the Westphalian administration was Napoleon himself. Westphalia was intended to demonstrate to the Germans the superiority of French administration, but does not appear to have lived up to his expectations. Indeed, some of Napoleon's own administrators, such as the envoy to the Court of Cassel, Reinhard, were also critical of the way the kingdom of Westphalia was organized: 'There was a drawback inherent in the application of the French system, namely the creation of posts and appointments entirely beyond the scope of the kingdom's resources. Without doubt, too many directorates were created; there were too many levels in the hierarchy, too much overlap in each post. It was in everyone's interest to apply too large a scale (to the administration) v. ...'[3]

This chapter attempts to give a more nuanced view of this kingdom, organized as it was at a decisive moment in the construction of the modern bureaucratic state.[4]

I   The Organization of the kingdom

Napoleon's initial project after his victory at Austerlitz in December 1805, was to turn Westphalia into a satellite state. However, after the Peace of Tilsit with Russia and Prussia in 1807, he expanded the project, founding a Kingdom of Westphalia comprising the provinces ceded by Prussia and some principalities occupied during the 1806/1807 war, namely Hesse-Cassel and the Duchy of Brunswick, making the new state far larger than originally intended. Certain former provinces of the Hanoverian Electorate, conquered after 1803, as well as former Saxon territory, were also incorporated into the kingdom. Indeed, there was great diversity among the twenty-nine territories incorporated into the Kingdom of Westphalia. The diverse past history of all these areas appears to have greatly influenced each territory's attitude to the newly-created state and, as such, the poor experience of French rule in Hesse-Cassel, its original core, should not be generalized for the kingdom as a whole.[5]

Origins of the populations integrated into the Kingdom of Westphalia[6]

Prussian territories			Hesse-Cassel	Brunswick	Saxe
Historically (longer than a century)	Recently integrated (former Ecclesiastical territories, towns of the Holy Roman Empire or Reichsstädte)	Hanoverian since 1806			
33%	18%	13%	22%	10%	4%

The Regency appointed by Napoleon and charged with the organization of the kingdom drew on the work of provisional officials, *Intendants*, stationed across the various territorial groupings during the initial military occupation; these officials were charged with producing a report on the existing administrative systems of the conquered countries. The report was compiled under ten subject headings, comprising (*inter alia*) the structure of provincial government, administrative institutions, territorial divisions, the judiciary system, the princely domains, the military system, taxation and religion. *Intendants* were assisted in this by local volunteers, although any interest on their part in the public good could prove to their disadvantage.[7]

Nevertheless, the many petitions sent by locals regarding the extraordinary taxation imposed by the French provided superintendents with accurate local data. The Regency also had precise details concerning the administrative personnel of the kingdom derived from questionnaires completed by public officials seeking to join the new Westphalian administration.[8]

The Kingdom of Westphalia is often represented as a rationally organized state,[9] without ever really questioning the nature of this rationality. The organizers used French terms to designate the regional territories within the Kingdom: departments received names based on watercourses (Elbe, Saale, Weser, Fulda, Leine, Ocker) and mountains (Harz), regardless of their traditional names. These departments were generally composed of territories taken from a number of principalities, thus forcing prefects to deal with widely differing situations within their departments. The Hanoverian departments (Nord, Aller and Elbe Inférieure) created in 1810, each receiving a portion of the former departments, were equally heterogenous. The constitution fixed the maximum and minimum population levels for departments and districts, ensuring that they did not stray too far from the French model. However, this model was loosely interpreted: eight departments were created, the minimum number as set out by the constitution, whilst the French model would have suggested five. In fact, compared to the departments of France itself or, indeed, the Hanseatic departments created in 1810, the Westphalian departments were relatively small and sparsely populated.

Officially, the division of territories was based on convenience for both administrators and subjects, and included such considerations as the accessibility of the principal population centres for the hinterland, in the various departments, districts and cantons. While administrative divisions (departments, districts and cantons) were certainly less unequal than the previous territorial divisions—the provinces, circles (*Kreise*) and segneurial jurisdictions—uniformity does not appear to have been a determining factor in their creation. The desire to break from the past, and not just simply from the random territorial divisions of the former seigneuries, especially influenced the cantonal distribution.[10]

The number of cantons per department appears, curiously, to have been established in line with the number of *juges inférieurs* (local magistrates) within a given territory. However, with a greater number of cantons, the authorities could employ more experienced administrators. On the particular point of the multiplicity of cantons, the Kingdom of Westphalia clearly distanced itself from the French imperial model. This stands in contrast to its uniform introduction in the four deparments on the left bank of the Rhine, the Hanseatic departments, and in the Grand Duchy of Berg. In all these territories each canton comprised approximately 10,000 inhabitants,[11] compared to 5,000 in Westphalia. In the Grand Duchy of Berg, only seventy-eight justices of the peace were created, whereas there had been previously been 156 *juges inférieures*.[12] In this category the number of Westphalian administrative personnel was particularly large, with 401 *juges de paix* (the French equivalent of *juges inférieures*) by 1812.[13] Whilst doing its best to respect the existing administrative divisions of the population, the Westphalian government nevertheless merged very small localities to create French-style communes; however, these groupings were much smaller than those in the Hanseatic and Berg departments, where the communes on average counted between 2,000 and 3,700 inhabitants, compared to roughly 700 in Westphalia.

Frenchmen occupied approximately 25 per cent of senior positions in the kingdom.[14] As with other satellite states, this figure represents a small minority of the administrative personnel:[15] based on personal files kept by these individuals, in 1812 there were 206 Frenchmen in the service of the King of Westphalia.[16]

Localization of French subjects in Westphalian service in 1812[17]

Cassel	In the departments	In the army
52%	21%	25%

Distribution by sector

King's Household and its administration	Conseil d'Etat	Secretariat of State, external relations, diplomacy	War	Justice	Interior	Finance and treasury	Haute Police	Postal service
17.8%	2.7%	6.4%	14.5% (Ministry) 27.3% (Army)	5.5%	2.3%	7.5%	4.5%	12%

Within the general directorate of personnel, French subjects occupied two thirds of the positions (14 out of 21 in 1808). At least 30 per cent of French subjects obtained their position (legitimately) through recommendations from friends or family members. The Minister of Justice considered it essential to employ French subjects in order to 'maintain and oversee the French institutions'.[18] Patronage thus assumed a role within the imperial system, as French subjects were thought to have a greater interest in the success of the new state than the locals. Alsatians, chosen for their linguistic ability, numbered 19 (nine per cent of all the Frenchmen in the service) whilst those from departments bordering the German-speaking lands numbered 63. However, their proportion at the lower levels was insignificant compared to the Germans: the town of Halle on its own had 205 public officials in

1808.[19] The role of Freemasonry in the control of the new State[20] should not be over-stated, however, particularly as regards provincial lodges, which the French usually infiltrated as a precautionary measure.

II A professional workforce brought to heel

Half (14) of the 27 prefects and deputy-prefects, named at the beginning of 1808, had previously served in administrative offices. The other half came from the nobility, although a fifth of these were local landed gentry who had served as provincial councillors (*Landräte*). At the level of sub-prefects, the Westphalian government sought to distance civil servants from their own areas, 50 per cent of sub-prefects were named to a territory that was not their own. However, like most prefects in the Empire,[21] they generally came from a neighbouring region to a district they administered.

The administration of direct taxation had rather more staff than under the ancien régime principalities, unlike that of indirect taxation, which in Prussia had had a great number of staff. Half of the eight departmental directors responsible for direct taxation came from ancien régime administrative chambers, but there was also a former *Landrat*; 25 of the 43 directors, inspectors and controllers had served in Prussia. Although the nobility constituted a small minority of this figure (eight out of the 43 officers), they did however dominate the senior posts (five of the eight directors).[22]

Staff from the former provincial law courts were, in general, reassigned to district tribunals. The creation of a graded judicial hierarchy for the district courts, which were far more numerous than the provincial courts, also allowed many of the *juges inférieurs* to climb the social ladder. The civil tribunal in Halle, in the Saale department, was thus composed of two former *juges de la basse justice* (local magistrates) and three other individuals who had not previously held fixed posts and who served simply as assistants (*referendaries*). In the Elbe department, 40 per cent of the intermediary magistrates were promoted during Jerome's rule. A similar example of social advancement can be seen in the hierarchy for the justices of the peace.[23] The vacuum left by *juges inférieurs* who had been promoted to district tribunals was filled by lower-level staff, such as secretaries and clerks. The relatively low salaries paid by the kingdom were thus only truly felt by the judges of the Prussian and princely provincial courts who now served on departmental and district tribunals.

While service to Westphalia was an economic necessity for some, for others it was an opportunity to wield some influence over the implementation of the reforms. A significant number of members of the intermediary administrative bodies were tempted to block Jerome's administrative, social and judicial reforms. The sub-prefect for Stendal, Comte de Schulenburg-Bodendorf, is a striking example of this. A former provincial councillor, he appears to have accepted the post of sub-prefect simply in order to preserve the old order, even though his new salary (6,000 francs) more than made up for any foreseeable losses that he would suffer following the introduction of the tax on aristocratic assets: of the annual 5,480 francs received from his Bodendorf estate, the count could only keep 4,811 francs in 1808; this dropped to 4,384 francs by 1812. Prior to 1807, the symbolic contribution made by the nobility (the *Lehnpferdegeld*) was about 10 thalers for Bodendorf, or 0.7 per cent of his total revenue.[24] His net worth of 160,000 francs made him one of the smaller landowners in his constituency (*Kreis*), which he had administered as provincial councillor (*Landrat*) and that had brought him less than 2,000 francs in return. To put this into context, the noble landowner with the largest estate got 50,000 francs from his lands. The Schulenburg-Bodendorf fief encompassed the villages of Bodendorf (where the count owned 95 per cent of all farmable land and the near-entirety of all forest land), Ivenrode and Hohenswarsleben (from which the majority of his seigneurial income came in money and in kind). In Bodendorf, the count maintained a paternalistic relationship with his dependants; they possessed nothing but their homes (*Häusler*) and were obliged to complete 52 days of forced labour (*corvée*) on land owned by the count on which they spent the rest of the time working as labourers. The *corvée* represented 24 per cent of workforce costs on his estate. After becoming the sub-prefect in another district, that of Stendal, the count had the prefect, his brother, appoint him as mayor of the commune of Bodendorf following the abolition of seigneurial jurisdictions by Jerome.

Schulenburg-Bodendorf also played a double game in his relations with the serfs and the *corvée*. In his official administrative reports, he expressed his opinions on agriculture and the commutation of *corvée* legislation, maintaining that the *corvée* prevented the peasantry from modernizing their farming methods. He thought immediate change was unlikely, however: 'The majority only reacts intuitively', he noted, 'and everywhere the matter is still too recent to have offered the opportunity to comprehend such notions.' Despite these remarks, he did everything possible to prevent his own peasants from breaking free of the *corvée* and their obligations. When peasants in Hohenwarsleben refused to pay their rent (*Lagergererchtigkeit*), thinking that the new legislation had abolished it, Schulenburg-Bodendorf took legal action. He also continued to impose a *droit de protection* (a feudal due) on the inhabitants of Bodendorf as it was not, in his opinion, covered by the decree abolishing serfdom.[25] When some villagers were summoned to appear before the justice of the peace in Neuhaldensleben in 1812 to be informed of the various rents and services which the law had not abolished, the Count asked the judge to suspend the summons in order to obtain a leave of absence from his post and attend the hearing in person. Thus, it is little wonder the government appointed prefects to territories other than those they owned.

The attitude of certain career civil servants towards government measures such as the new territorial divisions, the abolition of feudalism, the distribution of certain public positions and the appointment of communal agents, can also be described as hostile. The sub-prefect of Salzwedel, Ludwig von Westphalen was one such case. Of the 18 prefects who served Jerome at various times, at least five went over to the enemy, were arrested or disgraced. Prefects of questionable loyalty were promoted to Jerome's Council of State. Among the seven Westphalians who were made Councillors of State, six were nobles.[26] Relations with these old elites deteriorated after 1810.

Nevertheless, there were still administrators prepared to accept French principles of personnel management. Napoleonic administration functioned according to a number of principles which forced individuals within the system to follow governmental orders. Unlike earlier administrative structures, the Napoleonic administration rejected the principle of collegiality in decision-making. The bureaucratization process—the division of work by department rather than region, which largely depersonalized the service—sought to limit the autonomy of administrators; civil servants were deeply distrusted by the government, and not simply because the majority were originally Prussian. The creation of reasonably large territorial units alongside specialized administrative departments contributed to this process of depersonalization. With the exception of Weser, sub-prefects supervised on average about 120 mayors, and their administrative areas were three times larger and more populated than those under Prussian provincial councillors or those under councillors charged with supervising towns (*Steuerräte*). Before 1807 a Prussian councillor was normally charged with supervising three royal estates and was, in addition, specialized in a particular administrative department, although the department's catchment area usually coincided with the estates to which he was assigned. As director of the Westphalian estates, however, the same agent was charged with overseeing about 30 domains, with his remit limited to economic management. The pre-1807 councillor dealt with individuals and a small territory; the Westphalian administrator dealt with administrative objectives and a large territory. Prefectural control over directors of departmental administrative offices (including direct and indirect taxation, estates, waterways and forests) was purely theoretical, the individual offices answered to their respective ministries.

As in France, civil servants were organized into hierarchies and assigned grades the better to control them. Some prefectures and sub-prefectures were deliberately made more important, thus allowing the government to channel public servants into a hierarchy that could be scaled more rapidly if the individual followed governmental directives. The length of service prefects and sub-prefects were expected to complete varied hugely. Some sub-prefectures, such as Halle (in Saale) appear to have acted simply as a springboard to the post of prefect. The Halle district received an expenses budget of 9,000 francs—three quarters of sub-prefectures (14 out of 20) received only 5,000 francs each—and was administered successively by four sub-prefects under Jerome, the first of whom was the former Prussian councillor, Franz, appointed in 1807. By October 1808, Franz had already become prefect of the small Leine department (Göttingen), perhaps after having made a good impression on Jerome during his visit to Halle,[27] but perhaps also because the Minister of the Interior had learnt that the crown tax collector for the Giebichenstein estate, near Halle, was Franz's father-in-law. Franz was later transferred to the important Aller department. In financial administration, an individual's rise through the ranks could be meteoric, as in the case of Johann Caspar Philippe Hitzeroth who, at the age of 22 and with no university qualifications, joined the administrative offices in Magdebourg in 1803. As controller for direct taxation under Jerome, his salary rocketed from 555 francs to 2,000 francs. In 1812 he was summoned to Cassel by the Finance Minister, Malchus, who promoted him to chief clerk at the ministry with the rank of Inspector First Class and an annual salary of 3,544 francs.

Whilst the Westphalian system was often presented as a model for neighbouring states[28] it was criticized elsewhere in Germany, generally by Prussian administrators. The Prussian councillor, Koepken, based south of the Elbe, observed the installation of the new regime and composed a memo comparing the two administrative systems. His verdict on Westphalia's administration was damning, it set excessive workloads for prefects[29] who were too few in number and only assisted by privately contracted employees. Koepken felt the prefectoral corps should be a collegial body, appointed for life, as in Prussia. Prefects should not administer districts in which the prefecture is based, whilst mayors of cantons—an office peculiar to Westphalia—should become professional administrators and certainly not administer their own commune.[30]

III   Non-professional administrators and the situation of the subject

The institutions representing the Estates of the kingdom at the district councils, whose members were appointed by electoral colleges, were dominated by non-professional elites whose purpose was to maintain their privileges. The government, therefore, limited their spheres of influence and then finally dispensed with them altogether. Only municipal councils saw their responsibilities increased.

Jerome's subjects appear to have accepted their municipal posts without fuss: after the initial nomination process in April 1807, relatively few positions remained unfilled. In the Elbe department, only 9.1 per cent of mayors refused to take up their post, while in Harz a mere three per cent of posts were still vacant after the first round of appointments.[31] Only in the Weser department did the government initially prefer the limited solution of cantonal mayors, 59 to cover the whole department. However, once these territories were annexed directly to the Empire in 1810, French-style communes were introduced. The introduction of Westphalian communal institutions into the new 'Hanoverian' departments (integrated into the kingdom in 1810) appears to have caused few problems: of the 44 departmental communes in the Lower Elbe department only approximately a fifth of mayors were replaced following the initial appointments.[32] The nobility's attempt to infiltrate municipal institutions was always unlikely to succeed; however, the majority of noble landowners entering the Westphalian administration served at a local level.

Noble landowners in the service of the Westphalian state[33]

Department	Aller	Elbe	Fulde	Harz	Leine	Ocker	Saale	Total
Noble landowners in service of Westphalia	20	25	18	20	19	22	28	132
In local administration (communes and cantons)	16 (80%)	20 (80%)	9 (50%)	16 (80%)	19 (13%)	17 (77%)	27 (96%)	118 (89%)

Many municipal administrators came from the peasantry, and had been subject to the *corvée* before Napoleonic rule; therefore, they worked for the success of Napoleon's reforms. In the Halberstadt district of the Saale, for example, the prefect compiled a table of all civil servants, but also highlighted the landowning mayors and deputy mayors subject to the *corvée*. A third of mayors in the 64 rural communes and 42 per cent of deputy mayors were thus affected. In nearly 58 per cent of rural communes, one in two state agents had been obliged to fulfil the seigneurial *corvée*.[34] These figures encouraged Siméon, the Frenchman who was Minister of Justice, to make these communes the principal battleground in the drive to abolish seigneurial obligations. Consequently, whole communes, led by their mayors and deputies, refused to fulfil their seigneurial duties and often instituted judicial proceedings against their former lords. For example, peasants from three communes near Magdeburg had enough confidence in the new state to lodge a formal complaint against a seigneurial summons one week before Napoleon's crucial defeat at Leipzig in 1813 because they had been seriously damaged by armies crossing their territory.

Public opinion varied widely within the kingdom and across different social levels in its views of the new state. In Hesse and Brunswick, there were reported cases of mob justice against Westphalian administrators after the defeat of Napoleon. Hanoverians were known for their anglophile tendencies and continued to believe that the English would arrive to liberate them.[35] On the other hand, the director general of the state police (*Haute Police*), who investigated the conduct of both public servants and the population during the brief Russian and Prussian occupation of parts of the kingdom following the departure of the Grande Armée in 1813, paints a picture far more favourable to the Westphalian regime, particularly in the formerly Prussian territories. Of the 45 cantons evaluated by General Bongars, 27 were said to have behaved either 'very well' (four) or 'well' (23); seven more were described as 'calm' whilst a further two, despite a slightly favourable reaction to the arrival of enemy troops, were described as demonstrating 'a not entirely gangrenous attitude'. On 14 June 1813 in Arendsee, in the Altmark region, inhabitants armed with pitchforks and clubs and led by the mayor, chased off Prussian hussars who tried to requisition supplies. In Calbe, south of Magdeburg, a deputation of 60 inhabitants demanded the release from Russian custody of their canton mayor who had been arrested and mistreated because of his loyalty to the King of Westphalia. Only the attitude of the five Hanoverian cantons, integrated in 1810, was described as 'not at all good'.[36]

The contrast with the attitude of former subjects of Hesse-Kassel is clear. That said, the population's show of hatred towards certain mayors in the Werra department can be interpreted as a continuation of an old landgra-viate tradition, whereby the population often complained to the author-ities regarding village agents, in effect monitoring them.[37] The relationship between the prince and population in the smaller polity of Hesse-Cassel was probably no different under the larger Westphalian kingdom. Denunciation of administrators happened as much in the Westphalian Elbe department, whether in its ex-Prussian territories or the Hanoverian territories. In the end, however, from a relatively small total (61 cases of denunciation, of which 54 came from two districts, for nearly 1,200 mayors and deputy mayors), two thirds of complaints (40) were regarding conscription laws (sheltering or employment of draft dodgers) with 37 cases occurring in the two districts of Salzwedel and Stendal. Of this group, canton mayors, royal tax collectors and the nobility were by far the majority.[38]

This public monitoring system appears to have been more effective within the financial administration. Disappointed by the work of commis-sions charged with the taxation of the former privileged classes, thanks in no small part to their infiltration of the former by the latter, the govern-ment undertook to reorganize the land registries on a grand scale across the kingdom. At least 20,000 people were expected to participate in the process of reassessing land tax, including one commissioner for every two cantons, the mayors and municipal councils, tax regulators and other individuals appointed by the mayor. Minutes taken during this reorgan-ization process in the Saale department indicate that 'every landowner' participated.[39] Actual popular participation in this process therefore must have been far greater. This reorganization led to a standardization of fiscal obligations, an increase for some, a decrease for others, at the level of both commune and kingdom.

Napoleon had an empirical understanding of Parkinson's Law, that bureaucracies expand over time, and criticized the bloated administration in Jerome's kingdom, eventually preferring the more economical Grand Duchy of Berg as his model school for the system. Although personnel management in the Kingdom of Westphalia was run on French lines the state nevertheless received criticism from its subjects. The subsequent involvement of the wider population in breaking down administrative resistance by the privileged classes proved far more effective than is often acknowledged.

Notes

1. Armin Owzar, 'Vom Topos der Fremdherrschaft zum Modernisierungsparadigma—Zur Einführung', in *Modell und Wirklichkeit. Politik, Kultur und Gesellschaft im Großherzogtum Berg und im Königreich Westphalen 1806–13*, ed. Gerd Dethlefs, Armin Owzar, Gisela Weiß (Paderborn, 2008), 5. Thanks to Hamish Davey-Wright for the translation of this article.
2. For a summary of the views of the elites: Elizabeth Fehrenbach, *Traditionelle Gesellschaft und revolutionäres Recht. Der Kampf und die Einführung des* Code Napoleon *in den Rheinbundstaaten* (Göttingen, 1974), 103. Martin Knauer argues that the bourgeoisie welcomed Jerome with enthusiasm: 'Im Zeichen der Herrschaft, Staatskult und monarchische Repräsentation im Königreich Westphalen', in Dethlefs, *Modell und Wirklichkeit.*, 181–198. For the effects military and fiscal demands had on the regime's reception, see Helmut Berding, 'Das Königreich Westphalen als napoleonischer Modell- und Satellitenstaat (1807–1813)', in Dethlefs, *Modell und Wirklichkeit.*, 27, 29. Berding summarizes his own theories argued since 1973, based primarily on Heinz Heitzer, *Insurrektionen zwischen Weser und Elbe. Volkserhebungen gegen die französische Fremdherrschaft im Königreich Westfalen* (Berlin, 1959).
3. Archives du ministère des affaires étrangères, Paris, (hereafter AAE)/Correspondance Politique/Westphalie, V, 59, report from Reinhard to the Minister, 9 September 1810.
4. Bernd Wunder, *Privilegierung und Disziplinierung. Die Entstehung des Berufsbeamtentums in Bayern und Würtenberg* (Munich, Vienna, 1978).
5. Robert von Friedeburg, *Ländliche Gesellschaft und Obrigkeit* (Göttingen, 1997), 140.
6. For the project dated February 1806, AAE Mémoires et Documents, Allemagne, no. 118; the different territory percentages were calculated based on statistics compiled in 1807 and kept at the Service Historique de la Défense (Archives de l'Armée de Terre, Vincennes): 1 M 1526 (Prusse), AAE, Correspondance politique, Brunswick-Hanovre, 54.
7. Landeshauptarchiv Sachsen-Anhalt, Wernigerode depot (henceforth LHSAW) Rep. B 19 c, No. 5 B: 'Renseignements statistiques des villes et du plat pays de la Vieille Marche dédiés à l'intendant royal français... Monsieur Chivaille, par I . P. K. Preuss, citoyen'.
8. Geheimes Staatsarchiv Preußischer Kultur Besitz, Berlin (hereafter GSTAPK), Rep. B 4, No. 63–65, dossiers des personnes pour les possessions prussiennes, September–October 1807.
9. Ewald Grothe, 'Model or Myth? The Constitution of Westphalia of 1807 and Early German Constitutionalism', *German Studies Review*, 28/1 (February, 2005): 7.

10. Nicola P. Todorov, 'La division cantonale westphalienne. Instrument de la politique réformatrice napoléonienne', *Hypothèses 2001 Travaux de l'école doctorale de l'université de Paris 1*, 39–49. Idem, 'Le transfert du canton dans l'Allemagne napoléonienne', in *Le canton un territoire du quotidien?* Ed. Yann Lagadec, Jean Le Bihan and Jean-François Tanguy (Rennes, 2009), 61–72.

11. Ibid. 69–70.

12. Ibid. 70.

13. National Library of Russia, St. Petersburg (hereafter NLR), 993, Westphalian Archives, 3, No. 350–495.

14. Helmut Berding, 'Loyalitätskonflikte, unter napoleonischer Herrschaft. Die Situation der Staatsdiener im Königreich Westfalen', in *Europa im Umbruch 1750–1850*, ed. Dieter Albrecht (Munich, 1995), 243, based on F. A. K. von Specht, *Das Königreich Westfalen und seine Armee im Jahre 1813 sowie die Auflösung desselben durch den kaiserlich russischen General Graf A. Czernischeff* (Cassel, 1848); if we take into account ministry and head office staff, and based on office expense statistics, this proportion seems plausible: Archives nationales, Paris (henceforth AN) 400AP/94.

15. Stuart Woolf, *Napoléon et la conquête de l'Europe* (Paris, 1990), 177; the difference between satellite states and incorporated departments particularly in reference to Italy is discussed by Michael Broers, 'The Myth and Reality of Italian Regionalism; A Historical Geography of Napoleonic Italy, 1801–1814', *The American Historical Review*, 108/3 (2003): 688–709,

16. AN/BB/30/670, licence report; GSTPK/Rep. 26, no. 9, list of all commissions concluded, with the agents employed in these positions.

17. AN/BB/11/67–72, requests for licence reports of French subjects in Westphalian service, in accordance with imperial decree dated 26 August, 1811, BB/30, 669 and 670, Ministry of Justice, naturalizations.

18. AN/BB/30/670 Siméon to the French Minister of Justice, dated 14 March 1812.

19. LHSAW/Rep. B/27b, no. 224, role of individual taxation 1808.

20. Heinz Cürtler, *Deutsche Freimauerer im Dienste napoleonischer Politik; die Freimaurerei im Königreich Westfalen 1807–1813* (Berlin, 1942); on the other hand, see the composition of the Magdeburg lodge in Aemil Funk, *Geschichte der Loge Ferdinand zur Glückseligkeit* (Magdeburg, 1861).

21. Edward A. Whitcomb, 'Napoleon's Prefects', *The American Historical Review*, 79/4 (October 1974): 1089–1118.

22. Nicola P. Todorov, 'Finances et fiscalité dans le royaume de Westphalie', *Revue de l'Institut Napoléon*, II (2004): 7–46.

23. For Hesse: Stefan Brakensiek, *Fürstendiener, Staatsbeamte, Bürger. Amtsführung und Lebenswelt der hessischen Ortsbeamten 1750–1830* (Göttingen, 1999), 140; for Elbe: GSTPK/Rep. B4; no. 66; for the Saale LHSAW/Rep. 26, 2, no. 8.

24. LHSAW/Rep. H Bodendorf no. 358, and a similar contribution of 41 thalers for Hohenwarsleben. 'Estimation générale de la Valeur du domaine de Bodendorf'; no. 522, Etat de la caisse du 2ème district du cercle de bois, de 1800; no. 482, états annuels des recettes et dépenses de l'économie de la propriété. If we take into account the service charge that the inhabitants in Ivenrode paid in place of the corvée, the Comte de Schulenburg only paid 44.6 per cent of his workforce costs.

25. LHSAW/Rep. H Bodendorf, no. 259, 1–2, 25 February 1812.

26. Peter Burg, '"Geflissentlich beim Feinde Dienst gesucht" – Die Karrieren großherzoglich bergischer und königlich-westphälischer Beamter deutscher Herkunft',

in Dethlefs, *Modell und Wirklichkeit.*, 149. Burg wrongly sees in these nominations the sign of successful upward mobility. Livio Antonielli, *I prefetti dell'Italia napoleonica* (Bologna, 1983).

27. LHSAW, Rep. B 26, Nr. 3, Francke report, dated 24 May 1808.
28. Peter Burg, Geflissentlich, 154.
29. The workload was much lighter during previous regimes. Napoleon insisted on efficiency, one particular provisional budget goal being to limit personnel. The Westphalian Constitution even dictated the number of ministries. Guy Thuillier and Jean Tulard, *L'histoire de l'administration en France* (Paris, 1984), 26.
30. Landeshauptarchiv Sachsen-Anhalt, Magdeburg depot, Rep. A 9 b, XIV, no. 3, memo dated 13 March 1810.
31. Nicola P. Todorov, 'L'administration communal dans le royaume de Westphalie', *Annales historiques de la Révolution française*, 347 (janvier-mars 2007), 113–137.
32. LHSAW/Rep. B 19 D, Nr. 47
33. AN/400AP/94, table of noble landowners in the kingdom, 1812, lacking the Werra department.
34. LHSAW, Rep. B 26, 2, no. 30, 1809.
35. NLR, Fonds 993, Arch. West., 3, 897, statement, October 1812.
36. NLR Fonds 993, Arch. West., 12, 6041–6050.
37. Brakensiek, *Fürstendiener,* 134.
38. GSTPK, Rep. B. 3 no. 61, vol. I–IV.
39. LHSAW/Rep. B 30, a, Sp. II, no. 34, November 1811.

14

A Valorous Nation in a Holy War: War Mobilization, Religion and Political Culture in Prussia, 1807 to 1815

Karen Hagemann

Looking back at the aims of Prussian reformers and patriots between 1807 and 1813, Baron vom Stein wrote in 1823:

> Our chief idea was to rouse a moral, religious, patriotic spirit in the nation, to inspire it anew with courage, self-confidence, a readiness to make any sacrifice for independence from foreigners and national honour, and to seize the first opportunity to begin the bloody and hazardous struggle for both.[1]

As he had before, Stein emphasized in his reminiscences that after the devastating defeat in the 1806–07 War of the Fourth Coalition all aims of Prussian politics were subordinated to one universal objective, the military liberation from Napoleonic domination. He repeatedly stressed in his writings the dedication of all Prussian reform initiatives to the 'chief idea [of a] national rising'.[2] In his view this applied not just to policies for which he was responsible as leading minister of state between October 1807 and November 1808; the governments under Baron vom Stein zum Altenstein and Burggrave zu Dohna (1808–10) as well as Baron v. Hardenberg (from 1810) set similar priorities.

Some scholars like Thomas Nipperdey share this assessment at least partially, stressing that Prussia 'had to rebuild a state which had been defeated and sliced in two, and which was still bleeding from its wounds' and that until 1813, the three governments differed only in their specific responses to this challenge.[3] Other historians place more emphasis on the political differences between these governments and the various reform groupings in the administration and army.[4] What they frequently overlook though, is that, despite differences of opinion, the small circle of reformers agreed on the paramount immediate goal: the self-assertion of the Prussian state.

The Peace of Tilsit in July 1807, which Prussia and Russia were forced to sign after their defeat, starkly highlighted the debacle of the Prussian monarchy whose territory had been halved from 314,448 square kilometres to 158,008. The population fell from nearly ten million in 1804 to 4.6 million in 1808. Only eight of the original 23 administrative districts remained. The clearest evidence of the debacle was the French occupation of Prussia, which affected all provinces except West and East Prussia, for which reason Königsberg became the temporary capital.[5] While the Paris treaty of September 1808 ended the occupation of Prussia, it also set reparations at 140 million francs. This sum, upon whose payment the French withdrawal depended, was soon reduced to 120 million, but with interest, default interest and transfer fees at an extremely unfavourable exchange rate, all to be paid within 30 months. The French kept the fortresses of Stettin, Küstrin and Glogau with their arsenals of weapons and ammunition as collateral.[6] Six secret articles of the Paris Convention also stipulated that for a period of ten years the Prussian army could not exceed 42,000 men. Any additional levy of militia or volunteer forces was prohibited. This reduced the army to one sixth of its peacetime size of 247,000 in 1806.[7] Many soldiers and officers had to be discharged. Deprived of their livelihood, they represented a significant potential for political unrest. Not least because of their unfortunate social circumstances, they were among those who vehemently supported the rapid, secret rebuilding of the Prussian army and a war of revenge.[8]

After the defeat of 1806–07, this aim was long rendered illusory not just by the diplomatic circumstances, but also by the Prussian state's severe financial crisis, following its military defeat. From 1807 to 1815 the monarchy was constantly on the verge of bankruptcy and many civil servants had to be dismissed or their salaries and pensions paid only slowly or not at all for months on end. This, too, fuelled thoughts of revenge.[9] Prussia's economy also declined dramatically after the defeat. Many regions of Europe suffered between 1792 and 1815 from the wars and the accompanying trade and customs restrictions. Compared to the Confederation of the Rhine and the German-speaking regions directly annexed by France, however, Prussia's economic situation was especially precarious. The Continental System imposed by Napoleon in November 1806 particularly hurt the export sectors of its economy, mainly cereals in the eastern provinces and textiles in Brandenburg and Silesia. Unlike the western and southern states of the Confederation of the Rhine, closing the Prussian market to British goods did little to strengthen domestic production, since the French occupying power sought to create a new market in Prussia for its own industry by permitting imports of French manufactured goods at a modest tariff. The enormous payments in cash and kind that Prussia had to make to France until the renewed declaration of war in 1813 also crippled economic life.[10]

Under these catastrophic circumstances, there was little room for diplo-matic manoeuvre and little possibility of rearmament. The leading government and military circles agreed that in the medium term only military victory over France could restore the state's autonomy, as Stein rightly stressed in retrospect. The central political objective after 1807–08 was, conse-quently, to turn Prussia into a valorous nation able to lead the liberation struggle against Napoleon. Financial and military policy directly served this objective. Financial policy had to ensure that the Prussian state could afford reparations to France and support the occupying army, pay the costs of war and fund the necessary military reforms.[11] Military policy focused on the rapid reform of the Prussian military system, the self-cleansing of the army and preparation for general mobilization by promoting the popula-tion's spirit of bellicosity and self-sacrifice. This mobilization was regarded as essential since the virtually bankrupt Prussian state needed the material and political support of broad segments of the population to make war on France; that is, to introduce universal conscription, equip and supply the militia and volunteer units the state desired, care for the anticipated sick, wounded and crippled soldiers, and support the civilian victims of war, particularly widows and orphans.[12]

This essay concentrates on the third aspect of this program of prepara-tions for war, political mobilization for revenge. Though often overlooked in current scholarship on Central Europe in this period, both neverthe-less played an important role in political culture, especially where patri-otic national emotions were to be mobilized without the dangerous baggage of early liberal political demands.[13] I shall begin by analysing the internal debates on plans to promote a spirit of bellicosity and self-sacrifice among broad segments of the population between 1807 and 1813, which created the preconditions for rapid mobilization in spring 1813. Since the Protestant church was assigned a central role in these debates, the second part exam-ines whether and how these plans to enlist the churches were realized before and during the war of 1813–15.

A spirit of bellicosity and self-sacrifice

In a memorandum of 11 August 1808 on the condition of Prussia and government policy, the Minister of State, Stein, wrote:

> We must maintain the nation's sense of indignation at this oppression
> and at its dependence on a foreign, over-bearing people whose arrogance
> increases by the day, and ensure that the nation remains familiar with
> notions of self-help, of the sacrifice of life and property, the latter two
> will in any case soon be merely resources preyed upon by the dominant
> people; we must spread and stimulate certain ideas as to how to raise
> and conduct an insurrection. We shall find and apply various means to

this end, but without revealing the government's involvement; the latter, however, will avail itself of this spirit on the appropriate occasion and under favourable circumstances.[14]

Stein used this argument to try to win over the Prussian king, Frederick William III, to the project of a North German insurrection against Napoleon. The model he recommended to the monarch was the Spanish *guerrilla*. Stein regarded Spain as a model not just because it was the first occupied country that attempted to halt Napoleon's politics of conquest, but also because the Spanish fought in the service of absolutist monarchy and with the support of the Catholic Church, using intensive pamphlet propaganda that competed successfully with French counter-propaganda. Spain, Stein noted in his memorandum, proved what 'an armed people [could achieve] in concert with a standing army...when both nation and soldier, [are inspired by a shared] spirit of bellicosity [and a] patriotic will to sacrifice'. In the Prussian provinces too, 'affection for the ruling dynasty [and] bitterness [towards the] arrogant rapacious foe' was for him so great that such a popular uprising could be successfully realized 'with strength and good leadership'.[15]

Stein argued this case often over 1808–09.[16] Like other leading patriots and reformers he still assumed at this point that the Prussian people possessed a spirit of bellicosity, and were merely waiting for the signal to rise up and take revenge for the disgrace of the defeat of 1806–07 and French occupation. This is evident in the many memoranda, appeals and petitions that sought to convince the king of the possibility and necessity of insurrection.[17] Officers well beyond the narrow circle of army reformers around Generals Gerhard von Scharnhorst and August Neidhardt von Gneisenau lobbied Frederick William III determinedly to open hostilities. In 1808–09 they urged the king to place himself 'at the head of the nation [and] begin the struggle against the French'.[18] The number of petitions reached an initial highpoint in April 1809 when Prussia had to decide whether to join Austria's declaration of war against France. The numerous personal petitions to the king show how strongly caste motives, especially a highly developed code of honour, guided the so-called patriot faction (*Patriotenparthey*). Not surprisingly, aristocratic officers saw war with France as an opportunity to re-establish the individual and collective soldierly honour, so tarnished by the debacle by of 1806–07, and to secure their military position. So intent were they on both aims that they were even prepared to resort to the suspiciously revolutionary method of insurrection. With passion and patriotic-heroic pathos they invoked a life and death struggle and claimed that the honourable demise of the monarchy was always preferable to disgraceful subjugation.[19] More remarkable is the fact that many civil servants of both noble and middle class background used the same arguments for insurrection, as in a petition of May 1809 from high-ranking officials and officers strongly urging the Prussian king to ally with Austria:

> This expedient is also the most honourable, for the opportunity to take glorious part in the struggle for the fatherland is still open to YRH. Should we fall, we fall fighting for the throne. Should we prevail, we at least have a chance to regain our old splendour. Should we remain idle, we fall without the respect of the world and posterity.[20]

The king did not concur since he rightly doubted the Prussian population's readiness for insurrection, nor did he believe in an Austrian victory and realistically judged Prussia to be weak militarily.[21] The illusions harboured by leading military and civilian reformers in 1808–09 concerning the mood in the Prussian population, and their hopes that a quick popular rising would restore their battered individual and collective honour, appear to have been so strong that they equated the widespread mood of crisis hovering over the Prussian monarchy after 1806–07 with a readiness for insurrection. What is more, they projected their own value system, particularly their code of honour, as well as their personal sentiments and desires, onto the broader population. They only revised their assessment of the popular mood when Prussians failed to rise up in large numbers in response to the military insurrections begun by Prussian officers in northern Germany between April and July 1809 and when the anti-Napoleonic rebellions all failed.[22]

Since it was also clear that universal conscription, which was regarded as the best means of fostering a spirit of bellicosity, would not be introduced in the foreseeable future, the *Patriotenparthey* now began to reflect seriously on how the state could stimulate a spirit of bellicosity and self-sacrifice in broad segments of the population. The debate which ensued in letters, memoranda and personal petitions regarding the state's options for promoting that spirit of bellicosity and self-sacrifice was part of a discourse in wider patriotic circles on German national education.[23] For the patriots, there were three routes to this objective: first, publicity (*Publicität*), by means of which patriotic-minded writers were first and foremost to influence the educated men who shaped public opinion and simultaneously, a popular enlightenment would also seek to foster patriotism among the common man;[24] second, the education of male youth, whose civic and bellicose spirit was to be awakened as early as possible by schoolteachers and university professors;[25] and third, strengthening the general population's religious faith, upon which reformers believed that the willingness to sacrifice life and property for the fatherland was based. This final task was allotted to the Protestant clergy in the context of the state-controlled established church. Although it has often been overlooked in scholarship, religion played an important role in the reformers' plans for national education. Given the precarious diplomatic and domestic circumstances, patriots considered religion the central and safest means for the state to promote the spirit of bellicosity and self-sacrifice well beyond the small, educated elite.[26]

Stein was one of the first reformers to focus on religion in this undertaking. As early as November 1808, in his *Political Testament*, he argued vigorously for the necessity of 'reviving the people's religious sensibility' as the sole means of attaining 'loyalty and faith, love of king and country'.[27] He returned to this idea repeatedly; in an August 1811 memorandum for Chancellor Hardenberg he recommended measures—including specific guidelines for church services—designed 'to rouse, inflame and maintain religious sentiments' as central mechanisms for 'awakening public spirit'.[28]

The idea was not new. There was a long tradition of regulating the content and form of public worship, as well as war prayers and intercessions and the pulpit had always been used for official announcements and proclamations. Prussia's Protestant established church, like the other German established churches, was a state church until the Revolution of 1918 and as such subordinate to state interests. The king was *summus episcopus* (head of his state church) with significant rights to intervene in ecclesiastical affairs. He could even demand political services, which generally included—in addition to the regular announcement of official decrees and proclamations—religious services which would accompany the monarch's wars. During all early modern conflicts it was common for the faithful to ask God's blessing every Sunday in a war prayer; they celebrated victories with services of thanksgiving and, in the case of defeat, confessed their sins on specially instituted days of penance. In peace- and wartime alike, public instruction in church was and remained the only source of political information for large segments of the population, particularly in rural areas.[29]

Many patriotic pastors in Prussia were aware of this and there was much discussion in clerical periodicals of the time of the awakening of religious patriotism as a central task of church services in times of war and crisis. The authors agreed that 'the most necessary patriotic sentiments' could be spread 'most quickly, easily and best by the people's religious preceptors in church devotions'.[30] Under the circumstances, the paramount duty of the clergy was to preach obedience and loyalty to the king, and to call their flocks to 'patient endurance' and 'salutary self-sacrifice'.[31] In this they must consistently present their congregations with 'manful' models of 'active patriotism'.[32]

This discourse was picked up by leading civil servants and military reformers who, in concert with patriotic-minded pastors, assigned a central role to the Church in mobilizing for war.[33] Gneisenau was among those who took this idea furthest. His *Plan for the Preparation of a Popular Rising*, which he presented to Hardenberg and the king in August 1811, outlined a comprehensive programme for ecclesiastical mobilization for war, with clerics at its centre. His memorandum not merely recommended enlisting them to preach popular insurrection, but also suggested specific guidelines for the content of sermons and services. He deemed it particularly important that the liturgy should heighten the profound effect of the service and that the service should end with the congregation's oath of loyalty towards the king and obedience to the measures necessary to defend the country. He even wanted to make clergy responsible for organizing the popular rising in their communities if it occurred.[34]

Scholars consider Gneisenau's *Plan for the Preparation of a Popular Rising* an important forerunner to the Prussian *Landsturmedikt* of April 1813, which followed the introduction of the *Landwehr* in March 1813—both edicts together created the new militia, the *Landsturm* for the defence at home and the *Landwehr* for the support of the professional army. In the *Landsturmedikt*, military reformers codified the idea of warfare that fully incorporated civil society.[35] It was based on the radical notion of a war in which home became the front. The entire Prussian nation was to be a military fighting community.[36] The *Landsturmedikt* assigned the clergy a central role in mobilizing for war. According to Paragraph 28, they were to explain state war policy to the population and urge them to enact orders:

> My trust in the country's clergy, which has never been disappointed, assures me that they will explain and convey the spirit and purpose of all regulations to the people, and indeed that they will never lose sight of or abandon the congregations entrusted to their care, whatever the hardship or danger.[37]

The *Landsturmedikt* never came into effect—such a radical mobilization for war encountered widespread resistance and was controversial even among reformers—but was amended in July 1813. However once the war began, the plans devised before 1813 to enlist the church in mobilization were largely realized, along with Paragraph 28 of the *Landsturmedikt*.[38] This was possible because the plans corresponded to the self-image of most Prussian pastors as servants of the state.

The intensity with which leading reformers began reflecting in 1808–09 on how to mobilize the spirit of bellicosity and patriotic self-sacrifice would suggest the absence of such sentiments among broad segments of the Prussian population. Before 1813 only a small, albeit influential, minority of educated Prussian men—notably officers, officials, teachers and professors, pastors and writers, the so-called patriot faction—supported such a position and sought to influence others. Their commitment, however, was decisive for the formation of Prussia as a valorous nation between 1813 and 1815. This small circle developed, discussed and discarded diverse concepts and practices, intensively preparing the substance and methods for the rapid and effective mobilization for war in the spring of 1813. This included deliberately enlisting the Protestant church for the purposes of war.

A holy war

On 21 March 1813, six days after Prussia declared war on France, the Department of Public Worship ordered a universal church service on the following Sunday to celebrate the departure of the patriotic warriors. The king's appeal *To My People* was to be read from every pulpit in the land.[39] In order to increase the solemnity, Superintendent Hanstein of the diocese of Berlin had eight new patriotic religious songs printed, to be sung to the melody of familiar hymns.[40] He also ordered the tolling of all church bells and issued instructions for the liturgy. In early April 1813 Interior Minister Friedrich v. Schuckmann had a war prayer sent to all clerics, which they were to insert into the general prayers in future, following the sermon every Sunday and on high days. It asked God's blessing and aid for a people prepared to enter battle 'for liberty and independence, for God, country and king'.[41]

Immediately following the official declaration of war, leading officials and clerics in the Department of Public Worship began to realize plans they had long discussed among themselves. Although this enlistment of the church for the war effort was not new, the systematic way it proceeded during mobilization for the wars of 1813 to 1815 in Prussia seems to have assumed a new character. How far the Prussian state relied on clerical participation in promoting a spirit of bellicosity and self-sacrifice is evident from the appeal of 24 March 1813, by the head the Department of Public Worship, Georg Heinrich Ludwig Nicolovius, *To the Clergy of the Prussian State*, which begins:

> In order for the great beginning to succeed, we confidently call upon all those entrusted with the care of souls to rouse and maintain the proper spirit. It is up to the clergy to ensure that the sentiment which deems no sacrifice too great for the common good, and which dedicates itself with every desire and deed to that good, remains alive in every corner of the land. ... When all are inspired by the will to offer up, unasked, life and limb, worldly goods, son and brother, their nearest and dearest, for a higher purpose, when such a holy fire burns everywhere in the land, then God will give His blessing, and the great prize will be won with your vigorous aid.[42]

In the following months clergymen throughout Prussia received repeated orders to mark events of the war, especially minor and major victories. These included very precise instructions on the content and form of these services of thanksgiving and victory, which, according to press accounts, were generally well attended.[43] The pastors were also enlisted for numerous war-related duties in their communities: the accelerated confirmation of volunteers, wartime weddings, the blessing of departing volunteers and militiamen, the consecration of the flag, and the organizing of the militia. They furthermore had to assist with regular collections in aid of the medical care of sick and wounded soldiers and relief for war invalids, widows and orphans as well as the needy wives and families of soldiers.[44]

Following orders from the Department of Public Worship, dated 17 April 1815, the second war against Napoleon was likewise to open with a universal church service in which the king's second appeal was to be read to the assembled congregations along with 'suitable encouragement and invigoration'. In early May, a war prayer was again ordered for the closing of every Sunday and high day service. In addition, a decree of early June stipulated that evening prayers should be held in the churches for the duration of the war 'to preserve the religious mood in the people and to ask for God's aid in regaining the tranquillity that has been disrupted again'. With the first victories, services of thanksgiving and victory were again decreed. After the war it was the duty of Prussia's Protestant church to stage the official commemoration for fallen soldiers.[45]

There is much evidence that during the wars of 1813 to 1815, the Prussian clergy actively participated in the mobilization for war demanded by the state and military and preached religious patriotism. Contemporaries were firmly convinced of this,[46] but the many sermons published singly, in anthologies or clerical periodicals[47] and the press accounts of offerings and donations, as well as ceremonies and celebrations also point in this direction.[48]

The patriotic commitment of clerics focused on the sermon which, as part of Sunday services and the many holidays and patriotic celebrations, could reach people of both sexes, of all ages and social strata. For clerics, biblical language was the most powerful language. They found it eminently suited to addressing both hearts and minds equally. Since the words, expressions and idioms of the sermon were familiar to most people from childhood— the people prayed along with the clargy and memorized them—they were believed to have an especially intense rousing and moving effect.[49]

In the hope that their words might remain effective beyond the moment of preaching, a remarkable number of Protestant pastors published their patriotic sermons from the war years between 1813 and 1815. The sermons were printed alone or in collections and had been delivered mainly on special occasions such as the swearing-in of volunteers or militiamen or victory celebrations. Publishing them was intended to help preserve the collective memory of patriotic ceremonies and thus the religious patriotic spirit of the community. The dedications suggest that clerics frequently used the proceeds to finance wartime medical care and relief efforts.[50]

Overall, the high expectations the Prussian state and church leadership placed on the activities of clergymen during the wars of 1813 to 1815 seem to have corresponded to the aims of the patriotically engaged pastors. If we are to believe the printed sermons, they were actively trying to promote religious patriotism. It is hard to judge how representative the surviving sermons were, however, and we can also only speculate on their impact. But it seems very likely that sermons, because of their familiar religious language and emotionally accessible images, were indeed particularly effective. They may well have bolstered faith, hope, patriotism and self-sacrifice and helped people to cope emotionally with the consequences of all wars—fear, violence, pain, mourning and death.

* * *

Religion and the church played a central role in planning the patriotic mobilization for a war of revenge against Napoleon as discussed by the Prussian patriot faction after the defeat of 1806–07. Reformers were aware of the state-controlled Protestant church's utility in addressing, notably via the weekly sermon preached from the pulpit, much wider segments of the population than those reached by the other print media of contemporary political culture such as newspapers, periodicals and pamphlets. Iconography and spectacle, however—such as cartoons (displayed in bookshop windows), politically orientated fairground Punch and Judy shows, songs distributed by the army, and the rituals and symbols developed in the context of the state- and military-run patriotic ceremonies—packed a similar propaganda punch at the time since they spoke also to the illiterate majority in both country and city.[51] Most Prussian state officials and military (even patriots such as Stein and Gneisenau) were still deeply religious, and the majority of Prussian pastors traditionally considered themselves servants of both church and monarchy. No surprise then that before and during the 1813–15 Prussian Wars of Liberation they demanded and supported a policy which emphasized the role of the Protestant church and religion in war mobilization. They were right to assume the unlikelihood of anything achieving the same broad impact as the intense religious patriotic mobilization activities of the Prussian Protestant church, which began soon after the defeat of 1806–07, and increased significantly immediately after war was declared. These activities doubtless contributed significantly to strengthening the Christian-influenced, royalist regional patriotism that dominated Prussia long after the anti-Napoleonic wars.

Notes

I would like to thank Pamela Selwyn for the translation.

1. Heinrich Friedrich Karl Freiherr v. Stein, 'Erinnerungen ans Vergangene (Autobiographische Aufzeichnungen aus den Jahren 1823–24) 1757–1824', in *Briefe und Amtliche Schriften*, vol. 9, ed. Walther Hubatsch (Stuttgart, 1972), 864–910, esp. 878.

2. Ibid. 878–880.
3. Thomas Nipperdey, *Germany from Napoleon to Bismarck: 1800–1866*, trans. Daniel Nolan (Princeton, N.J., 1996), 21 and 23. Paul Nolte, *Staatsbildung als Gesellschaftsreform. Politische Reformen in Preußen und den süddeutschen Staaten 1800–1820* (Frankfurt/M., 1990), 97.
4. On the literature, see Bernd Sösemann, 'Die preußischen Reformen: Forderung und Herausforderung', in *Gemeingeist und Bürgersinn. Die preußischen Reformen*, ed. idem (Berlin, 1993), 11–24. Matthew Levinger, *Enlightened Nationalism: The Transformation of Prussian Political Culture, 1806–1848* (Oxford, 2000), 3–14. Karen Hagemann, 'Männlicher Muth und Teutsche Ehre'. *Nation, Militär und Geschlecht zur Zeit der Antinapoleonischen Kriege Preußens* (Paderborn, 2002), esp. 45–53. Katherine Aaslestad and Karen Hagemann, '1806 and its Aftermath: Revisiting the Period of the Napoleonic Wars in German Central Europe', *Central European History* 39/4 (2006): 547–579.
5. Ilja Mieck, 'Preußen von 1807 bis 1850. Reformen, Restauration und Revolution,' in *Handbuch der Preußischen Geschichte*, vol. 2, ed. Otto Büsch (Berlin, 1992), 3–292, esp. 17–18.
6. Ibid. 33. Wilhelm Treue, 'Preußens Wirtschaft vom Dreißigjährigen Krieg bis zum Nationalsozialismus,' in *Handbuch*, ed. Büsch, vol. 2, 449–604, esp. 501.
7. Heinz Stübig, *Armee und Nation. Die pädagogisch-politischen Motive der preußischen Heeresreform 1807–1814* (Frankfurt/M., 1971), 13.
8. Karen Hagemann, '"Desperation to the Utmost": The Defeat of 1806 and the French Occupation in Prussian Experience and Perception', in *The Bee and the Eagle: Napoleonic France and the End of the Holy Roman Empire*, ed. Alan Forrest and Peter Wilson (Houndsmills, 2008), 191–214.
9. Ibid.
10. Treue, 'Preußens Wirtschaft', 501–505.
11. Friedrich-Wilhelm Henning, *Handbuch der Wirtschafts- und Sozialgeschichte Deutschlands*, vol. 2 (Paderborn, 1996), 276–282.
12. Hagemann, 'Desperation'. Dierk Walter, *Preußische Heeresreformen 1807–1870: Militärische Innovationen und der Mythos der 'Roonschen Reform'* (Paderborn 2003), 235–325.
13. See for example, Levinger, *Enlightened Nationalism*; but also Christopher M. Clark, *Iron Kingdom. The Rise and Downfall of Prussia, 1600–1947* (London, 2006), 345–408.
14. Stein, 'Denkschrift, Königsberg 11.8.1808', in Stein, *Briefe und Amtliche Schriften*, vol. 2, part 2, ed. Walther Hubatsch (Stuttgart, 1960) 808–12, esp. 810.
15. Ibid. 812–813.
16. 'Immediatbericht Steins, Königsberg 14.8.1808', in ibid. 812–813; 'Denkschrift Steins, [Königsberg], 8.9. [1808]', in ibid. 850–852.
17. For example, 'Zwei Denkschriften Scharnhorsts, [Königsberg Mitte August 1808]', in ibid. 821–24. 'Immediateingabe, Berlin Mai 1809', in Geheimes Staatsarchiv Preußischer Kulturbesitz, Berlin-Dahlem (Gh. Sta.), Rep. 92, no. 37, 11–17.
18. 'Immediatbericht des Generalleutnants v. Tauentzien, Berlin 19.4.1809', in Gh. Sta, Rep 92, no. 36, 212–314, esp. 214.
19. 'Immediatschreiben des Hauptmanns a.D. v. Pfuhl, Potsdam 1.4.1809,' in Gh. Sta., Rep. 92, no. 36, 11–15, esp. 13; Bernd v. Münchow-Pohl, *Zwischen Reform und Krieg. Untersuchungen zur Bewußtseinslage in Preußen 1809–1812* (Göttingen, 1987), 82–90.
20. 'Anonyme Immediateingabe, Berlin Mai 1809,' in Gh. Sta., Rep. 92, no. 37, 11–17.

21. 'Aufzeichnung Friedrich Wilhelms III., Königsberg 24.6.1809,' in Gh. Sta., Rep. 92, No. 38, 162–3. Thomas Stamm-Kuhlmann, *König in Preußens großer Zeit. Friedrich Wilhelm III. der Melancholiker auf dem Thron* (Berlin, 1992), 232–398.

22. Münchow-Pohl, *Zwischen Reform*, 82–8 and 132–170.

23. Helmut König, *Zur Geschichte der bürgerlichen Nationalerziehung in Deutschland zwischen 1807 und 1815*, 2 vol. (Berlin, 1972 and 1973) vol. 1, 298–356. Stübig, *Armee und Nation*, 239–256.

24. 'Denkschrift Steins, Brünn, März 1810', in Stein, *Briefe und Amtliche Schriften*, ed. Walther Hubatsch (Stuttgart 1961), vol. 3, 292–98, esp. 294.

25. Ibid. 295–297. see also König, *Zur Geschichte*, vol. 2, 81–177 and 286–302.

26. 'Stein an Götzen, Brünn 8.6.1809,' in Stein, *Briefe*, vol. 3, 148; Gneisenau, 'Plan zur Vorbereitung eines Volksaufstandes', in Georg Heinrich Pertz, *Denkschriften des Ministers Freiherrn vom Stein über Deutsche Verfassungen*, vol. 2, (Berlin, 1865), 112–42.

27. 'Politisches Testament Steins, Königsberg 24.11.1808', in Stein, *Briefe*, vol. 2, part 2, 988–992, 991; see also Erich Foerster, *Die Entstehung der Preußischen Landeskirche unter der Regierung König Friedrich Wilhelms des Dritten nach den Quellen erzählt* vol. 1, (Tübingen 1905 and 1907), 124–169.

28. 'Denkschrift Steins für Hardenberg, Prag 24.8.1811', in Stein, *Briefe*, vol. 3, 570–572.

29. Foerster, *Die Entstehung*, vol. 1, 124–99 and 172–175.

30. Pastor Kunze, 'Von der notwendigen Verbreitung der Vaterlandsliebe durch Volkslehrer in kirchlichen Andachten, welche den großen Begebenheiten unserer Zeit angemessen sind', *Journal für Prediger (JfP)* 59/1 (1814): 29–46, esp. 30.

31. 'Was hat der Prediger in Kriegszeiten zu thun?', *JfP*, 52/2 (1807): 150–180.

32. 'Über das Verhalten des Predigers bei der politischen Abtretung seiner Provinz', *JfP*, 56/4 (1810): 375–429.

33. 'Denkschrift Scharnhorsts, "Organisation einer Anstalt, um das Volk zur Insurrektion vorzubereiten um im eintretenden Fall zu bestimmen" [August 1808],' in *Die Reorganisation des Preußischen Staates unter Stein und Hardenberg*, ed. Rudolf Vaupel, part 2: *Das Preußische Heer vom Tilsiter Frieden bis zur Befreiung 1807–1814*, vol. 1: 1807–1808 (Leipzig, 1938): 555–557, esp. 556.

34. Gneisenau, 'Plan zur Vorbereitung eines Volksaufstandes', 8.8.1811, in Pertz *Denkschriften*, vol. 2, 112–142, Stübig, *Armee*, 221–225 and 138–139; Foerster, *Entstehung*, vol. 1, 148–150.

35. Stübig, *Armee*, 222.

36. Maximilian Blumenthal, *Der Preußische Landsturm von 1813* (Berlin, 1900), 161–178.

37. Ibid. 168.

38. Ibid. 74–127.

39. Rudolf Jungklaus, 'Wie die Ereignisse der Freiheitskriege zu ihrer Zeit in Berlin kirchlich gefeiert worden sind', *Jahrbuch für Brandenburgische Kirchengeschichte*, 11/12 (1914) 304–30, esp. 304–307.

40. Ibid. 306–311.

41. Ibid. 312 and 311–14.

42. Foerster, *Entstehung*, vol. 1, 198–199.

43. Jungklaus, 'Wie die Ereignisse', 313–315.

44. Ibid. 304–306. See also Gerhard Graf, *Gottesbild und Politik. Eine Studie zur Frömmigkeit in Preußen während der Befreiungskriege 1813–1815* (Göttingen, 1993), 36–7.

45. Jungklaus, 'Wie die Ereignisse', 323–5. Karen Hagemann, 'Tod für das Vaterland. Der patriotisch-nationale Heldenkult zur Zeit der Freiheitskriege', *Militärgeschichtliche Zeitschrift*, 60/2 (2001), 307–42.

46. Josias Friedrich Christian Löffler, 'Predigten, Reden und Entwürfe in Beziehung auf die Ereignisse der Zeit. Vorwort', *Magazin für Prediger*, 8/1 (1815): 75–76.

47. Fifteen German-language periodicals for Protestant clergymen existed between 1806 and 1816, all of which regularly published sermons; see Joachim Kirchner (ed.) *Bibliographie der Zeitschriften des deutschen Sprachgebietes bis 1900*, vol. 1, (Stuttgart, 1969): 119–133.

48. Hagemann, *Männlicher Muth*, 416–426.

49. *Dank-Gebeth welches statt der gewöhnlichen Collecta vor dem Altar in der St. Georgen Zucht- und Waisenhaus-Kirche mit der ganzen Versammlung auf den Knien, am 19. Sonntag nach Trinitatis, also am 1. Sonntag nach der dreytägigen Schlacht und Eroberung von Leipzig mit Sturm ist gehalten worden wegen Errettung der Stadt* (Leipzig, 24 October, 1813) p. 1.

50. C. F. W. Herrosee, *Rede bei der Vereidigung einiger Kompagnien der Züllichauschen Landsturmmänner, gehalten in der königlichen Schloßkirche am 3ten Junius 1813 und auf Verlangen in Druck gegeben*, [Züllichau, 1813].

51. See Hagemann, *'Mannlicher Muth'*.

Part IV

The Italian Peninsula and the Illyrian Provinces

Introduction

Michael Broers

Napoleon's First Italian Campaign, 1796–97, brought the Italian peninsula directly into the Revolutionary wars and then under French control. By 1798, the mainland was effectively in French hands; the Italian rulers had been expelled and new, pro-French sister republics created almost everywhere, the most important of which was the Cispadane (later Cisalpine) Republic centred on the ex-Austrian-ruled province of Lombardy, around Milan. By 1799, Austro–Russian forces had pushed the French out of the peninsula completely, except for the Ligurian coast, where the Ligurian Republic (the Revolutionary successor to the Republic of St George), held out. 1799 saw revolts against the French and their local collaborators all over Italy, from the Army of the Holy Faith (the *Sanfedisti*) led by Cardinal Ruffo in Calabria, to the rebels of the peasant valleys of the Piedmontese Alps, in the north-west. The violence and widespread nature of these revolts left bitter divisions between pro- and anti-French factions at every level of Italian society, everywhere.

The Second Italian Campaign of 1800 restored Italy to French control. In 1802, after a brief period of interim government by pro-French patriots, the mainland states of the House of Savoy (the Piedmont region around Turin), became five French departments; the Savoyard king, Victor Amadeus III, fled to Sardinia where he remained until 1814. The Cisalpine Republic was re-founded and renamed the Italian Republic in 1802, with Napoleon as president and Melzi d'Eril, a pro-French noble who had been a supporter of the reforms of the Habsburg Emperor Joseph II, as vice-president and its effective ruler; it was to become the Kingdom of Italy in 1805, in line with the transition from republic to empire in France in 1804, with Napoleon as its king and with Josephine's son by her first marriage, Eugène de Beauharnais, as viceroy. The Italian Republic was expanded to include the Duchy of Modena and the Papal territory around Bologna, the Legations. These regions received the full set of Napoleonic administrative and judicial reforms and the Concordat (the Italian Republic had its own Concordat, broadly similar to that of France), simultaneously with France. Napoleon permitted the Ligurian Republic to survive but handed the Republic of Venice to Austria as compensation for the loss of Lombardy, as he had previously done, briefly, in 1797. All the other Italian rulers were allowed to stay after having been restored by the allies in 1799. This settlement remained in place until after the War of the Third Coalition in 1805. What followed was the most sweeping reordering of the Italian peninsula in its history to that time. In 1805 the Ligurian Republic was abolished and its territories annexed to France as three departments; the Duchy of Parma-Piacenza was to follow suit in 1807. Napoleon deposed the Neapolitan Bourbons in 1805, who fled to Sicily where they were protected by the British. In 1806 Napoleon's elder brother Joseph became king of the mainland possessions of the kingdom of Naples and was replaced by their sister, Caroline, and her husband, Murat (Napoleon's cavalry commander), when Joseph became King of Spain. Austria now lost Venice to the Kingdom of Italy and the region became six departments ruled from Milan. These changes were spurred on by the support given by the rulers of these territories to Austria in 1805. The next series of changes were driven by Napoleon's attempts to enforce the Blockade along the Italian coast. By 1808 Napoleon deposed the Spanish Bourbons he had installed in Tuscany in 1801 (renamed the Kingdom of Etruria). In theory, Tuscany now became a Grand Duchy under his sister, Elisa, but effectively it was three French departments. Finally, in 1809, Napoleon deposed Pius VII and annexed the rump of the Papal states, Umbria (the region around Perugia) and the Patrimony of St Peter around Rome became two French departments. By 1810 the Italian mainland peninsula was split into three blocks, the fourteen imperial departments in the north-west and west, and the Kingdoms of Italy and Naples; this was the highest degree of unity since Roman times, the three blocks replacing twelve pre-revolutionary polities. Each of these annexations was followed by popular revolts, most of which were easily put down. However, there were serious, widespread rebellions in central and north-eastern Italy in 1809 and unrest in Calabria, in the south of the kingdom of Naples, which was only contained in 1811.

In 1814, the Savoyards returned to Turin and were granted the Ligurian departments as part of the policy of encircling France; the Austrians regained Lombardy and Venice, but Modena was restored to its Duke, and the Legations to the Papacy. Parma-Piacenza was restored as a state, but given to Napoleon's wife, Marie-Louise, the daughter of the Austrian Emperor, Francis I. Tuscany was restored to Ferdinand III, a Habsburg who had been deposed for the Spanish Bourbons in 1801. Pius VII had already been returned to Rome by Napoleon. Caroline and Murat were initially allowed to keep Naples, but when Murat defected to Napoleon in the Hundred Days, they were deposed and the Bourbons returned from Sicily in 1815.

The Illyrian Provinces comprised territories that Austria had seized on the abolition of the Venetian Republic, mainly the coastal and inland areas of modern Croatia, together with the independent city state of Ragusa (modern Dubrovnik) on the Adriatic coast, Carniola (a good deal of modern Slovenia), Carinthia and part of the Tyrol (traditionally parts of the Austrian Monarchy and in modern-day Austria). Their capital was Laibach (modern Ljubljana). Its coastal areas, Istria and Dalmatia, had been seized from Austria and given to the Kingdom of Italy in 1805 and transferred to France in 1809 as punishment for Austria's leadership of the war. From 1809 until 1814, the provinces were ruled as French departments, by French administrators, but never formally annexed. They existed to deny Austria access to the sea, tighten the Blockade in the Adriatic, and secure trade links with the Ottomans. The French introduced Napoleonic institutions into these areas to enforce conscription, but with minimal success. In 1814, these regions reverted to Habsburg rule.

15
The Napoleonic Kingdom of Italy: State Administration

Alexander Grab

'In the beginning was Napoleon. His influence upon the history of the German people, their lives and experience was overwhelming'.[1] This statement by the German historian Thomas Nipperdey applies to Italy as well. The Napoleonic invasion into northern Italy launched the *epoca francese* (1796–1814), laying the foundations of modern Italy and marking the beginning of the long march towards the Peninsula's unification. During that period Napoleon brought the French Revolution to the Peninsula. He deposed old dynasties, abolished aristocratic and ecclesiastical privileges, united regions, established uniform legal, administrative, fiscal, conscription and educational systems. The years 1800–14 were the most important years of French rule in Italy. During those years Napoleon reshaped its map at will, ultimately consolidating the Peninsula into three parts: the northern Italian Republic, which became the Kingdom of Italy;[2] the Kingdom of Naples;[3] and areas annexed to imperial France, including Piedmont, Tuscany, and Rome.[4] This essay will discuss the creation and operation of the central administration in the northern Republic and Kingdom of Italy (1802–14). It will focus on the administration of conscription and finances and will discuss their achievements in strengthening state power.

In January 1802, Bonaparte created the Republic of Italy and became its president. In March 1805, after becoming emperor, Napoleon transformed the Republic into the Kingdom of Italy (*Regno d'Italia*) with him as its king. The Kingdom of Italy lasted until Napoleon's fall in 1814. The Republic consisted of regions that belonged to several old regime states: the Austrian Empire, Piedmont-Sardinia, the Venetian Republic, the Papal State and the Duchy of Modena. Napoleon expanded the Kingdom's territory three times, annexing to it the Veneto (1806), the Marche (1808), and the Alto Adige (1810). At its peak, the Kingdom extended over an area of 84,000 square kilometres and possessed 6.7 million inhabitants.

The principal accomplishment of Napoleon in northern Italy was the unification of regions that previously had belonged to different states into a single state with uniform and increasingly effective political, legal, and

administrative structures. Indeed, the Republic-Kingdom of Italy constituted one of the best examples of an efficient central state in what Michael
Broers named the 'inner Napoleonic empire', namely those countries
where Napoleonic rule succeeded in implementing its reform policies and
in leaving a profound institutional legacy that remained after Napoleon's
fall from power.[5] The northern Italian state was modelled on the French
system. The republican constitution established a powerful executive.
Napoleon and his vice-president in Milan, Francesco Melzi d'Eril, had
the final say on establishing internal policies, appointing top administrators and running foreign policy. Seven ministers (war, finance, treasury,
interior, religion, justice and foreign relations) reported to them. The legislative branch, on the other hand, was divided into three bodies and had
limited power. The Legislative Council prepared laws while the Legislative
Body voted on them. An electoral body, consisting of three colleges of
landowners, merchants and the intelligentsia, elected the members of the
legislature.

Melzi played a key role in running the Republic, but his aspiration to
establish an independent Italian state led to tension with the First Consul.
After Napoleon became emperor, he replaced Melzi with his obedient
stepson, Eugène de Beauharnais, as his viceroy. Napoleon's power became
highly authoritarian. Indeed, Eugène, who was young and inexperienced
and who owed Napoleon his military career, was more submissive to the
Emperor than other relatives who ruled other satellites.

In 1802 Melzi laid the foundations of the central administration, basing it
on the French system. He divided the Republic into departments, districts,
and towns (*comuni*). The twelve departments in the Republic increased to
24 with the expansion of the Kingdom. They varied in size but possessed a
uniform bureaucratic structure. The lynchpin of the entire system was the
prefect, who headed the department and was appointed by Napoleon and
was responsible to him.[6] The prefect was responsible for enforcing the laws,
maintaining public order, and supervising the military draft and education. He was an indispensable link between the centre and the periphery.
The prefects were helped by department councils and sub-prefects who ran
the districts while the mayors, *sindaci*, ran the *comuni*. The sub-prefects
and mayors of towns of more than 5,000 people were appointed by the
central government. As the system became increasingly more centralized,
the Kingdom's bureaucracy became larger, more reliable and efficient.
Administrators were chosen increasingly on the basis of skill and gained in
experience and professionalism.[7] However, administrative efficiency varied
among departments depending on the duration of French rule, effectiveness
of earlier reforms and resistance to the government. Socially, most ministers,
prefects and mid-level administrators came from the landed classes, while
the rest were merchants, professionals, or from the intelligentsia. Of the 52
prefects who served during the Republic and the Kingdom, 30 were nobles

while 22 belonged to the bourgeoisie,[8] demonstrating Napoleon's efforts to amalgamate both classes into a new propertied elite.

Military conscription

The success of the state's administration was epitomized in the military area, the most important function of the Napoleonic state. As in other satellites, the Napoleonic authorities invested much effort in conscripting and training tens of thousands of young men and forming a new Italian army which was incorporated into the *Grande Armée*. No other policy contributed as much as conscription to the consolidation of the Italian state and its administration.

The core of the new military system was an annual mandatory conscription proclaimed on 13 August 1802, modelled on the French system.[9] Every year the state drafted thousands of men between the ages of 20 and 25 for four years. Married men, widowers with children, seminarists and the handicapped were exempt . The law divided conscripts into five groups, one per year of age, and ranked them by birth date with the youngest the most likely to be drafted. Conscripts could buy themselves out of the service. The authorities supervised conscripts' movements, requiring out of state travellers to have a passport and to return home by a specific date.

Enforcing conscription was a complex process, requiring the collaboration of state, department and municipal officials. The draft started when the government announced the annual number of draftees, *requisiti*, assigning each department a quota depending on population. Department councils then divided their share among the districts, and the latter divided their quota among their *comuni*. The district's councils compiled lists of draftees and sent them to the prefect and war minister. On a specific date all the draftees assembled in the district principal town and were escorted to the department capital where military officers received them. The prefects invested more time and energy in conscription matters than in any other area. In the Kingdom of Italy the government improved the conscription process.[10] Prefects headed a new body, the Department Council of Levy, and were given stronger control over lower officials. Districts were divided into cantons where a Cantonal Committee of Levy formed a contingent of troops. In early 1807, however, the authorities replaced the canton with the *comune* as the basis of recruitment, placing the responsibility for providing troops directly on local officials, who were also ordered to carry out an annual public drawing of lots, *sorteggio*, to determine the ranking of draftees.[11]

Conscription constituted an entirely new challenge for most Italians. It was the greatest sacrifice the Napoleonic regime imposed on the recruits, most of whom were peasants. It disrupted their life, separating them for many years from their families, farms and communities. Unaccustomed to conscription and lacking national consciousness, conscripts found military service abstract and alienating. Hence, conscription aroused widespread opposition in Italy as it did throughout Europe.[12] Thousands of conscripts dodged the draft and deserted. At times, conscripts rioted and attacked officials. Many deserters joined bandit bands, thereby threatening public order. This resistance was not stimulated by nationalist feelings but constituted an attempt by rural Italy to protect its communities and way of life.

Obviously, the government could not tolerate the widespread resistance to conscription and responded by improving and expanding the repressive conscription apparatus. As Isser Woloch has stated regarding France, 'With Napoleon, conscription became the battleground, the ultimate contest of wills between individuals and local communities on the one hand and a distant impersonal state on the other'.[13] Under the Kingdom in particular, the government strengthened the conscription machinery. They centralized the drafting process, established new courts, stiffened punishments and expanded the police force. The efforts to enforce conscription more effectively were responsible more than any other policy for the build-up of state power.

Concentrating more power in the hands of prefects constituted the most important administrative change designed to improve the execution of the draft.[14] As heads of the Department Council of Levy, they gave the final approval to the lists of conscripts and strengthened their control over the district and canton levy councils. The sub-prefects supervised the drawing up of the conscript lists, visited the cantons to check the lists and, with a physician, examined those who requested exemptions.[15] Through the sub-prefects and their dominant position over the entire conscription hierarchy, the prefects maintained tight control over municipal officials.

The war minister received reports on recruitment from the prefects and sent them instructions. He exhorted them to make every effort to guarantee the swift completion of conscription and eliminate breaches in the law.[16] Highlighting the importance of conscription, ministers often used national and civic rhetoric. In 1807, Augusto Caffarelli stated: 'It is just that every citizen has a duty to defend the state. Without the armed forces...the liberty and security of the citizens will be compromised.'[17] Prefects, for their part, applied pressure on the officials of the *comuni*, ordering them to follow conscription regulations, meet deadlines and arrest deserters.[18]

The *gendarmerie* constituted the main tool for combating violators of the conscription law. On 20 February 1801, the government imitated the French example[19] and instituted the *gendarmerie* for the maintenance of law and order, establishing its force at 1,326 men, 25–35 years old.[20] One of the *gendarmerie*'s major duties was to arrest deserters. In 1804 Melzi raised the number of gendarmes to 1,941 men, stipulating that regular troops could become gendarmes. The *gendarmerie*'s presence scared deserters and citizens who sheltered them. In the department of Brenta, gendarmes arrested 180 deserters from November 1809 to February 1810 and in Bacchiglione 122 deserters and refractories were apprehended from January to May 1811.[21] In 1809, the government assigned fifty soldiers in each department, a parallel force of the French *colonnes mobiles*, to help the *gendarmerie* in its police missions, including the hunting down of deserters and *briganti*.[22] This additional force yielded some positive results, as the prefect of Brenta reported.[23]

Establishing new courts and harsher penalties for deserters constituted an important step in bolstering the Kingdom's repressive system. On 18 May 1808, the authorities created new military courts, the *consigli di guerra speciali*, to try deserters.[24] Modelled on the French *conseils de guerre*, these courts' verdicts could not be appealed against. Penalties were harsh. The death penalty was prescribed for soldiers deserting to the enemy or abroad a second time, for deserters who stole a horse or arms, or for leaders of a desertion plot. Ten years in prison chained to an iron ball was the penalty for deserters who fled abroad, stole military equipment, or escaped from prison. The severer penalties were not, however, as intimidating as the authorities had hoped, both because numerous deserters were tried *in absentia* and because many soldiers believed that life in prison was preferable to service. The billeting of soldiers with deserters' families, a hardship frequently inflicted in France, was used only sporadically in the Republic-Kingdom.

Finally, the state also used the clergy to combat opposition to conscription. Bovara, the minister of religion, ordered bishops and priests to urge their flocks to obey the conscription law. There was no contradiction between Catholicism and military service, he wrote, 'one of the most sacred duties of the Government was to establish a national [military] force'. Prefects frequently ordered priests to assist in battling desertion, disseminating information, and reading conscription decrees from the pulpit.[25] The bishop of Bergamo, Gianpaolo Dolfin, praised a military career as 'one of the most noble and most glorious', insisting that conscription was needed for the defence of people and their property.

How successful was the implementation of conscription in the Republic-Kingdom of Italy? Despite the persistence of draft dodging and desertion, the Napoleonic state won the conscription battle with civil society in northern Italy, as it did in France.[26] The conscription machinery, undoubtedly, succeeded in accomplishing its two main goals of drafting thousands of men annually and of gradually expanding the Italian army. During 1802–14 the authorities drafted 155,000 soldiers altogether. At its peak in 1812, the Italian army numbered more than 70,000 men. Over the years the government established an increasingly elaborate set of conscription laws, institutions and officials, turning the draft procedure into an annual routine to which many people became accustomed. The growing experience of conscription bureaucrats and gendarmes also contributed to improving the implementation of the law. The new measures and reforms reinforced the conscription apparatus, centralized the recruitment operation and tightened its rules, thus enforcing the draft more vigorously and efficiently. Conscription officials and gendarmes reached remote villages thereby compelling their population to acknowledge the state and obey the law. Indeed, the number of draft dodgers declined and from 1807 to 1812 the draft proceeded more rapidly and smoothly than before. In 1808 Eugène wrote to Napoleon that '[conscription] progresses easily and calmly. It has gone without complaint'.[27] In sum, by means of the annual draft, more than by any other policy, the state increasingly became a reality the governed were unable to ignore. Yet we must not overlook the limits of conscription policy and the fact that it contained internal contradictions regarding state power. As the most controversial Napoleonic policy it drew strong resistance from tens of thousands of citizens. More than any other policy, this opposition reflected the unwillingness of the population to accept the Napoleonic state, causing estrangement between the government and the governed and, by challenging the administration, undermining stability.

Financial policies

Aside from the military draft, the financial exploitation of the satellite states (*pays conquis*) and annexed territories (*pays réunis*) was the most important Napoleonic policy in occupied Europe. Especially after 1806 Napoleon based his imperial fiscal policy on the concept that 'war should support war'.[28] It is estimated that, during the 1804–14 period, occupied lands paid half of Napoleon's military expenses.[29] Aside from taxes and requisitions, the French emperor also compelled satellites to maintain costly national armies and pay for the upkeep of French armies stationed on their soil. In sum, the financial exploitation of Europe was crucial to Napoleon's Empire.

Napoleon's financial exploitation of northern Italy began in his first Italian campaign in 1796. Heavy taxes, requisitions of food supplies and plundering were widespread. This fiscal extraction of resources became more systematic during the Republic and Kingdom of Italy. The Emperor considered Lombardy a rich country and was unconcerned with the impact of his financial policies on its inhabitants. In January 1810, despite a growing deficit, Napoleon declared that 'the Kingdom of Italy is rich and possesses several important resources'.[30]

As in many Napoleonic satellite states, well over 50 per cent of the Kingdom's budget was devoted to military expenses. This included maintaining the Italian army and French troops on Italian soil. The rest of the expenses were spent on paying public debt, Eugène's court and the costs of various ministries. Most of the state's revenues derived from direct and indirect taxes supplemented by customs, the lottery and sale of national property. Direct taxes included property tax, personal tax and mercantile tax. Indirect taxes consisted of taxes on products, including the profitable fees on salt and tobacco.

The chief financial administrator was finance minister Giuseppe Prina, who ran the financial administration very efficiently. A highly competent administrator, Prina demonstrated total devotion to Napoleon. Through his reforms, Prina modernized the financial system, rendering it more efficient, uniform and remunerative. The Emperor had a very high opinion of Prina, stating: 'There is no person who is more essential than the finance minister; he is a hard worker who knows his field' and 'The finance minister is the only man (with) common sense and character'.[31] To respond to Napoleon's rising fiscal pressure, Prina raised existing taxes, restored taxes levied in Austrian Lombardy and devised new ones. Prina's efforts to increase state revenues were helped by the Kingdom's territorial expansion and the addition of tens of thousands of tax payers. He built an effective fiscal machinery, thereby strengthening the state and undermining the regional elites who had controlled the financial system under the old regime.

Prina created a loyal administration based on merit, designed to routinize tax collection, eliminate fiscal privileges and reduce costs. He stressed the political benefits of financial standardization: 'unifying the different systems of finance of the various provinces that compose the Republic, will strengthen the moral union of its diverse population'.[32] In sum, Prina's financial goals and accomplishments were tied with Napoleon's political and administrative objectives of creating a strong state with a uniform bureaucracy.

Property tax was the most important revenue. Its most serious flaw was the absence of uniform property evaluation, resulting in great inequalities among tax payers. The Interior Minister complained of 'enormous disparities of between tax payers in the departments of Mella and Serio'.[33] A standardized property survey was needed to eliminate this problem. Prina and Eugène strongly supported a uniform system. The latter stressed the advantages of such a reform: 'This operation...will augment the profits of the Treasury and at the same time establish just equality among tax payers.'[34] Moreover, a cadastre was designed to strengthen state control over the tax system and add to its political power. With the expansion of the Kingdom, the need to rationalize the property tax grew more urgent. Launching a uniform property survey controlled by the government was part of the effort to integrate the different provinces into a unified state. On 12 January 1807 the Emperor ordered the initiation of a land survey and on 13 April the government published measurement and mapping rules.[35] This coincided with land assessments in France and the Kingdom of Holland. In the Kingdom of Italy each department was divided into surveyed *comuni* and surveyors had to prepare a register specifying the landowners's name, size, quality of property and product. The operation progressed effectively. In 1811, 415 assessors were surveying property in fifteen departments. By the end of 1812, close to 50 per cent of the state had been assessed. Prina expected to complete the enterprise by 1817. Even though the Napoleonic regime never managed to complete it, the land survey constituted a very significant reform that increased tax revenues. No less important, it established uniformity and equality among tax payers, strengthened the central government and undermined the traditional autonomy of the local elites.

The new financial administration was based largely on the French model. The ministries of Treasury and Finance were staffed by professional bureaucrats, including general controllers, accountants, inspectors, cashiers and archivists. The Treasury ministry received the tax revenues and other types of income and was in charge of paying the bills. More significantly, the Finance Minister was in charge of ensuring the collection of direct and indirect taxes and revenues from customs and national property. The addition of new taxes and the annexation of new territories to the Kingdom required a restructuring of the financial organization. Prina wished to introduce a greater degree of specialization and aimed to gain complete ministerial control over property tax (*censo*), which under the Republic he had shared with the Interior Minister. On 7 June 1805 the government placed the administration of the *censo* under the Finance Ministry. On 28 June 1805 the authorities formed seven separate departments, *direzioni nazionali*, in the Finance Ministry: customs; salt, tobacco, snuff, and consumption fees; national property and consolidated duties; *censo* and direct taxes; lottery; mints; post office.[36] The *direzioni*, headed and run by *direttori generale*, were represented by lower officials throughout the departments. The latter reported about conditions in their areas to the *direzioni*. Officials also received assistance from local administrators. In sum, Prina constructed a hierarchical machinery designed to enable him to control the financial system. The large size of the staff employed by the Finance Ministry was another indicator of the increasing number of its functions and rising specialization. The Finance Minister had 245 employees and employed 5,198 throughout the state.

The success of the financial system depended on efficient tax collection. Prina invested much effort to improve it and placed tax collectors under tight scrutiny. On 26 March 1804 the authorities restructured direct tax collection, modelling it on the French system.[37] Communal tax collectors were required to sign a three year renewable contract and were forbidden from suspending collection except in emergency situations. Their salaries, paid by the *comune*, could not exceed three per cent of the collected sum. These tax collectors were selected through an auction; the winner was the bidder who asked for the lowest compensation. Late tax payers paid a fine, which collectors kept. After fifteen days delay, collectors were authorized to confiscate the indebted tax payer's property. The prefect constituted the ultimate authority in assuring that all the rules were followed. At the end of their three year term, collectors had to submit their accounts to the Finance Minister. Many of these norms applied to departmental collectors as well. The latter received their salaries from the state.

For the purpose of collecting indirect taxes, the Republic was divided into 22 financial districts: 12 *regolatorie* and ten *delegazioni di finanza*. The former collected taxes in the 12 departments while the *delegati* did the same in the ten major cities. The government employed 2,351 subordinates to carry out that task. In June 1805, the authorities transformed these offices, labelling them *intendenti*, placing them under the *Direzione generale* of salt, tobacco, snuff, and consumption fees.[38] The number of *intendenti* rose to 27 when the Kingdom expanded. They were assisted by the *Guardia di Finanza* numbering more than 2,000 men.

How successful was Prina in achieving his financial goals? He succeeded in increasing state revenues. Between 1802 and 1812 income rose from 81 to 141.1 million lire, a 74 per cent increase. The rising revenues enabled the government to meet the expanding military expenses and to pay close to 300 million lire towards the cost of the French army in Italy, the development of the infrastructure, and the liquidation of the public debt. As we saw, Prina's reform policy played a central role in augmenting state revenues. He initiated reforms, issued instructions and appointed and supervised state functionaries. He increased existing taxes, restored old ones, introduced new imposts and restructured the financial system. The Napoleonic state could count on a growing number of capable and loyal cadres of officials who were ready to contribute to its prosperity and strength. The division of the various financial branches into separate *Direzioni*, each in charge of a particular area, was a departure from past administrations and increased bureaucrats' efficiency and expertise. The heads of the *direzioni generali* received a constant flow of information from their representatives in the departments, which Prina used when preparing the annual financial reports he sent to Paris.

Essential to the new financial system was the centralized structure of taxation and the cadastre constituted a key part of it, forming as it did a unified, precise and reliable property assessment. It established equality among landowners and eliminated abuses and past exemptions. The government was in charge of assessment. Tax collection underwent major changes and became increasingly bureaucratized. The government fixed tax rates, regulated deadlines, established rules and ensured that taxes would be collected and transferred rapidly to the national treasury. Yearly collection costs amounted to a mere 8.5 per cent of the amount raised, comparing favourably with other countries, especially France. Moreover, each year the authorities were able to collect about 90 per cent of the taxes by the end of the fiscal year and to raise most of the outstanding revenues within a year.

These figures notwithstanding, it must be emphasized that Prina's reforms and efforts did not yield the same results for the collection of all the taxes throughout the state. Tax collection in the Veneto and the Marche, which were annexed to the Kingdom later, was less effective than in the older departments. Property owners in the Veneto protested vociferously about the *estimo*. Lombard landowners had had an accurate assessment since the

Austrian period and property tax collection there progressed without difficulty. Collection of personal tax in walled towns faced resistance and salt and tobacco were stolen and smuggled. Mountainous departments were not as accessible to tax collectors as departments located on the plain.

More importantly, however, the rising pressure from Napoleon on the Kingdom increased the fiscal difficulties for the authorities, especially during the last years of French rule. In August 1808 Prina complained that the financial situation posed a 'major burden'. By 1809 the accumulated deficit from previous years amounted to 7.4 million lire. In 1810 the budget could be balanced only through the sale of bonds. In 1811 the deficit rose to five million. In April 1812 Prina insisted that 'every tax has been pushed to the highest level, the ordinary resources can barely suffice for the current expenses'.[39] In 1812 state expenditure rose to 149.4 million lire and the deficit reached four million lire. The Kingdom's authorities appealed to Napoleon to reduce his demands. Eugène wrote: 'The present situation of the treasury of your Kingdom of Italy necessitates, Sire, that Your Majesty comes to its aid through some extraordinary means', and proposed that Napoleon reduce the 30 million lire annual payment for the French army in Italy.[40] He implied that such a move would be politically wise since 'it will make a good impression on the public opinion'. Napoleon refused to make any concessions. For 1813, Prina proposed to cover a deficit of 21 million lire by increasing land tax and granting special import licenses.[41] The Finance Minister concluded his report with a gloomy statement, 'the financial situation in Italy is not what Your Majesty would desire'. In 1813, the government resorted to desperate measures to increase state revenues. In August, it increased land tax and in November required the wealthiest property owners and merchants to lend the government three million lire. It also issued two sets of government bonds worth 24 million lire. Yet those measures were to no avail. Military expenses were rising rapidly and the treasury was near bankruptcy. The Kingdom was no longer able to sustain tax increases without threatening social and political stability. Prina's policies consolidated the financial machinery and increased the state's resources, but did so at the cost of ever-increasing fiscal pressure on the Kingdom's population. This caused a growing discontent and hostility towards the Napoleonic state in general and the Finance Minister in particular, that cut across class lines. Due to his devotion to Napoleon, he was identified as the embodiment of an oppressive French system. The propertied classes were furious with the rise of departmental and, especially, communal taxes and resented the loss of their fiscal privileges. The lower classes accused Prina of raising indirect taxes and introducing the hated personal tax. Practically everybody resented the growing effectiveness of the state in collecting taxes.

In late 1813 the Austrians invaded the Kingdom, forcing Eugène's troops to retreat toward Milan. Three opposition groups conspired to dissolve the Kingdom of Italy. The anti-French climate culminated in an uprising in Milan on April 20 1814 when a Milanese crowd, incited by a group of nobles, murdered Prina. This uprising and Prina's death marked the end of the Napoleonic regime in northern Italy and prevented the creation of an independent Kingdom under Eugène.[42] Shortly thereafter the Austrians entered Milan and restored their rule in Lombardy-Veneto.

Notes

1. Thomas Nipperdey, *Germany from Napoleon to Bismarck, 1800–1860* (Princeton, 1996), 1.
2. Carlo Zaghi, *L'Italia di Napoleone dalla Cisalpina al Regno* (Turin, 1986). Alain Pillepich, *Milan capitale napoléonienne 1800–1814* (Paris, 2001). Alexander Grab, 'From the French Revolution to Napoleon,' in *Italy in the Nineteenth Century*, ed. John Davis (Oxford, 2000), 35–41.
3. John Davis, *Naples and Napoleon: Southern Italy and the European Revolutions (1780–1860)* (Oxford, 2006).
4. Michael Broers, *The Napoleonic Empire in Italy, 1796–1814: Cultural Imperialism in a European Context?* (Basingstoke, 2005).
5. Michael Broers, *Europe under Napoleon 1799–1815* (London, 1996), 181.
6. Livio Antonielli, *I prefetti in Italian napoleonica* (Bologna, 1983).
7. Carlo Capra, *L'età rivoluzionaria e napoleonica in Italia 1796–1815* (Turin, 1978), 242.
8. Zaghi, *L'Italia napoleonica*, 330.
9. *Bollettino delle leggi della Repubblica italiana* (henceforth, *Bdl*) (1802), 234–252. On conscription in the Republic/Kingdom of Italy, see Franco della Peruta, *Esercito e società nell'Italia napoleonica* (Milan, 1988). Alexander Grab, 'Army, State and Society: Conscription and Desertion in Napoleonic Italy (1802–1814)', *The Journal of Modern History* 67 (March 1995): 25–54.
10. *Bdl*, 14 July 1805, 397–407. Della Peruta, *Esercito*, 151–152.
11. *Bdl*, 11 January 1807, 22–23.
12. For resistance in France, see Alan Forrest, *Conscripts and Deserters: The Army and French Society during the Revolution and Empire* (Oxford, 1989).
13. Forrest, *Conscripts*, viii. Isser Woloch, 'Napoleonic Conscription: State Power and Civil Society,' *Past and Present*, 111 (1986), 101.
14. *Bdl*, 14 July 1805, 397–407. Della Peruta, *Esercito*, 151–152, 168–79.
15. *Bdl*, 4 August 1806, 835–837.
16. *Archivo di stato di Milano*, (henceforth *ASM*), *Ministero della Guerra*, (henceforth *MG*), *cartella* (henceforth c.), 785, 23 May 1805; c. 285, 26 April 1808.
17. Princeton University Library, EBA, box 38, folder 2, 4 February 1807.
18. *ASM*, *MG*, c. 796, prefect of Olona, 20 October 1809; c. 795, prefect of Mincio, 20 November 1809.
19. Forrest, *Conscripts*, 201–206.
20. Della Peruta, *Esercito*, 61–62.
21. *ASM*, *MG*, c. 287, prefect of Brenta, 10 February 1810; c. 294, prefect of Bacchiglione, 7 June 1811.
22. Antonielli, *I prefetti*, 445–46. Forrest, *Conscripts*, 211–213.
23. *ASM*, *MG*, c. 293, 26 September, 1812.
24. Della Peruta, *Esercito*, 278.
25. *ASM*, *MG*, c. 285, 9 May 1808; c. 287, 12 January 1810.

26. Woloch, 'Military Conscription', 127.
27. *ASM, Aldini*, c. 80, 27 March 1807.
28. Louis Bergeron, *France under Napoleon* (Princeton, 1981), 40.
29. D.M.G. Sutherland, *France 1789–1815 Revolution and Counterrevolution* (New York, Oxford, 1986), 413.
30. Melchiore Roberti, *Milano capitale napoleonica La formazione di uno stato moderno 1796–1814* (Milan, 1946–47), vol. II, 372 no. 2.
31. *Correspondance de Napoléon* (Paris: 1858–1870) 7 June, 1805, vol. 10, 490; 5 August 1805, vol. 11, 64.
32. Roberti, *Milano capitale*, vol. II, 343.
33. ASM, *Censo*, p.m. c. 132, 25 February 1804.
34. ASM, *Aldini*, c. 97, letter to Napoleon, 24 October 1807.
35. *Bdl* (1807), 193–203.
36. *Bdl* (1805), 347–55.
37. *ASM, Censo*, p.m. c. 496. *Bdl* (1804), 149–60. On France Bergeron, *France under Napoleon*, 47, 50.
38. *Bdl* (1805), 344–46.
39. *ASM, Aldini*, c. 103, Aldini to Napoleon, 19 April 1812.
40. *ASM, Aldini*, c. 103, 17 April 1812.
41. *ASM, Aldini*, c. 103, 21 December 1812.
42. John Rath, *The Fall of the Napoleonic Kingdom of Italy (1814)* (New York, 1941) 37–43.

16
The Imperial Departments of Napoleonic Italy: Resistance and Collaboration

Michael Broers

The French annexed over one third of the Italian peninsula between 1802 and 1810. Piedmont, Liguria, Parma-Piacenza, Tuscany, Umbria and Rome all became French departments, fourteen in all. The *ancien régime* histories of these different states were very different in many ways, particularly on the level of institutions, yet remarkably similar in their geographical (indeed, topographical) profiles and so offer a mixture at once complex and varied, but also often comparable experiences of Napoleonic rule. First, however, Napoleon had to deal with what he found.

I From the crisis of the *ancien régime* to annexation

Napoleon's First Italian Campaign of 1796–97 was a stunning military success and, by the early months of 1798, the entire Italian mainland had fallen to the French and all the indigenous states had been shaken by their presence. By the time the French were driven back over the Alps by combined Austro-Russian armies and internal popular revolts in spring 1799, it was already clear who were friends of the new French order and who opposed it. These divisions (that would plague the years of Napoleonic rule) and the sources of support for the French were located in the bloody events of 1799, 'the black year', as Italian historians often refer to it.[1]

The French also found states in crisis almost everywhere. By the last decades of the eighteenth century, the economies and societies of the Italian states had suffered the strains of demographic growth in areas least able to support it, for the most part on the Apennine spine. Piedmont, Liguria, Parma-Piacenza, Tuscany and the Papal states all had clear centres and peripheries; their centres were lowland plains in the major river valleys (or in the case of Liguria, of the Mediterranean coast) where the major urban centres were located, and where large-scale commercial agriculture had produced an underclass of impoverished, landless, rural day labourers. These were the political and administrative hearts of the *ancien régime* states. Beyond and above them, the valleys of the Apennines formed the little-governed periphery, areas of small peasant subsistence farming, transhumance and transit trade that often overlapped with, and tipped into, banditry and smuggling. For all their other differences, the states of the future imperial departments shared the same merely ephemeral control over, or regular contact with, these regions. Here, a lethal combination of peasant land-hunger, over population and the increasing rapaciousness of landlords pushed many of these communities to the limits of endurance by the 1790s. Traditionally secure leases were broken, on the one hand, their terms and prices increased in line with spiralling inflation, and on the other, families sub-divided their already small holdings in response to population pressures, thereby undermining productivity on land that was often agriculturally marginal. These conditions were noted by Piedmontese provincial *intendants*, by Genoese patricians, by the bishops who were the provincial governors of the Papal states and by the Church everywhere, all with a deep concern matched by their inability to deal with the crisis.[2] The only state to embark on a policy of concerted economic and institutional reform was Tuscany, under its Habsburg archduke, Peter-Leopold. During the 1780s, he had attempted a comprehensive, fundamental series of reforms to secure the peasantry of the valleys in their tenure, while also establishing internal free trade. The twin policies proved incompatible, however, free trade drove up prices already high as a result of bad harvests, and private landlords did not follow Leopold's lead on land reform. All this was compounded by religious reforms (much disliked) that sought to curb popular piety. The result was the ferocious *Viva Maria* risings, which ended the reforming impulse permanently.[3] They did not end the crisis, however. Elsewhere rural unrest grew, although it did not target the state as in Tuscany. Well before the French invasion and its own depredations, the fragility of the Italian states was clear, especially to those who governed them. The French inherited these conditions when they pushed aside the weak polities of the old order.

The violence of 1796–99, *il triennio*, drew together this structural crisis and the political convulsions brought by revolution and occupation. The peasant revolts that broke out, from the southern borders of the Papal states to the Alpine valleys of Piedmont, were fuelled by longer term dislocation but triggered by the brutal rapaciousness of the French and by the renewed reforming policies of the Italian patriots who supported them and ran the new sister republics.[4] When the French retreated in 1799 they were harassed the length of Italy by the peasantry of the periphery, and their supporters felt the vengeance of the popular and restored ruling classes alike. When Napoleon returned in 1800, this was what he had to contain, govern and repair.

II   Resistance: from invasion to annexation

The events of the *triennio* led the French to expect trouble everywhere in Italy in the initial stages of annexation. Indeed, upon the re-occupation and annexation of all the individual Italian states, revolts took place immediately, following sequentially the creation of the imperial departments. But because the French had seen it before, they were usually better prepared to deal with it than in 1796–99. At this juncture however, these many brief, small-scale disturbances had a different significance for the French because when they annexed territory after 1800, the French had come to stay, to rule and, above all, to enforce conscription on the hinterlands. Whilst open rebellions were crushed quickly, and seldom repeated themselves, the degree of initial resistance indicated that French rule was, and would continue to be, resented. Thus, although resistance and resentment remained so atomized as to pose no threat to the security of French rule, it was also widespread and intense enough to ensure that the new regime seldom proceeded smoothly from day to day.

Piedmont was the Italian region longest under French rule and one where the latter successfully reformed a generally disorderly society; along the Apennine frontier with Liguria smuggling and banditry were part of the local economy, dove-tailing with paramilitary communities, and the *barbetti* had long been charged by the Savoyard monarchy with the defence of the Alpine border with France. Piedmont witnessed peasant revolts in Aosta and its Alpine valleys from 1800 to 1802, and Liguria underwent unrest along the Apennines which often centred on the ex-fiefs of the nobility, traditional safe havens for smugglers and bandits. By about 1803, however, the French had silenced the determined, brutal guerrilla war of the *barbetti* around the passes into Provence and, by 1807, once the resistance of the bandit-smugglers of the southern border had been broken, good order prevailed. Piedmont was furthermore notable for its peaceful response to regime change in 1814, in contrast to the widespread violence of the early years, although local anti-conscription revolts persisted to the end.[5]

On the other hand, the revolt of the Piacentino came as bolt from the blue for the French, for the region had never shown a capacity for collective, large-scale revolt during the *triennio*, although it had seen much localized resistance to both French and Russian marauding. In late 1805, however, whole villages across several valleys rose at once, in a well-organized fashion, to attack local officials. The introduction of conscription was certainly the trigger, but the rebels' petitions and proclamations pointed equally to the new, unprecedented forms of taxation, to the disruption of religious life and to the requisitioning of their mules. The last point was, in their eyes, far from trivial or transient; the rebels saw it not only as economically ruinous in the short term, but also as part of a more pervasive policy of destroying the haulage trade of the bandit-smugglers. Though the valleys were quickly overrun by the rebels, a coordinated assault from Liguria and Piacenza broke them by the first weeks of 1806. Napoleon was infuriated that such an uprising had broken out at all, in a region so far from the frontline. But the real lesson learnt, in fact, was regarding the power of his state; a rebel force estimated at a hard core of 7,000–8,000, and able to muster several times that number on occasion, had been destroyed by virtually the last line of the regime's coercive forces, the Gendarmerie.[6]

On the annexation of Tuscany, in 1808, the twin pillars of resistance in 1799—the Aretino in the south, and the hills around Pisa and Pistoia, in the north— sprang to life. The presence of the Gendarmerie was enough to prevent them taking the major cities of Siena and Pistoia, unlike in 1799, although in Tuscany it needed a considerable influx of regular troops to push the Aretino rebels back into the swamps of the Maremma.[7] In all these cases, mass revolt would not rear its head again, but the French perceived a need for constant vigilance. They had learnt that the end of collective resistance did not equate with true pacification.

Resistance to conscription perpetuated collective violence against the new regime all over Napoleonic Europe, but in the Italian Apennines it also helped foster genuinely anti-statist attitudes that sprang from centuries of freedom from regular, systematic intrusion by any form of civil authority. What is notable in many cases in Piedmont, Liguria and the Piacentino—where French rule was longer than in Tuscany or the Papal states— are numerous cases of the leaders of the revolts of the *triennio* and the early annexation, transforming themselves into managers and facilitators of draft dodging by peaceful, as well as violent means. Behind them, emerges the solidarity of rural communities—themselves traditionally riven by vendettas—in the face of the threat of the blood tax, as conscription was known. Siste Quaglia, a notary in the hamlet of Arquata in eastern Liguria, was a man who did not change his view of the new regime. He adapted his methods of resistance to the French over a period of 15 years and carried his community with him, as the threat changed from violent military invasion to conscription. Even before the French invasion in 1795, he recruited volunteers locally for the Habsburg army; a year later, he was one of the leaders in the risings against the advancing Army of Italy. After annexation in 1805 onwards, Quaglia made full use of his legal training to help the young men of the area avoid conscription by legal means. It was not wholly altruistic—the French police seemed almost relieved to report how rich Quaglia had become through the families and whole villages that would dig deep to save their sons— although they also hinted that his wealth probably came from the high demand for his services, more than the price he charged. The real fear was the formidable popularity and support he had gathered around him. It took until 1813 to trap him, withdraw his notarial license and jail him for 'conscription frauds'.[8] In 1813, the French Director-General of Police in Turin believed that Quaglia still posed a threat because of the loyalty he retained among the families of the youths he had helped. Alongside the old guard like Quaglia was a new generation. Stefano Grondana, a young notary in the Polcevera valley in Liguria, involved himself, like Quaglia, in helping families avoid conscription by legal or quasi-legal means and used his position to agitate against it; he spent some of his income to get his children a private tutor. a priest known for his anti-French views.[9] There were less subtle resisters in the hills. In 1810, Bruno Levrero, a leader in the *triennio,* was condemned to death in Genoa for killing a tax collector. The imposing collective support for Levrero— expressed by the menacing crowds at his trial who descended from the hills for the event—worried the authorities more than the murder itself. The French prefect of Genoa considered the whole valley guilty, but the Director-General was unnerved by the support Levrero got from his lawyers, who defended him *gratis* and 'who went to great lengths for their client'.[10] The combined efforts of notaries, lawyers and other elements of the local elite, to say nothing of the inter-clan rivalries which dominated life in the Ligurian Apennines,[11] reveals how the leveller of conscription—which could strike any family unable to purchase a replacement—maintained solidarity across social classes, even creating it where it had not existed before. In 1814 these valleys saw organized revolts against conscription and French rule.[12] It is debatable how politicized this kind of resistance was in terms of support for an outright restoration of the old order and it is probably best described as anti- rather than counter-revolution.[13] Nevertheless, the evolution of resistance on the periphery, from violent collective revolt to collective reliance on the law—both to protect violent offenders and avoid conscription—was made possible by the active participation of the local elites. The manner in which forms or resistance mutated in these communities is even more striking than the persistence of collective violence in the face of a powerful state. It is arguable that the activities of men like Quaglia, Grondana and Levrero's lawyers betoken the emergence of an articulated, focused opposition to the new regime, even if that opposition did not correspond readily to the desire for an integral restoration of the old order. What can be said with certainty, however, is that support for the French, and readiness to collaborate with them, was as thin as the soil of the Apennines.

The answer to lack of cooperation was the intrusion of a permanent, diffused force. By establishing the Gendarmerie throughout the Italian hinterlands, the French took a momentous step in the history of the relationship of the Italian peripheries to their political centres. The change in the presence and power of the state in the lives of the mountain communities of the Apennines was nothing short of seismic for, almost overnight, these unpoliced upland valleys suddenly had the strong arm of the Napoleonic state thrust directly and permanently into their midst. The Gendarmerie was established throughout the empire and had sister services in all the satellite kingdoms,[14] but there were few parts of the empire where its arrival entailed so ruthless a break with the past, as in the imperial departments of Italy. Each canton received a six-man brigade and the state ensured that at least four gendarmes were always French, usually housed in barracks apart from the communities they served, and paid by the central government; most of those Italians who made up the remainder of the corps were Piedmontese, sent into Liguria, the Duchies and the Papal states, as foreign and unwelcome as the French themselves.[15] This was how conquest was made lasting and complete; and in particular, this was how conscription (the hard reality of the new order) was enforced. As often as four times a year, the prefects toured their entire departments, visiting each cantonal seat, where they worked with the local Gendarmerie brigade to ensure those conscripted were rounded up, by force if required. Obviously, these operations often provoked armed resistance and legalistic evasion almost everywhere—administrative success should not be interpreted as acquiescence —but the new state won the violent confrontations, thus extracting most of the conscripts it demanded. It is true that the process of conscription fostered banditry in areas where it had not been especially rife before, as in Tuscany, and often broadened the scope of the latter if it was deeply rooted, as in southern Piedmont and the Papal states, where the bands became rallying points and nuclei for young men trying to evade the Gendarmerie.[16] However, unlike any coercive power before them, the French returned and returned, sweeping collective, open resistance aside. Indeed, the effectiveness of the Gendarmerie in the imperial departments—certainly in Piedmont, Liguria and the Duchies, less so in the Papal states—marked an important difference between the experience of Napoleonic rule between these regions and the Kingdom of Naples, where the convulsed conditions there prevented the Gendarmerie ever being distributed in settled brigades across the national territory. South of Rome, the Gendarmerie remained a sporadic presence, deployed in flying columns rather than local units.

Aversion to these peripheries, however, was not only a French issue. It was almost a trope among the Italian elites in their lowland and coastal urban centres. The Counter-Reformation Church, through Jesuit missions to the isolated uplands, and the military incursions of more determined rulers, like the House of Savoy, had tried to tame them.[17] None had succeeded. The determination of the French to master the Apennines was one of the strongest potential sources of collaboration available to the new rulers. But there was more to it than this.

III   Collaboration: the painful birth of the new regime

The allied victory of 1799 was as sweeping and complete as Napoleon's three years previously and the old order was restored everywhere in the future imperial departments. This was only partially overturned after Napoleon's comprehensive military victories in 1800, however. Piedmont and Liguria

were brought swiftly back into French orbit, the former as French departments, the latter as a sister republic, but elsewhere, the old order remained.
In Parma-Piacenza, Tuscany and the Papal states, the traditional elites
continued to struggle with the structural crisis, now intensified by the
burdens of French occupation and the political divisions of the *triennio*.
Thus, each successive occupation confronted the French with similar sets
of internal reactions and similar patterns of support and opposition to their
rule. With this background in mind, the importance of the gradual spread
of annexation in Italy becomes significant.

When the French annexed Italian territory, they inherited a complex
political world for two distinct reasons. First was the varied nature of the
ancien régime states; Piedmont, Liguria, the Duchies and the Papal states
could not have had more different political cultures or institutional frame-
works, at least at national level. Second, the Italian states had all been torn
apart during the *triennio*. Minorities of enlightened reformers had aligned
with the French, as had many embattled local administrators who simply
sought to preserve order and stem the tide of social anarchy by accepting
help from the French, often the only viable source of order left. The restored
governments and the popular classes had turned on them in 1799, creating
divisions and vendettas deeper and more intractable than was conceivable
before the phenomenon of foreign intervention. Thus, the French inherited both the diverse political heritage of the old Italian order, alongside
the bitter civil war between their own supporters (the patriots or Jacobins)
and the supporters of the *ancien régime*. Upon this myriad complexity, they
sought to impose the uniform system of government and justice that had
emerged under the Revolution and Napoleon, and this occurred in different
states, at wide intervals between the annexation of Piedmont in 1801–02
and that of the Papal States in 1809.

The patterns of collaboration and the degree of successful participation in
Napoleonic government by the elites of the imperial departments depended
on the pre-conditions of their respective *ancien régime* political cultures
and their responses to the immediate circumstances of the *triennio*, but
perhaps even more, on the views the French formed of them in the course
of the occupation and the stage the First Empire had reached at the point
of annexation. All the Italian departments contained conservative elites
imbued with Post-Tridentine Catholic values, for whom the new regime was
anathema, and these were feelings that often intensified rather than diminished after the annexation of the Papal states and the imprisonment of Pius
VII in 1809. Families like the D'Azeglio in Turin, the Patrizzi in Rome or
the Stoffa in Umbria recoiled in horror at the prospect of their sons serving
the empire as civil servants, and worse still as soldiers.[18] The most ancient
noble families of Turin and Florence largely ignored the Bonaparte courts
set up to attract them and shunned official occasions. The great Roman
families generally obeyed the Pope's injunction not to serve his jailers. Few,

anywhere, availed themselves of the new *lycées*, preferring to hire clergy—often ex-Jesuits or reluctantly secularized regulars—as private tutors for their children. None of this was unique to Italy or news to the French, who had witnessed similar reactions in France itself. There were large sections of the elites for whom *ralliement* was a dead letter. That being said, the spectre of a convulsed periphery and threats to their rural property could soften even the most recalcitrant, as when the notoriously anti-French, deeply pious Scotti-Douglas family of Piacenza used their influence to help Junot quell the Piacentino revolt.[19] This spirit of cooperation ended with the crisis, however, and when exiled Roman clergy arrived in the city after 1809, the Scotti were among their most generous patrons and protectors.[20]

The French had a twin-pronged political policy towards the elites of the empire, described in detail elsewhere in this volume: *ralliement*, being general support for the regime; and *amalgame*, which meant active participation in it. There was a reasonable degree of *ralliement* among some sections of the urban elites, but not always among those the French wished to cultivate. In Piedmont, where they ruled longest, support came from the bourgeoisie of the smaller provincial towns, rather than from the ranks of families which composed the service-nobility of the old order. They were among the few elements of the Italian elites with whom the French felt real affinity, as the products of an absolutist regime modelled closely on that of Louis XIV. However, most of this group—nobles educated at the University of Turin in civil law or in its progressive military schools—did not rally. The problem here was largely deep-rooted loyalty to the native dynasty, but the French also met with disappointment in Tuscany, though for different reasons. Whilst the Piedmontese represented the hopes for the absolutist aspect of the Napoleonic regime, the Tuscans—supposedly supporters of Peter-Leopold's reforms—were their hope for its enlightened reforming aspirations. Here too the French were mistaken, finding the Tuscan aristocracy more dominated by conservative, Catholic values than they had foreseen. This was a cultural rather than a political problem, for the rapidly shifting fortunes of the Archduchy did not foster dynastic loyalties; indeed, the Tuscan elite had supported the Spanish Bourbons foisted on them in 1801, largely because the latter perpetuated the conservative policies of the Habsburg, Ferdinand III.[21] In contrast, the French knew enough about the Genoese patricians and the Romans not to place real hopes in them as active participants. Few political cultures were as alien to that of the Napoleonic regime as those of Papal states or the Republic of St George; the former was run by the Church—bishops ran provinces, the College of Cardinals doubled as the central government—while the latter relied on the patrician families of Genoa to serve as administrators and magistrates on the Rota, whose name denotes the amateur, voluntary terms of public service. In both states, professional qualifications were, quite literally, optional. This sat incongruously with a regime that created the *Grandes Écoles* to train future bureaucrats. In 1811, when asked to supply Paris with the details of magistrates who might be the equivalent of French *parlementaires*, with a view to appointing them to the senior courts, the prefect could but reply that Genoa had never had a professional magistracy.[22] Not surprisingly, few Ligurians entered public service. This was repeated everywhere outside Piedmont.

The incompatibility of the Italian elites with Napoleonic norms left huge gaps in the judiciary and administration. The void was filled either by the patriots of the *triennio* or by the French themselves. Patriots confessed openly that the vendettas of 1799 had left them with nowhere else to turn. Barrocchio, the mayor of the Piedmontese town of Alessandria, probably spoke for all of them when he noted: 'My political existence depends on the fate of the government; its enemies are my enemies.'[23] The patriots were too small in number, however, and often seen as incompetent by the French; by and large, they occupied subordinate posts in the administrative and judicial hierarchies, save for a few Piedmontese, notably Ugo Vincenzo Botton di Castellamonte and Luigi Peyretti di Condove, both of whom rose high in the French courts, the former remaining in France in 1814.[24] All but one of the prefects of the 14 Italian departments, and many of the sub-prefects, were French or Piedmontese, as were the public prosecutors and most of the senior magistrates on the Courts of Appeal; the French and Piedmontese dominated the Criminal Courts, as they did the Gendarmerie. In practice, the French on the ground not only despised the reactionary elements of the elite as degenerate and priest-ridden, they also had little time for their Piedmontese colleagues. Future events often leant this irony. Ferdinando Dal Pozzo, a Piedmontese patriot from the provincial town of Vercelli, was a lawyer who rose to the most senior positions on the French courts of Genoa and then Rome, but his competence was always suspect among his French colleagues. Dal Pozzo's work in the creation of the tribunals in the Roman departments was attacked bitterly in the general inspection reports of 1810[25] and continued to be ridiculed by French magistrates who inherited his work. A seemingly bland remark on Dal Pozzo's work was all the more damning. On the eve of the creation of the new Cour Impériale, the French procurator said simply that, 'in the new structures, it will be very important to have capable men as public prosecutors, because honesty, of itself, is not enough'.[26] In the years after 1814, however, Dal Pozzo emerged as a sage of now lost Napoleonic jurisprudence and a beacon of progressive politics. His legal meditations, much sought after in elite, reforming circles, were published in ill-concealed anonymity.[27]

Conclusion

The significance of annexation was seminal, although the influence of direct rule from France was neither predictable nor uniform for any of these territories. If the Italian elites learnt from the Napoleonic example for the process of reform and reunification, it was largely as spectators, at least outside Piedmont. As so often elsewhere, their first contact with the modern state left the masses more oppressed, bullied and exploited than at any previous time in their experience. Nevertheless, the profundity of the Napoleonic legacy is indisputable. The decades immediately after 1814 saw policies of reaction and forgetting, as was the case in other parts of post-Napoleonic Europe, alongside concerted attempts to absorb at least some essential parts of the Napoleonic regime into the restored orders. The Piedmontese instituted an intensive reaction, but kept the Gendarmerie, renamed the Carabinieri Reale; Pius VII retained many French reforms; Marie-Louise ruled Parma-Piacenza almost as a French department. Everywhere, the imprint of French judicial and administrative practices was deep. Equally, harsh French repression, the brutal imposition of conscription and the cultural callousness of their religious reforms left scars across the social spectrum and so, almost inadvertently, gave the restored regimes a certain amount of political capital to help them weather the difficult circumstances of post-war Europe. For better and for worse, in negative and positive ways, the experience of Napoleonic rule in these varied parts of Italy left indelible marks.

Notes

1. For a survey in English: Michael Broers, 'The Parochial Revolution: 1799 and the Counter-revolution in Italy,' *Renaissance and Modern Studies*, 33 (1989): 159–74.
2. For an overview, in English, setting disorder in its economic context: John A. Davis, *Conflict and Control. Law and Order in Nineteenth Century Italy* (Basingstoke, 1987), 17–65.
3. Gabrielle Turi, *'Viva Maria': La Reazione alle riforme Leopoldine, 1790–1799* (Florence, 1969).
4. Alice Raviola Blythe, 'Le rivolte del luglio 1797 nel Piemonte meridionale', *Studi Storici*, 39 (1998): 401–47.
5. Michael Broers, *Napoleonic Imperialism and the Savoyard Monarchy, 1773–1821. State Building in Piedmont* (Lampeter, 1997). Steven Clay, 'Le brigandage en Provence du Directoire au Consulat, 1795–1802', in *Du Directoire au Consulat (3) : Brumaire dans l'histoire du lien politique et de l'État-Nation*, ed. J. P. Jessene (Rouen, 2001), 70–71.
6. Michael Broers, *The Napoleonic Empire in Italy, 1796–1814. Cultural Imperialism in a European Context?* (Basingstoke, 2005), 83–93. Vincenzo Paltrinieri, *I moti contro Napoleone negli stati di parma e Piacenza (1805–1806)* (Bologna, 1927).
7. Broers, *Napoleonic Empire*, 48–51.
8. Arcvhivio di Stato, Genoa (ASG) Prefettura Francese, Pacco 116, fasciolo 155 (Alta Polizia) S. Prefect, Novi to Prefect, 13 April 1813.
9. ASG Prefettura Francese, Pacco 170, fasciolo 230 (Polizia) Barrabino, *Maire*, San Cypriano to D'Auzers, 30 March 1809.
10. Archives Nationales, Paris (ANP) F7 (Police-Générale) 8822 (Gênes) D'Auzers to Min, 3 arrond., 3 July 1810. Prefect to Min, 3 arrond., 26 April 1810. D'Auzers to Min, 3 arrond., 3 July 1810.
11. Osvaldo Raggio, *Faide e Parentele. Lo stato genovese visto dalla Fontanabuona* (Turin, 1990).

12. ANP F7 8797 (Apennines) D'Auzers to Min, 3 arrond., 5 February 1814. F7 8833 (Gênes) D'Auzers to Min, 3 arrond., 7 March 1814.
13. For the distinction: Colin Lucas, 'Résistances populaires à la Révolution dans le sud-est', in *Mouvements populaires et conscience sociale*, ed. Jean Nicolas (Paris, 1985), 484. Roger Dupuy, *De la Révolution à la Chouannerie* (Paris, 1988).
14. Clive Emsley, *Gendarmes and the State in Nineteenth Century Europe* (Oxford, 1999), 155–172.
15. Michael Broers, 'War and Crime in Napoleonic Italy, 1800–1814: Regeneration, Imperialism and Resistance', *Criminal Justice History*, 16 (2002): 21–52.
16. Broers, *Napoleonic Imperialism*, 318–325. Paul Bergounioux, 'Brigandage et répression dans les Bouches-du-Tibre: 1810–1813', *Annales historiques de la Révolution française*, 345 (2006), 93–114, http://ahrf.revues.org/document7063.html (19 November 2009).
17. Adriano Prosperi, *Tribunali della coscienza: inquisitori, confessori, missionari* (Turin, 1996). Giorgio Lombardi (ed.) *La guerra del sale (1680–1699). Rivolte e frontiere del Piemonte barocco*, 3 vols (Milan, 1986).
18. Candido Bona, *Le 'Amicizie'. Società e rinascita religiosa (1770–1830)* (Turin, 1962). On the Scotti-Douglas, see Broers, *Napoleonic Empire*, 269–270. On the Patrizzi, see ibid. 270–271. On the Stoffa, see ibid. 237–240.
19. Broers, *Napoleonic Empire*, 83.
20. Michael Broers, *The Politics of Religion in Napoleonic Italy. The war against God, 1801–1814* (London, 2002), 164.
21. Franz Pesendorfer, *Ferdinando III e la Toscana in età napoleonica* (Florence, 1986).
22. ANP BB5 (Organisation Judiciaire) 296 (Gênes) Prefect to Min. Justice, 11 March 1811.
23. ANP F7 (Police-Générale) 8836 (Marengo) Barrocchio to Min, Police-Générale, 18 May 1809.
24. Giorgio Vaccarino, 'Ugo Vincenzo Botton di Castellamonte: l'esperienza giacobina di un illuminista piemontese,' *Bolletino Storico Bibliografico Subalpino*, 63 (1965): 161–202. On Peyretti, see Broers, *Napoleonic Imperialism*, 449.
25. ANP BB5 313 (Rome) 'Rapport sur l'organisation judiciaire des États romains,' Coffinhal to Min. Justice, undated (1810).
26. ANP BB5 313 (Rome) Proc. Cour d'Appel to Min. Justice, 15 June 1811.
27. Ferdinando Dal Pozzo, *Opuscoli d'un avvocato milanese*, 8 vols (Milan, 1817).

17
The Feudal Question in the Kingdom of Naples
Anna Maria Rao

Joseph Bonaparte's abolition of feudalism, enacted on 2 August 1806, was hailed by contemporaries as a fundamental legal initiative that ended an ancient system of oppression and administrative inequality. A new state had been born and the people, as Vincenzo Cuoco wrote in the very first issue of his newspaper, the *Corriere di Napoli*, could now rediscover 'the fullness of their powers and civil freedom'.[1]

Even historians have seen this law as the symbol of a real break with the past,[2] the lynchpin of the modernization policy of the new government. Joseph Bonaparte immediately demonstrated that it was possible to pass directly from planning and theory to action. The abolition of feudalism had long been discussed and desired by Neapolitan reformers during the late eighteenth century, but all they had managed to obtain from the Bourbons was a few very biased measures limiting the jurisdiction of the barons. Vincenzo Cuoco was an intellectual product of that hothouse of reform and was well aware of conditions in the provinces. He had read closely the great works of Antonio Genovesi and Gaetano Filangieri, which denounced the feudal system, identifying it as the principle obstacle to renewal in the kingdom. So Cuoco, in his first article of 16 August (and later in *Corriere di Napoli*) laid out with great clarity what the abolition of feudalism fundamentally implied, namely: the elimination of delegated jurisdictions, themselves enacted in a very specific way, and the general reform of judicial administration; the redimensioning of the role of professional legal activity, which had always had a prominent place in southern Italian society; the re-ordering of the fiscal system along the lines of a single type of property taxation; the affirmation of the sanctity of private property; and the stimulation of the economy through internal free trade. Moreover, it was thought that the abolition of feudalism would fundamentally affect politics. With the barons deprived of their noble titles derived from feudal lands, they would no longer be able to claim the role of an intermediary body within the state, a role which they had enjoyed since the seventeenth century; henceforth, their hopes of playing an active role in the state would be as landholders within a new political landscape, characterized by private property.

The application of the law, however, was not an easy business. Historians in the early twentieth century criticized the limited impact the law had on the peasantry: abolition did not improve their lot because it did not bring about a redistribution of property, nor did it favour the formation of small- and medium-sized peasant smallholdings. Feudal demesnes remained firmly in the hands of ex-feudal lords or large landowners.[3] In the 1980s, historians began to contest this negative assessment, underlining the overall economic stimulus given to the economy by large enterprises.[4] It is now accepted that it is no longer possible to have a uniform view of the results of the feudal laws for all the different regions of the kingdom. The burden of feudalism was not felt in the same way, everywhere, and so abolition produced different results, depending on specific economic, geographic and social conditions. Even feudal lords fared differently: some transformed themselves into private property owners retaining a large part of their property, whilst others saw themselves as worse off.[5]

John Davis' recent volume on the Kingdom of Naples in the Napoleonic period[6] raises new doubts as to whether the law abolishing feudalism and the measures put in place to enact it really did represent a break with the past. Taking a broader chronological perspective, Davis claims that the breakdown of the feudal system had already occurred in the last decades of the eighteenth century, partly through reform, but largely because of the economic context. Davis disputes the idea of the backwardness traditionally associated with the Kingdom of Naples. Rather, he emphasizes the vibrancy of the social transformations and the political struggle which characterized the late eighteenth century. Thus, he significantly dilutes the generally held conviction that Napoleonic government brought about a modernizing break with the past. But even Davis finds himself obliged to underline one undeniable fact, fundamental for understanding the importance and influence of the Napoleonic abolition of feudalism: 'the law of August 1806 demonstrated that it was one thing to abolish feudalism where it no longer existed, but something quite different in Naples where it was a pervasive and deeply contentious reality'.[7]

One way to measure the radical nature of the rupture represented by the abolition legislation is that the majority of the communities in the kingdom (the *universitates*) were subject to feudal jurisdiction; at the beginning of the eighteenth century only about a 100 out of 2,000 were under royal jurisdiction. This number grew in the 1760s when certain feudal families died out and their fiefs were transferred to the royal treasury under the law of devolution. According to data collected by the nineteenth-century historian, Lodovico Bianchini, out of the approximately 2,000 *universitates* in 1786, 384 were crown demesnes, with a population of slightly more than a million, whilst 1,616 were feudal demesnes, with 3,376,504 inhabitants.[8]

The exercise of jurisdiction was a powerful instrument in the hands of the barons, with it they were able to control economic production, the circulation of foodstuffs and social relations within the feudal demesne.[9] From the royal administration, the feudal system represented not only a dismemberment of sovereignty, but also entailed a fiscal system based on inequality, based on the concept of the kingdom as the king's personal property.

The eighteenth-century reforming enlightenment movement in Naples, beginning principally with Antonio Genovesi, had developed an increasingly critical anti-feudal polemic. As Jacques Rambaud, the greatest historian of Joseph Bonaparte's reign in Naples, wrote in 1911, 'national genius had anticipated the French'.[10] The reforming polemic attacked not only specific abuses, themselves long criticized by legal tradition, but also challenged the very legitimacy of the justice delegated to the barons. Gaetano Filangieri's *La scienza della legislazione*, published in 1780–85, launched a violent attack on feudalism as the dismemberment of sovereign authority, which by its very nature should be indivisible, and sought to create a codified legal system. Filangieri, who was himself the younger son of a feudal family, attacked the juridical institution of *fedecommesso* or entail, a legal construct whereby the aristocracy was able to prevent alienation (the break-up of inherited family demesnes), in fact this system immobilized the property market, impeding the free circulation of land.

The anti-feudal polemic developed precisely in the years in which economic and political changes began to weaken the power and wealth of the barons. Economic growth and price rises favoured not the barons (who remained largely distant from the direct management of their feudal lands) but rather the barons' agents and their tenants. When Calabria and Messina were hit by the earthquake of 1783, Ferdinando Galiani, then secretary of the Magistracy of Commerce, thought this catastrophe should be welcomed as an opportunity to reduce baronial power and abuses. In the early 1790s a great debate arose concerning the project whereby feudal lands devolved to the crown would no longer be resold as feudal lands but as fully private property, without jurisdiction. In the end, the involvement of the Kingdom of Naples in the anti-French war in 1793 drastically raised the State's financial needs, forcing the adoption of measures limiting some feudal fiscal privileges.[11]

For all these reasons, many historians consider the abolition of feudalism as a long process, rather than an act of individual will by Joseph Bonaparte. Another important stage in this long process was reached in 1799, when the government of the Neapolitan republic, after a stormy debate, passed the first law abolishing feudalism, which abolished noble titles and related jurisdictions, and seigneurial rights on persons without compensation, whilst *censi e diritti* (taxable rights) on objects were refunded and could even be redeemed. In its second and final version, promulgated on 26 April, the law also provided for the transfer of all feudal demesnes to the communes, whilst the law of 7 March reserved a quarter of these demesnes for the barons. The abolition never transpired, however, because of the overthrow of the Republican government.[12]

This emphasis on the long process of the debate, and earlier legislative action which prepared the ground for the abolition law of 1806, does not render the law less radical but simply shows how the new government managed to intervene so swiftly in a problem which had lasted for centuries. Moreover, the abolition of feudalism and the reacquisition of alienated taxation had a completely different significance for Napoleon Bonaparte. For him, these measures were first and foremost designed to serve as a channel for funds. As early as 6 March 1806 he sent his brother forthright instructions for the raising of war contributions totalling thirty million francs:

> Thirty million is nothing for the Kingdom of Naples.... You have gold everywhere because you have fiefs and alienated taxation everywhere. Make sure you avoid entrenching the abuses of the ancien régime; in two or three weeks, either by a decree from you or me, everything must be identified, all alienation of demesnes and also alienation of tax... should be examined, and a uniform and severe system of taxation be set up.[13]

He was promptly obeyed, not only with the immediate promulgation of the anti-feudal legislation, but through the equally rapid enactment of fiscal reform based on a property tax and on the reacquisition of alienated taxes.[14]

Conversely, the new government could not have begun its legislative career otherwise, the abolition of feudalism was in fact the first essential step in any attempt at state reform. As the report that accompanied the law of 2 August 1806 noted, the feudal system was 'one of the largest obstacles to the regeneration of a state'. It would not have been possible to enact financial and judicial reform without first abolishing feudalism; as the same report noted, in order to 'establish a uniform, fair and well-governed system for the collection of contribution', it was necessary to abolish feudalism, to eliminate the differences between properties of different types, whilst at the same time assuring the barons of their full property rights on their lands and compensating them for the rights they had just lost.[15]

In the end, these laws did in fact abolish feudalism and all feudal jurisdictions, all feudal lands were now subject to the common law of the kingdom. However, unlike in 1799, the hereditary nobility was preserved. Devolution duties and feudal taxes were suppressed since the ex-feudal lands were now subject to the same fiscal regime as other property. Personal duties and prohibitive duties (monopolies on the use of tools and other such items, the so-called banalities) were abolished with compensation. All rivers and waterways were declared public property. The barons conserved their full property rights over mills and other machinery or structures on what had been feudal lands. Royal rights were preserved unless the communities contested them in the courts. The tithe on oil, traditionally gathered from the feudal olive presses in the province of Lecce, was preserved. The feudal demesnes (which the law of 1799 had reserved for the communes) remained in the hands of the ex-barons, but the people preserved their rights of use until a new law could be passed which would determine how the lands should be divided up. Subordinate fiefdoms (*suffeudi*) were abolished.[16]

The royal bureaucrats well understood the importance of the mediating role traditionally played by courts in the political and social life of the Kingdom. Eighteenth-century reformers frequently denounced the inefficiency of the judges with respect to the punishment of seigneurial abuses and the complicity of those judges with the barons. The system was slow, confused and corrupt. Cuoco believed there were as many as 30,000 court cases running at that time between the communities and the barons, a real 'civil war in the courts', 'a real scourge'.[17] In 1799, Mario Pagano, during the debates on the feudal law, proposed that the barons' property deeds be verified not by the ordinary courts, whose failings (the deliberate delay of trials and the bias towards the powerful) were all too familiar, but by 'a commission of seven honest citizens', entrusted with making a decision in three months; past this date, the barons' possessions would be 'forever forfeit'.[18] A similar decision was taken by Joseph Bonaparte's government, fully aware that only an extraordinary magistracy could enact the legislation on abolition. On 9 November a Feudal Commission was created for the verification of the barons' title deeds regarding *piazze* (taxes on sales) and customs rights. The Commission, which was supposed to finish its work within two months, was finally dissolved on 21 June 1810. On 11 November 1806, another commission was created to judge and definitively resolve, before 1808, the many cases, then running between communities and the barons. This commission, too, was not to be dissolved before 20 August 1810.[19] As Vincenzo Cuoco wrote in his review of the book, *Storia degli abusi feudali* by Davide Winspeare (ex-president of the Feudal Commission), it was not sufficient simply to declare that feudalism was abolished, 'what was needed was an executive procedure that would tear out its roots'.[20]

Notwithstanding the enthusiasm of Vincenzo Cuoco (who was a member of the Commission appointed on 11 November 1806), contemporary criticism of these provisions were not slow in coming. Some thought that the law favoured the barons, transforming them into property owners but without destroying the 'tyranny' of feudalism. Indeed, application of the law had been transferred to the judiciary. However, both the nobles and the judges of the ordinary courts protested against the creation of extraordinary organs of justice. The liberal leaning noble, Prince Strongoli Francesco Pignatelli, accused the Feudal Commission and the justice minister, Giuseppe Zurlo, of despoiling and persecuting the barons.[21] Even Queen Caroline Bonaparte bemoaned the fate of the Neapolitan nobility. On 24 August 1810 she wrote to Murat that the poor nobles could not even afford suitable clothes for presentation at Court because a day did not go by when 'that damned commission' sent another noble to his ruin. She emphasized the great political and economic risks inherent in this. In Paris, people claimed 'that there is no king in Naples; it is the Revolution on the throne'. The experience of revolution showed the dangers of deposing the nobility, because the people, 'after having destroyed the nobles, never fail to overturn the throne'. This argument against the radicalism of the legislation— that the nobility and their lifestyle were beneficial to society and the economy of the capital—is particularly interesting; for Caroline, the ruin of the nobles was the ruin of the whole city.[22]

Despite these and other complaints, Murat continued to support Zurlo and the Feudal Commission, while the barons continued to resist fiercely and protest against the communes. The communes, however, appeared unable to profit from the moment. In September 1808, the Intendant of Calabria Ultra, Giuseppe de Thomasis, noted the apathy of the communes there; they appeared hesitant to approach the Feudal Commission to resolve their claims, perhaps from fear of reprisals. In the same year, the Intendant of Principato Ultra noted that the population was still under the influence of the old feudal aristocracy.[23] Nevertheless, the Commission of 11 November 1806 achieved a great deal. On its dissolution almost four years later it had judged over 5,000 cases and pronounced 1,700 decisions.[24]

Lauded by some contemporaries and despised by many others, the abolition legislation has continued to excite the praise and criticism of historians. In the nationalistic climate of the early twentieth century, Italian historians were little inclined to recognize the benefits of Napoleonic government in Naples. Romualdo Trifone, in particular, held that the legislation of the French decade had not favoured the increase of small- and medium-sized properties, nor effected substantial changes in the condition of the peasantry; for Trifone, they had been better served by the reforming actions and judicial activities of the ancien régime.

More recently, though still recognizing the limits of this legislation and its application, historians place greater emphasis on the critical role which this legislation played in the general reform of the state, rather than on its effect (or lack of it) on the redistribution of property, an area where it had little chance of success. As Pasquale Villani has observed, the abolition of feudality 'cannot be considered a failure simply because it did not manage to ensure the success of the division by quota and the sharing of the land amongst the poor peasants. Indeed, to expect that poor peasants would benefit from the ruin of the barons is ingenuous, to put it mildly. There was only one possible, more or less legitimate, heir to the barons namely, the gentlemen or *galantuomini*, that is, the various levels of the middling types in the towns and countryside of the kingdom'.[25]

The methods of application of the abolition legislation and their effects on the kingdom differed greatly from zone to zone and from family to family.

For the provinces of the Terra di Lavoro, the Principato Ultra, the Principato Citra (all three make up modern Campania), the data collected by Villani leave little doubt about the effectiveness of this legislation:

> In one respect the abolition laws and the application of the new civil code had more immediate effects with more important medium- and long-term consequences. For the provinces of Campania, an early Murat-period report noted that in the Terra di Lavoro, at the barons' expense, 26,878 *moggia*[26] of land became communal demesnes and 75,884 were allotted for civic use, whilst in the writer of the report's opinion, an 'infinite' number of *colonie* (farms) received legal recognition; in the Principato Citra, at the barons' expense, 87,000 *moggia* became either communal demesnes or were allotted for civic use and *colonie*, only 48,000 *moggia* received legal recognition; in the Principato Ultra, at the barons' expense, 58,000 *moggia* became either communal demesnes or were allotted for civic use and 60,000 *moggia* were freed from the burden of *terraggio* (a feudal cultivated-land tax). At this point began the controversial procedure called *quotizzazioni demaniali* (the sharing out by quota of demesnes) which was to last for more than a century and which, contrary to what is generally thought, should be seen as one of the principal measures which led to the creation of the peasant small holding... unstable peasant crop cultivation was often the guarantee of the survival of the large landholding via the practice of *terraggio*. The transformation of this typical sort of unstable cultivation into a now more or less definitive *colonia* and the sharing out by quota of communal lands were the most important contributions which the abolition laws gave to the formation of the peasant smallholding.[27]

In the same provinces, the legislation had even more radical effects on the economy, especially in manufacturing where traditional bonds were shattered—notably the textile mills in Arpino and Piedimonte d'Alife—and in the field of prohibitive duties; as for the sharing out of feudal demesnes and dismantling laws on the common use of land, the results were slower and remain more disputed.[28]

Different effects were seen in Molise. In some feuds belonging to the Francone family and later to the Caracciolo di Torella family, the decisions handed down by the Feudal Commission significantly modified the situation, reducing the income from tithes and *terraggi* and assigning a part of their feudal demesnes to the communes in compensation for the loss of civic use of land assigned with full property rights to the Caracciolo family.[29]

The numerous studies of the provinces in Puglia reveal a varied situation:

> In Terra di Bari, in the coastal parts and in the southern central region above Murgia, the land privatization process and the widespread practice

of wood cultivation had already modified the previous agrarian communitarian regime which the abolition laws had hoped to get rid of. The reform was therefore limited to the recognition and establishment of peasant possession; and whilst it did not remove the duties (*canoni* and *censi*) on that land, preferring to render them legitimate within the new system, in certain circumstances it did allow those duties to be redeemed. In cereal-pastoral Murgia the effects were on the other hand more radical, favouring the appropriation of the land either by the sheep farmers of the Dogana di Foggia, by large middling-type landowners, or by ex-feudal landowners. In this case, possibilities for industrial concerns to enjoy intense capitalist exploitation opened up, as in fact happened, but much later on, in the Capitanata.[30]

As regards the balance of property ownership in the countryside, the law on the division of demesnes took much longer to enact, not only as a result of local conflicts, but also because of the exceedingly complicated and controversial measurement problems faced by the agents appointed to oversee the partition.[31]

Analysis of individual noble families also reveals differences. For many, the legislation, in addition to redefining their noble status and lifestyle, radically affected the size and composition of their estates. They were hit by the property tax and the loss of at least part of their demesnes, and the produce derived from banalities (traditional fees) and jurisdictional duties. So many ex-feudal lords, though preserving a good deal of their estates and even, at times, increasing them with the purchase of national properties, saw their incomes decrease. For the Doria d'Angri family 'the power of their estate to offer a significant income was not even remotely challenged'; indeed, their property increased.[32] Conversely, the Caracciolo di Torchiarolo family saw the income from their baronial court estate, Salcito in Molise, reduced by a third.[33] The Serra di Gerace family saw their income of the Calabrian properties (Terranova, Gioia, Gerace) from *terraggio* and rents drop significantly, and the whole of their feudal demesne at Terranova was divided equally between the ex-feudal lord and the communes.[34] The Saluzzo di Corigliano family was hit hard by the abolition of feudalism, but worse still for them was the loss of their income linked to public debt; however, their lengthy presence at Court allowed them to make good their losses and to recover their wealth.[35] In southern Calabria, the powerful Ruffo di Scilla and Ruffo di Bagnara families, already hard hit by economic changes in the eighteenth century and by the earthquake of 1783, had their income significantly reduced under the French, not only because of the loss of their seigneurial rights but especially through the land tax, thereby losing the dominant role they had exercised for centuries in local society.[36]

For some of the families endowed with feudal lands in the Capitanata, the weakening of their social control through the loss of jurisdiction and seigneurial rights proved fatal: the Maresca di Serracapriola lost much of their income and new social groups rose to prominence in their former fiefs in the Valle del Fortore; however others, such as the Pignatelli di Bisaccia, managed to keep their estates on a relatively even keel.[37]

In Terra d'Otranto, the great Caracciolo di Martina family in the eighteenth and nineteenth centuries was hit more by disease and early deaths than by the legislation, although it contributed to their permanent removal to Naples and definitive transformation into the great Court nobility.[38]

The judgements of the Feudal Commission on the very many cases pending between the ancient D'Avalos family and the communities in their ex-feudal demesnes were decisive in significantly reducing their income from duties, land and feudal rights; in 1806 the last member of the family, Tommaso, followed the Bourbons to Palermo, only to die there shortly after.[39] The pro-Bourbon nobility in exile was hit by the sequestration of property in addition to the abolition legislation, but even in these cases, many families got their lands and prestigious duties back after the Restoration.

The transition for many families was from feudal lands, to Court, to public administration, such as the Tocco dei Montemiletto who were endowed with feudal lands in a strongly commercialized grain zone in Principato Ultra, which explains their mercantile pretensions throughout the eighteenth century.[40] With reference to the Tocco family, Michèle Benaiteau notes how this society, which was suffering the serious political and military upheavals of the turn of the eighteenth and nineteenth centuries, faced a grave crisis. In the Tocco's feudal lands, the peasant economy had almost reached the lowest subsistence level and the abolition of feudalism would not have pulled it back from the brink. She agrees with John Davis: 'Whilst the legislative and operative results of the so-called Napoleonic decade suited the wider aspirations of the country, they also significantly accelerated the breakdown of peasant society, subjecting the kingdom to a war economy in the service of Napoleonic imperialism.'[41]

The patrimony of another great Puglian family, the Muscettola di Leporano, received a definitive blow from the legislation, as studied by Maria Antonietta Visceglia. They provide 'a historiographical perspective which does not give the reforms of the Napoleonic period such a revolutionary scope as to impose a violent and radical change in the structures of production, but one which would rather consider the abolition of feudalism as a century-long process, beginning in the middle of the eighteenth century with the far-reaching transformations for socio-economic life, felt post 1764 and continuing throughout the first half of the nineteenth century.'[42] For Visceglia, even today, 'the history of the selection which the abolition legislation operated upon ranks of the feudal aristocracy is yet to be written'.[43]

Notwithstanding either the hit taken in terms of traditional prerogatives, or noble protests, the aristocracy did not, in general, put up much resistance to the abolition legislation, unlike their fierce opposition in 1799. By 1806, the abolition of feudal jurisdiction seemed inevitable. By the late eighteenth century, many grand nobles saw it as a useless burden; even the Bourbon ministers, in exile in Palermo, had no doubts on the matter when, after a restoration, Ferdinand IV consulted them about the re-ordering of the kingdom. In a report written between late 1806 and February 1807, they wanted the French law of 2 August abolished, but only in order to promulgate new legislation, little different from that of Joseph Bonaparte except for one particularly delicate point, revealing of their pro-baronial prejudices: they wanted the feudal demesnes to remain the completely independent property of the barons.[44]

Little is known about the consequences of the abolition legislation in the provinces, their juridical status, or their boundaries, relative to the people who lived there. The definitive dissolution of the great feudal estates— those collections of properties (often straddling provincial borders) belonging to a single family—was one of the most important effects of the transformation of the ancient families from feudal lords to rent-collecting property owners.[45] However, feudalism also contained within itself a whole system of patronage and assistance (dowries for poor girls, for example) which for many years, at least in certain areas, had preserved paternalistic relationships. It embraced large clientage networks, and research is needed to be done to asses at what point these networks collapsed or to what extent they were used by the nobles and common people as a means of resisting Napoleonic 'modernization'. The abolition of feudalism must be studied from a much wider perspective than simply land assets or state reform.

Recent studies have examined the cultural effects of the abolition legislation. The relative impoverishment of the feudal families brought with it a diminution of their presence in the world of art and book collecting: in patronizing the arts, and in theatre-based sociability; there were conspicuous changes in ownership of their ancient book and art collections.[46] Their absence was only partly filled by the sociability of the middle classes. Nevertheless, new impulses were given to Court life and the royal collection, especially during Murat's reign.[47]

In conclusion, the laws abolishing feudalism were willed by Napoleon Bonaparte to extract the maximum amount of money from the Kingdom of Naples, not from a desire for modernization. Indeed, Napoleon suggested his brother grant feudal titles to Frenchmen in his entourage to ensure their loyalty.[48] He also repeatedly advised him to show no pity to 'the *lazzaroni* who kill with the stiletto' and to have them shot. Joseph should make sure first and foremost that he was feared: 'It is only by a salutary terror that you will impose yourself upon the Italian people.'[49] His memory of the Sanfedista uprising of 1799 must still have been quite fresh.[50]

Joseph was able to draft the abolition legislation relatively rapidly because of the accumulation of debates and projects on the subject. The promulgation of the law of 2 August did not meet with resistance from the feudal aristocracy who, by this point, had long been ready to abandon its juridical rights and become a class of landowners. The complicated and delicate problem of the enactment of the legislation was entrusted to the judiciary; judicial power thus continued to play an influential political and social role. The mediation of the judiciary was typical not just in the administrative but also in the political life of the Kingdom of Naples, but the creation of an extraordinary judiciary made the mediation more trenchant and effective after 1806. The abolition of feudalism did not, and could not, bring about substantial changes in the condition of the peasantry. It was, however, the preliminary condition, as well as the strongest lever, for a radical reorganization of the state. The abolition of feudalism is one of the measures of Napoleonic government which best shows the linkage of force and consensus characteristic of its orientations and actions. As Lodovico Bianchini wrote in the early nineteenth century—himself by no means gentle in his judgements on the revolutionary and Napoleonic periods—that in Naples 'that government was successful in its enterprise, not only by force of arms but also by force of opinion'.[51]

Notes

1. Vincenzo Cuoco, 'Osservazioni sulla legge dell'abolizione della feudalità', in *Corriere di Napoli*, n. 1, 16 agosto 1806. *Scritti giornalistici 1801–1815*, ed. Domenico Conte and Maurizio Martirano, 2, *Periodo napoletano* (Naples, 1999), 9.
2. On the description for French decade, see Anna Maria Rao, 'Il "Decennio francese": appunti su una denominazione', *Due francesi a Napoli, Atti del Colloquio internazionale di apertura delle celebrazioni del Bicentenario del Decennio francese (1806–1815), Napoli, 23–24–25 marzo 2006*, ed. Rosanna Cioffi, Renata de Lorenzo, Aldo Di Biasio, Luigi Mascilli Migliorini, Anna Maria Rao (Naples, 2008), 177–194.
3. Alfonso Perrella, *L'eversione della feudalità nel napolitano. Dottrine che vi prelusero. Storia, legislazione e giurisprudenza* (Campobasso, 1909). Romualdo Trifone, *Feudi e demani. Eversione della feudalità nelle provincie napoletane. Dottrine, storia, legislazione e giurisprudenza* (Milan, 1909). Francesco Lauria, *Demani e feudi nell'Italia meridionale* (Naples, 1923).
4. See especially Elio Cerrito, 'Strutture economiche e distribuzione del reddito in Capitanata nel decennio francese', in *Produzione, mercato e classi sociali nella Capitanata moderna e contemporanea*, ed. Angelo Massafra (Foggia, 1984), 133–265.
5. For a survey, see Anna Maria Rao, 'Mezzogiorno e rivoluzione: trent'anni di storiografia', in *Studi storici*, 37 (1996): 981–1041, 1025–1030.
6. John A. Davis, *Naples and Napoleon. Southern Italy and the European Revolutions 1780–1860* (Oxford, 2006).
7. Ibid. 235.
8. Lodovico Bianchini, *Della storia delle finanze del Regno di Napoli*, second edition augmented and revised by the author (Palermo, 1839), 405.
9. See the instructions sent by the barons to the agents in Luca Covino, *I baroni del buon governo: istruzioni della nobiltà feudale nel Mezzogiorno moderno* (Naples, 2004).

10. Jacques Rambaud, *Naples sous Joseph Bonaparte 1806–1808* (Paris, 1911), 403.

11. See Anna Maria Rao, *L"amaro della feudalità'. La devoluzione di Arnone e la questione feudale a Napoli alla fine del '700* (Naples, 1997) (1st edition Naples, 1984). *Ead.*, 'Nel Settecento napoletano: la questione feudale', in *Cultura, intellettuali e circolazione delle idee nel '700*, ed. Renato Pasta (Milan, 1990), 51–106. *Ead.*, 'The feudal question, judicial systems and the Enlightenment', in *Naples in the Eighteenth Century, The Birth and Death of a Nation State*, ed. Girolamo Imbruglia (Cambridge, 2000), 95–117.

12. See Anna Maria Rao, 'La Repubblica napoletana del 1799', in *Napoli 1799–1815. Dalla Repubblica alla monarchia amministrativa*, ed. Anna Maria Rao and Pasquale Villani (Naples, 1995), 9–121, 37–47.

13. See Vincent Haegele (ed.) *Napoléon & Joseph. Correspondance intégrale 1784–1818* (Paris, 2007), 165. Napoleon was to harp on the same theme in successive letters.

14. Renata De Lorenzo, *Proprietà fondiaria e fisco nel Mezzogiorno: la riforma della tassazione nel decennio francese (1806–1815)* (Salerno, 1984).

15. Trifone, *Feudi e demani*, 175. More in general, on state reform, see Costanza D'Elia and Raffaella Salvemini (eds) *Riforma e struttura. L'impatto della dominazione napoleonica nel Mezzogiorno fra breve e lungo periodo* (Naples, 2008).

16. The text is published in Romualdo Trifone, 176–178. For an examination of the dispositions for abolition, see also Giuseppe Galasso, *Il Regno di Napoli. Il Mezzogiorno borbonico e napoleonico (1734–1815)* (Turin, 2007), 1052–1057.

17. Vincenzo Cuoco, *Osservazioni sulla legge dell'abolizione della feudalità*, 9–10.

18. See Rao, 'La Repubblica napoletana del 1799', 41.

19. See Trifone, *Feudi e demani*, 181–190.

20. Vincenzo Cuoco, 'Storia degli abusi feudali, di Davide Winspeare, dedicata al Re, tomo I, Napoli 1811', in *Monitore delle Due Sicilie*, n. 197, 18 settembre 1811, in *Scritti giornalistici*, 2, 387.

21. See Pasquale Villani, 'Il decennio francese' in Rao and Villani, 179–284: 232.

22. Letter cited in ibid. 233.

23. Letters cited in ibid. 225–226. See also Armando De Martino, *La nascita delle intendenze. Problemi dell'amministrazione periferica nel Regno di Napoli 1806–1815* (Naples, 1984), 388, 391.

24. See Manfredi Palumbo, *I comuni meridionali prima e dopo le leggi eversive della feudalità. Feudi, università, comuni, demani* (Montecorvino Rovella (Salerno), 1910), 36.

25. Villani, 238; see also useful remarks on Trifone, *Feudi e demani*, 226–228.

26. One moggio equals approximately three-quarters of an acre.

27. Pasquale Villani, 'L'eredità storica e la società rurale', in *Storia d'Italia. Le regioni dall'Unità ad oggi, La Campania*, eds Paolo Macry and Pasquale Villani (Turin, 1990), 3–90: 30–31. For a broader view of the picture, essential reading is Pasquale Villani, *La vendita dei beni dello stato nel Regno di Napoli (1806–1815)* (Milan, 1964).

28. Aurelio Lepre, *Terra di Lavoro*, in *Storia del Mezzogiorno*, vol. V, *Napoli capitale e le province* (Rome, 1986), 95–234, esp. 203–214.

29. Angelo Massafra, 'Orientamenti culturali, rapporti produttivi e consumi alimentari nelle campagne molisane tra la metà del Settecento e l'Unità' in *Campagne e territorio nel Mezzogiorno fra Settecento e Ottocento*, ed. idem (Bari, 1984) especially 68–72.

30. Pasquale Villani, *Introduzione*, in *Economia e classi sociali nella Puglia moderna* (Naples, 1974), 1–16: 11. On the Capitanata see Angelo Massafra, 'Note sulla

geografia feudale della Capitanata in età moderna. Nobiltà e feudalità nel Mezzogiorno moderno: problemi e orientamenti di ricerca', in *La Capitanata in età moderna. Ricerche*, ed. Saverio Russo (Foggia, 2004), 17–47; Anna Maria Rao, 'L'eversione della feudalità', Il Decennio francese in Capitanata (1806–1815)', in *Atti del 12° Convegno nazionale Preistoria, protostoria e storia della Daunia, San Severo 14–16 dicembre 1990*, ed. Giuseppe Clemente (San Severo, 1991), 15–28.

31. Francesca Maria Lo Faro, 'Ingegneri, architetti, tavolari: periti "di misura" nel Regno di Napoli fra Settecento e Ottocento', in *Storia e misura. Indicatori sociali ed economici nel Mezzogiorno d'Italia (secoli XVIII–XX)*, ed. Renata De Lorenzo (Milan, 2007), 305–361, esp. 344–346.

32. Maria Luisa Storchi, 'La questione del patrimonio fondiario di Marcantonio Doria, in Eboli, nel primo quarantennio del XIX secolo', in *Studi sulla società meridionale* (Naples, 1978), 127–164.

33. Angelo Massafra, *Orientamenti culturali*, 72 n. 44.

34. Agnese Sinisi, 'Le aziende calabresi dei Principi Serra di Gerace nella prima metà del XIX secolo', in *Problemi di storia delle campagne meridionali nell'età moderna e contemporanea*, ed. Angelo Massafra (Bari, 1981), 91–116. *Ead.*, 'I contratti di affitto delle "gabelle" dei feudi di Gioia e di Terranova, nella Calabria Ulteriore, nell'età moderna', in *Archivio storico per le province napoletane*, 17 (1978), 359–384; John Davis, *Società e imprenditori nel Regno Borbonico. 1815–1860* (Roma-Bari, 1979), 95–107.

35. Giovanni Montroni, *Gli uomini del re. La nobiltà napoletana nell'Ottocento* (Rome, 1996), 29–31. For more detail on the Saluzzo see Raul Merzario, *Signori e contadini di Calabria. Corigliano Calabro dal XVI al XIX secolo* (Milan, 1975).

36. Giuseppe Caridi, *La spada, la seta, la croce. I Ruffo di Calabria dal XIII al XIX secolo* (Turin, 1995), 222–233.

37. See Saverio Russo, 'Agricoltura e pastorizia in Capitanata nella prima metà dell'Ottocento', in Massafra *Produzione, mercato e classi sociali*, 267–320, esp. 297–308; Idem. 'Distribuzione della proprietà stratificazione e mobilità sociale a Cerignola nell'Ottocento', *Il Mezzogiorno preunitario. Economia, società e istituzioni*, ed. Angelo Massafra (Bari, 1988), 883–899, esp. 886; Idem. *Storie di famiglie. Mobilità della ricchezza in Capitanata tra Sette e Ottocento* (Bari, 1995), 30.

38. Elena Papagna, *Sogni e bisogni di una famiglia aristocratica. I Caracciolo di Martina in età moderna* (Milan, 2002), 186–189.

39. Flavia Luise, *I D'Avalos. Una grande famiglia aristocratica napoletana nel Settecento* (Naples, 2006), 164–171, 369.

40. Valeria Del Vasto, *Baroni nel tempo. I Tocco di Montemiletto dal XVI al XVIII secolo* (Naples, 1995).

41. Michèle Beaniteau, *Vassalli e cittadini. La signoria rurale nel Regno di Napoli attraverso lo studio dei feudi dei Tocco di Montemiletto (XI–XVIII secolo)* (Bari, 1997), 368.

42. Maria Antonietta Visceglia, 'La vicenda dei Muscettola tra XV e XIX secolo', in *Il bisogno di eternità. I comportamenti aristocratici a Napoli in età moderna*, ed. Maria Antonietta Visceglia (Naples, 1988), 253.

43. Ibid. 255. For details concerning on Neapolitan noble families see also *Ead.*, *Identità sociali. La nobiltà napoletana nella prima età moderna* (Milan, 1998), 9–58.

44. Antonio Mele, 'La legge sulla feudalità del 1806 nelle carte Marulli', in *All'ombra di Murat. Studi e ricerche sul Decennio francese*, ed. Saverio Russo (Bari, 2007), 87–112.

45. See also the case of the Doria family and their feudal estate in Melfi, reconstructed in Agnese Sinisi, *Il 'buon governo' degli uomini e delle risorse. Gestione di*

uno 'Stato' feudale e governo del territorio nel Mezzogiorno fra Settecento e Ottocento (Naples, 1996).

46. See Paola Fardella, 'Riflessi della Repubblica sul collezionismo privato napoletano', in *Novantanove in idea. Linguaggi miti memorie*, ed. Augusto Placanica and Maria Rosaria Pelizzari (Naples, 2002), 231–246, esp. 240–241. Flavia Luise, 'Aristocrazia e raccolte librarie', in *Cultura e lavoro intellettuale: istituzioni, saperi e professioni nel Decennio francese, Atti del primo seminario di studi 'Decennio francese (1806–1815)'*, ed. Anna Maria Rao (Naples, 2009), 235–261.

47. Ornella Scognamiglio, *I dipinti di Gioacchino e Carolina Murat. Storia di una collezione* (Naples, 2008); *Idem., La figura del collezionista tra affermazione sociale e nuovo gusto 'borghese'*, in Rao, *Cultura e lavoro intellettuale*, 263–275.

48. Letter by Napoleon to Joseph, dated Paris, 8 March 1806, in *Correspondance intégrale*, 167.

49. Letter dated 6 March, ibid. 165.

50. See Anna Maria Rao (ed.), *Folle controrivoluzionarie. Le insorgenze popolari nell'Italia giacobina e napoleonica* (Roma, 1999).

51. Bianchini, *Della storia delle finanze*, 525.

18
The Illyrian Provinces

Reinhard A. Stauber

The Austrian Empire had been comprehensively defeated at the end of the disastrous encounter at Wagram in 1809.[1] On the day the Peace Treaty of Schönbrunn was signed, 14 October 1809, Napoleon issued a terse administrative decree creating the Illyrian Provinces.[2] To those parts of his hereditary lands that Francis I had to cede to the French (and which cut off the Habsburg Monarchy's access to the Adriatic Sea) were added Dalmatia, the territory of Ragusa/Dubrovnik and the bay of Cattaro/Kotor. In the far eastern part of the Tyrol, the judiciary districts of Lienz, Sillian and Windisch-Matrei were added in 1810–11.[3]

Motives for annexation

As one of the artificial states typical of the Napoleonic era, the Illyrian Provinces comprised areas that had previously belonged to a number of different states:

- Habsburg territories, mainly in central Austria (*Innerösterreich*): the western part of Carinthia, Gorizia, Carniola, Trieste and the central part of Istria; and the eastern parts of the Tyrol;
- coastal areas and islands of the former Republic of Venice and given to the Habsburgs in 1797 when the Republic was dismantled, comprising western Istria and the Dalmatian coast—these areas were initially given to the Kingdom of Italy;
- parts of the Kingdom of Croatia, an associated country of the Kingdom of Hungary, south of the river Sava, including (from 1776) the city of Rijeka/Fiume;
- six regimental districts on the Military Border with the Ottoman Empire, which the Habsburgs had built up since the re-conquest of Hungary; and
- the city and territory of the republic of Dubrovnik/Ragusa, nominally under Ottoman rule but in fact independent.

In total, the Illyrian Provinces covered an area of about 55,000 square kilometres, a conglomerate of completely different traditions and cultures that spreads over five states on today's map. At the time, the provinces were home to an ethnically mixed population of about 1.5 million people (made up of about one half Croatians and Serbs, about one third Slovenes, and the remaining sixth German and Italian speakers). The seat of the central administration was not located in Trieste, the largest city, but for strategic reasons in Ljubljana/Laibach, today's Slovenian capital. Eighty-five per cent of the Illyrian Provinces' population were Catholic, and the rest predominantly Orthodox and living on the Military Border and in Dalmatia.[4] The term Illyria, derived from the name of a pre-Roman tribe, is imprecise. Sometimes it referred to Balkan Slavs in general; at others it meant simply Croatians, Bosnians and Dalmatians. In the nineteenth century the Southern Slav tongues, most frequently Croatian, were identified as the Illyrian language.[5]

Constitutionally, the Illyrian Provinces were a part of the French Empire in the sense that they were ruled directly from Paris. Yet, like Catalonia for example, they did not form a constituent part of the Empire as they had not been formally incorporated into the French state by a Senatorial resolution.[6] Their 'special status'[7] was reflected in the fact that the French system of *départements* was not introduced into their administrative structure and that the military character of their administration remained evident.

Napoleon's motives in creating this artificial state can be found at a number of different levels. Joseph Fouché thought that Napoleon had several plans for the future of the Provinces, and that he often alternated between them. We cannot overlook military-strategic considerations on the eastern and south-eastern borders,[8] centred on the creation of a buffer zone against Russia, and the continuation of the tradition of maintaining a Military Border against the Ottoman Empire. The main factor, however, was shaped by the continental blockade and continental system, both essential to French hegemony. The Illyrian Provinces ensured, at least on paper, that the eastern Adriatic coast was closed to British ships and goods. The Provinces were intended to encourage trade with Constantinople via the land route, through which France and Italy mainly imported cotton.[9] To this extent, the purpose of the most important building work of the French period in the Balkans, the *Route Impériale No. 5 de Laybach en Albanie*, went beyond purely military requirements.[10] Begun in 1807 in the area around Dubrovnik, by 1810 Route 5 extended as far as Kotor and joined up with existing sections of road linking Laibach, Zadar/Zara and Split. The route should also be viewed in the context of the increasingly aggressive nature of Napoleon's policy of expansion and extending the outer empire, particularly in the years 1809–10,[11] namely: the annexation of the Papal States in May 1809; the annexation of Holland in July 1810; the seizure of the whole of Germany's North Sea coast with the large harbours of Emden, Bremen, Hamburg and Lübeck (considerably reducing the territory of the Kingdom of Westphalia) and the parts of Holstein between Hamburg and the Baltic Sea, wiping out the Duchy of Oldenburg; and in December 1810 the removal of the Valais (with its important road connections to northern Italy) from the Swiss Confederation and transformation into the *Département* Simplon.

In his major study of the European state system, Paul Schroeder points out that there was probably also a political-strategic component to the foundation of the Illyrian Provinces. Napoleon was aware of how highly the imperial state of Austria valued these areas, now that she was entirely landlocked.[12] Even in 1810, in discussions with the new Austrian chief minister, Metternich, Napoleon at times held out the Provinces as objects of negotiation or exchange, at one point for example, in return for what was left of Galicia, whose northern section had become part of the Duchy of Warsaw. Metternich's correspondence and memoranda show that regaining the Illyrian regions was a high priority for him. When, in March 1812, Metternich agreed to provide an Austrian army corps for Napoleon's Russian campaign, Napoleon dangled the prospect of Austria gaining either Prussian Silesia or the Illyrian Provinces as a reward. At the negotiations in Dresden, in June 1813, as his final attempt to appease Napoleon before he joined the Allies, Metternich still demanded the evacuation of the Grand Duchy of Warsaw by the French and its repartition among the three eastern powers, the restoration of the Hanse towns and Danzig to Prussia, and the Illyrian provinces to the Habsburgs.

Administrative organization

The Illyrian Provinces were divided into administrative units late in 1809, initially into ten provinces/intendancies and reduced to seven from 1811. Each one was headed by an intendant whose duties were, in principle, the same as those of a prefect. The part of Croatia that had previously been part of the Habsburg Military Border retained its special status, however. The intendancies were sub-divided into around twenty districts under *sous-délégués* (the number changed over time), the districts were sub-divided into cantons (the area of jurisdiction of justices of the peace) and finally the cantons into municipalities (*arrondissements communaux*). The larger towns were under a mayor (*maire*).[13] All leading functionaries were appointed in Paris, not elected.

The senior administrator in the Provinces was the Governor-General. The first person to fill this position, from 1809 to 1811, was Marshal Auguste de Marmont, Duke of Ragusa (1808), an artillery officer who had been at Napoleon's side since the siege of Toulon, in 1794.[14] He had gained administrative experience as Governor-General of Dalmatia and took his seat at Laibach in November 1809 after defeating Archduke Charles on the

Province (1811–12)	Capital	Share of Population (%)
Carinthia	Villach	10
Carniola	Ljubljana	25
Istria	Trieste	16
Croatia (Civil)	Karlovac	14
Dalmatia	Zadar	15
Dubrovnik	Dubrovnik	4
Military Province (Croatian military border)		16

battlefield of Znaim/Znojmo (10–11 July 1809) and being created a marshal by Napoleon. His pay, as was usual, was drawn from the *domaine extraordinaire* provided by the newly occupied areas.

The Governor-General was assisted by a Justice Commissaire, Joseph Coffinhal-Dunoyer, and a General Intendant of Finances who, in practice, headed the entire internal administration. This last position was first filled by Luc-Jacques-Éduard Dauchy—who, with Marmont, had headed Dalmatia's financial and domain administration since 1806, and had gained experience as a Prefect in Italy—and later by Charles-Godefroy Redon de Belleville and André-Christophe Count Chabrol de Crouzol, respectively.[15] As everywhere in Europe, these three top positions were filled exclusively by Frenchmen, though the position of Intendant could be different. The first generation of French administrative officials had been in the country since the military occupation of the Austrian parts of the Adriatic in July 1809, initially subordinate to the military commander, Baraguey d'Hilliers. Almost all were very young (in their twenties) and had only been appointed at the beginning of 1809 as auditors at the Council of State, the Napoleonic state's most important reservoir of elite administrative staff. When the Provinces were formally created and a French civil administration established in the autumn of 1809, they stayed in post for the time being, but 'found themselves on ground that tested their certainty in the universal applicability of their system of government'.[16]

The territorial divisions of the Illyrian Provinces, established at the end of 1809, had been fixed by Marmont—his guiding principle was to preserve the historical units of his eclectic state in preference to a rational restructuring. When General Intendant Dauchy tried to oppose this process, Marmont persuaded Paris to recall him in June 1810. In the course of this dispute, Marmont was also to dismiss several of the young intendants in the region of Carniola and Gorizia and replace them with men from the Illyrian Provinces. Thus 25-year-old François-Marie Fargues was replaced by Baron Janez Baselli von Süssenberg as *Intendant de la Haute Carniole résidant à Laybach*.[17]

In 1811, Marmont was himself recalled and given command of the French army in Portugal, his successor as Governor-General of the Illyrian

Provinces from 1811 to 1813 was the specialist engineer, General Henri-Gatien Bertrand. Bertrand was replaced in 1813, first by Andoche Junot, Duke of Abrantès (a purely nominal appointment, however, since Junot was by this time mentally ill), and then by Joseph Fouché, Duke of Otranto, who had been dismissed as Police Minister in 1810.[18] But Fouché had no time to administer. Two weeks after the Frenchman's staged entry into Laibach on 29 July 1813, Metternich declared war on the French Empire and Beauharnais withdrew all imperial troops to the western bank of the Isonzo River to protect the northern Italian heartlands. Fouché withdrew with the retreating army, moving his official headquarters first to Trieste at the end of August and then to Gorizia at the beginning of September, from whence he sent Napoleon his final report on Illyrian affairs at the beginning of October 1813. Thereafter, he left for Parma.

The final Organizational Decree for the Illyrian Provinces, in effect their constitution, was a highly detailed document with 271 articles, dating from 15 April 1811. In it Napoleon imposed his centralizing policy over attempts by the first Governor-General, Marmont, to secure certain exceptional rights for these peripheral provinces.[19] Subsidiary to the provisions of the Organizational Decree, the French *Code civil* came into force from 1 January 1812.[20] Criminal procedures were regulated by an ordinance from the Governor-General dated 25 September 1811.

It is difficult to establish to what extent the French civil code was actually implemented in practice, as the relevant authorities had to be set up first, and the tribunal districts were not defined until the beginning of 1812. According to the decree of 15 April 1811, the stages of judicial appeal began with the justices of the peace in the cantons, then went to eleven tribunals of first instance (those in the capitals of the provinces also functioned as criminal courts), three courts of appeal (in Ljubljana, Zadar and Dubrovnik), and finally either to the *Cour de Cassation* in Paris or the *Petit Conseil* of the Illyrian Provinces (consisting of the Governor-General, the Justice Commissar and two appeal court judges), a body which also functioned as the Administrative Court. The new administration of justice applied to the entire population, just as much to the previously privileged aristocracy and clergy as to vassals; furthermore, the patrimonial courts previously conducted by landowners were abolished. The Organizational Decree of 1811 also swept away personal feudal obligations, while feudal rights were privatized and made commutable. Thus, the new justice and taxation system effectively did away with the patrimonial jurisdiction of landowners.

Education and the language issues

A school reform abolished Maria Theresa's three-tier Primary School Regulations (*Volksschul-Ordnung*) of 1774 and the Church's right to inspect schools. An integrated primary school with four classes was introduced instead, and the network of secondary schools offering instruction to the lower classes was expanded.[21] More academic secondary schools, *lycées*, existed in Trieste, Koper and Gorizia, and these were intended for those who planned to go on to study at university, or as a preparation for joining the administrative service. In November 1811, the Central School in Laibach was transformed into a university (*Académie*) with five departments; two to three hundred students were taught there in German, French and Latin. By making it possible to study at a university in the Illyrian Provinces, the French sought to bind students to their country and educate a local elite. A vocational school was also founded in Laibach. Financing the primary schools and lower secondary schools, for which the municipalities were responsible, presented a structural problem. As many municipalities lacked the money, schools quickly closed and many planned openings never took place.

Language policy in the Illyrian Provinces was a complicated matter. The official language was French; regionally, German and Italian were also used. The official gazette of the Provinces, the *Télégraphe officiel*, was published in all these languages between 1810 and 1813. There was no vernacular edition because at that time the Slovenian language did not contain developed legal or administrative terminologies.

The leading Slavic philologists in the region, Valentin Vodnik and Bartholomäus/Jernej Kopitar,[22] first had to convince Governor-General Marmont and his General Inspector of Education, Raffaele Zelli, previously the head teacher of a secondary school in Zadar, that Illyrian was not a single language. They explained that it existed in two basic forms: one spoken by the Serbs, the other by the 'Slovenci'.[23] Consistent with the programme of Slavic linguistic nationalism endorsed by the two intellectuals, the first decree on education in the Illyrian Provinces, dated 4 July 1810, stipulated that the Slavic vernacular (*langue du pays*) was to be introduced both as a subject and as the language of instruction in primary and secondary schools. Just one year later, however, when Bertrand replaced Marmont, the equality accorded the Slavic idiom in higher secondary schools was reversed.

During the transitional period in July 1811, Zelli pointed in vain to the integrative function of the regional language. Referring to the Napoleonic programme of *amalgame*, he explicitly linked the language with a (fictional) Illyrian nation:

> The Illyrian Provinces are composed of peoples so different in language, customs and morals that it cannot be repeated too often than whatever the educational system adopted, it must seek to unite these people into the body of the nation and lead them, step-by-step, to adopt the same ideas and to make them feel the same way.[24]

Vodnik, a friend of Zelli's, had written a grammar for the new Slovenian language primary schools in 1811 (*Pismenost ali Grammatika sa perve shole*) and, in addition to his teaching position in a secondary school in Laibach, he had accepted the post of Director of Primary Education in the Illyrian Provinces. In this capacity he wrote numerous textbooks in Slovenian. He believed that a written Illyrian language should be synthetically created from the closely related dialects of Slovenian and Istrian–Dalmatian, and then used in the schools of the various provinces as a common language of teaching and administration.

Only after the reintroduction of the Austrian three-tier school system in 1813 did the number of school-age children attending compulsory school in the Slovenian-speaking region actually increase substantially: in 1817, one in seven school-age children attended a school; in 1847 the figure was one in three.[25]

Unrest and the reform of landownership

From 1789 to 1790 in the Alpine–Adriatic region peasants rose up against landowners for the first time, sometimes with arms.[26] In 1809 and from 1811 to 1813 further unrest was directed against the French. As everywhere in Europe, taxation and conscription drove the revolts. However, it should be noted that conscription was introduced at different times in different regions. In the previously Austrian parts of the country and on the Croatian Military Border it was not imposed until 1812.

An intense debate developed around the reform of landownership in the Illyrian Provinces. In 1810, Marmont ordered a 20 per cent reduction in tithes and ground rent. At the same time, however, he introduced a land tax and a poll tax on the French model, soon known disrespectfully as *fronki*.[27] As already mentioned, the Organizational Decree of 1811 abolished personal feudal obligations without compensation, as well as the patrimonial legal jurisdiction of feudal landowners. Ground rents were declared the product of a contractual relationship under civil law, transformed into mortgages and entered in the appropriate registers. In principal, such mortgages could be redeemed by an appropriate payment. Compulsory labour service was unaffected.[28]

Although Paris delayed the transfer of the French regulations of 1790 concerning the commutation of ground rent to the Illyrian Provinces, to 1812, Justice Commissar Coffinhal drafted a decree on the abolition of feudalism modelled on the measures that had been introduced in the annexed north German departments in December 1812. This would have entailed the abolition of all legal claims relating to personal service and the creation of standard procedures for the commutation of legal claims arising from property (compulsory labour, taxes, tithes). Paris continued to delay these reforms, however. The Justice Ministry referred the matter to the Council of State, which did not act until the autumn of 1813. The General Intendant Chabrol de Crouzol had already complained to Junot in June 1813 that the Emperor refused to countenance any change in the administrative system of the Illyrian Provinces. The last Governor-General, Fouché, repeated this criticism even more strongly in October 1813, but by now French rule in the Adriatic was collapsing. The basic attitude criticized by Crouzol and Fouché was mirrored in Napoleon's policies in the second half of his period of rule, when he became more interested in the nobility and less in social improvements, and also reflected the pressure of military priorities from 1812. Ultimately, all efforts to abolish the system of serfdom were unsuccesful, while the introduction of the equal division of property encouraged the fragmentation of landholdings and, potentially, an increase in the sub-peasant classes.

One of the most important elements of continuity in domestic policy between the French–Illyrian Provinces and the Austrian Kingdom of Illyria was that the landlords' judicial rights, which had been connected with the right to levy direct state taxes, were not restored. Local jurisdiction was transferred to newly-created district authorities (*Bezirks-Kommissariate*), whose areas of authority were relatively large and rationally organized. In most cases, the Austrian state brought together general domestic administration, tax administration and the administration of justice.[29]

Conscription and the costs of war

Conscription on the French model was first introduced in the former Austrian territories in 1810. The Army of Illyria was created in December 1809 out of Marmont's corps in the Armée d'Allemagne, the ex-Armée de Dalmatie. The first quota of 18,000 conscript soldiers was designed to bring numbers up to 29,000 men by the beginning of 1810; this target was drastically reduced to some 14,000 later in the same year. Even though the quota of conscripts was not very high (3,000 at each levy) and punishments for draft avoidance were severe (including fines and the occupation of municipalities by troops) it was hard to prevent evasion. Anti-conscription riots broke out across the provinces and deserters joined bands of brigands. Naval service (which had its own conscription system after 1811) was unpopular and the construction of ships in the dockyards of Trieste could not be revived. Early in 1811, French naval forces in Illyria consisted of only twenty vessels, none of which were fit for active service. The situation was different in Military Croatia where Marmont retained the Austrian system of militarized peasants and incorporated twelve battalions of Croatians as a garrison detachedto the army of Illyria.[30]

Rising military costs left inadequate funds for other branches of administration. The Illyrian government had to spend up to 75 per cent of its budget on military and naval expenses in 1812. The army was the main cause for the French regime's financial crisis and also became its main victim. In spite of the introduction of the uniform administration of direct taxation on the French model, and notwithstanding Napoleon's expectation that the new regime should be self-sufficient, the revenues of property and personal (head) tax (the latter extremely unpopular) did not provide the revenues the French had hoped for. The result was a continued deficit from the outset that exceeded six million francs in 1810. Even though Napoleon put the Illyrian Provinces under the direct control of Paris for fiscal purposes in 1811, Illyria's revenues never covered the expenses of the General Government and heavy taxation, exacted with coercion, together with the failure of the state to meet its payments, undermined public confidence in Napoleonic rule.

The Illyrian authorities failed to enforce the Continental blockade to prevent the smuggling of British goods, itself the primary reason for annexation. Indeed, smuggling on the rugged Dalmatian coastline proved impossible to eradicate. With the small island of Lissa/Vis, 50 kilometres off the Dalmatian coast near Split, acting as a main British military base and trading centre in the Adriatic, the French could do nothing to undermine British naval supremacy in the region. For the people of the Illyrian ports, 'smuggling...took on the aspects of a national industry',[31] whereas direct control of customs administration was wielded from Paris and denied the French General Government of the provinces. 'The continental system, which gave birth to Illyria, was also its grave.'[32]

A provisional solution for the Illyrian Provinces under Habsburg rule

From mid-1813 one of Metternich's key demands had been the return of the Illyrian Provinces to the Austrian Empire. After the complete military occupation of the Adriatic region by November 1813, Austria did not turn the clock back to pre-French times but, on the whole, retained the French legal and administrative system of the former Illyrian Provinces.[33] As early as August 1813, Francis I had decreed that the formerly Austrian lands were to be provisionally administered in accordance with existing regulations, and that changes were to be made only where there were special reasons for doing so.[34] The formal act of taking possession of Illyria by means of a patent of incorporation (*Einverleibungspatent*) took place on 23 July 1814. On the other hand, the official languages in use locally before 1809 were to be reintroduced in 1814; and in a number of stages between 1814 and 1816, the *Allgemeine Bürgerliche Gesetzbuch* (Austrian civil code) of 1811 gradually replaced the French civil code.

After detailed debate in a special Court Commission and also in the Council of State (*Staatsrat*), decrees of 13 June and 3 August 1816 finally created a new state as part of the Austrian Empire, in which the Illyrian Provinces continued to exist, now renamed the Kingdom of Illyria.[35] The name was Metternich's idea, apparently drawing on recommendations made by Jernej Kopitar and Sigismund Baron von Zois in Laibach, which he had visited in May 1816.[36] The Kingdom of Illyria existed in this form until 1849. Dalmatia, however, was elevated into an independent kingdom, administered directly from Vienna.

Illyrism and Metternich's plans for reform

The Napoleonic designation of Illyrian Provinces obviously drew on regional references to antiquity and the allegedly original population of south-eastern Europe. Contemporaries used the term Illyrians primarily for the inhabitants of Croatia, Bosnia and Dalmatia and in a wider sense for all Southern Slavs.

To some extent, Illyrism, a mostly Croatian cultural–political movement mainly of the nineteenth century, can be seen as a postscript to the Napoleonic Illyrian period in the Alpine–Adriatic region. In the 1830s, Ilyrism expressed itself in the struggle, personified by Ljudevit Gaj,[37] to forge a Croatian written language. This created language, which emerged from the three main dialects spoken at the time, was a bid for Illyrians to hold their own against the Magyars. In the course of this process, demands were also voiced (by Janko Count Drašković, for example) that Croatia be united with the associated regions of the Military Border and Dalmatia with the aim of forming a single state, to which Slavic-speaking Carniola would be added in order to create a Greater Croatia as a territorial core around which all the Slavs in the Balkans could unite. This was to be given the national collective name Illyria.[38]

Within this territory of the Austrian Kingdom of Illyria, a national historical interpretation of the French–Illyrian period developed, which highlighted many continuities with the territory reorganized under Napoleon, and this interpretation still colours contemporary scholarship. As in Italy, with the increasing rejection of the Austrian Habsburg state over the course of the nineteenth century, the Napoleonic period became glorified in retrospect and came to be seen as a time of greater independence, greater participation in decision-making, and as the nucleus of national independence.[39]

Thus, an almost proto-Yugo-Slavian vision was projected back onto Napoleon and the French emperor was presented as the liberator and promoter of Southern Slav unity. In reality, however, it was Austrian Chancellor Count Metternich, the personification of a political reactionary, who had established the Kingdom of Illyria as a Southern Slav empire (or *Mittägliches slawisches Reich* to use the words of his submission to the Emperor of 24 May 1816),[40] in an attempt to create a counterweight against Russian influence among the Southern Slav Catholic population of the multinational Habsburg Empire. His proposals—shelved by the Emperor Francis I and never even partially realized—would have provided an effective formula for 'the cardinal idea of unity plus multiplicity ... [for] ... the equal partnership of all of the ... regions of the Empire', and could have served as a functioning model for turning the empire into a federation.[41]

Notes

1. Translation: Dr. Angela Davies, London.
2. See Josip Kolanović and Janez Šumrada (eds) *Napoléon et son administration en Adriatique orientale et dans les Alpes de l'est 1806–1814. Guide de sources* (Zagreb, 2005), esp. Šumrada's introduction 'Statut juridique et organisation administrative des Provinces Illyriennes', 21–41. Janez Šumrada (ed.) *Napoleon na Jadranu—Napoléon dans l'Adriatique* (Koper, 2006). Almerigo Apollonio, *L'Istria Veneta dal 1797 al 1813* (Gorizia, 1998). Frank J. Bundy, *The administration of the Illyrian provinces of the French empire 1809–1813* (New York, 1987). Melitta Pivec-Stelé, *La vie économique des Provinces Illyriennes* (Paris, 1930). Short surveys include: Alexander Grab, *Napoleon and the transformation of Europe* (Basingstoke, 2003), 188–196. Sergij Vilfan, 'Von den französischen Illyrischen Provinzen zum österreichischen Königreich Illyrien', in *Napoleonische Herrschaft in Deutschland und Italien—Verwaltung und Justiz*, Christof Dipper, Wolfgang Schieder and Reiner Schulze (eds) (Berlin, 1995), 93–120.
3. Ferdinand Hirn, *Geschichte Tirols von 1809–1814* (Innsbruck, 1913), 46–62, 85, 313–316. Reinhard A. Stauber, *Der Zentralstaat an seinen Grenzen. Administrative Integration, Herrschaftswechsel und politische Kultur im südlichen Alpenraum 1750–1820*, (Göttingen, 2001), 367, 374, 382–385.
4. Kolanović and Šumrada, *Napoléon et son administration*, 12.
5. Miloš Okuka and Gerald Krenn (eds) *Lexikon der Sprachen des europäischen Ostens* (Klagenfurt, 2002), 282, 504, 951.
6. Kolanović and Šumrada, *Napoléon et son administration*, 39.
7. Stuart Woolf, *Napoleon's Integration of Europe* (London/New York, 1991), 51.
8. Paul W. Schroeder, *The transformation of European politics 1763–1848* (New York, 1994), 382.
9. Woolf, *Integration*, 30.
10. Pivec-Stelè, *La vie économique*, 79–117. Bundy, *Administration*, 247–250.
11. The concepts of an inner and outer empire are introduced by Michael Broers, *Europe under Napoleon 1799–1815* (London/New York, 1996). See also Michael Erbe, *Handbuch der Geschichte der Internationalen Beziehungen, vol. 5: Revolutionäre Erschütterung und erneuertes Gleichgewicht. Internationale Beziehungen 1785–1830* (Paderborn, 2004), 332f. Geoffrey Ellis, *The Napoleonic empire* (2nd edn, Basingstoke, 2003), 55–58. Owen Connelly, *The French Revolution and Napoleonic Era* (3rd edn, Fort Worth, 2000), 259–262; cfr. Erbe, *Handbuch*, 334.
12. Schroeder, *Transformation*, 406f, 466, 470f; cfr. Erbe, *Handbuch*, 334.
13. For detailed surveys see Kolanović and Šumrada, *Napoléon et son administration*, 52–54, 887–903. Jože Žontar (ed.) *Handbücher und Karten zur Verwaltungsstruktur in den Ländern Kärnten, Krain, Küstenland und Steiermark bis zum Jahre 1918. Ein historisch-bibliographischer Führer* (Graz, 1988), 34–49. For the following scheme, see Vilfan, *Von den Illyrischen Provinzen*, 98, 118.
14. Jacques-Olivier Boudon, 'Marmont, gouverneur général des Provinces illyriennes, et ses mémoires' in Šumrada, *Napoleon na Jadranu*, 221–232.
15. 'While Bertrand concentrated on military affairs, Chabrol ran civilian matters and soon became the most influential official in Illyria' (Grab, *Napoleon*, 190).

16. Michael Broers, 'The Napoleonic Empire', in *The Bee and the Eagle. Napoleonic France and the End of the Holy Roman Empire 1806*, Alan Forrest and Peter H. Wilson (eds) (Basingstoke, 2009), 65–82, esp. 73. Becoming aware of the '"otherness" of the outer empire', the Intendant of Dubrovnik took stock of his experiences as writing in 1813: 'We are dealing with peoples who are too ignorant, too estranged from civilisation and, above all, too poor to hope to attain it quickly or without help. In the hopes of giving our laws to these people—who know none—at a stroke, before their levels of intelligence are sufficiently developed, we shall only create a further, hindering source of estrangement between them and our government'.

17. See Janez Šumrada and Adrijan Kopitar (eds) *Nastajanje Napoleonove Kranjske—Avenement de la Carniole Napoléonienne. Korespondenca Françoisa-Marie Farguesa, francoskega intendanta za Kranjsko in Gorenjsko, 1809–1810* (Ljubljana, 2004).

18. Michel Vovelle, 'La dernière mission de Joseph Fouché en Illyrie', in Šumrada, *Napoleon na Jadranu*, 233–248.

19. Kolanović and Šumrada, *Napoléon et son administration*, 34–40. Jean Tulard, 'Provinces Illyriennes', in *idem*. (ed.) *Dictionnaire Napoléon* (Paris, 1987), 910.

20. Vilfan, *Von den Illyrischen Provinzen*, 100–102.

21. Peter Štih, Vasko Simoniti, Peter Vodopivec, *Slowenische Geschichte. Gesellschaft–Politik–Kultur* (Graz, 2008), 219–230. Joachim Hösler, *Slowenien. Von den Anfängen bis zur Gegenwart* (Regensburg, 2006), 62–70.

22. For biographical information, see Ingrid Merchiers, *Cultural Nationalism in the South Slav Habsburg lands in the early nineteenth century. The scholarly network of Jernej Kopitar [1780–1844]* (München, 2007), 23–75.

23. Štih et al., *Slowenische Geschichte*, 230.

24. Janez Šumrada, 'Les principaux traits de la politique napoléonienne dans les Provinces illyriennes', in *idem., Napoleon na Jadranu*, 43–58, esp. 55.

25. Joachim Hösler, *Von Krain zu Slowenien. Die Anfänge der nationalen Differenzierungsprozesse in Krain und der Untersteiermark von der Aufklärung bis zur Revolution, 1768–1848* (München, 2006), 139–152.

26. Dana Zwitter-Tehovnik, *Wirkungen der Französischen Revolution in Krain* (Wien,1975) 97–112.

27. Štih et al., *Slowenische Geschichte*, 228.

28. Šumrada, 'Les principaux traits', 47–52.

29. Werner Drobesch, *Grundherrschaft und Bauer auf dem Weg zur Grundentlastung. Die 'Agrarrevolution' in den innerösterreichischen Ländern* (Klagenfurt, 2003), 23.

30. Bundy, *Administration*, 408–438; Pivec-Stelè, *Vie économique*, 191, 324.

31. Bundy, *Administration*, 258–407; quote on 348.

32. Pivec-Stelè, *Vie économique*, 130–136, 220–263; quote on 338. Cf. Grab, *Napoleon*, 191–195.

33. Dipper et al., *Napoleonische Herrschaft*,14. Vilfan, *Von den Illyrischen Provinzen*, 103–109.

34. Arthur G. Haas, *Metternich, reorganization and nationality 1813–1818. A story of foresight and frustration in the rebuilding of the Austrian empire* (Wiesbaden, 1963), 36–42, idem., 'Kaiser Franz, Metternich und die Stellung Illyriens', in *Mitteilungen des Österreichischen Staatsarchivs*, 11 (1958): 373–398.

35. Haas, *Metternich*, 97–101. Peter Vodopivec, 'Der Alpen-Adria-Raum 1815 bis 1848', in *Alpen-Adria. Zur Geschichte einer Region*, ed. Andreas Moritsch, (Klagenfurt/Wien, 2001), 319–338, 319–321; Drobesch, *Grundherrschaft und Bauer*, 15–47 and map 1.

36. Luka Vidmar, '"Et in politicis propheta": politični komentarji v korespondenci med Žigo Zoisom in Jernejem Kopitarjem—"Et in politicis propheta": Political Commentaries in the Correspondence between Žiga Zois and Jernej Kopitar', in *Slavisticna Revija* 54 (2006): 753–775, 766–772.

37. Elinor M. Despalatović, *Ljudevit Gaj and the Illyrian Movement* (Boulder, 1975).

38. Cf. Helmut Rumpler, *Eine Chance für Mitteleuropa. Bürgerliche Emanzipation und Staatsverfall in der Habsburgermonarchie (Österreichische Geschichte 1804– 1914)* (Vienna, 1997), 188–200. Merchiers, *Cultural nationalism*, 131–221. Moritsch Andreas (ed.) *Der Austroslavismus. Ein verfrühtes Konzept zur politischen Neugestaltung Mitteleuropas* (Vienna, 1996) esp. the introduction 11–23.

39. As in Walter Markov, 'Die illyrische Paradoxie', in *Mitteilungen des Österreichischen Staatsarchivs*, 25 (1972), 587–594.

40. Haas, *Metternich*, 175.

41. Rumpler, *Chance für Mitteleuropa*, 202.

Part V
Spain and Portugal, 1800–14

Introduction

Michael Broers

Spain had had a long-standing alliance with France before the Revolution, the family compact, so-called because both countries were ruled by branches of the Bourbon dynasty. When Louis XVI was overthrown in 1792 Spain fought against France in the War of the First Coalition, but in October 1800 Napoleon and Charles IV, the Spanish king, re-established the traditional alliance, although the Spanish chief minister, Godoy, kept Spain out of the war with Britain until 1804. The Spanish fleet fought at Trafalgar on 21 October 1805 and was all but destroyed. Spain proved an ineffective ally, partly because of the instability within the royal family that culminated in the King and Godoy turning on Ferdinand, Charles' son and heir, arresting him in October 1807 as they feared he was plotting to overthrow them. Godoy and Charles became increasingly unpopular with the Spanish elites and in March 1807 there was a military coup against them supported by a popular revolt, the disturbance of Aranjuez, named after the royal palace where it took place. Godoy was arrested, Charles abdicated and fled to France, and Ferdinand became king, as Ferdinand VII. Fearing that Spain would become dangerously unstable Napoleon poured 80,000 troops under Murat into the country from 1807–08.

In May 1808 Napoleon met with Charles and Ferdinand at Bayonne to resolve the crisis. Both agreed to renounce their claims in favour of Napoleon's older brother, Joseph. Charles retired to Rome; Ferdinand went to live (until 1814) in the chateau of Valençay, the home of Napoleon's Foreign Minister, Talleyrand. The news from Bayonne provoked a mass uprising in Madrid on 2 May 1808 (three days before the abdications became formal), in favour of Ferdinand and against Joseph, which was brutally suppressed by Murat. However, the revolt then spread across most of the major cities of Spain in the spring-summer of 1808. Joseph entered Madrid as king on 20 July, but the following day a French army was defeated at Bailen and he fled. These successes prompted the creation of a government of resistance, the *Junta Central* (the central committee), to lead Patriot Spain, but Napoleon entered Spain with his elite troops in November. By December he had defeated the Spanish, restored Joseph and driven a small British force under Moore into the sea in Galicia, in the far north-west. This was the only time Napoleon fought in Spain in person. By 1809, the French had defeated several Spanish armies and secured most of the major cities, but localized, fragmented, irregular resistance was taking shape all over Spain, known as the *guerrilla* (the little war). By 1810 the French held most of Catalonia and advanced into Andalucia taking Seville, the seat of the *Junta Central*, which was soon overthrown from within. Before its collapse the Junta had called elections for a national parliament, the Cortes; somehow, elections—often very democratic in character—were held throughout Spain in 1810, even in French occupied zones. The Cortes convened in Cadiz in September, protected by the British Navy, and was generally acknowledged as the rightful government of Patriot Spain. There were bitter ideological divisions within the Cortes, however. The Royalist, reactionary elements—*los serviles* (the loyal, the servants)—saw the Cortes as nothing more than a regency for Ferdinand; they were opposed by the liberals—the first time this term was used to denote progressive, reforming politics—who won the parliamentary debates and gave Spain a democratic constitution in 1812, as well as driving through reforms of the Church, taxation and the law. This all remained theoretical, however. The Cortes had little effective power across Spain, even among the guerrillas and provincial governments who claimed to fight for it. The reforming impulses in Cadiz were partly driven by competition from Joseph's government, which included prominent progressive Spanish intellectuals and administrators, the *afrancesdados,* who had sided with him because he represented reform, as embodied in his Constitution granted at Bayonne.

The *guerrilla* ensured Joseph's rule was never secure anywhere, but until 1812 the only parts of Spain entirely free from the French were Cadiz and Galicia, which was close to British-controlled Portugal.

Portugal's history in these years was very different from Spain's. Traditionally allied to Britain, she had come under intermittent pressure from France and Spain to cut these ties until, in 1807, with Spain now an active French ally, Napoleon ordered a French army to invade the country. Lisbon was occupied by Junot on 30 November; the Portuguese royal family had fled to Brazil three days earlier. Oporto, the second largest city, rose against the French in June 1808; it was able to link with the Spanish patriots in Galicia and a British force arrived in support. By the Convention of Cintra, 31 August 1808, the French were forced out of Portugal. By 1809 the country was under a British viceroy, Lord Beresford, a virtual dictator who mobilized its entire society and economy for defence against repeated French assaults. The same year Wellington assumed command of all British and Portuguese land forces and built impregnable defences for Lisbon, the lines of Torres Vedras. These eventually became the springboard for the reconquest of the Iberian peninsula.

Before Napoleon withdrew significant numbers of troops for the Russian campaign in 1812, all Wellington's attempts to break out of Portugal had failed. Weakened and thinly stretched thereafter, the French were also harassed by guerrillas who were now more easily supplied by the British, often acting as local armies. In May 1813 Wellington successfully pushed across northern Spain, crushing Joseph at the battle of Vitoria on 21 June; by November he had driven the French over the Pyrenees. Ferdinand returned in March 1814, dissolved the Cortes with the support of the *serviles*, repudiated the 1812 Constitution and arrested most of the liberals. Many of the *afrancesados* fled to France. The Portuguese royal family, by contrast, did not return to Lisbon until 1821. Both Spanish and Portuguese monarchs faced serious revolts from disappointed liberals in 1821, but survived, although their countries, with war-torn economies, remained unstable for decades to come.

19
The Monarchy at Bayonne and the Constitution of Cadiz

Emilio La Parra López

Specialists in constitutional history have emphasized the different treatment accorded to the figure of the king in the two Spanish Constitutions produced by the War of Independence, namely the one approved in Bayonne in 1808 and that of Cadiz, in 1812. It is not my intention here to retrace old ground, nor to analyse both constitutional texts, the subject of numerous excellent studies. My sole aim is to indicate some elements that may help explain the differences often pointed out between them, focusing particularly on the political context that produced them.[1]

The Constitution of 1808 was drawn up by an assembly convened on the orders of Napoleon in Bayonne, which discussed different projects presented by the emperor. Its terms implicitly supported a division of powers, but it made clear that the will of the monarch was superior to that of the parliament; that the king was the key, the true director of policy, with the power to intervene in every branch of the state. This Constitution did not dedicate a specific section to the powers of the monarch, precisely because it did not limit his power, and therefore his attributes were not those considered in the text but rather all those not expressly renounced. Thus, as Fernández Sarasola maintains, any power not explicitly attributed by the Constitution to another organ, must be understood as reserved to the king.[2] The king therefore is not a just another repository of state power, a co-participant in government, but the true sovereign, on whose shoulders rests the power of the State. In Busaall's words, this Constitution establishes a royal autocracy without effective checks or, as Fernández Sarasola argues, 'a strongly authoritarian constitutional monarchy'.[3]

The monarch was treated differently in the Cadiz Constitution. Here, the king was simply a constitutional functionary and, as Joaquín Varela has pointed out, this had serious judicial consequences for the concept of the monarchy.[4] Broadly speaking, Cadiz established a constitutional monarchy because the origin and limits of royal power derived from the Constitution, however in a narrow sense it ceased to be a constitutional monarchy but was, more correctly, a democratic monarchy, with a system of government closer to that of the French Constitution of 1791.[5] Although the king had a real role in directing policy, the parliament (the Cortes) predominated in state affairs. This model was based on the principle of national sovereignty, the rigid separation of powers, and it limited the role of the king for circumstantial and personal reasons rooted in the distrust of the person embodying the Crown, Ferdinand VII.[6]

In Bayonne, as Fernández Sarasola has explained, the monarchy is the State. This was not a consequence of the constitutional text, but the root of its vision of royal power. The king is not a constituted organ, he precedes the Constitution, Bayonne was a Granted Charter. Napoleon declared Joseph King of Spain on 6 June 1808, and the Constitution was approved one month later.[7] Furthermore, it was the king who took the initiative in constitutional reform.[8] Conversely, the Constitution was drawn up according to Napoleon's instructions and was based on the constitutional norms of the Napoleonic régime, which broke with the parliamentary norms of the French Revolution. Much of the Bayonne Constitution was a literal reproduction of the Senatus Consultus of 28 Floreal, Year XII (1804); some parts of it were inspired by the Constitution of Year VIII (1799) and the Constitutions of the satellite kingdoms of Holland (1806), the Grand Duchy of Warsaw (1807), Westphalia (1807) and Naples, promulgated as recently as 20 June 1808.[9]

In Cadiz, however, the monarchy was not the state but was a branch of government, which could be reformed should the representatives of the nation gathered in the Cortes so decide; the king was excluded from the constituting power.[10] The liberals who met in Cadiz considered that, by intervening in another country during the Bayonne negotiations, Napoleon had contravened the people's rights. Thus, the renunciations of the throne by Charles IV and Ferdinand VII were coerced and, as a consequence, Joseph was not a legitimate king but an intruder. The Liberals understood that if a monarch was to acquire legitimacy the consent of the nation was obligatory. Ferdinand VII, however, had renounced the crown without consulting the nation, which meant that, in practice, he was defying fundamental Spanish laws, something that kings could not do. Ferdinand VII, therefore, had ceased to be king of Spain in Bayonne, not because Napoleon had so decided (obviously, all the Spaniards who took up arms in 1808 denied that Napoleon had these powers), but because he relinquished his rights without consulting the nation.[11] This resulted in an exceptional situation in which it fell to the nation to assume sovereignty and itself form a new monarchy, as well as to designate the person to wear the crown. Thus, the nation, which had come together in the Cortes, had the authority to draw up a Constitution that could not only define the nature of monarchy—'The Government of the Spanish nation is a moderate, hereditary monarchy' (article 14)—but also explicitly decide who was to be king: 'The king of the Hispanias is the Lord Ferdinand VII of Bourbon, who reigns at the present time' (article 179). The result was the establishment of a new kind of monarchy, as well as a new monarch, for it is clear that the King Ferdinand of the 1812 Constitution was not the same king who ascended the throne on 19 March 1808. He was no longer an absolute but a constitutional monarch, a constituted organ whose prerogatives were explicitly articulated in the Constitution (articles 170–171 and 172), as were the limits of his authority. Furthermore, the king was obliged to swear an oath to the Constitution (article 173).

The models for monarchy established by the two Constitutions are clearly different. The key to explaining this difference lies in the political context of 1808 rather than in any theoretical influences. The Bayonne Constitution was the product Napoleon's wishes and had the clear objective of ensuring the pre-eminence of royal power and the French ruling dynasty, hence the enormous emphasis Bayonne accorded to issue of the succession, to which Title II is devoted.[12] The Constitution 'set out to be at one and the same time the form through which [Napoleon] organized the State and the formal instrument through which he transferred the Crown to his brother Joseph Bonaparte' as a result of the legitimacy acquired in the Bayonne renunciations.[13]

The Cadiz Constitution had an altogether different aim, at least as far as the Liberals were concerned, that of freeing Spain from any prospect of tyranny. However, faced with the circumstances of the War of Independence, taking sides was unavoidable. Manuel José Quintana, like the Liberals, chose to 'free my country from Bonaparte's tyranny and all forms of tyranny', for 'the time had come to correct the political ills of Spain'.[14] When the critical moment came the Spanish were deprived of their king, but in exercising their sovereignty they decided to preserve the monarchy and provided themselves with a king who, fundamentally, was king through the will of the nation, regardless of whether he had already been one under different circumstances.

However, the manner in which Napoleon's plans for Europe took shape in the Bayonne Constitution, and the patriots' reaction, was only possible because an exceptional situation had already arisen in Spain. Indeed, it was the result of the severe political divisions that predated the Napoleonic invasion, namely, the bitter struggle between by the followers of Charles IV and Godoy on the one hand and, on the other hand, a heterogeneous block united almost exclusively by their hostility to Godoy—in which the most active sector, if not the only one, was a group of aristocrats and clerics usually known as the Fernandine party. The dispute took place not only at court level, but had a wider, more important political dimension when it infiltrated public opinion and therefore drew in Spanish society as a whole.

The Fernandines opposed the system of extreme absolutism established by Charles IV and Godoy after 1801, when the latter was named Generalísimo. There were two kinds of reaction: that of the privileged orders, who believed that their status was at risk and felt excluded from political decision-making; and that of other, very varied social sectors, who attributed their problems to Godoy's personal ambition and bad government. The Godoyists, for their part, opposed the backward-looking and anti-reformist stance of the privileged classes and, in keeping with Enlightened thinking, assumed that only a strong monarchy was capable of enacting effective reforms. And yet there were contradictions in both attitudes: the Fernandines did not reject despotism, but rather the person who embodied it (Godoy); the Godoyists did not consider dispensing with the nobility and clergy as pillars of the monarchy. Charles IV's own, archaic concept of monarchy was very influential on this point.

This dispute was not confined to political debate—though this was nevertheless very intense and unfolded within state institutions—but was pursued also through handbills and, above all, in public gatherings and even in the street. Censorship and police control made it impossible to conduct debate in the press or though other public processes. The conflict thus assumed a physicality which had serious consequences. The first was the Conspiracy of El Escorial, discovered on 27 October 1807, and the Aranjuez riots of 17–19 March 1808.

The intensity of this internal conflict made public opinion aware of Spain's decadence and weakness and spurred calls for the regeneration of the monarchy. Even before the El Escorial conspiracy was uncovered, that is before the political confrontation within the court became public, the two opposing groups already understood that the resolution of their rivalry, which was tending towards mutual annihilation, could not come about internally. Only an external arbitrator, from abroad, could halt the conflict, and Napoleon was the only candidate. Inevitably, both groups approached him, requesting his support to further their causes.[15]

The result was to encourage Napoleon's hopes for a successful intervention in Spain. He presumed that his plans for dynastic change would be achieved without great difficulty provided he took certain precautions, mainly the military control of strategic points in the Peninsula and the cultivation of Spanish public opinion, together with the careful manipulation of Charles IV and Ferdinand VII. The message to be conveyed to the Spanish was obvious: Napoleon sought the regeneration of the monarchy, to endow it with the vigour of which both factions had sapped it. However, in order to achieve this it was necessary to place somebody new on the throne, naturally a member of his own dynasty, which, being the most powerful in Europe, offered the greatest guarantee for dealing with the crisis faced by Spain and its empire. Convinced of his ability to please everyone, Napoleon believed that this was feasible, as he wrote on 10 April 1808 to Murat. Napoleon had charged Murat with making it widely known that it was his intention not only to preserve the integrity of the monarchy and the independence of the country, 'but also the privileges of all classes'.

Napoleon's promises—which Murat undertook to propagate through considerable, though in practice, unsuccessful propaganda—coincided in

one essential point with the general feeling of the Spanish for the maintenance of the institution of the monarchy and the safeguarding of the integrity of the empire. The Spanish believed that any solution to the internal
crisis would necessarily involve the continuity of the monarchy. In 1808
there was no thought of establishing a republic because this system had
been discredited by the experience of the Jacobin Terror and because an
intense defence of the monarchy had been mounted in Spain in the 1790s
as a reaction to the French Revolution. The word republic, previously used
widely in Spain without negative connotations, began to be avoided or
referred to in a critical sense.[16]

In 1808 the king remained the key element in the system, as in the eighteenth century, and yet his person was no longer worshipped as before. At
the same time theoretical writings began to appear which raised doubts
about the role of the monarch, even though the monarchy was still defended
as an institution.[17] As for the nobility, they continued to argue that absolute monarchy had seriously damaged the country, precisely because the
monarch was no longer tempered by them, a thesis long held by the aristocratic, or Aragonese, party.[18] Above all, according to this thesis, those close
to the monarch were to be feared, particularly his counsellors, whether
an individual (such as Godoy) or a group (such as the quasi-privy council
constituted at the beginning of Ferdinand VII's reign by Escoiquiz, the
Duke of the Infantado and the Duke of San Carlos, through whose hands all
important matters passed).

In 1808, then, everyone claimed to be trying to save the monarchy, but
there were doubts as to who should occupy the throne in these changed
circumstances once the internal crisis had been resolved. Supporters of
Charles IV and Godoy had no difficulty in accepting the solution offered by
the Bayonne Constitution. They had no alternative, since the propaganda
against Godoy (which also implicated Charles IV) had had a profound
impact on Spanish society. They disliked the prospect of a foreign king,
but it was the lesser of two evils. Moreover, Napoleon and Joseph promised to preserve Catholicism, the independence and territorial integrity of
the Spanish monarchy, and they promised regeneration and enlightened
reforms, which amounted to the programme that had characterized the
reign of Charles IV to which Godoy was committed, at least in theory.

The other faction, which post-May 1808 called itself patriotic since it denied
Napoleon's authority, experienced a different problem. Fundamentally, it
had mixed feelings about Ferdinand VII. On the one hand, it accepted the
potent image of him that had been forged, of the innocent, virtuous prince,
prepared to restore the happiness of his kingdom, even going so far as to
sacrifice himself for the cause. This propaganda justified Ferdinand's journey
to Bayonne and his renunciation of the throne as a result of Napoleon's
deceit and threats.[19] Nevertheless, Ferdinand also incarnated the spirit of
the Old Regime and had shown unmistakeable signs of absolutist tendencies

during his brief tenure of power, March 1807–April 1808. Naturally, this did not convince those soon be known as liberals, and yet, despite everything, they found themselves obliged to accept Ferdinand VII because, when the uprising against Napoleon took place, he had become a myth that penetrated Spanish society to its heart. The Supreme Councils made lavish declarations that the main objective of the struggle was to restore him to his throne. Ferdinand was identified with Spain and he was raised to the status of principal victim of the invader, more even than the dead of 2 May in Madrid.[20] 'Ferdinand was the name and watchword that sustained the popular spirit against Napoleon's stealth and military might', as J. L. Villanueva put it, once the war had ended.[21] In short, as Álvarez Junco concludes, '...those mobilized [against Napoleon] undoubtedly felt "Spanish", but what they truly worshipped was not some abstract idea, but a real person, Ferdinand, a sacrosanct figure, immune to all criticism; they were definitely following the time-honoured custom of invoking the king as the personification of the collective, especially in circumstances of war'.[22]

At the Cadiz Cortes, it was the liberals, not the Fernandine party, who controlled events. However, they shared the Fernandines' aversion to Godoy and so rejected all possibility of the restoration of Charles IV and, since they were naturally uncompromisingly opposed to Joseph I, they had no alternative but Ferdinand VII. Even so this sparked many misgivings in liberal ranks. First, there was the question of Ferdinand's character, especially his propensity for allowing himself to be led by his intimates (the privy council mentioned above), which did not inspire confidence in the liberals. In their writings, Flórez Estrada and the Count of Toreno harshly criticized the behaviour of these counsellors, as did several deputies in the Cadiz Cortes.[23] Second, there were fears that Ferdinand could be used by Napoleon to end Spanish resistance. An extensive debate on this took place in the Cadiz Cortes in the last weeks of December 1810, when the Cortes had only been assembled for three months and therefore before discussions on the Constitution began. At this point, the deputies, both liberal and royalist (this coincidence should be borne in mind) anticipated some of the fundamental ideas on the place of the monarch in the political system that would later be included in the constitutional text, although these debates have been little-used by historians.

The debate arose from news concerning Ferdinand's behaviour during his stay in Valençay. The Cadiz deputies learnt that Ferdinand had written asking Napoleon to accept him as his adoptive son.[24] It was also rumoured that Ferdinand had married an Austrian Archduchess, or was negotiating such a marriage under Napoleon's protection. Both items of information, which were not mere speculation (particularly the first which was completely true), so alarmed the deputies that they dedicated the parliamentary sessions of 29–31 December 1810, and that of 1 January 1811, to discussing a proposition presented by Francisco Xavier Borrull, one of the most combative royalist deputies: 'That any acts or agreements that the Kings of Spain may carry out while in the power of enemies and which may cause any harm to the Kingdom are declared null and void and have no legal force whatsoever.'[25]

Obviously, the deputies were in agreement with Borrull's proposition, regardless of their ideological positions. But it is significant that the parliamentary discussions revealed a general distrust of the hitherto idolized king. It was said that, given the impossibility of obtaining a military victory, Napoleon might make use of the voluble and impressionable Ferdinand to end Spain's resistance, sending him back to Spanish territory with the appearance of having restored his crown, but in reality having transformed Ferdinand into his puppet. Nevertheless, what stands out most is that at such a relatively early date and, above all, before discussion of the constitutional project began, it was perfectly obvious that the deputies did not consider the king to be above the nation, but subordinate to it, 'rather than love the King' said Pérez de Castro, 'they taught me to love my Nation, although for me my Nation, King and Country go hand in hand...'.[26] The deputy Huerta argued that 'everyone wants to put Nation before King; everyone meeting in this Congress agrees on that point, as do the spectators.' [27] A few days earlier, López Pelegrín had been very explicit; for him, Ferdinand VII 'is not King of Spain as his father was; he is so because Your Excellencies [the Cortes] have recognized him (as such) and because you wish it' and, as a result, everything done 'outside the will of the nation' is counterproductive.[28]

In keeping with this view—which coincides, as we have seen, with that expressed years later by Flórez Estrada—and after the exceptional situation provoked by the Bayonne renunciations and Napoleon's intervention in Spain, Ferdinand VII's legitimacy did not derive from history (dynastic continuity, as in the case of Charles IV), but from the will of the nation.

In conclusion, the speakers who intervened in these sessions openly rejected the possibility that Ferdinand could act on the basis of his dynastic interests to recover the crown. They explicitly and continuously referred to the principle of national sovereignty and emphasized that the Fundamental Laws of the Kingdom (the frequently invoked historical tradition) did not determine an absolute monarchy, but established limits on the power of the king.[29] Along with the affirmation of these principles, all of which were included later in the constitutional text of 1812, certain opinions about the person of Ferdinand were expressed, betraying the scant confidence he inspired in Cadiz. Distrust of Ferdinand VII's person flourished in the Cadiz Cortes, even before the constitutional debate commenced, because of the monarch's behaviour in Bayonne and in Valençay. Yet, despite these misgivings, the deputies, including the liberals, could not dispense with Ferdinand VII because, in the struggle against the foreign tyrant, the nation had invoked him as its talisman.

In the text produced after the debate, the Decree XIX of the Cortes written in 1811 and so prior to the approval of the Constitution, the contradictions (and fears) of Cadiz liberals are laid bare in respect of the person of Ferdinand VII. At that point in time he was indispensable but evidently inspired scant trust. The precautions built into the Constitution were a response to these fears, but it is clear that the myth of the prisoner king had made so profound an impression on Spanish society that it was not difficult for Ferdinand and the supporters of absolutism to abolish the Constitution once the war had ended. This meant, in turn, the end of the Bayonne Constitution, a text which despite everything that had happened, was never received with enthusiasm by the Spanish, in contrast to Ferdinand, the monarch who intended to reign in accordance with its absolutist injunctions.

Notes

1. There are abundant studies of the Cadiz Constitution, although they generally do not devote much space to the constitution's treatment of the figure of the monarch. Important exceptions in this sense are the papers by Joaquín Varela Suanzes-Carpegna, some of which are collected in his volume entitled *Política y Constitución en España (1808–1978)* (Madrid, 2006). The Bayonne Constitution, on the other hand, has not attracted the same degree of attention among scholars and, until recently, it was necessary to resort to two monographs from the beginning of the twentieth century: Pierre Conard, *La Constitution de Bayonne (1808). Essai d'édition critique* (Paris, 1910) and Charles Sanz Cid, *La Constitución de Bayona* (Madrid, 1922). A considerable change has come about recently, as will be seen by the studies cited in the course of these pages, the most outstanding of which are those by Ignacio Fernández Sarasola and Jean-Baptiste Busaall. Also important, in addition, is the doctoral thesis (unpublished) by Xavier Abeberry Magescas, *Le Gouvernement Central de l'Espagne sous Joseph Bonaparte (1808–1813). L'efficacité des institutions monarchiques et de la justice royale,* Université de Paris XII-Val-de-Marne, 2001.
2. Ignacio Fernández Sarasola, 'La forma de Gobierno en la Constitución de Bayona', *Historia Constitucional* (Electronic Journal) 9 (2008), http://hc.rediris.es. See also idem, *La primera Constitución española: el Estatuto de Bayona,* Biblioteca Virtual Miguel de Cervantes Saavedra, 2003, http://cervantesvirtual.com and *La Constitución de Bayona* (Madrid, 2007), 59–60.
3. Jean-Baptiste Busaall, 'Le règne de Joseph Bonaparte: une expérience décisive dans la transition de la Ilustration au libéralisme modéré', *Historia Constitucional* (Electronic Journal) 7 (2006), http://hc.rediris.es. Fernández Sarasola, 'La forma de gobierno'.
4. Varela Suanzes-Carpegna, *Política y Constitución,* 21.
5. Varela Suanzes-Carpegna, *Política y Constitución.* Ángeles Lario, *Monarquía y República en la España contemporánea* (Madrid, 2007), 40.
6. Joaquín Varela Suanzes-Carpegna, 'Rey, corona y monarquía en los orígenes del constitucionalismo español: 1808–1814', *Revista de Estudios Políticos,* 55 (1987).
7. This point is manifested in the preamble to the constitutional text: 'Joseph Napoleon, by the grace of God King of Spain and the Indies, having heard the National Assembly, gathered in Bayonne on the instructions of our dearest and

beloved brother Napoleon, Emperor of the French ... have decreed and hereby decree the present Constitution so that it may be respected as the fundamental law of our States and as the basis of the agreement binding our peoples with Us and Us with our peoples'. The difference with the Cadiz Constitution is evident. The preamble to the latter highlights the fact that the constitution is the product of the Assembly representing the Spaniards: 'The extraordinary general parliament of the Spanish nation ... decrees the following political Constitution for the proper governance and correct administration of the State'.

8. This is established in article 143: 'The present Constitution shall gradually be enacted successively by means of Royal Decrees or Edicts, so that all of its provisions may come into effect prior to January 1st, 1813'.

9. San Cid, *La Constitución de Bayona*, devotes ample space to showing the coincidences between the three drafts presented in Bayonne and the constitutional texts of the Empire, particularly the Senatus-Consultus of Year 12.

10. See José Mª Portillo Valdés, *Revolución de nación. Orígenes de la cultura constitucional en España, 1780–1812* (Madrid, 2000), 171 and ff. and José Álvarez Junco, 'El primer liberalismo y el concepto de nación', in *Lecturas sobre 1812* (co-ord.) A. Ramos Santana (Cadiz, 2007), 13–20.

11. This idea is set out in great clarity by Flórez Estrada in his *Representación hecha a S.M.C. el Señor Don Ferdinand VII en defensa de las Cortes* [1818], in *Obras* (Madrid, 1958) vol. II, 169: '...you, with your absence and your renunciations, you lost all right to the crown and... the Spanish nation was left with the most absolute freedom to establish itself as it might see fit'.

12. Various studies have highlighted the central role in the Napoleonic imperial constitutional system of the combination of the concept of hereditary monarchy with the plebiscite-based Caesarism (Bonapartism is a combination of the prestige of Napoleon's family and the dynastic privilege with popular support). See Marcel Morabito and Daniel Bourmaud, *Histoire constitutionnelle et politique de la France (1789–1958)* (Paris, 1991), Luca Scuccimarra, 'El sistema de excepción. La construcción constitucional del modelo bonapartista (1799–1804)', in *Fundamentos*, 2 (2000): 273–357.

13. Fernández Sarasola, *La Constitución de Bayona*, 56–57.

14. Manuel José Quintana, *Memoria sobre el proceso y prisión de don Manuel José Quintana en 1814*, ed. Ferdinand Durán López (Cadiz, 1996), 77 and 83–84.

15. Regarding the role of mediator in the Spanish dynastic dispute attributed to Napoleon, see Emilio La Parra, 'El mito del protector. Napoleón y la crisis de la monarquía española (1806–1808)', in *Napoleão. História e Mito*, co-ord. Antonio Ventura (Lisboa, 2008), 41–54.

16. Javier Fernández Sebastián, 'El momento de la nación. *Monarquía, Estado y nación* en el lenguaje político del tránsito entre los siglos XVIII y XIX', in *1802. España entre dos siglos. Monarquía, Estado, Nación*, co-ord. A. Morales Moya (Madrid, 2003).

17. This was the case of Ibáñez de la Rentería and Martínez Marina, where they argue that kings show a natural tendency to despotism. See Javier Fernández Sebastián (ed.) *La Ilustración Política. Las 'Reflexiones sobre las formas de gobierno' de José A. Ibáñez de la Rentaría* (Bilbao, 1994). Francisco Martínez Marina, *Obras* (Madrid, 1962) vol. I, 57.

18. At the beginning of the nineteenth century, the echoes of the famous text of 1793 by the Count of Teba, later to become the Count of Montijo, had not yet faded, and they illustrate the feelings of the nobility led by Aranda; his title is

sufficiently expressive: *Discurso sobre la autoridad de los ricoshombres sobre el Rey y cómo la fueron perdiendo hasta llegar al punto de opresión en que se halla hoy (Speech on the Authority of the First Lords over the King and on how it was lost to the point of oppression in which it now stands).* The Fernandine party reflected, in part, this way of thinking, which was also upheld, from a different perspective and with some nuances, by outstanding figures of the Enlightenment, such as Jovellanos (see Ferdinand Baras Escolá, *El reformismo político de Jovellanos [Nobleza y Poder en la España del Siglo XVIII]* [Zaragoza, 1993]).

19. On the construction of the image of Ferdinand VII in 1808, see Emilio La Parra, 'El príncipe inocente. La imagen de Ferdinand VII en 1808', in *La trascendencia del liberalismo doceañista en España y en América,* ed. M. Chust and I. Frasquet (Valencia, 2004) 31–50 and idem. 'El mito del rey deseado', in *Sombras de mayo. Mitos y memorias de la Guerra de la Independencia en España (1808–1908),* ed. Christian Demange et al. (Madrid, 2007), 221–236.

20. Richard Hocquellet, *Résistance et révolution durant l'occupation napoléonienne en Espagne, 1808–1812* (Paris, 2001).

21. Joaquín Lorenzo Villanueva, *Vida Literaria* (London, 1825), modern edition (Alicante, 1996), 232.

22. José Álvarez Junco, *Mater Dolorosa. La idea de España en el siglo XIX* (Madrid, 2001), 73.

23. Álvaro Flórez Estrada, *Introducción para la historia de la revolución de España,* in *Obras,* vol. II, Conde de Toreno, *Historia del levantamiento, guerra y revolución de España* (Madrid, 1953), 52. For the speeches before parliament, see, among others, those by Argüelles on 12 September 1811 (*Diario de Sesiones de las Cortes Generales y Extraordinarias* [Madrid, 1870], 1,830) and that by Antonio de Capmany, at the session held on 15 October 1811 (*Diario de Sesiones,* 2,080).

24. This fact is of capital importance, owing to the role that the constitutional regulations of the Empire granted to the Emperor's adopted children.

25. *Diario de Sesiones,* session held on 29 December 1810, T. I, 246. The proposition was approved at the session held on 1 January 1811, and enacted in Decree XIX of the Cortes (*Colección de decretos y órdenes que han expedido las Cortes General y Extraordinarias* [Cádiz, 1811] T. I, 43).

26. *Diario de Sesiones,* session held on 1 January 1811, I, 280.

27. *Diario de Sesiones,* session held on 30 December 1810, I, 269.

28. *Diario de Sesiones,* session held on 14 October 1810, I, 261.

29. *Diario de Sesiones,* speech by García Herreros at the session held on 20 December 1810, I, 263001E264: 'The Monarchy is not absolute, as it had never been previously; the laws establishing it [referring to the *Partidas*] restrict the exercise of sovereign power to vary narrow limits.'

20
Popular Resistance in Spain

Jean-René Aymes

The Peninsular War has one specific, fundamental negative characteristic which sets it apart from the wars of the ancien régime: it was not a confrontation between two monarchs or two regular armies engaged in pitched battle.

At the outset of the conflict, the Supreme Junta of Granada published a proclamation concerning Spanish resistance to Napoleonic troops and the implications of this document are important. First, it highlighted the concept of 'nation', and second, it announced that 'the people' would play a more decisive role in the struggle: 'Spain has shown that the wars of Nations are not the wars of Kings and that a people which has risen up as one has never fallen beneath the yoke of tyranny'.[1]

This popular activism, as imagined by the proclamation, presupposed a widespread awareness of the purpose of the fighting and of the issues at stake. Indeed, the prologue to the book in which the proclamation was published argued that, as a result of both the factual information it communicated and the Junta's propaganda, the people would emerge from the ignorance in which they had been kept by bad government. The convergence of people's opinions with their hopes would then give form and content to a new reality, namely 'public opinion', also called 'the public voice of the nation'.[2] For the struggle against the enemy to be effective and eventually successful, it went on, the people ought not to be divided. This notion of the people (*pueblo*) was not only seductive, it was indivisible, but it had to be distinguished from the term used by Napoleon and Joseph in their attempts to discredit insurrection and resistance, namely, the populace (*plebe*).

Propaganda addressed to the *pueblo:* problems of social class and gender

The remarkable, admirable arrival of the *pueblo* in the political arena made it possible for patriotic propagandists to counter the contemptuous stereotype (commonly found outside Spain, especially in France) of the Spanish as inert, submissive, idle, easily deceived and manipulated. Spanish Patriotic writings therefore vaunted the rebirth of the nation, extolling the people's innate virtues which hitherto had lain buried and inert. They proclaimed that whilst the inhabitants of Madrid had, in May 1808, expressed 'opinions of justice and honour', in the rest of the country 'the whole majesty of the Spanish people had emerged, as had their energy and heroic character in the generous affection they express and demonstrate'.

There were even attempts to appropriate the populace (*plebe*, normally differentiated negatively in comparison to the *pueblo*) into the semantic group centred on the concept of nation, thereby glorifying and ennobling it. The title of a text *Elogio [Praise] of the Spanish Plebe/Populace*, signed by a mysterious I.Q.,[3] is of particular interest in this respect. The *plebe*/populace is initially defined as follows: 'You, a respectable group of humble and unknown men, the most useful members of those who constitute the great national family, you are the object of my veneration, gratitude and amazement.'[4] Despite the fact that the terms *Plebe/Pueblo* are never fully assimilated, later in the text there is nevertheless a semantic slip by which the word *plebe* appears metaphorically to melt into the word *pueblo*, a word that could not inspire contempt. Nor is this the only new feature in this text. It also bears the double novelty, and indeed ideological audacity, in a simultaneous denunciation of the Old Regime and criticism of the elites— the leading scholars, the army, the clergy and the notables—men who ought to be encouraging the patriotic uprising, leading it and fighting against traitors and waverers:

> You, the magnanimous and sublime *pueblo*, you have done it all. Though cast into darkness, though scorned, though crushed by so many years of horrible oppression, you have done it all. The learned were silent, arms lay still. As for your leaders, either they betrayed you, basely wrought your ruin and were the first to abandon you, or they were overcome by cowardice and wavered. Few ministers of the altar dared take courage from the gospel and raise the cry.[5]

Nevertheless, the mysterious I.Q., who was definitely not of humble origins, feared that this admirable people, having once risen up, would succumb to unbridled frenzy, revel in anarchy and seize power.

The problem of social class in patriotic literature of this kind is superimposed upon that of gender. There is a significant body of brief patriotic pieces and poems by women, but it is difficult to identify the social origins of their authors. In the *Colección del Fraile*, there are texts signed by 'the widow of Martín Peris', 'the widow of Agustín Laborda' or 'the widow of Vázquez'. The modern reader has the overwhelming impression that these women were not shepherdesses, seamstresses or servants. For these women the death of their respective husbands appears to have given them permission to take up the pen. These surnames may have been pure invention, but the impression remains that these, possibly middle-aged, ladies were the counterparts or disciples of the small number of women who took part in the Patriotic Ladies' Associations, such as that of the Marquesa de Villafranca. It would appear that the Peninsular War was not seized upon by women as an opportunity to become fully empowered citizens.

Why did members of the popular class join the resistance?

One of the problems facing patriotic propagandists was rousing Spaniards of all classes to fight, to aid the combatants and to make sacrifices. Their policy was to emphasize the horrors of the French invasion and, later, the occupation. Pamphlets, newspaper articles and plays depicted requisitioning, looting, rape, forced labour and extra taxation, usually in the countryside. A proclamation of June 1808 is interesting in this context. It is probably less well known than the weighty, solemn sort of patriotic propaganda that focused on the famous trinity of King, Religion and Country. Rather, it catalogues the 'squadron of evils' threatening the inhabitants of Las Cabezas.[6] With the exception of married women at risk of rape, monks, and those called up by Napoleon's army, the common people do not seem to be threatened by these evils. The author appears concerned only with the titled and the wealthy, people who could be prevented from enjoying their socio-economic superiority. In contrast to the powerful, the lower classes had nothing to lose under the French occupation.

Passive resistance

Whilst the rural population did not always take up arms, they did possess many alternative ways of demonstrating their hostility to the invasion and their support for the military and guerrilla struggle, notably by providing the latter with shelter, lodging and supplies.

French soldiers refer in their memoirs to villages deserted because the inhabitants had fled before them. Peasants often hid their stores of wheat and wine before leaving; they burned their unharvested fields to deny the French food. The consequence of this was that the French were forced to steal, to take reprisals and to impose extra taxes where villages were not abandoned.

In the cities under French occupation, passive resistance encompassed refusing to swear the oath of obedience to the 'intruder king', refusing to enlist in the Civic or Honourable Militias (which were to be French auxiliaries), absenting oneself from military parades, or not attending French organized plays or bullfights.

Active resistance: 'the nation in arms'?

The French invasion of Spain was based upon a monumental, catastrophic miscalculation. In Bayonne in May 1808, Napoleon confided to Canon

Escoiquiz, that (with the exception of the *plebe*) the Spanish people had neither the ability nor the will to resist him. Escoiquiz replied by listing the innumerable obstacles that the Napoleonic army would inevitably encounter, arguing that the French 'will face an enemy composed of all the inhabitants of the country, and innumerable groups of people will present them with insuperable difficulties on all sides'.[7]

Despite the fact that two historiographical schools exist in Spain, today (especially in 2008 as a result of governmental or local political initiatives) the thrilling picture of 'the nation in arms', of a people rising up unanimously against the invader, of a class-ridden society coming together for the defence of the country and the deposed king, has tended dominate.

In the spring and summer of 1808, and throughout the conflict, the propagandistic celebration of popular heroism became increasingly politicized, bestowing attributes on the resistance that were not exclusively linked to the defence of country, king and religion, principally liberal concepts of 'national sovereignty' and the 'sovereignty of the people'; from these stemmed the schism between liberals and absolutists.

In his newspaper *Spanish Robespierre*, Fernández Sardino criticized the *servile* (reactionary) Miguel de Lardizábal because the latter was a staunch adversary of the Sovereignty of the People who associated that concept with 'the introduction and propagation of Republican maxims and democracy'. Sardino went on to stress delightedly (in 1811) that the popular uprising was now a widespread, radical and beneficial revolution, in which he himself had participated.[8] The extreme, subversive and provocative character of the *Spanish Robespierre* made it an extraordinary periodical. It paid homage ('veneration, gratitude and amazement') to that 'obscure and ignored group of men and women, the most useful members of those who make up the great national family…. It was they who first launched the cry of independence'. Indeed Sardino gives the impression of having found inspiration in the 1808 text of the mysterious I.Q. However, three largely original themes mark I.Q.'s apology for the *plebe*: first, that the people took the initiative to revolt as a consequence of the passivity, resignation or cowardice of the great and the good, the military commanders, the clergy and the educated; second, the text powerfully and generally condemns the ancien régime governments who long persisted in rendering the people 'brutish and degenerate'; third, I.Q. takes pains not to alarm his readers or to give the impression of placing his hopes in a 'revolution with a guillotine', like the Jacobin Terror, assuring them that the process will soon end and the people will return to 'their natural gentleness', content with their period of sovereignty, and will be docile and obedient to the new authorities they have chosen.[9]

Two years later, in a well-known article published in *The Spanish Robespierre* at the end of September 1810, Fernández Sardino renewed the accusation that the elite had been terrified and vacillating, that the only group to act had been '*plebe*, which had been swept up in a holy fury'.[10]

The French press was under strict government control and the propaganda it presented to the public was centred on the image—soon to become fossilised and stereotyped—of armed resistance fed not by the people but by marginalized individuals from the dregs of society. Thus, in the *Moniteur Universel* of 9 July 1809, an article referred to some guerrilla bands active in the Toledo region:

> The majority of their troops, which total no more than one hundred men, are thieves, condemned fugitives from the law, who have formed into companies of smugglers and to whom the Junta (of Seville) has granted military ranks and honours.[11]

After 1814, publications sometimes contrasted the spontaneity and energy of the rebellious Spanish people in arms with the passivity, double dealing, cowardice and treachery of the aristocracy and the wealthy. This was a minority and controversial trend in the literature, but one of its best examples is an episode where the French General Leopoldo Hugo pursued the guerrilla chief Juan Martín Díez, 'The Undaunted', in Old Castile:

> While the grandees and the nobles of the Spanish monarchy, forgetting the oath of obedience to Ferdinand, paid homage to King Joseph in Bayonne...some simple farmers, unknown craftsmen who had not received favours from the Bourbons or the brilliant honours of the court, were arming themselves to defend princes known only to them through the vexations of their ministers, but to whom they paid homage. None of the illustrious names of the Spanish nobility is to be found among the leaders of those guerrillas who have harassed the French army with such vigour and courage.[12]

Enlistment in the army and guerrilla bands

The most radical, tangible and obvious form of patriotic commitment by the popular class was their incorporation into the guerrilla bands and the regular army.

In the middle of August 1808, an edict of the Supreme Junta declared that harvest and field work would no longer be reasons for peasants to avoid enlistment. With farmers and day labourers now liable for service, almost the entire population was called to arms.

There are three historiographical problems surrounding the *guerrilla*: their composition; their effectiveness; and, finally, their relationship with the population and the authorities. The contemptuous interpretation of the French memoirists and the official press should be ignored here. Contributions by contemporary historians are of greater interest, particularly when they provide statistics. In this respect, Ronald Fraser has examined a small group of 300 recruits from the Andalusian town of Morón de la Frontera. His study reveals that:

> The day labourers who made up almost half of the population were only little more than 10 per cent of the conscripts…. Among those whose professions were registered, no landowner from Morón is named, and there are only seven master craftsmen. It was usually their journeymen or occasional apprentices who responded to the call-up. Once again, as in Madrid during the events of May 2nd, the shoemakers, cobblers and bricklayers constituted the majority, followed by barbers and carpenters.[13]

Fraser has an original theory for the low number of day labourers, faced with the possibility of an excellent harvest, the landowners pressured them not to answer the call-up lest 'the first good wheat harvest of the century should lie unharvested in the fields'. Nor do the nobility, themselves, seem to have rushed headlong into the new armies.

The Juntas

The appearance and conduct of individuals from the popular class at the heart of the Juntas poses another historiographical problem, which has yet to be fully clarified, although the recent studies of Richard Hocquellet, Antonio Moliner and Jean-Marc Lafon have brought new insights.[14] Some years ago, I modestly pioneered a non-systematic, non-statistical investigation of several cases suggesting that in general, given their composition, the local juntas did not reflect the structure of society, because the grandees predominated to the detriment of popular representatives.[15] Hocquellet's views seem too radical, however, when he argues that the people alone never formed Juntas; for Hocquellet, the patriotic Juntas were a matter for the local authorities and do not emerge spontaneously from the rebellion.[16] It is more likely that the situation in Villagarcía, near Santiago, was more or less mirrored elsewhere. Here, the provisional president of the Junta of armament and defence was not a popular fighter, but rather a field marshal with full powers to distribute weapons to the populace, or withhold them.[17]

Although the local juntas were, arguably, potentially revolutionary insofar as they sometimes replaced the municipal councils and might act autonomously, that revolutionary potential was constrained, not least because of both the composition of the Juntas and their natural inclination to defend the interests of the majority of their members. This is born out by the composition of the Supreme Junta of the Government, which forbade the use of weapons, ordered the closure of the theatres and maintained the courts. Who would be so foolish as to expect revolutionary measures from a Junta composed of five clergymen (an archbishop at their head), four magistrates, three noblemen, two generals, two representatives of the city, a tradesman and just one representative of the people? Far from reflecting the proportions of different social classes, the Juntas scarcely admitted the third estate; the rural world is notably absent.

A socio-political revolution?

In principle, the only enemies facing the Spanish were the French and their collaborators, soon labelled traitors or 'bastard sons of the Motherland'. This may have been the justification for the killing, abuse or arrest of representatives of the military or civil authorities who had had dealings with the occupying forces or who were simply hesitant in the spring of 1808.[18] On closer examination, however, the motives which emerge had little to do with patriotism. Some commoners refused to pay the tithe, citing worsening poverty as the pretext; this sort of tax strike was totally unrelated to the patriotic struggle since it expressed a willingness to question one of the ancestral privileges of the Church. Certain historians and ideologues have noted that in some places during the spring and summer of 1808 the landless poor, unopposed, seized arable land or meadows, thus identifying the rich landowners with the intolerable injustices of the ancien régime, and see in this the sparks of a French-inspired revolution.

Ronald Fraser has examined in depth two sets of events in the Extremaduran village of Don Benito in November 1808.[19] There, the 'ill-intentioned rebels' (as the anonymous author of a report calls them) insulted the 'honourable inhabitants', demanding that 'the rich who are those who have something to lose should go to war…. The malcontents do not accept that the sons of the powerful should escape from the obligatory call-up under a false pretext or by paying substitutes to go in their place'. Despite Fraser's promise of numerous comparable examples with subtitles in chapters such as 'Wage demands', 'The farmers' revenge', 'Conflict in Extremadura' and 'Revolt of the Asturian smallholders', the truth is that although these genuine revelations are of great interest, they represent only isolated rebellions or social revolutions on a purely local scale and no more. Apart from their insignificant number, the overwhelming impression remains that, in most places, the victims were people accused of having supported the French for quite some time or, latterly, for being excessively passive or hesitant patriots.

Conversely, probably of greater importance was the feeling of fear experienced by the grandees and the local authorities when faced with the possible avalanche of collective action considered to be dangerously revolutionary. Historians have perhaps not placed sufficient emphasis on the frequency and force of the calls for calm and order made by local notables and directed at the angry or agitated people. In May 1808 the Marquis of Camareno la Real demanded an end to 'the popular tumult' caused in Cartagena by women and children who, instead of being 'contained and held in check by their parents', prevented 'good honest nobles from pursuing their rightful interests'.[20] For the members of the Vich Junta, in what appears to be an address to peasants possibly considering illegal land seizures, the maintenance of public order presupposed the sanctity of property rights.[21] One of the surprising consequences of this denunciation of popular violence when it degenerated into public disturbances and crimes against private property is the similarity between the literature it provoked on both the patriotic side and that of the French occupiers. Thus, in April 1808, Murat, in his address to Prince Antonio, was careful to 'reassure owners, businessmen and peaceful inhabitants of all classes', attributing the spread of 'anarchy' to the excesses of the 'people', whom Murat called 'rabble'.

Oblique or corrupt forms of popular resistance

Leopoldo Hugo was correct that, at the beginning of the conflict, it was principally members of the popular class who rose up, while the powerful hesitated. However, he could not see the (sometimes shameful) reasons that led the poor to join the *guerrilla*. The French commanders' view that all guerrilla fighters were bandits is, of course, unacceptable. However, as has been usefully indicated by Charles Esdaile[22] and Ronald Fraser, there was no shortage of guerrillas whose conduct was not driven by patriotic or religious imperatives or impulses. Some men entered the guerrilla bands to avoid conscription; discipline was much stricter in the regular army than in a gang of ruffians. Others were attracted by booty, and this led Esdaile to conclude that 'the evidence that the guerrillas were more motivated by booty than by patriotism is overwhelming'.[23] Yet others—regular soldiers taken prisoner by the French who had escaped—preferred the freer life of the guerrillas rather than returning to their units. Others were out for revenge, having seen their house or the village church set on fire, or members of their families murdered. British and French soldiers often agreed in their exceedingly harsh view of guerrilla looting and extortion, and even acting against their British allies. Espoz y Mina, the guerrilla chief in Navarre, eliminated some of his men whose indiscipline and lack of respect made his army unpopular. Esdaile tends to see the majority of guerrillas as mere bandits, 'barely interested in questions of ideology or patriotism', and cites the case of 'the lads from Santibáñez', a group of highwaymen from the Plasencia region. They always claimed to be guerrillas, but in reality most of their victims, whom they usually treated with atrocious cruelty, were shepherds, migrant day labourers, muleteers and peasants.[24] Some contemporary proclamations occasionally infer that the popular rising against the French could have dishonourable motives or was unrelated to the defence of king, religion and country. Whilst the defence of throne and altar did inspire countless heroic actions, it also produced ugly deeds, executed under false pretexts and devoid of legitimacy.

Women could provoke particular criticism. Although celebrated for 'their extraordinary spirit and effort' when they fought alongside the men in the defence of besieged cities,[25] they could also be criticized for abandoning their homes to take part in indecent activities on the barricades. The Marquis of Camarena la Real enjoined 'good patricians' to mete out just punishment to those women who violated 'the dignity of their sex':

> Although it has been remarked with admiration that the women who for reason of their sex should withdraw from the popular tumult have in fact withdrawn into their homes in those moments, it has been noted with concern that some, out of a spirit of curiosity, others for less straightforward principles, have gone in great numbers into the mêlée, adding to it with angry, and perhaps even irritating voices....[26]

Then, with laudable nobility, the Marquis requested that women show 'greater consideration for all foreigners'. Presumably, he meant the defeated French soldiers, although it is well known, from the testimony left by soldiers of General Dupont, how brutally the defeated of Bailén were treated on the road to Cadiz, in some cases by women in a crazed state. In his *Memoirs*, the future General de la Bourdonnaye recounts how 'inhabitants of all ages and condition rushed en masse along our route and harassed us with curses and threats. The women were the most agitated; they expressed their rage with horrible grimaces and seemed to announce to us, by their fierce gestures, that before long they would make us pay for all the ills the French were inflicting on the Spanish'.[27]

The intentions and behaviour of the people of Cadiz towards the defeated French at Bailén are recounted in the little-known testimony of Governor Tomás de Morla, who was asked to execute all prisoners on the prison ships. He first notes that this slaughter would have had the unfortunate effect of provoking and legitimating 'tragic and horrible consequences', presumably meaning massive reprisals. He then goes on to praise the triumphant soldiers who had behaved with humanity, before finally adopting the relatively noble and daring position of deriding the baseness of anyone who would request the extermination of the now defenceless enemy. There is, however, a slight contradiction in his long letter: at one point he seems to blame the 'rabble' alone, for this shameful conduct, despite the fact that he had previously accepted that this same 'rabble' had been the stimulus which spurred the educated classes of Cadiz to behave like gentlemen, with decorum and charity. With Morla, we are light years from the *Praise of the Populace* penned by the mysterious I.Q. and, later, by the *Spanish Robespierre*. Elsewhere in the letter, Morla does not conceal the fact that people have indeed behaved basely and that it was the cowards, the clever and the hypocrites who railed against the prisoners on the pontoons, demanding the most barbarous revenge instead of behaving correctly towards them.

A popular struggle of an ideological nature?

Naturally, right at the heart of the intense popular patriotic propaganda stands the struggle between two types of adversary: the first, the outsiders, are the French invaders; the second, from within, are the Spaniards who are prepared to collaborate. However, it should be borne in mind that when certain commentators took to the literary stage and adopted the pose of spokesmen for the incorruptible and innately good people, they targeted in their books, pamphlets and newspaper articles not just the French and their own treacherous compatriots but also—completely unexpectedly—those Spanish men who, by defending the reforms of Cadiz, had 'prejudiced religion and endangered the mother country'. This last quote comes from the *Protection against Irreligion* by Father Vélez. Claiming to express the opinions and feelings of the Spanish people, this furious opponent of liberalism and freemasonry went so far as to write: 'Up to now we have been fighting against enemies from outside; the enemy within is more fearsome.'[28] Father Vélez had a dualist vision of the people conditioned by the chronology of the war; the people of 2 May 1808 were exemplary because they rose spontaneously against the much-hated French and because they meekly obeyed the laws of the Church. Unfortunately, according to Father Vélez, the *philosophes*—the liberals of the Cortez—had taken advantage of the (appalling) press freedom, thus undermining the foundations of the nation by spreading their irreligious, anti-traditional maxims. There is an inherent contradiction here: the Spanish people, so admirable in the spring of 1808 for their patriotism and rectitude, have allowed themselves to be infected by evil or, to be precise, liberalism, freemasonry and immorality imported from France. The Spanish people are not, then, incorruptible. For Father Vélez, as for the Bishop of Orense and other advocates of absolutism, popular resistance to the penetration of the reformist or revolutionary programmes of the French, the supporters of Joseph Bonaparte and the liberals, is just as important as resistance to the Napoleonic invasion.

* * *

At risk of appearing excessively schematic, the six years of conflict and popular resistance presented in three phases, unequal in length.

In the spring and summer of 1808, the massive, predominantly popular, uprising directed against the invaders exhibited on different occasions characteristics that, for the great and the good, the clergy and the powerful, presaged general anarchy, bloody revolution and the curtailment of ancestral privileges and economic interests. The elites then, either individually or in groups, emerged almost everywhere to direct and guide the popular uprising in order to limit it to the struggle against the French and their collaborators, so as to preserve the social order.

In the following years, once the danger of a Spanish version of the Robespierre-esque Terror had disappeared, popular armed resistance became formalized, taking place within the traditional framework of the regular army, within the less orthodox framework of the guerrilla, and within the geographically specific framework of the besieged cities.

In the third phase, particularly during the years 1810–13, the people, although not ceasing to play an active part in the struggle against the French, became a public which demanded information and explanation. In this war of opinion, the adversaries—French military leaders, Joseph's supporters, liberals and absolutists—sought to inform the people and to influence them politically and ideologically. In this war of ideas, the concept of popular resistance became distorted as the opposing sides tried to shape and strengthen popular resistance against their ideological adversaries. This popular resistance was more a receiver than a producer of discourses.

At the end of the war, in 1814, the reformist work only just begun by the Joseph's authorities was easily abolished by Ferdinand VII. This fact alone suggests that the two revolutionary bombs in the hands of the people (French Jacobinism and Spanish liberalism), had been defused. Although this defeat was not definitive, it was to last for some considerable time.

Notes

1. *Demostración de la lealtad española. Colección de proclamas, bandos, órdenes, discursos* ... (Madrid, 1808) 2, 80 III.
2. *Demostración*, Prologue: 'The Printer to the Reader', 1.
3. 'Elogio de la plebe española', *Demostración*, 3, 152–155.
4. Ibid. 153.
5. Ibid. 154.
6. 'Vecinos de Las Cabezas', *Demostración*, 1, 23–25.
7. 'Memorias de Juan de Escoiquiz', *Memorias de tiempos de Fernando VII* (Madrid, 1957) 97 (I), 131.
8. *El Robespierre español*, 12 (1811): 187–188.
9. 'Elogio de la plebe española', *Demostración*, 3, 152–155.
10. Text cited in part by Jean-René Aymes in *La guerra de la Independencia en España (1808–1814)* (Madrid, 2008), 56.
11. Jean-René Aymes, 'La guerre d'Espagne dans la presse impériale (1808–1814)', *Annales Historiques de la Révolution française*, 336 (2004): 137.
12. Joseph Léopoldo Hugo, *Mémoires du général Hugo* (Paris, 1934), 242.
13. Ronald Fraser, *La maldita guerra de España—Historia social de la Guerra de la Independencia (1808–1814)* (Barcelona, 2006), 213. The following examples are taken from the same work.
14. Richard Hocquellet, *Résistance et révolution durant l'occupation napoléonienne en Espagne, 1808–1812* (Paris, 2001). Antonio Moliner, *Revolución burguesa y movimiento juntero en España* (Lerida, 2004) notably chapter I 'El pueblo en armas', 35–89. Jean-Marc Lafon, *L'Andalousie et Napoléon—Contre-insurrection, collaboration et résistances dans le midi de l'Espagne (1808–1812)* (Paris, 2007).

15. Jean-René Aymes, *La guerra de la Independencia en España (1808–1814)* (Madrid, 1973).
16. Hocquellet, *Résistance et révolution.*
17. Aymes, *La guerra de la Independencia*, (2008 edn), 94.
18. See the account of the assassination of the Marquis of Solano in Cadiz, in Théophile Geisendorff-Des Gouttes, *L'expédition et la captivité d'Andalousie (1808–1810)* (Geneva, 1930), 284–285.
19. Fraser, *Maldita guerra*, 292–293 and Ronald Fraser, 'Historia y mitos de la resistencia popular en la Guerra de la Independencia, Bailén a las puertas del bicentenario: revisión y nuevas aportaciones' in *Proceedings of the seventh meeting on the Battle of Bailén and contemporary Spain, Bailén City Council / University of Jaén* (Bailén, 2008), 55–67.
20. 'Bando de Cartagena', *Demostración*, 1, 9.
21. Fraser, *La maldita guerra*, 237.
22. Charles Esdaile, *La Guerra de la Independencia—Una nueva historia* (Barcelona, 2003), 318. The following examples are taken from the same work.
23. Esdaile, *La Guerra de la Independencia*, 148.
24. Ibid. 151–152.
25. See for example the proclamation of Palafox, entitled 'Aragoneses y soldados que defendían a Zaragoza...', *Demostración*, 4, 42.
26. 'Bando de Cartagena', *Demostración*, 1, 9.
27. In Geisendorff-Des Gouttes, *L'expédtion*, 147.
28. In Javier Herrero, *Los orígenes del pensamiento reaccionario español* (Madrid, 1973), 15 and 312 for the following quotations.

21
Imperial Spain

José M. Portillo Valdés

Spanish historians have always found it surprising that the greatest colonial loss ever suffered by a European monarchy did not bring about an intellectual reflection in the 1820s and 1830s similar to that which followed the loss of a handful of islands in the Caribbean and the China Sea in 1898. In fact, neither Ayacucho (the last battle in Peru in 1824) nor the hopeless resistance of Spanish troops in San Juan de Ulúa, Mexico, after 1821, produced a reaction of a national mourning or reflections on the place of Spain and Spanish civilization in the world. On the contrary, if there was any common ground in the analyses made at the time, it was the emphasis on the inevitability of the process understood as emancipation. Whilst some questioned the more or less opportune timing of the event, it was generally felt that the maturing of the American territories was always, sooner or later, going to lead to their independence, like a son who leaves home, guardianship and dependence on paternal authority to begin his own life. It is not surprising therefore that upon independence war gave way to expressions of familial reconciliation. During the negotiations for mutual diplomatic recognition between Mexico and Spain, finally established in 1836, such language was clearly expressed by the Spanish delegate: 'This [negotiation between Spain and Mexico] must be entered into, not as a treaty of peace, recognition and commerce between two different nations, but adopting the principle of the reconciliation of two members of the same family by means of which we may obtain commercial advantages greater than those enjoyed by more privileged nations....'[1]

The compelling liberal essay by José Manuel de Vadillo, written at the height of the crisis, perfectly reveals the climate of public opinion as regards American independence among liberal Spaniards at the end of this process of imperial decline. Although Vadillo's argument was contradicted by some leaders of American public opinion, such as the Mexican Lorenzo Zavala, the basis of his thesis rested on an interesting paradox that stressed both the natural need for, and the inconvenience of, the independence of Spain's possessions in America. Incorporating the discourse on the benevolence of the Spaniards' conduct in their overseas domains, Vadillo wanted to demonstrate that if independence as emancipation was unavoidable, there was no reason why it should come about through chaos and disorder, something which would serve only the interests of the British and North Americans. The work of liberals in Spanish America, argued Vadillo, might have made it possible to 'bring about emancipation in a calm, orderly manner, and one therefore more useful to itself [Spanish America] than through bloody and anarchical revolutions'.[2]

In the years following the death of Ferdinand VII in 1833, when Francisco Martínez de la Rosa was recalled from exile by the Queen Regent, María Cristina, to strengthen the throne of the infant Queen Isabel II, and when the Royal Statute of 1834 was being drawn up, which created a parliamentary regime, public opinion began to blame the despotic regime of Ferdinand VII (from 1814 to 1820 and again from 1823 to his death in 1833) as the main cause of the family rift between Americans and Spaniards. José Rivera Indarte, the Argentinian poet from Cordoba, an opponent of José Manuel Rosas, the omnipotent governor of Buenos Aires, addressed Martínez de la Rosa, the Spanish poet from Granada and Prime Minister at the time, hailing him as the man responsible for restoring the freedom of Spain and explaining to him his thoughts on the advantages of Spanish recognition of the American republics. This was above all, as Vadillo also believed, a philosophical issue. If the war had lasted for years, this was solely because 'the party of fanaticism and oppression refused to acknowledge the sovereignty of the people ... '. Rivera Indarte insisted on the advantages, namely that the regularization of family relations with Spain would give the Americans legal security and commercial convenience.[3]

In short, at the time of the transition from despotism to a new constitutionalism (1834–37) Spanish liberals finally reached a conclusion very similar to that expressed by most eighteenth-century European thinkers, empires were morally acceptable only if conceived as commercial entities. If independence was as normal as the emancipation of a son who leaves the parental home on marrying or taking holy orders, all that remained was the familial bond that could ensure commercial advantages. Several writers concerned with the problem of how to deal with the fact of American independence felt that some kind of Spanish commonwealth was the most Spain could hope for: ' ... it is necessary to show the Spanish that their prosperity is intertwined with that of their brothers, the Americans, and that their true interest lies in extending the sphere of their trade, suppressing the enormous jealousy and rancour of the old, exclusive system, and in making the Americans see that no one wishes to reign over them, but engage in trade together.'[4]

By the 1830s all that remained, along with some goodwill and no small amount of refinement and good manners, was mutual trade. Nevertheless, in the previous two decades in the wake of the unprecedented crisis faced by the Spanish monarchy in 1808, many other possible ways of politically reconfiguring a Hispanic space had been formulated; and some had even been attempted. The American empire could become several independent political entities, or it could be imagined as a commonwealth, governed as a federal monarchy or as a group of peoples organized in a politically autonomous manner, linked by a single constitution and monarchy in the same body politic. Possible partitions of the monarchy into different American kingdoms, endowed with their own royal prince and federated under the Spanish monarch as emperor, had been envisaged by the end of the eighteenth century. However, from the time of the 1808 crisis onwards, the re-imagination of the Spanish Atlantic as a common body required some kind of constitutional solution. It was no longer about how the monarchy organized itself but about how the nation reconstituted the monarchy.

As for the 1808 crisis itself, it was not without precedent. It had been preceded by an imperial political crisis that had emerged from the wars of Spanish Succession (1701–13) and the Seven Years War (1756–63). In fact, by 1763 it had become more than evident to most Spanish intellectuals and officials of the monarchy that the Catholic Monarchy as it had been conceived from the sixteenth century was dying.[5] Indeed, ministers as prominent as Pedro Rodríguez de Campomanes, President of the Council of Castile, or José de Gálvez, Minister of the Indies, openly proposed that Charles III transform the monarchy into a commercial empire. It was felt that the religious discourse did not correspond to the concept of modern empire which assumed a moral background of empire related more to commerce than to religion. In his influential works, Montesquieu had criticized the Spanish monarchy as a clerisy and regarded its empire as ancient in character, founded on occupation. Many other European intellectuals followed him in reproducing an image of Spain as a peculiar form of monarchy, half European, half Asiatic. The interesting point here is that this same interpretation was widely accepted by Spanish intellectuals and royal officials. The traditional argument that spiritual conquest justified the enlargement of the Spanish Catholic monarchy no longer made sense in the context of commercial empire. The models to be followed by Spain were no longer Rome or Israel but Britain, France and Holland. In order to save their monarchy, they believed, the Spanish kings Charles III and his son Charles IV had to transform it into a veritable commercial empire. Henceforth, a language of empire, metropolis, colonies and their commercial interrelation was employed by the royal bureaucracy. It was also the moment when some essential reforms were introduced into the administration of Spanish America, specifically the reorganization of viceroyalties, the introduction of the system of intendancies for territorial government and of free trade.

Notwithstanding the efforts made in the 1770s and 1780s to imperialize the monarchy, by the end of the war with the French Republic in 1795, the impossibility of reviving Spain in the imperial European game was evident. On the one hand, Spain was definitively caught between the British Empire, reshaped after the independence of North America, and the new, emergent French republican empire. On the other hand, at the heart of the Spanish court the confrontation between two factions led respectively by Charles IV and the Prince of Asturias escalated by the turn of the century into a power struggle, although both factions agreed over the need to submit to France and its new leader, Napoleon Bonaparte. This submission intensified the Spanish imperial crisis which preceded the crisis of the monarchy in 1808.

1808 was a key moment in this lengthy imperial crisis that occurred simultaneously with a crisis in the monarchy itself. The eighteenth-century European debates about Spain and its significance for European civilization—the assumption that the Spanish monarchy needed to be put under foreign tutelage, evident in the writings of intellectuals like Montesquieu or Edmund Burke, and the formulation of the concept of Spain as a type of monarchy intermediate between Britain and the Ottoman Empire—contextualize the failure of the attempts to transform the ancient Catholic monarchy into a new competitive, commercial empire.[6] The decision of Bonaparte to intervene in the politics of the monarchy itself in May 1808 with the dynastic substitution of the Bourbons by his own family can be seen as the vindication in the enlightened European mind of the incapacity of Spain to manage her own empire. The imperial crisis and the monarchical crisis thus coming together in 1808 proved fatal to the traditional Catholic Monarchy and favoured the blossoming of a new notion of the Catholic Nation as a concept capable of replacing the king as the incarnation of sovereignty, as the Constitution of 1812 would state in its first articles. The purpose of this essay is to show how the imperial and monarchical crises, originating in the field of the *ius gentium* (international law), would evoke an initial response immediately after the publication of the transfer of the crown to Napoleon in terms of *ius civile*. This was manifest in the setting up of the Juntas and the conviction that they were the trustees of the king's sovereignty, taken from the doctrine of civil law, and later in the constitutional solution formulated in Cadiz between 1810 and 1812. International, civil and constitutional law were, thus, the scenarios where the Spanish crisis evolved from imperial to national.

Revolution and imperial mediatization of the monarchy7

In the 1770s, European *literati* were surprised to see how the British settlers in America succeeded in expressing their opposition to the parliamentary and royal despotism from London through a constitutional revolution. Pennsylvania, North Carolina and Virginia then produced constitutional governments that left European readers in astonished admiration. The French philosophers Denis Diderot and Gabriel Bonnot de Mably waxed lyrical about these texts, while the Italian intellectual Gaetano Filangieri asked Benjamin Franklin for his help in order to move to Philadelphia and participate in the American republican epic at first hand. Filangieri was never to reach America, but the texts and reports of that revolution would continue to arrive, demonstrating on the one hand that the independence of territories dependent on a European crown was somehow feasible and, on the other, that republicanism was practicable beyond the dimensions of a city state. Both lessons were of most relevance for the Hispanic conglomerate of kingdoms spread over America since local elites there could see how North Americans demonstrated that Jean Jacques Rousseau's idea of republicanism as a local manifestation could be successfully amplified to larger territories than the city state.[8]

It is true that Spain supported the American Revolution because it followed an international policy shaped by its alliance with France and because that Revolution would seriously weaken Britain, but it could not remain immune to its consequences, as the Count of Aranda saw immediately and as practically all of the commentators of the Spanish crisis of 1808 would reiterate.[9] Unlike France, Spain had enormous overseas domains and its metropolitan constitution was far removed from the principles driving the North American political experiment.

The start of the constitutional revolution in France in the summer of 1789 made it clear that from now on there would be a change in the political order of the old European monarchies. The first revolutionary regime, enshrined in the constitution of 1791, despite maintaining the presence of the king was radically hostile to the political traditions of the monarchy.[10] With a great tradition of civic and openly republican historiography behind it, the revolution of 1789 took a deliberate decision to produce a constitution as a purely political invention with no ties to history.[11]

Between 1776 and 1789, then, the Spanish monarchy had to face the fact of revolution. Whilst Spanish ministers tried first to isolate Spain from the extraordinary events in France, after the trial and execution of Louis XVI in January 1793 the monarchy could not remain immobile. The War of the First Coalition (1793–98) was the context in which Manuel de Godoy, the factotum of Spanish politics, was definitively raised to unfettered power, which was to last until the crisis of 1808. Although the war went badly for Spain, Godoy managed, en route, to get rid of the court party led by the Count of Aranda—who were more inclined to recognition of the French republic—and to organize his own faction in support of the king in the latter's decision to wage war against the regicides. In this context, the Treaty of Basle (1795) could be presented as a success, since Spain did not suffer territorial losses, and it also seemed as if the political situation in France was becoming more moderate by 1795.[12]

However, if the French 1795 constitution offered an end to the revolution and the consolidation of a stable constitutional regime, this did not mean that France had lost its powerful presence in Europe.[13] On the contrary, one of the bases for the consolidation of Napoleon's growing prestige after 1799 was precisely his imperial conception of the French republic and the promotion of the constitution as the reinforcement of state power.[14] By the time Napoleon took power in France in 1799, Spain had already redirected its foreign policy, returning to the traditional family compact with France. The Bourbons on the Spanish throne, Philip V in 1733 and 1743 and Charles III in 1761, both signed the so-called family treaties with their French cousin, Louis XV. The notable difference in 1795 was that there was no longer a royal family on the French side of the agreement, but a republic that was rapidly becoming an empire.

The Treaty of San Ildefonso in 1796, by which Spain readopted the policy of allying with France, marked the beginning of a process of imperial mediatization of the Spanish monarchy which culminated in the Treaty of Fontainebleau of 1807. During the decade that separates both pacts, Spain progressively put its overseas empire at the service of the emerging French empire, thus increasingly showing its dependence on France in terms of *ius gentium*.[15] The failure of the Peace of Amiens (1802) and the resumption of hostilities between France and Great Britain appreciably accentuated Spanish involvement in French imperial strategies, as witnessed by the Treaty of Subsidies (1803), which to all intents and purposes placed the fiscal revenues of the Spanish Empire at the service of France. As Emilio La Parra has pointed out, there was no turning back. In the years to come, dependence on France would become both the guarantee that allowed Charles IV and his own court faction, led by Manuel de Godoy, to hold on to power, and the dagger that would deal the death blow to the monarchy.[16]

The Treaty of Subsidies demonstrated how far the imperial mediatization of the Spanish monarchy by the French imperial project actually reached. Because it envisaged an economic compensation in the highly probable case that Spain could not assist France with troops and, since Spanish fiscal revenues were literally exhausted, it implied the necessity of transferring funds to France from the imperial revenues of the monarchy. As a consequence, in 1804 the Spanish government extended to America a Royal decree of 1798 forcing the transfer of the monetary wealth from financial institutions (mostly ecclesiastical) to the Royal Treasury in order to consolidate the Spanish public debt (known as *Vales Reales*). This monetary wealth, which came mostly from New Spain (the financial backbone of the empire), was redirected to meet the commitments made to France. Spanish Americans were experiencing both the politics of ministerial despotism and the consequences of the imperial mediatization of the Spanish monarchy.

The treaty of Fontainebleau, signed in October 1807, can be considered as the culmination of this process. By this treaty the Spanish king, completely without precedent, allowed French troops free passage across the heartland of the monarchy, while still more troops were billeted on the border ready to enter the Peninsula, as they eventually did. Officially headed for Portugal to join with Spanish troops to invade and partition its neighbour, the French army immediately garrisoned strategic fortresses and cities in

Spain, effectively dividing Spain along two lines, one from the French border to Burgos, Valladolid and eventually to Madrid, and the other from the border to Catalonia. The idea of placing Spain under foreign tutelage had finally become a fact.[17]

On the day the new treaty was ratified by the king a plot to overthrow Manuel de Godoy and force the abdication of Charles IV was discovered, centred on the Prince of Asturias. Some prominent courtly aristocrats (such as the Duke of Infantado and the Marquis of Astorga) and the Prince's closest advisors (notably the cleric Juan Escoiquiz) seemed to be involved in the plot, although the special court charged with its investigation never found conclusive evidence. The plot, in any case, revealed the open hostility between the two courtly parties. Originally the so-called aristocratic party had been formed around the idea of a constitutional regeneration of the monarchy, but by now it was mainly fuelled by the desire to control the government. In fact, the two parties were basically in political agreement, above all in following an international policy of alliance with France, and fought only for power. This naturally made Bonaparte's plans of intervening in the monarchy easier to fulfil.

1808: mediatization of the monarchy and general crisis

Although it is already part of a well-established historiographical discourse to speak of a French invasion of Spain at the end of 1807 and beginning of 1808, it is nevertheless technically wrong, for the large French army entered the Peninsula with the acquiescence of the sovereign. However, Napoleon did not have the authorization of a signed treaty to garrison strategic places or to organize a vice-regal government in Spain and entrust it to Marshal Murat, although he did exactly this. The occupation of Spain was the consequence of the previous mediatization of the benefits of empire and the projected mediatization of the monarchy itself. Bonaparte was acting according to the logic of the combination of these two processes and not according to the text of the treaty of Fontainebleau. It is worth considering the difference created by the crisis of 1808, for it affected not only the imperial part of the monarchy and its revenues, but Spain itself. With some thousands of troops inside Spain, a de facto government in the hands of Murat and, from the end of April 1808, with the Spanish royal family in France, Napoleon completed the mediatization of the monarchy in the succeeding months. In terms of the international law doctrine *ius gentium*, Spain ceased to be a nation and had to be more properly considered a colony or dependent part of France.

On 19 March a new plot in Aranjuez, one of the royal residences near Madrid, succeeded in overthrowing Manuel de Godoy and forced Charles IV to abdicate in favour of his son, the Prince of Asturias. Ferdinand VII rapidly sought French imperial favour, as his father did immediately the next day in order to declare his abdication illegal. The political behaviour of both kings shows to what extent they had accepted the submission of the Spanish monarchy and its destiny to the decisions of the French emperor. If, as is probable, Napoleon had already made the decision to replace the Bourbon dynasty with his own, the Spanish royal family certainly made it easier.

There were early signs that Ferdinand and his court did not fit into Napoleon's imperial plans for Spain. At his entrance into Madrid, the new King was rudely ignored by both Murat and the French ambassador. Later, when the King's delegates went to treat with Murat for recognition of his legitimacy as King of Spain by the French Emperor, he learnt that Napoleon had already decided to include Spain in his projected confederation of southern Europe. The removal of the whole royal family to France in April 1808, including the favourite Manuel de Godoy and the royal princes, completed the plan of leaving Spain bereft of the entire the royal family. Moreover, in Bayonne, Charles IV immediately announced his willingness for Murat to become the Governor of Spain.

The Emperor, who considered Charles IV as the rightful King of Spain and dealt with him accordingly, literally bought the hereditary rights to the Spanish monarchy from father and son, between 5 and 10 May 1808. In exchange for properties and fabulous pensions for life, Charles IV renounced his rights to Napoleon (describing the latter 'as the only man in the current state of affairs who can restore order') under the sole condition that the kingdom be kept united and no religion other than Catholicism be permitted. Likewise, Ferdinand renounced 'as far as necessary the rights he holds as Prince of Asturias'.[18]

After Bayonne, the Spanish monarchy was completely mediatized by Bonaparte. Although nominally it continued to exist under the new Bonaparte dynasty, in terms of *ius gentium* Spain had literally disappeared, absorbed by the French empire. As noted above, the *ius gentium* or international law did not comply with a systematic and positive regulation of international norms but was rather a juridical culture that informed how relations between States or sovereign nations should be established making use of wars, treaties, alliances and federations. It was a juridical culture that only took account of political bodies endowed with their own, independent sovereignty. In this culture, the fact that a sovereign political body should be detached from any other was not an indispensable requisite for it to be considered as an independent nation, since it might well be linked through federations or other types of contract providing protection or aid. That had been the case of the Swiss Confederation before the French intervention in 1798 and, as the second President of the United States, John Adams, wrote in 1787, it was also the case of some other republican governments incorporated to monarchies, like the case of the Basque province of Biscay in Spain.[19] The differentiating factor between nation and country in Emmerich de Vattel's terms was that the former might be able to act for itself in the context of international relations, and this was precisely what Spain lost between October 1807 and May–July 1808.

Taking control of the Spanish monarchy through the (illegal) surrender of the royal family, Napoleon went on to give Spain a new regime and a new king. The first he did with notable speed, for Murat immediately convened a meeting of notables in Bayonne to whom the emperor presented a constitutional text that, after being slightly altered upon review in Bayonne, was approved at the beginning of July.[20] This, the Constitutional Act of Spain, rendered the monarchy's lack of independence in the sphere of *ius gentium* explicit. On the one hand, article 2 recognized the hereditary rights of the Bonaparte dynasty and, on the other, article 124 established Spain's dependence on France in matters of international policy. There was also Napoleon and his brother Joseph's treaty of 5 July 1808 relating to Joseph's dynastic rights, which was signed three days before the promulgation of the Bayonne constitution and added to it en bloc. This treaty not only encumbered Spain with the costs of the purchase of the dynastic rights from Charles IV and his son (estates included) but established far more systematically the subordination of the Spanish monarchy to the French empire in international relationships. A secret clause, moreover, allowed French commerce to use the Spanish trading circuit in exchange for its protection.

The model of monarchy set out in this agreement and the constitutional text of Bayonne consisted of a conglomeration of metropolis and colonies in which both parties were in turn subordinate to the French empire. Both parts of the monarchy, metropolis and colonies, were also to be represented in the Cortes, although in different ways since the American provinces had only corporate representation, notably less numerous than that of the metropolis. The Napoleonic model made no distinctions between the economic and commercial spheres, establishing an open system from which French commerce could benefit, embodied in the treaty between Joseph and his brother Napoleon. In this sense, unlike the Cadiz constitution, the Bayonne constitution embodies fairly faithfully eighteenth-century Spanish enlightened projects to establish an empire in the Hispanic Atlantic based on commerce.

The consequence of this operation to implant a dynasty and subordinate the Spanish monarchy to the Napoleonic international order confronted the kingdom with the need either to choose to accept this situation as the one most convenient for Spain, or to resist it, refusing to obey the new king. The first of these positions was not without attractions, since Joseph I could very easily present himself as the enlightened monarch for whom most of the Spanish elites of previous decades had so longed. In fact, above all in metropolitan Spain, those in favour of accepting a king who presented himself with a constitutional text in hand (and with the promise of legal codes and the rationalization of the administration) understood that the situation of subordination in the international order which it also entailed might be worth the price. This explains why a very significant part of the intellectual elites connected to the government and administration were inclined to recognize the new monarch.[21]

Resistance to the process of imperial mediatization of the Spanish monarchy in its entirety (as a monarchy and as an empire) required exceptional determination, flying as it did in the face of the most important magistracies of the monarchy (the Council of Castile, law courts and chanceries), which had nodded to the deals done in France. The first to move were the municipal councils, followed immediately by the emergency institutions, the juntas, which came out against the new dynasty implanted in Bayonne. Their main objective was to present themselves as institutions able to absorb the traditional legitimacy of the monarchy in order to avoid being seen solely as rebels with no commitment to order or devoid of legal status. The interesting thing here is that the second response to the events of May 1808 in Bayonne spread to both monarchy and empire and so, unlike the previous dynastic crisis at the beginning of the eighteenth century, the 1808 crisis had an Atlantic dimension that would characterize it until its culmination in the independence of the American territories.[22]

Notes

1. 'Noticias para un tratado con México' (1835) in Luis Miguel Díaz and Jaime G. Martini, *Relaciones diplomáticas México-España* (Mexico, 1977), 69. This text was published in a previous version in *Secuencia. Revista de historia y ciencias sociales*, commemorative number, 2008.
2. Alberto Gil Novales (edition and introduction), *José Manuel de Vadillo y la independencia de América (1828–1836)* (Madrid, 2006), 228.
3. José Rivera Indarte, *El voto de América, o sea breve examen de esta cuestión: ¿Convendrá o no a las nuevas repúblicas el reconocimiento de su independencia, enviando embajadores a la corte de Madrid?* (Buenos Aires, 1835).
4. Antonio Salas, *Memoria sobre la utilidad que resultará a la nación, y en especial a Cádiz, del reconocimiento de la independencia de América, y del libre comercio del Asia* (Cádiz, 1834), 4.
5. Juan de Solórzano had argued in 1647 in his influential *Política Indiana*—the key text on the nature of the monarchy for Spanish jurists and royal officials until to the late eighteenth century—that the Spanish monarchy was best understood as the realization of a divine plan to catholicize the world.
6. Eva Botella, 'Era inevitable 1808? Una revisión de la tradición de la decadencia española', *Revista de Occidente*, 326–327 (2008): 47–68.
7. By imperial mediatization I mean the process of intervening in that part of the Spanish monarchy that constituted her colonial wealth and of directing it to the benefit of a different metropolitan European power, namely France.
8. José M. Portillo, 'Ilustración y despotismo ilustrado' in Miguel Artola (dir.), *Historia de Europa* (Madrid, Espasa, 2007). The need to read the *Social Contract* (1762) as the result of local Genevian political experiencies is stressed by Helena Rosenblatt, *Rousseau and Geneva. From the 'First Discourse' to the 'Social Contract', 1749–1762* (Cambridge, 1997).

9. Manuel Lucena, *Premoniciones de la independencia Iberoamericana* (Madrid, Mapfre-Doce Calles-SECIB, 2003).
10. François Furet, *La monarchie republicaine. La constitution de 1791* (París, 1997).
11. Jacques de Saint-Victor, *Les racines de la liberté. Le débat français oublié 1689–1789* (Paris, 2007). Ramón Maiz, *Nación y revolución: la teoría política de Emmanuel de Sieyès* (Madrid, 2007).
12. Emilio La Parra, *La alianza de Godoy con los revolucionarios (España y Francia a fines del siglo XVIII)* (Madrid, 1992).
13. Michel Troper, *Terminer la Révolution. La constitution de 1795* (París, 2007).
14. Steven Englund, *Napoleon. A Political Life* (Harvard, 2004).
15. *Ius gentium* is Latin for International Law. More than a positive law, *ius gentium* referred to a doctrine that had been recently reformulated by Emmerich de Vattel, *Le Droit des Gens ou Principes de la Loi Naturelle* (1758). According to which *ius gentium* was about free nations with a capacity to commit themselves freely through the means of treaties (commerce, assistance, war and peace) or to wage war against others. Peoples with no such capacities were not properly nations but colonies or dependencies. My argument here is that, in terms of *ius gentium*, Spain would be reduced from a nation to a dependent part of the French republican empire. For the principles of the *ius gentium* at the time see Marti Kosekenniemi, *From Apology to Utopia. The Structure of International Legal Argument* (Cambridge, 2005), chapter 2.
16. Emilio La Parra, *Manuel de Godoy. La aventura del poder* (Barcelona, 2002).
17. Pablo Fernández Albaladejo, 'Entre la *gravedad* y la *religión*: Montesquieu y la *tutela* de la monarquía católica en el primer setecientos', in *Constitución en España*, ed. J. M. Iñurritegui, J. M. Portillo (Madrid, 1998), 25–49.
18. These treaties of renunciation by King Charles IV and Prince Ferdinand are cited in their reproduction translated from the French version that José María Queipo de Llano, Count of Toreno, included in an appendix, *Historia del levantamiento, guerra y revolución de España* (1835–1837) (Pamplona, 2008) (edition by Richard Hocquellet). The classical collection by Alejandro del Cantillo, *Tratados, convenios y declaraciones de paz y de comercio que han hecho con las potencias extranjeras los monarcas españoles de la casa de Borbón desde el año de 1700 hasta el día...* (Madrid, 1843) also drew on this documentation.
19. John Adams, *A Defence of the Constitution of Government of the United States of America* (London, 1787), letter IV.
20. Carmen Muñoz de Bustillo, *Bayona en Andalucía: el estado bonapartista en la prefectura de Xerez* (Madrid, 1991).
21. Miguel Artola, *Los afrancesados (1953)* (Madrid, 1989).
22. Jaime E. Rodríguez O., *The Independence of Spanish America* (Cambridge, 1998).

22
The New Spanish Councils[1]

Marta Lorente

I The Emperor's legacy

1 The argument

Let us imagine that a group of Spanish lawyers, not particularly interested in history, were asked which, in their opinion, was the most important judicial or institutional legacy bequeathed by Napoleon to nineteenth-century Spain. Even if there were constitutional experts in the group, no doubt none of them would recall the Constitutional Statute of Bayonne, whereas, in all probability, all or almost all of them would state quite categorically that throughout the nineteenth century, Spanish legal culture absorbed two things of Napoleonic origin or inspiration, the Civil Code and administrative jurisdiction—the latter understood as a necessary pre-condition for the legal formulation of a new concept of civil administration in Spain, modelled on that of Napoleonic France. It has become commonplace among Spanish legal historians to emphasize the French origin of Spain's legal codification and the administration of justice, just as it is now usual to see them as a year zero in the history of European, and particularly Spanish, judicial-political culture.[2] These foundations are based on two fundamental premises with a shared logic. Both the Code and administrative jurisdiction permitted a genuine change in the paradigms of the legal culture intrinsic to the Old Regime: on the one hand, the Code revoked the old statutes;[3] while on the other, the emergence of the new system of administration destroyed the institutions and procedures that fed the government of justice that had determined and managed the control of order within pre-modern societies for centuries.[4]

Even the most superficial reading of the history of nineteenth-century Spain demonstrates that both one, the ultimate Code, the Civil Code and the other, administrative jurisdiction, became realities although long after 1814. Up to 1845 and 1889 respectively, Spain lived without administrative jurisdiction and without a Code: thus, Napoleon only triumphed on Spanish soil after his death. This essay eschews the complicated history of the Code in Spain;[5] rather, it concentrates on the equally difficult transplantation to Spain of an institution, the Council of State, understood fundamentally as the highest court of appeal for administrative jurisdiction.

2   Of names and things

Between 1808 and 1845, a series of institutions emerged in Spain whose names may confuse the non-specialist. Thus, when they entered the Peninsula Napoleon's armies came across an old and tattered Council of State[6] which formed part of the special Hispanic polysynody, a system of government based on different but interrelated councils.[7] Hispanic constitutionalism made a point of reformulating the Council of State; Joseph Bonaparte appointed a Council of State as prescribed by the Bayonne Constitution.[8] At the same time, the Cortes of Cadiz did the same thing in its first statute.[9] The unconstitutional return of Ferdinand VII restored the traditional institution, although it was henceforth mortally wounded and shortly after Ferdinand's death in 1833 the Councils of the Spanish Monarchy were dissolved.[10] From among the ashes of the old polysynody, a new council, the Royal Council of Spain and the Indies, was created; its State Section, not without difficulty, attempted to reincarnate the old institution.[11] Dissolved in 1836 because of its manifest incompatibility with the restoration of the constitutional regime, it was not replaced until a reforming regime finally succeeded in forming a new Council in 1845. Named first the Royal Council and later the Council of State, it has existed to this day, although not without undergoing an endless series of transformations.[12]

The similarity of names notwithstanding, clearly only Joseph's Council and that created in 1845 bear any relation to the Napoleonic paradigm. The irregular chronology of the life of this institution, as well as its specific aspects, make it possible to suggest the existence of a kind of rejection of the institutional surgery of grafting the Council onto the Spanish body politic. However, this view of the process is diametrically opposed by another, widespread perception, which regards the erection in Spain of a system of administrative justice copied on the French model as a rationalization of the exercise of power. To put it another way, what is perceived is a process of institutional transformation culminating naturally in the construction of the administration of the Liberal State and its modern Administrative Law.[13]

However, the history of institutions must go beyond the description of their internal affairs and embrace that of culture and society.[14] The history of Spanish administrative jurisdiction may be extended beyond the particular interests of the different legal disciplines, whose search for their origins is effectively a justification of their current identity. In this latter context, the implantation in Spain of the Napoleonic model of special administrative jurisdiction meant less a transplantation, than a perversion of the original model caused by the corporate nature of Spanish society. This, in turn, definitively preconditioned the particular institutional structure of the emerging Spanish state which, in its turn, provoked an attitude of resistance to the project of the modern, Napoleonic model of the state, an attitude wholly commensurate with the profound anti-individualism that permeated Spanish juridical culture in the nineteenth century, which was based on supposedly liberal principles.

II   The origins of administrative justice and the Council of State

There is a critical current of historiography in contemporary Spain, determined to set the history of administrative justice and the Napoleonic Council of State in the wider context of rethinking the origins and nature of administrative justice, often called Administrative Law. This is a vast debate, but some of its basic premises are summarized here.

1   Administrative justice: some considerations about its antiquity and nature

The existence of Administrative Law prior to the French Revolution is the subject of much scholarly debate.[15] However, the most plausible school of thought interprets Administrative Law as the need to have an independent administration of justice that may sacrifice the rights of individuals without their consent in the name of the collective, public interest.[16] However, these assumptions come into direct conflict with the medieval idea of the governance of justice which, although obsolete by the early nineteenth century, lingered on until the eve of the crisis of the Old Regime.[17] This concept, in turn, determined for centuries the institutional structure and procedures of the French and Spanish monarchies,[18] whose most important arbiters of public discourse, lawyers, always understood bureaucracy as an offshoot of justice and not as an independent branch of government.[19] Conversely, many have argued that the creation of administrative justice enshrined the French version of the principle of the separation of powers included in the Declaration of the Rights of Man and the Citizen of 1789.[20]

2   The Emperor's divan: the fundamental attributes of the Council of State

In part, the process of state reform was consolidated in France by the creation of a new institution, the Council of State.[21] A superb instrument of Napoleonic authoritarianism, the Council of State was instituted by the Constitution on 22 Frimaire, Year VIII (14 December 1799). Its members were nominated at the discretion of the Head of State, who could remove them or second them for other duties, as required. Although the Council did not have any juridical independence since all of its deliberations had to be approved by the Head of State before being implemented, it was difficult, if not impossible, to govern without its aid. The Council was responsible for drawing up all legislation, interpreting bills, formulating all administrative regulation; it was responsible for all departments and municipalities and for consultation on all questions of an administrative nature that were sent to it by the Head of State or his ministers. The famous article 75 of the Constitution of 1799 definitively protected administrators from the magistracy, while at the same time it made the Council the definitive arbiter of the management of this protection. The shielding of bureaucrats from the courts was now enshrined in the Napoleonic Constitution.[22]

Although the constitutional text did not speak specifically of the administrative jurisdiction of the Council, this was the natural consequence of enacting two great fundamental laws, one on departmental administration (17 February 1800) and the other organizing the courts and recruitment of magistrates (18 March 1800). Finally, the Decrees of 11 and 22 June 1806 created the Disputes Committee within the Council, chaired by the Minister of Justice and made up of six *maîtres de requêtes* (appeal judges) and six auditors. They were charged with the investigation and preparation of all the reports on any contentious matters on which the Council was to hand down a pronouncement, as well as with deciding how to proceed with regard to its new committee.

3   Recapitulation. On the essence of administrative jurisdiction: Rule of Law v. *droit administratif* (administrative jurisdiction)

When Napoleon invaded Spain in 1808, the Council of State was a new, healthy and original entity, not a (re)formulation of ancient institutions or an unavoidable consequence of the Revolutionary dictum of the separation of powers. It consolidated the paradigm shift away from the old model of governance of justice, which was significantly different, if not damaged beyond repair, after 1789. The essence of Napoleonic administrative jurisdiction was rooted not so much in the administrators' appropriation of judicial affairs that took place in the first years of the Revolution, as in the shielding of bureaucrats as individuals from normal justice. This raised a constitutional question through the inclusion of article 75 in the first law of Year VIII. As Duverger de Hauranne pointed out in 1828, article 75 was not an enactment or new formulation of the Revolutionary Law of 1790, but a Napoleonic interpretation of the same, because at the outset of the Revolutionary reforms it was the Assembly and not an authoritarian executive that retained the power to send the administrators before judges in the event of denunciations by private individuals.[23]

Article 75 not only removes responsibility from the Administration, but above all establishes a double chronological and geographical frontier between juridical cultures. Tocqueville best explains the chronology of this evolution:

> It frequently occurred, in the old Monarchy, that the *parlements* would decree the arrest of a public servant who was guilty of a crime. Sometimes

royal authority would intervene and have the process annulled. Despotism was then revealed in all its nakedness, and obedience was seen to be no more than submission to force. We have, then, stepped back from the point reached by our parents, since, under the guise of [administrative] justice, we allow to be done and consecrated in the name of the law that which could only be imposed upon them by violence.[24]

The geographic extent of the concept of Administrative Law was set out in A. V. Dicey's *Introduction to the Study of the Law of the Constitution*.[25] Notwithstanding the text's errors, for decades this work not only traced a dividing line between the countries that belonged to the Administrative Law club and the rule of law club, but also offered a comprehensive criticism of the Administrative Law club, based on the fundamental repugnance English lawyers felt for the infamous article 75, rather than in the rejection of the existence of a judicial order specializing in administrative matters, per se, which in turn generated a particular Law. For Dicey:

> In many continental countries, and notably in France, there exists a scheme of administrative law—known to Frenchmen as *droit adminis-tratif*—which rests on ideas foreign to the fundamental assumptions of our English common law, and especially to what we have termed the rule of law. This opposition is specially apparent in the protection given in foreign countries to servants of the State, or, as we say in England, of the Crown, who, whilst acting in pursuance of official orders, or in the *bona fide* attempt to discharge official duties, are guilty of acts which in themselves are wrongful or unlawful.... It forms only one portion of the whole system of *droit administratif*, but it is the part of French law to which in this chapter I wish to direct particularly the attention of students.[26]

The constitutional English-language world held firm on a principle it had shared with the continental Monarchies of the ancien régime, that the status of public servant should not protect those who abused their office. Such offenders became mere private individuals answerable to the public.

As well as consolidating the definitive break with the old judicial culture of common law, the Napoleonic version of the Council of State and administrative jurisdiction came into direct conflict with many premises of liberal ideology, as its critics undertook to point out throughout the Restoration and the July Monarchy.[27] However, the Council of State not only survived the fall of Napoleonic authoritarianism,[28] it emerged unscathed from all the vicissitudes of French constitutional history.

While not false, this outline constitutes an idealized and superficial vision of the fortunes of the Council of State. Its survival in France can only be explained in terms of the adjustments it underwent, some of which occurred at points when its demise seemed imminent.[29] In turn, the success of the Council of State as an institutional model depended to a large extent on the adaptations it underwent in its various, complex introductions to many of the states of nineteenth-century Europe. These processes undoubtedly perverted the original character of the institution. This is how both the failure and the specific perversion of the Spanish Council of State should be examined.

III   The complex Spanish transplant

1   Administrative justice, constitutional justice: Bayonne v. Cadiz

The Councils of State created by the Constitutions of Bayonne and Cadiz were utterly different from each other. Joseph's Council was modelled exactly on Napoleon's,[30] while the Cadiz Council was a consultative organ subject to the Parliament or Cortes. The Cadiz Council was not a jurisdictional body, whereas Joseph's Council represented the apex of what was known as retained jurisdiction. If anything characterized Cadiz constitutionalism, it was its direct refusal to create a judicial order that differed from the common law. However, the most important difference from the Napoleonic model was its complete rejection of the concept of immunity for public servants from the courts in all that related to their duties in the administration of justice. Cadiz's constitutionalism abolished legal privileges (with the exception of military and ecclesiastical privileges), making a constitutional point that it was now possible for everyone who wielded authority, including the clergy, to be accused by the citizenry of committing breaches against the Constitution before their superiors, magistrates or, in the final instance, even before Parliament itself.[31]

The continuation of a traditional concept of responsibility of public officers was still considered a guarantee of good administration by the framers of the Cadiz constitution. Moreover, this concept was now endowed with a fresh point of reference, the terms of the Constitution itself governed all the actions of any public authority. The constitutionalization of the old jurisdictional order implied the upholding of two principles: first, any legal, governmental or even normative measure that affected declared rights could be transformed into a lawsuit; and second, no public servant could hide behind his rank to prevent being taken to court.[32] This concept was accepted in Spanish America through the adoption of the Cadiz Constitution in the overseas territories, which in turn was reformulated in Spanish American constitutionalism after the Wars of Independence. It is therefore hardly surprising that administrative justice is completely unknown in most Latin American states.

In opposition to this legalistic perception, stood the Constitution of Bayonne—deeply rooted in the concept of administrative justice—which, even allowing for the difficulties created by the war, was a complete failure.

Those in Bayonne responsible for the adaptation of the constitutional text to the Spanish Monarchy demonstrated not so much hostility as a notable lack of understanding regarding what the Council of State and administrative justice were meant to be. Thus, while for some the institution was superfluous, for others the creation of the new Council did not necessarily imply the dissolution of those already in existence.[33] The old cumulative logic that presided for centuries over the institutionalization of the Catholic Monarchy was wielded on various occasions in Bayonne. It was equally surprising that nobody noticed or wished to notice the significant novelty of article 54, the key to the retained jurisdiction,[34] which bestowed on the Council the instruments necessary to determine unilaterally a jurisdictional sphere completely independent of the common law.

The absence of discussion did not augur well for the future of this institution. Although from the outset the King vehemently wished to form his Council himself, as he made clear in the solemn inaugural act of installation (3 May 1809), the subsequent life of the Council did not live up to the brilliance of its inception. Little by little, the Council was excluded from its role of legislative assembly, having to endure attacks on it from detractors or competitors.

A full account of the vicissitudes of the Council cannot be given here. Rather, the emphasis is placed on the existence of a significant contradiction which, marking its origins, accompanied the Council throughout its short life. It was hampered by hastily drafted regulations that organized its workings, and it neglected to develop the specific article that involved its powers over internal disputes (2 May 1809). However, and hence the contradiction, the Council not only gave priority to its dispute-related duties to the detriment of more general legislative activity (which was developed in the Regulations), but finished by dedicating itself almost exclusively to resolving administrative questions.

Bayonne put the cart before the horse. Given that a series of reforms of justice, municipal administration and finance did not exist or had not been properly implemented, it was difficult, or rather impossible, to separate justice from civil administration, and increase the latter to the detriment of the former. Nevertheless, Joseph did try to create a modern state out of the system he inherited from the old Monarchy, as seen in the Decree dated 17 April 1810, which divided the Kingdom into prefectures, but the even the most superficial reading of this and other edicts reveals that Joseph's plans consisted of not so much creating an administrative jurisdictional order separate from the common law, as of hoping that an effective administration would dominate government, leaving room only for recognition of the specialized jurisdiction for finance. In any case, this difficult process gave the Council of State the final decision on legal action against public officials.

Even if it had ever been implemented, Joseph's dream would have become unmanageable. The grievances provoked by the ploughing of fields, opening of canals and the creation of public works that lurked beneath the term civil government would have led to the search for legal redress on a vast scale—as the Cadiz Cortes could well attest, as citizens and institutions of all kinds and classes filled it to bursting with petitions and complaints throughout its short but eventful existence.

2   From the Royal Councils of Spain and the Indies to the Royal Council (of State)

The experience of Cadiz and the failure of the Josephine kingdom reveal that the crisis of 1808 did not suddenly efface the traditional corporative structure of Spanish society. The old order was marked by the plurality of ordinances and centres of power, the multitude of privileges and, in short, the understanding of politics in terms of harmonization, rather than the hierarchical imposition of decisions deriving from a single legislative source. This panorama persisted until the death of Ferdinand VII in 1833, although by that time Spain had lost its American empire, more corporative in its structure even than that of the metropolis. From 1834 onwards, the voices crying out for the creation of an administrative jurisdiction on the French model increased manifold, though the foundations of that jurisdiction were only laid down in 1845.[35] Nevertheless, by 1834, criticism of the 'confusing of matters of justice and government' brought about the dissolution of the old Councils but without proposing any alteration of the two principles which composed the negative aspect of Napoleonic administrative jurisdiction: Government proceedings could turn into judicial matters; and individuals from the civil administration could be put before a judge. In short, the old jurisdictional mechanisms continued to thrive in 1830s Spain.

If this analysis is accepted, it must be asked how the solution of 1845 was reached. It is certain that throughout the preceding decade a series of basic premises were established for the Spanish Administration: division into provinces, the creation of the Ministry of Public Works and its sub-departments, the reform of the judicial system, and so on. However, it should be added that one fundamental characteristic of the old apparatus of the Monarchy was preserved, the plurality of privileges, which persisted until 1868. Nor was this all, from 1834 onwards the consultative bodies multiplied ad infinitum, to the point where even institutions of a revolutionary nature (the famous Juntas of the mid-1830s) called themselves consultative. Thus the two most essential powers of the original imperial council were disseminated in a multitude of instances within the prevailing Spanish Administration, which only underlines the weight of its heritage.

In these circumstances, the creation of an administrative jurisdictional order may be identified with a radical surgical operation to excise the other existing orders, in the same way that the creation of the Council might have supposed the modernization of the famous consultative function. However, no such thing occurred; thus, the new administrative jurisdiction continued to compete with other jurisdictions, as well as with ordinary procedure, and the new Council of State consulted in the same way as the General Commission for Codification, charged with drawing up draft codes, acts and even regulations. The cumulative logic that Joseph I had permitted, continued to set the pace for the construction of the contemporary Spanish Administration. Therefore, it is not surprising that the Provincial Councils, initially conceived as the first instance of the administrative order, were largely inactive. Nevertheless, the administrative revolution of 1845 was less the creation of an administrative jurisdiction, with the Council as the last recourse of appeal, as the creation of a new set of privileges, or in the granting of a charter of its own to the only Ministry bereft of privileges, the Ministry of Governance.

3   Conclusion: the Spanish state and weak individualism

Historians have long abandoned the thankless task of trying to squeeze Spanish events into the mould offered by the canonical version of the French revolution in order to defend the existence of a genuine Spanish revolution. However, the French models of legal and administrational institutions still explain the emergence of the illiberal contemporary State: the division into departments illuminates the Spanish division into provinces, the subdelegates of the Ministry of Public Works are comparable to prefects, the Supreme Court to the Court of Cassation, and the Council of State and the administrative jurisdiction are similar to those of the Napoleonic system.

Although it is certain that the men of 1845 invoked the name of the Emperor again and again, it is equally the case that their edifice had little to do with the original paradigm. Moreover, if it resembled anything, it was precisely a kind of reformulation of an institutional policy deeply rooted in the reformism of the late eighteenth century. Nonetheless, 1845 introduced a key innovation, the so-called authorization to judge, an imitation of the famous article 75, which completely transformed the rules of the game. Spain joined that club so fiercely criticized by Dicey, given that henceforth, administrators as individuals could not be called before a judge. This, in turn, meant that everything touched by them became, as if by magic, an administrative matter and was not therefore subject to legal responsibility. There was only scope to speak of the so-called disciplinary liability.

This state of affairs did not exactly contribute to promoting a culture of rights, thus opening the way for the emergence of modern individualism. All of this was reflected in Spain's judicial culture, which, for almost a whole century, was content to reformulate a series of images, categories and discourses that can be properly described as *epigonal ius commune*, the final presence of a common law, shown to be scarcely compatible with the profound transformations undergone by continental legal culture as a result of the advent of the Code and the laborious formulation of contemporary Administrative Law.

Notes

1. SEJ 2007–55448-C02–02.
2. Eduardo García de Enterría, *La lengua de los derechos. La formación del Derecho público europeo tras la Revolución Francesa* (Madrid, 1994).
3. Jean-Louis Halperin, *Histoire du droit privé français depuis 1804* (Paris, 1996).
4. See for all, Antonio M. Hespanha, *Cultura Jurídica européia. Síntese de um Milenio* (Florianópolis, 2005).
5. Marta Lorente, *La Voz del Estado. La publicación de las normas (1810–1889)* (Madrid, 2003).
6. On its status, see Feliciano Barrios, *España 1808. El Gobierno de la Monarquía* (Madrid, 2009).
7. Feliciano Barrios, *El Consejo de Estado de la Monarquía española, 1521–1812* (Madrid, 1984).
8. Tomás de la Cuadra-Salcedo, 'El Consejo de Estado en las Constituciones de Cádiz y Bayona', in *Documentación Administrativa* 244–245 (1996), in *Historia y Política* 19 (2008): 151–171. Marta Lorente, 'La frustración del sueño imperial: El Consejo de Estado de la Constitución de Bayona' (in press).
9. Fernando Martínez, 'De la función consultiva y del Consejo de Estado gaditanos', in *Historia Contemporánea*, 33 (2006-II): 557–580.
10. Josep Fontana, *De en medio del tiempo. La segunda restauración española* (Barcelona, 2006).
11. Marta Lorente, 'La supresión de los Consejos y la creación del Real de España e Indias', in *Actas del XV Congreso del Instituto Internacional de Historia del Derecho Indiano* (Cordoba, 2005), vol. II, 1099–1144.
12. Juan Ramón Fernández Torres, *La formación histórica de la jurisdicción contencioso-administrativa (1845–1868)* (Madrid, 1998).
13. This is, in essence, the interpretation offered by García de Enterría, *La lengua de los derechos*.
14. António M. Hespanha, *A história do direito na história social* (Lisboa, 1978). Idem *Cultura Jurídica*.
15. Sylvain Soleil, 'La justice administrative avant 1789. Retour sur trente ans de découvertes', in *Regards sur l'histoire de la justice administrative. Journées d'études du Centre d'histoire du droit de l'Université de Rennes I*, ed. G. Bigot and M. Bouvet (París, 2006), 3–30.
16. Luca Mannori, Bernardo Sordi, *Storia del diritto amministrativo* (Roma-Bari, 2001).
17. An excellent synthesis of its main characteristics in: Alejandro Agüero, 'Las categorías básicas de la cultura jurisdiccional', in *De la Justicia de Jueces a la Justicia de Leyes: hacia la España de 1870*, coord. Marta Lorente (Madrid, 2006), 19–54.
18. Carlos Garriga, 'Justicia animada: Dispositivos de la Justicia en la Monarquía Católica', in ibid. 59–99, and Carlos Garriga, 'Gobierno y justicia: el gobierno de la justicia' (in press). (My thanks to the author for allowing me to consult this work).
19. Here the arguments of Luca Mannori are reproduced: 'Per una 'preistoria' della funzione amministrativa. Cultura giuridica e attività dei pubblici apparati nell'età del tardo diritto comune', in *Quaderni Fiorentini*, 19, (1990): 323–504. Idem, 'Centralisation et fonction publique dans la pensée juridique de l'Ancien Régime; justice, police et administration', in *Actes du Colloque d'Orléans, 30 septembre, 1er et 2 octobre*, Orléans, Presses Universitaires d'Orléans, 1993. *Idem,*

'Giustizia e amministrazione tra antico e nuovo regime' in *Magistrati e potere nella storia europea*, ed. R. Romanelli (Bologna, 1997), 39–65.

20. Eduardo García de Enterría, 'Le contrôle de l'administration. Techniques, étendue, effectivité des contrôles. Contentieux administratif objectif et contentieux administratif subjectif à la fin du XXe siècle: Analyse historique et comparative', in *Colloque du deuxième Centenaire. La Revue Administrative du Conseil d'État français*, 53 année (2000) (special number, 3), 125.

21. A. Regnault, *Histoire du Conseil d'État depuis son origine jusqu'a ce jour* (Paris, 1851) 2–21. M. de Villaidan, *Histoire des Conseils du Roi* (Paris, 1856) vol. 1, V. L. Aucoc, *Le Conseil d'État avant et depuis 1789. Ses transformations, ses travaux et son personnel. Étude historique et bibliographique* (Paris, 1876), 26.

22. Article 75: 'The agents of the Government may not be prosecuted for facts relative to their functions but as a result of a decision by the Council of State'.

23. M. Duverger de Hauranne, *De l'ordre légal en France et des abus d'autorité* (Paris, 1828), 293.

24. Alexis de Tocqueville, *De la démocratie en Amérique* (Brussels, 1837), vol. I, 194. The translation and the addition in brackets are my own.

25. I am using the ninth edition of this work, enlarged with an introduction and appendix by E.C.S. Wade, and published in London, 1945 (the first edition dates from 1885). For decades this work influenced English-language understanding of *droit administratif*, regardless of the fact that many held it responsible '...for a good deal of misunderstanding among Frenchmen and Englishmen of each other's systems'. From Wade's introduction, *Introduction*, xiv.

26. Ibid. 234.

27. Here it is enough to cite as an example two very critical pieces of writing: G. de la Rochefoucauld, *Des attributions du Conseil d'État* (Paris, 1829) and M. H. Colombel, *De la jurisdiction administrative* (Paris, 1840).

28. Bernard Pacteau, *Le Conseil d'État et la fondation de la justice administrative française au XIXe siècle* (Paris, 1977).

29. Marc Bouvet, *Le Conseil d'État sous la Monarchie de Juillet* (París, 2001).

30. Xavier Abeberry Magescas, *Le Gouvernement central de l'Espagne sous Joseph Bonaparte (1808–1813). Effectivité des institutions monarchiques et de la Justice Royale, (thèse pour l'obetention du doctorat en droit)*, 2 vols (Université de Paris XII-Val-de-Marne, 2001).

31. Marta Lorente, *Las infracciones a la Constitución de 1812* (Madrid, 1988).

32. Carlos Garriga, Marta Lorente, *Cádiz, 1812. La Constitución jurisdiccional* (Madrid, 2007).

33. I am using the collection of texts that make up the first volume of the collection directed by Miguel Artola, *Las Constituciones españolas*, ed. I. Fernández Sarasola, *La Constitución de Bayona (1808)* (Madrid, 2007).

34. This law made it possible for the Council to decide jurisdictional competences of administrative and judicial bodies, deal with the contentious part of the administration and, finally, determine whether to summons agents employed by the Public Administration.

35. Juan Ramón Fernández Torres, *Historia Legal de la jurisdicción Contencioso-administrativa (1845–1998)* (Madrid, 2006).

23

Political Paradoxes in Napoleonic Europe: The Portuguese Case

Fernando Dores Costa

I find it absurd that you set against me the opinion of the people of Westphalia.... If you listen to the opinion of the people, you will do nothing at all. If the people refuse their own happiness, the people are anarchic, they are guilty, and punishment is the first duty of a prince.

Napoleon to Jerôme

I am not so stupid as to place the interest of the inhabitants before serving Your Majesty.

Junot to Napoleon 14 February 1808

Before the upheavals of the Revolution of 1789, there was broad sympathy for, and considerable interest in, limiting the powers of ministers and the State. A social reorganization was envisaged in which the role of informed public opinion would increase and the possibility of arbitrary government would be eliminated, or at least reduced. We know that within this general perspective, there were many differences of opinion. However, the way in which the French army entered Portugal, led by Junot, meeting no resistance and occupying Lisbon with raw recruits in the unfavourable weather conditions of November 1807, brutally revealed that in the intervening period Europe had changed. The prospect of a Europe of free, republican peoples in which government was less powerful, had disappeared beneath the shocking efficiency of a France that had become an Empire. In 1803 Clausewitz speculated whether the French would become the new Romans. The idea that force and force alone ruled the world had triumphed. Paradoxically, the State and *raison d'état* had triumphed. This change may be best illustrated by the development of Fichte's thought, by Hegel's creation of a political theory heavily influenced by Napoleon, and also by the thinking of one of the most influential theoreticians of war, Clausewitz. This is not to say that this development was confined to Germany; indeed, the sense that might was right and that force alone could ensure a political regime, now seemed to pervade Europe.[1]

The kingdom of Portugal became part of Napoleon's continental empire after a lengthy diplomatic game. Since 1796 Portugal had maintained an unstable relationship with both France and Great Britain. Finally, in 1807, the Prince Regent of Portugal left for Brazil, a possibility long foreseen but postponed until it became inevitable. He left the field open for conciliation, exhorting the Portuguese to collaborate with the approaching Napoleonic army. Although an intense debate about military reform had taken place after the War of the Oranges in 1801 and a reorganization of the army had been announced in 1806, the possibility of the armed forces being ordered to confront the invading troops had been rejected. For a while some councillors of state had been demanding that Portugal should abandon fence-sitting diplomacy and join the Napoleonic system. But this option would have handed over the colonies, in particular Brazil, to French protection. In any event, by 1807 Napoleon was at the peak of his power and Portugal would find no support if it attempted to resist.

Under Junot, Portugal had its longest period of Napoleonic government lasting from December 1807 to August 1808. There was another brief period of Napoleonic rule in the city of Oporto, under Soult, in 1809. The operation in November 1807 was to seize the Portuguese navy and was directed at Lisbon.

The objective was not achieved; the Portuguese navy was taken by the British. However, the order to advance as far as Lisbon is only comprehensible, on the one hand within the framework of the alliance with Godoy's Spain and, on the other, because Napoleon's objective was the ships and the naval fortifications in Lisbon. The Treaty of Fontainebleau planned the division of the kingdom into three zones, one for Godoy. The French needed to secure Portugal properly after the capture of Lisbon, and they needed the Portuguese fleet; that is, the Portuguese alliance was considered important by Napoleon, but Junot needed more troops to ensure it happened. This was made possible by the Spanish alliance. The taking of Lisbon was a delicate military operation as would be demonstrated later. With Lisbon in Junot's hands, Napoleon obviously intended to apply the continental blockade in Portugal, removing the English from the Tagus. The presence of the Russian fleet on the Tagus made it possible, in theory, for the Portuguese fleet to combine with the Russians against the French and Spanish. The British viewed the Russian presence as a danger. 'We all deserve to be damn'd for letting the Russian fleet get into Lisbon. But of this, we must not now say a word…. I now propose burning the Portuguese and Russians in the Tagus, which I believe to be practicable without risking our line of battle ships.'[2] Lisbon could be the point of support for other initiatives. At the end of May 1808, Napoleon would ask Junot how many transport ships greater that 300 tons he could supply in the event of one of his squadrons appearing in Lisbon 'in order to mount an expedition to Brazil'.[3]

It is more interesting to observe how, in a few months, from December 1807 to July 1808, Junot found himself facing the dilemma of governing Portugal in the context of imperial demands. The objective was conquest and it is difficult to imagine that the Portuguese saw this as the path to liberty. The general disarming of the population (taken to the point where any armed individual was considered an irregular combatant and a permit was necessary to go hunting), the dissolution of the army, the posting of the best officers and troops to France through the formation of the Portuguese Legion, the creation of a so-called deputation to Napoleon made up of the men judged most influential and as potential leaders of a resistance movement, the execution of individuals for brawling with French troops for commonplace, apolitical reasons, were measures that were unquestionably marks of conquest and instruments of Portugal's incorporation into the orbit of the empire.

Eliminating the most basic capacity to wage war, notwithstanding such an integration, might still bring about beneficial social and economic changes. Yet these changes, which had been the aspirations of the Revolution in its initial phase, now carried a different meaning. The Napoleonic project was a unique way of restoring the state's authority by conquering France and imposing a Napoleonic dictatorship. This reinforced the French State to an unprecedented extent through the elimination of intermediaries; this was an ironic result of the reforms of the Revolution, which had created the concept of equality among citizens through the abolition of privilege, but also the abolition of all bodies such as the *Parlements* which stood between the individual and the state. It was embodied in the abolition of feudalism and the implementation of equality before the law. There were no intermediary authorities or bodies between the individual and the State. These reforms did not, in principle, constitute a strengthening of the State, but of the individual. However, from the perspective of a new Machiavellianism, this could easily be turned into the atomization and isolation of the individual in the face of bureaucracy. Above all, on the periphery of the empire, it might begin to be perceived as an instrument of conquest. As Georges Lefebvre stated in his *Napoléon*: 'In his mind, the implantation of his system of government should first and foremost establish his supremacy; it was of great importance to him that his power, and that of his vassals and allies, should go unchallenged: intermediaries, privileges, feudalism should therefore disappear so that everyone could become a direct subject of the State.'[4] What, in the early days of the Revolution, had been the emancipation of the middle classes and even of the peasantry (far beyond what, strictly speaking, the liberal programme actually entailed) had become, on the fringes of the empire, a policy to eliminate the capacity to resist military occupation.

Likewise, the elimination of mechanisms that traditionally sustained the nobility greatly empowered the Napoleonic regime because, before 1789, the nobility was seen as the potential leadership of resistance. Lefebvre writes: 'It was also appropriate for the laws of succession to cut great fortunes down to size, thus making the aristocracy a creature of the sovereigns and the priests, their servants.' The obligation of all members of the Great Empire was to provide money and men. What was at issue in the political forms of the old order was their inefficiency: 'The Ancien Régime, with its chaotic and sluggish administration did not mobilize the country's resources sufficiently quickly; it was necessary to start afresh and replace it with Napoleon's bureaucracy.'[5]

The famous Civil Code was the preferred model for social organization: 'The essentials of this social policy were embodied in the Civil Code and this is why the emperor was so determined to introduce it everywhere. Since 1807, he sought to impose it on the Hanseatic cities, on Danzig, on his German protectorates, and, of course, on Holland and Westphalia; in 1808, his mind turned to Portugal; in 1809, to Spain.' The adoption of the Code in these countries would correspond to the creation of a civil society with the characteristics necessary to serve the State. National differences would disappear: 'what suits the French suits everyone, for', he wrote to Eugène, 'there is really very little difference between one people and another'.[6] We know, however, that at the same time Napoleon believed it was inevitable that people would rebel, and that his own prejudices led him to underestimate their ability to do so consistently (as in the case of the peoples of the Iberian peninsula). In letters to Joseph, King of Naples in 1806, he criticized Joseph for not taking the measures and precautions necessary to defend the himself from the conspiracies and revolution that would inevitably occur.[7] Thus, we can easily understand the extent to which the conditions created on the imperial periphery favoured the propagation of a counter-revolutionary discourse which exploited fear and simplified conflicts in extremist terms. After Junot's retreat, there was an upsurge in the publication, and wide dissemination, of pamphlets demonizing Napoleon and the French in general as Jacobins, men who wanted to destroy society and plunge society into chaos.

After the taking of Lisbon, Napoleon's plan for Portugal was defined in a letter dated 3 January 1808 and put into effect by Junot on 1 February, when he suppressed the Council of the Regency (which Prince João had left behind, like the shadow of a sovereignty he no longer exercised). The decree said that the whole Kingdom of Portugal would be governed by and in the name of the Emperor through the general-in-chief of his army, but only until conditions were right for the treaty between France and a defeated Portugal to be implemented. According to Junot's report to Napoleon, that decision would have been well received, the 'Portuguese nation is pleased to see the French take up the reins of power, and they will be happy with us given that they have not been handed over to Spain'.[8] The partition anticipated by the Treaty of Fontainebleau was condemned by the Portuguese because of an alleged concern that they might be absorbed by Spain, and Junot played on this discontent at the carving up of Portugal. The general-in-chief expressed to the Emperor his commitment to his new task of governing the kingdom: 'It will be extremely difficult for me to succeed in organizing this land.' One remark reveals Junot's new-found commitment to Portugal: 'This Kingdom truly deserves a good Government; I believe its topography and the very nature of its soil resist any division.'[9] If ingenuousness is discounted, it seems Junot enjoyed his role as governor. In a letter dated 14 February 1808, Junot restated his opposition to the partition of Portugal, expressing his satisfaction on discovering that Napoleon agreed. In fact, Napoleon had only written that partition should be postponed until circumstances made it possible to publish the treaty. Junot wanted to persuade the Emperor to change his position, 'But Sire, this Treaty divides Portugal, and Portugal is not divisible'. He again praised the kingdom, with its provinces united 'this will always be one of the most beautiful Kingdoms in Europe', while 'the port of Lisbon is the best placed in Europe'.[10] Portugal could also be a source of funding: 'Under the heading of finances... enjoying the benefits of the Napoleonic Code and administered like France, it must yield, exclusive of customs revenues, or the civil list, at least 40 million (francs).' The role attributed to the introduction of the Code in this context is noteworthy; it was expected to encourage the private ownership of property and the creation of wealth, which would then be translated into a rapid increase in State revenues. Portugal might even become a source of soldiers, which reveals that Junot used the defence of Portugal to absorb Portuguese troops into the French army. He did not have enough forces of his own to do otherwise: 'Its inhabitants are likely to be excellent soldiers; they have spirit and courage and are not in the least soft.'[11] Junot believed that this human raw material, given its 'purity' or 'roughness' (the idea that a soft life made men unfit for war was a commonplace in the eighteenth century), might be put to good use. The idea that conquest was a means to create reservoirs of manpower was no baseless cliché of anti-Napoleonic propaganda.

Junot could even adopt the stance of defending Napoleon's orders as reasonable. Imposing a levy of 100 million francs was the hallmark of conquest *par excellence*. Junot did not approve of the amount: 'The levy has no doubt caused a great stir, but Sire, it is obvious that this is too much.' It would not be possible to pay it without selling off parts of their properties and precious objects. He urged Napoleon to show benevolence: 'If Your Majesty deigned to reduce the contribution by half, You would be doing this country a great service; half the amount could be collected easily, from now to the end of the year, your army's provisions would be assured, and your name would be blessed: permit me to repeat that this contribution is not possible in its entirety.'[12] Napoleon would approve this reduction, saying, 'half will be in silver and the other half in Crown property'.[13]

The most interesting divergence between the two men arose from the thorny problem of the Civil Code. 'Is there any reason not to enforce the Napoleonic Code in Portugal?' Napoleon asked Junot.[14] The latter answered in a way that differs from his earlier view, which associated the Code with great economic dynamism, and everything suggests this shift in opinion demonstrated the influence of those around him. Junot sought a smoother relationship with the upper classes of the occupied country: 'I believe there would be considerable disadvantages if the various legal codes were to be published at this point in time: the laws of this country are too different from our own, especially in respect of inheritance. I could do with some men with expertise in this matter to disentangle the present legislative structure and demonstrate to Your Majesty the disadvantages or the benefits of promulgating the new codes, or else indicate the changes that local issues and the spirit of the country provide.'[15] Napoleon insisted on the introduction of the Code; Junot's position represented cautious resistance.

In the meantime, Junot faced great difficulties in governing because of the economic and financial effects of the disruption of the trade routes: on 29 April, he reported that not one ship had arrived from the Portuguese colonies since his occupation of Lisbon; before the arrival of the French troops, the English (he said) had exported wines for two years; but the dispatch of wine aboard American ships that he had authorized (and which would bring in some welcome cash) was emphatically forbidden by Napoleon.[16] 'You violate the law of the blockade against England in Portugal, and you receive neutral ships loaded with colonial goods supposed to come from America, and which everyone knows have come from London.'[17] For Napoleon, the governance of conquered countries should be based on his armies' need for provisions, but the senior administrators felt they had to build more collaborative relationships with the ruling elites, a view shared by at least some of those elites.

There was another brief experience of Napoleonic rule in Portugal in April–May 1809 after Soult's troops' incursion into the northern provinces as far as the city of Oporto. Soult adopted a policy of moderation to win over the Portuguese, giving rise to the idea that he was promoting himself as a future king of Portugal. Although it is possible that this rumour spread through intrigue among the French, it is certain that it circulated in printed form.[18] As with Junot, Soult's objective was the preservation of Portugal's political unity and the status of the Portuguese ruling classes within the Napoleonic Empire. It is interesting that, faced with the unprecedented social chaos which engulfed Portugal, the French might have been seen by the elites as saviours, since they guaranteed order against the fury of the plebeian masses. A fundamental contradiction of Imperial government on the periphery is confirmed, that the representatives of the empire faced an insoluble dilemma. They had to sustain the imperial army and so they had to impose taxes on the population and rebuild the economy while, at the same time, under the pressures surrounding them, they were tempted to become protectors of the country, opting for moderate and conciliatory measures.

Could the French presence have raised expectations among the Portuguese who had been influenced by French ideas? I believe that it could not be thought in 1808 that Napoleon's armies would bring about the 'freedom of the people'. It was obvious that his policy was one of domination. However, groups of Portuguese did try to take control of the situation.

Their initiatives were intended to try to maintain the political unity of the kingdom and thus the social status of the Portuguese nobility (in its broadest sense, encompassing all the elites). They tried to avoid the partition of the kingdom, preventing it from being a mere reserve on which Napoleon could draw as he needed, as foreseen by the Treaty of Fontainebleau. Collaboration with the occupying power sought to negotiate a reduction in taxes. It was a matter of self-preservation within the Napoleonic empire. They were asking for a prince of their own and a Constitution comparable to that of the Grand Duchy of Warsaw. All that differed was how national representatives were to be elected, a duty entrusted to Parliament, 'better to confirm our old customs'. Modernizing aspects went hand in hand with this political unity, however. The programme was clearly not revolutionary in character. The limited scope of the social reforms it envisaged should be emphasized. Traditional religion was maintained, although freedom of worship was to be established. Properties in mortmain belonging to corporations could now be sold. This measure was disputed by all those charged with financial affairs and had already been projected (in tentative form) in Minister Dom Rodrigo de Sousa Coutinho's ecclesiastical tithe of 1796. Debates about the best financial use of church property continued for many years. The crucial element was the Napoleonic Code. Were its objectives liberating or modernizing? A strong sense of Portuguese nationalism grew throughout the nineteenth and twentieth centuries, in opposition to British political domination of the country under the guise of protection. Paradoxically, this allowed the dissemination of exactly those moderate and liberal ideas that were critical of the British. These same liberal ideas came to be attributed to the Napoleonic armies, who were regarded as the first to introduce them. The fact that the first liberal revolution in August 1820 had been unleashed by a military uprising motivated by the wish to expel those British officers remaining in the Portuguese army, led to the acceptance of this simplistic interpretation from the outset. The Napoleonic Code established a concept of civil society based around landowners who controlled their own properties and families, and thus organized the basis on which the State would rule and from which it took the resources it required. But the foundation of the State was not this civil society. The State had to let this civil society develop without interference (this is what distinguished Napoleon from the Jacobins), but it could not leave it to decide the future of the State.

The landowners were just defending a narrow and particular point of view.[19] Furthermore, the civil code was only one of the codes of the Napoleonic power edifice and must be seen relation to the penal code and, naturally, the effective absence of representative assemblies.

This is the first aspect of the paradox. The second, the British command of the Portuguese forces and their integration into Wellington's army, cannot be examined here, but is equally crucial. The central paradox is the relationship between State and nation. Patriotism is the political legitimacy of State action, but patriotism is not a useful source of military organization. National defence is organized patriotism by imposing a discipline that is not (easily) understood, in contrast to patriotism.[20]

The new kind of war, that nations, opposed to princes, a type of conflict that was already a commonplace in the Napoleonic era, hides the fact that the State, as an abstract entity, implies the concealment of its leaders' interests. The novelty thus lies in the possibility of leaders instilling fear into the populace in order to extract more resources. Napoleon's restoration of the empire is certainly the best example of this and was imitated throughout Europe.

Notes

1. J. G. Fichte, *Machiavel et autres écrits philosophiques et politiques de 1806–1807* (Paris, 1981). A. Philonenko, *Essai sur la philosophie de la guerre* (Paris, 1976). S. Avineri, *Hegel's theory of the modern State* (Cambridge, 1995 [1972]). J. Hyppolite, *Introduction à la philosophie de l'histoire de Hegel* (Paris, 1983). E. Cassirer, *The Myth of the State* (New Haven, 1974 [1946]). F. Meinecke, *Machiavellism. The doctrine of Raison d'État and its place in modern history* (New Brunswick, 1998). P. Paret, *Clausewitz and the State* (Oxford, 1976).
2. Letter from W. Wellesley to Arthur Wellesley, 2 December 1807. On that date the Portuguese ships had already left for Brazil. The Russian fleet remained in the Tagus until the French defeat, and was later evacuated through an agreement with the British army.
3. Napoleon, *Correspondance publiée par ordre de l'Empereur Napoléon III* (Paris, 1858-) vol. 16, letter no. 14,023, 271–272.
4. G. Lefebvre, *Napoléon* (Paris, 1935), 427–430.
5. Ibid.
6. Ibid.
7. For example, letter no. 504 dated 24 May 1806 in *Correspondance de Napoléon: six cents lettres de travail (1806–1810)*, ed. Maximilien Vox (Paris, 1943), 328–329.
8. Letter dated 4 February 1808, in Cristóvão Ayres, 'O diário de Junot na primeira invasão francesa em Portugal', *História orgânica e política do exército português. Provas.*, 12 (1908) 156.
9. Ayres, 157.
10. Letter dated 14 February 1808, in Ayres, 162.
11. Ayres, 163.
12. Letter dated 17 March 1808, in Ayres, 181.
13. Napoleon, *Correspondance*, vol. 16, letter no. 13, 973, 222.

14. Napoleon, *Correspondance*, vol. 16, letter no. 13, 896, 155–156.
15. Letter dated 24 May 1808, in Ayres, 201.
16. Letter dated 29 April 1808, in Ayres, 189.
17. Napoleon, *Correspondance*, vol. 17, letter no. 13, 764, 29.
18. Soult explained his project to Napoleon in his letter dated 30 May 1809, Nicole Gotteri, *Le Maréchal Soult* (Paris, 2000), 326–327. The Ricard circular, dated Oporto, 19 April 1809, was published by Charles Oman, *A history of the Peninsular War*, vol. II (London, 1995), 632–633.
19. This victory of the State is central in Hegel's work and was widely disseminated through his Philosophy of Law. Avineri, *Hegel's Theory*, 142–143.
20. Fernando Dores Costa, *Insubmissão. Aversão ao serviço militar em Portugal no século XVIII* (Lisbon, in press).

24
Conclusion: The Napoleonic Empire in the Age of Revolutions: The Contrast of Two National Representations

Annie Jourdan

Strangely enough, the revolution of 1789–91 was to be revived with the creation of the First Empire. This revival is rarely noted and relatively unknown.[1] Yet the social pact that Napoleon concluded with the French people on 2 December 1804 indeed suggests that the Empire was going to be a constitutional monarchy, founded on a written constitution and a social pact. The latter was meant to maintain the liberties of the French and to protect the rights of the constitutional bodies. It was only under these conditions that the Senate and the Corps Législatif had agreed to proclaim Napoleon Emperor of the French. Discussions about this decision started in April 1804 and ended one month later. Meanwhile, the Tribunate and the Senate discussed the changes they wanted to bring about in the French government. For some of their members, the issue was to re-establish the government on a constitutional basis and to put an end to what they called the Consulate's dictatorship. All agreed, however, that something had to change and those changes were to be inspired by the first revolutionary reforms. Before explaining in detail what it was about, I want to argue that the First Empire retained more revolutionary achievements than is normally assumed—also by the present author—but in a very special way.[2] To be sure, only a detailed study of the political, juridical and cultural institutions can prove the soundness of this argument and allow us to see how and why it happened. Evidence may have been given by Napoleon himself when in St. Helena, he said that his Civil Code would endure. This conviction could apply to other great imperial accomplishments, such as architecture and civil engineering.[3] Napoleon was very proud of these civil achievements and was aware of their value for post-revolutionary France. Tackling this problem will enable me to invalidate theories that see the First Empire simply as a military state.[4] My argument is that it is far more complicated.

A dictatorial Consulate

First of all, Napoleon inherited from the age of Revolutions the conviction that a people must be governed by a written constitution.[5] The Consulate's constitution, a complex compromise between the drafts of Sieyès, the Daunou commission and the ideas of Napoleon Bonaparte himself, implemented a republican regime with four or five organs of government, a structure that gave the impression that authority would be divided and well balanced—as in Britain or America.[6] The legislative body voted on the laws; the Tribunate discussed them; the Senate controlled them and decided whether they were to be enforced; while the Consuls, helped by the Council of State proposed them. The Senate and Tribunate were both institutions Sieyès had desired since 1795 as a means to protect the rights of the French. Daunou shared those convictions and also had thoughts of a third power—a *tiers-pouvoir* as Marcel Gauchet put it.[7] However, and as Necker rightly argued, the division of powers was nonsense, as only the First Consul had the means to put them into action or not.[8] Nonetheless, the Consulate had a written constitution which contained a number of republican institutions, including elections, civil laws and representation. The same can be said about the Consulate for Life, through which the elections became even more liberal.[9] The First Empire did not abolish these laws. Indeed, it barely changed the earlier constitutions. Only the roles the Senate, the Tribunate and the Corps légis-latif were going to play actually changed. The Senate acquired more rights to the detriment of the lower house, and the Tribunate, which initially was meant to be the voice of the Nation, simply disappeared in 1807. The Corps législatif had no right to speak, whereas the hereditary Senate was compro-mised by the so-called senatories and had to be satisfied with illusory powers so as not to come up against the political ambitions of Napoleon.[10] All these constitutional changes, too, are well known.

The real point is that the form of the institutions was still republican, whereas the content was not, for the functions of the representative bodies regressed discreetly. Furthermore, there was no longer a Bill of Rights.[11] From 1799 until 1815, the Napoleonic regime did not go back to 1789 as far as this was concerned. Nevertheless, it is true that from 1799 onwards, even the republican Daunou came to believe that the Declaration of Rights had to be the Holy Book of the representatives alone—and no longer of the French People.[12] These discussions would resurface in 1804.

What of sovereignty? From the outset, Napoleon recognized the sover-eignty of the people, but saw himself as being its one and only incarnation. He maintained this argument to the end. 'La France est en moi', France was in him, he said until 1815.[13] The source of sovereignty remained the people, but the exercise of that power passed into the hands of the Head of State. If Napoleon could boast as he did it was because of his plebiscites. Representatives were no longer the intermediaries between the executive power and the people. The executive power communicated directly with the people, via the plebiscite.[14] It gave Napoleon a certain legitimacy and discredited the parliamentary bodies, which no longer had the means to address public opinion. This change is another difference from the French Revolution, in which the National Assembly had secured that power. All this is well known and the point does not need to be laboured.

If politics had been restored to the bureaucracy, and specifically into the hands of the First Consul and then the Emperor, and if the Bill of Rights had disappeared as quickly as it had been implemented, the codification would allow us to argue that rights still existed if in a rather particular way. They were to be confined to the social or private sphere.[15] Civil society became the first concern for the Consulate and the Empire and human rights were to be placed within this sphere. What the Civil Code in fact reveals is that it protected revolutionary equality, social liberties and individual property. When Napoleon later spoke of his liberal laws, he meant in fact the Civil Code, which he considered the greatest achievement of his reign. Thereby, he showed that what was important to him was the modernization (or rather the homogenization) of society and not the democratization of politics. Furthermore, the Consulate—and the Empire—can be seen as an important step towards the 'possessive individualism', which Pocock invokes, when he discusses modernity and the domestication of virtue, dear to Gordon Wood.[16] On this point, the Empire was perpetuating the revolution—mainly that of the Directory in which participatory democracy had given way to a representative one and in which civic virtue was gradually replaced by civil values.[17] The real difference between these two conceptualizations was that under Napoleon the representative bodies lost almost all their powers to the head of state.

From the outset, Napoleon Bonaparte presented himself as a civil servant, as can be seen in the paintings he commissioned during the Consulate.[18] From the Revolution onwards, the executive body had indeed lost its sacred status and become a secular power, dependent on the will of the people and motivated by what the king or the leader did rather than by who he was. Louis XVI—as Joël Félix brilliantly argued[19]—should have become the first magistrate of France. This understanding of kingship was doomed to failure because the heir of the absolutist Bourbons clung too much to his traditional role. He betrayed the revolution and was never a true constitutional monarch. Napoleon tried to fulfil this role in his own particular way, as an authoritarian and liberal ruler, whose interventions in the Council of State or orders to his ministers conformed to that understanding.[20]

Another institution which can be seen as a legacy of the Revolution is national education, implemented from 1802 onwards. Here, the form was military but the content was classical.[21] The clergy was no longer excluded but the curriculum remained secular, even though political and ideological topics were becoming more and more taboo.[22] What mattered here, however, was that Napoleon saw it as his duty to reorganize the whole educational system, so that the French would become increasingly civilized. He interpreted his policy firstly as a civilizing mission; and later as a propaganda campaign for his dynasty and national glory.[23] This was also the purpose of the Napoleonic Museum that was transformed into a universal temple of fine arts during the Empire.[24]

To cut a long story short, at the end of the Consulate France was still a republic with an authoritarian leader who by 1802 had seized more and more power: that is, Bonaparte then had the right to appoint the other two consuls; to select his own successor; to conclude peace treaties; and to appoint up to forty new senators by which he could strengthen his grip on the Senate itself. These prerogatives were probably too much for the other political bodies who had dreamed of something completely different. The Cadoudal conspiracy was to be the trigger that provoked them to consider further reforms that would be more compatible with their fundamental aspirations.

Back to 1789

During the spring of 1804, after the royalists had tried to murder Napoleon, a propaganda campaign launched an appeal to the French asking for an hereditary title for the Saviour of France and thus the creation of a new dynasty. The petitions that came from all the municipal and provincial bodies and from the armies were published in the official *Moniteur.* These initiatives were an incentive for the Tribunate to propose transforming the Consulate into a hereditary regime and to create a French Empire. Between April 28 and May 18, the Tribunes discussed this fundamental change and explained their reasons for this unexpected decision.[25]

Let us look first at the issue of an hereditary title which might have seemed to betray the aspirations and achievements of the Republic. Nothing would be less true if the Tribune Curée were to be believed, heredity would actually be necessary to strengthen the achievements of the French Revolution. It would secure and maintain the immense results 'for which 30 million French men and women rose up in 1789', and it would discourage new attempts on the life of the Head of State. Curée also reminded his colleagues that heredity had not been not condemned in 1789. The Nation had wanted to keep its king, as shown by the Cahiers de Doléances. That it had not succeeded could be ascribed to the king himself who had never accepted being 'the king of the French'. Worse, 'born king, he could not consent in good faith to becoming a simple magistrate' and had betrayed the covenant between himself and the people. But that pact had been reciprocal; it had bound the nation to the king and the king to the nation.[26] Once it had been violated, the covenant had been broken and the Nation had been free to make a new deal. It had become an elective republic.[27]

Yet, even this regime would not have been a workable choice because the republican government was condemned to be provisional and heavily divided; conflicts and factions had been weakening the nation. Napoleon Bonaparte was the only one who succeeded in ending the revolution and restoring civil order and internal peace. With the Civil Code, everything for which the people fought was now maintained and strengthened; equality and law were now the norm. If France wanted to preserve all these achievements, concluded Curée, it must make the Bonapartes hereditary rulers, 'whose leader was and still is the first soldier of the Republic and now her first magistrate'. Other Tribunes shared this opinion and stressed how important it was to establish a social contract which would protect the rights of the nation and maintain the intermediate bodies and the high-ranking civil servants. In the wings, Fontanes and Talleyrand wanted more; an actual representation.[28] Indeed, this last wish signified not only the maintenance of the constitutional bodies, but greater power for the Senate, the Legislature and the Tribunate. Therefore, the issue here was not so much the people's sovereignty as the rights of national representation—rather like 1789.[29]

But how to justify the dynastic shift legally? The Tribunes felt Britain pointed the way. It served as a useful model because it had proclaimed the rights of the people—the source of sovereignty—to change its government, and it had deposed the unfaithful Stuarts in preference of a new king, William of Orange. History kept repeating itself and showed that a nation had the right to dethrone a degenerate king and replace him with a great man able to achieve the great destiny of a Great Nation. In other words, the prince served the people rather than the people serving the prince. Or better still, 'the prince is for the nation and not the nation for the prince'.[30]

Be that as it may, the Bourbon monarchy was condemned as feudal and thus arbitrary and this alone was a reason to repudiate it. The Tribunes rejected the feudal regime entirely, regarding it as pernicious, but they also rejected elective government because of the conflicts it engendered. Look at Poland, argued other Tribunes, and you will see how dangerous election is to the well-being of a realm. But in exchange for the new power and title given to Napoleon, the nation would get institutions which protected civil and political liberties. To Carnot, who opposed this convoluted argument and instead invoked the despotism that could be derived from such a construction, Carrion Nisas answered:

What! Because the first magistrate will be called emperor; because he will be hereditary, there would be neither fatherland nor liberty in France! We would have neither law, nor social pact! That was not what Rousseau, this sincere republican, was saying! He said that all legitimate government based on laws was republican. Who says here that we are going to put a man above the laws? The Emperor of the French Republic will be neither the owner of France nor of its inhabitants: he is the Head of the French because they want him to be so....[31]

The discussions that followed show extremely well how great were the expectations of the Tribunes—and of the other constitutional bodies. They anticipated true representation, that the parliamentary powers would vote on taxes and enforce the laws, that the judicial power would be independent, the ministers be responsible to the assemblies, and civil and political liberties be respected. Such, in short, was the content of the social pact the French wanted to conclude with their Emperor. It was also a subtle strategy for putting an end to what some of them called the Consular dictatorship.

The interpretations the Tribunate put forward about the Revolution and the Empire are very interesting, for they shed light on the expectations of the representatives of the new regime and show that they still believed in the republican ideals and the great achievements of the Revolution.[32] They also make clear that their actual aims were first the destruction of the feudal system—when opposing the Bourbon monarchy—and second the return to order and stability—when referring to the Directory. The form of the government—and I will come back to this point—was of less importance to them. What really mattered was the content of the constitutional oath: liberty; equality; maintenance of the revolutionary laws—among these the sale of *biens nationaux* or national lands; as well as, and primarily, genuine power and independence for the constitutional bodies.

On 4 May 1804 the Senate presented a draft text to Napoleon. Like the Tribunate, the Senate asked for constitutional provisions that guaranteed 'the independence of the higher authorities; a free and informed vote on taxes; the security of property; individual liberty; freedom of the press and of elections; ministerial responsibility and the inviolability of the constitutional laws'.[33] Thereby, the Senate made no secret of its republican opinions and political intentions. These principles were not at all what the future Emperor envisioned. The text was rejected and the Senate invited to write a new one inspired by Napoleon's wishes. On December 2, coronation day, François de Neufchateau, president of the Senate, took the new text to Notre Dame where Napoleon was to take the famous Constitutional Oath:

> I swear to maintain the integrity of the territory of the Republic, to respect and cause to be respected the laws of the Concordat and the liberty of worship, to respect and cause to be respected equality of rights, political and civil liberty, the irrevocability of the sales of the national lands; not to raise any taxes, nor to establish any tax except in virtue of the law; to maintain the institution of the Legion of Honour; to govern in the sole view of the interest, the welfare and the glory of the French people.[34]

Some articles had disappeared: freedom of the press; independence of the higher authorities and ministerial responsibility. But still, the oath guaranteed the political and civil liberty of all French citizens. The end of the oath is also striking. To quote Neufchateau: 'This noteworthy oath seems to have been written by the whole nation. It is the price to be paid if you want the nation to be faithful to you. The two oaths are linked; they guarantee each other'.[35] Here again, what the Revolution had changed can be discerned; the people had to conclude a contract or a covenant in which their rights were protected and that had to be reciprocal.[36]

But why an emperor? Was it because the revolutionary victories had made France an empire on the model of Rome? True, the term Empire was used as early as 1775 to describe France. In 1792 the death penalty was reintroduced to punish anyone who tried to dismember the (French) Empire. During the Directory, the French annexations and the creation of sister republics popularized the idea even more. Republicans and neo-Jacobins prided themselves on the Republic of Gauls, or emphatically referred to the Empire of Gaul described by Julius Cesar. Thanks to the Republic, France had thus become an Empire and deserved to have its Emperor.

The legislators tried time and again to justify their choice and to prove to their colleagues and the French people that an emperor was not incompatible with a republic. One of them even said: 'an empire is a republic adapted to a one-headed government, whose duty is actually to maintain the republic'. Another added that the empire was a contract in which the nation gave its leader—and not its master—the power to ensure the people's rights. Napoleon could become emperor on condition that the nation's rights would be respected and that the corresponding duties would be fulfilled.[37] This modern emperor was to be seen as a civil servant and a victorious Consul—as in Rome. Another useful precedent was found in Germany, where the emperor was the chief of a monarchical republic and had nothing to do with feudality. However, the Hero of France was too great to be a mere king or a consul. According to Neufchateau, he had to wear a finer title more in keeping with national majesty and liberty.[38] Furthermore, this new title would allow the French Republic to distance itself from the feudal Bourbon monarchy, while harmonizing its institutions with those of Europe, restoring its dignity and consolidating its stability. All this could bring an end to wars and restore general peace. At this point, more than one Tribune launched an attack on the 'degenerate' Bourbon dynasty which would have weakened and humiliated the French nation. Napoleon, on the other hand, had taken France to unknown heights. Thanks to him, France was to play 'the first role among the European powers'. Here lay a key element in the French Empire's creation.

Since the beginning of the French Revolution, and particularly after the victories of the Directory, French nationalist sentiment actually had increased. Afterwards, the Tribunate, the Senate and the Corps législatif used amazing hyperbole to describe the new France: 'the greatest and happiest Empire'; 'the most beautiful empire'; 'the first Empire in the world'; that had to be protected—but not extended—for the glory of the Great Nation. So, in a way, the proclamation of the Empire crowned this Great Nation. I need not stress how dangerous this ambition was for the future. The legislators indeed wanted not only stability and order, but also grandeur and glory. Yet, national stability and glory never get on very well together.

A broken pact

The rest of the story is well known. Napoleon went his own way and took little account of the oath. He raised conscripts and levied new taxes when he needed them. He did not respect the constitutional bodies and he implemented censorship. He violated the liberty of the press while imprisoning opponents and paid scant attention to the Senatorial Commission on Personal Liberty—an institution created in 1804 to protect individual rights and which was unable to function properly because of the police.[39] Here again, there had seemed to be republican bastions against arbitrary power at first. But the attractive form of the institution masked its deceptive content. Nevertheless, the 1804 reforms revealed that the French had not abandoned their revolutionary ideals and that they were ready to cut them from a quite different, imperial, cloth.

After the campaign of 1814 and the defeat of the imperial army, the Senate, which would depose Napoleon, published a text to justify its disaffection. This text has never been taken seriously, either by historians or by political scientists, because they ignored the oath of 1804 and focused on the prerogatives the Senate wanted to keep.[40] Yet, after years of frustration, the Senators were finally able to express their grievances on April 3 1814; Napoleon, they said, has broken the pact he made with the French people, for this reason 'the imperial government no longer exist[ed]'. But these grievances did have some basis and remind us that Napoleon had indeed violated the oath he took in 1804.[41] Thus, the Senate was right to speak as it did and to draft a new constitution[42] to include a new pact and a popular plebiscite. It would bring France back to the failed 'republican turning point' of 1804. The measures the constitutional draft of 1814 announced were indeed based on the Senate text of 1804 that had been rejected by Napoleon: the senatorial constitution included freedom of voting and of opinion (also political opinion), freedom of the press, of religion and of conscience, as well as a proportional equality of taxes, the career open to talent, the independence of the judiciary, ministerial responsibility, the maintenance of the jury and of the two senatorial commissions for individual freedom and freedom of the press and, last but not least, the right for the constitutional bodies to propose and to discuss laws.[43] The new king, Louis XVIII refused to join the Senate.[44] For him, the revolution was well and truly over, even though he, too, had to make some compromises.

Conclusion

I hope I have made my argument clear that the Empire ought to have become far more republican than the Consulate. It was a failure, as we well know. Even so, the representative bodies still dreamed of a real constitutional government with a separation of powers and checks and balances, with individual liberties and equality, and respect for the nation's rights. Their drafts let us see how influential the revolutionary ideals remained.[45] In fact, some of these achievements were implemented by the Civil Code and thus restricted to the social and private sphere.[46]

During the Empire, there were actually three spheres: the political, dominated by Napoleon (and his bureaucracy); the military, dominated by the same (and his marshals); and the civil, where the people were able (at least in principle) to live in freedom and equality. Napoleon himself lived in all three spheres. Here again, the great painters of his age enable us to distinguish the three features: as supreme magistrate, Napoleon was painted in his office, working night and day; as chief of the army, he was very often represented on his (white) horse, at some distance from the troops he inspired and commanded. Paintings of him as a private person became scarcer after the Consulate. Indeed, his private life became more and more political.[47] Thus, when he was represented with his family or with his wife and son, we do not see the man and the father, but the founder of a new dynasty. He alone had no civil or public life and this sacrifice might have given him a certain legitimacy.

However, if one were to believe the diverse representations of Napoleon, he was and remained a republican emperor because of his liberal laws, his achievements for the French people and the dialogues he had with them via the plebiscites. Beside Napoleon's authoritarianism, the great difference with the revolution and the first French Republic was that the people's sovereignty was no longer represented by the legislators but by the Emperor himself. That was not enough at the time to grant him full legitimacy in the eyes of the French political elite, who firmly believed that the best regime had to be a constitutional and/or a parliamentary one, with representative bodies to restrain the executive, and with fixed laws to protect the nation's rights. Monarchy, republic or empire, the form of government was less important. After Waterloo, Fouché and the legislators of 1815 would again speak of political guarantees and of a national covenant. Among the guarantees the right to consent taxation was still very important,[48] as was the independence of the constitutional bodies. As far as these principles were concerned, the Restoration would be an improvement, even if it kept more imperial features, and it can be described more as a limited monarchy than as a parliamentary one.[49]

During the Age of the Eighteenth-Century Revolutions, the source of power thus changed radically. Legitimacy had to be given by the people, but the exercise of sovereignty was to become less participatory and more

representative than in the first phase of the Revolution, while the constitution was based on a social compact instead of a declaration of rights.
Napoleon did not deny these principles, but saw himself as the sole *persona
repraesentans*.[50] While he chose form over content, the legislators—who also
saw themselves as the people's true representatives—preferred content to
form, but could not convince the Head of State to share their convictions.

Notes

1. See also my 'Le Premier Empire: un nouveau pacte social', *Cités 20* (Paris, 2004), 51–64. This new contribution goes deeper into the matter.
2. In his groundbreaking book, Martin Lyons conversely seems to think that 1804 is the end of the Revolution. M. Lyons, *Napoleon Bonaparte and the Legacy of the French Revolution* (Basingstoke & London, 1994), 299. Most French historians say so. I did too in *L'empire de Napoléon* (Paris, 2000) because, and like most historians, I didn't pay attention to the discussions of 1804 and to the text of the oath. That is not to say that the Empire was really a democracy or a representative republic, as we will see.
3. Las Cases, *Mémorial de Sainte-Hélène* (Paris, s.d.), vol. II, 119–125, 504–505.
4. Think of David Bell's last book, *The First Total War* (Boston & New York, 2007) and Jean-Paul Bertaud's *Quand les enfants parlaient de gloire* (Paris, 2006). Both interpret the Empire as a military state. See also Howard Brown, 'The Search for Stability' in *Taking Liberties. Problems of a New Order from the French Revolution to Napoleon*, eds H. Brown & J. Miller (Manchester, 2002), 33. When one focuses on the military dimension of the Empire, it is not difficult to find more evidence on the matter. But when one focuses on its civil dimension, the same is true. A comprehensive perspective is essential here.
5. He was so sure about this necessity that he enforced a constitution in all the monarchies he created. In the Netherlands, Napoleon implemented a constitutional monarchy with a constitutional pact in 1806, as would also happen in Spain and Westphalia. See J.-B. Bussaal, 'Le règne de Joseph Bonaparte: une expérience décisive dans la transition de la Ilustración au libéralisme modéré', http://hc.rediris.es/07/pdf/03.pdf and for the German text, E. Grothe, 'Model or Myth? The Constitution of Westphalia of 1807 and Early German Constitutionalism', *German Studies Review*, 28 (2005): 1–19.
6. Lucien Bonaparte even wanted to follow the American example. Boulay de la Meurthe. *Théorie constitutionnelle de Sieyès. Constitution de l'an VIII. Extraits des mémoires inédits de Boulay de la Meurthe* (Paris, 1836), 5.
7. Marcel Gauchet, *La Révolution des pouvoirs. La souveraineté, le peuple et la représentation* (Paris, 1995).
8. Jacques Necker, *Dernières vues de politique et de finance (s.l.,* 1802).
9. About the elections during the Napoleon's regime, Josiane Bourguet-Rouveyre, 'La citoyenneté à l'épreuve du conformisme et de l'uniformité sous le Consulat et l'Empire', *Terminée la Révolution*, ed. M. Biard (Calais, 2002) Bulletin des Amis du Vieux Calais, hors-série, 89–100.
10. Jacques Godechot, *Les Constitutions de la France depuis 1789* (Paris, 1995).
11. In the constitution of Year VIII, there were only *dispositions générales* about the right to be judged by law and not to be convicted without reason. In the constitution of 1802, the (next) first consul had to swear to maintain the constitution;

to respect freedom of conscience; to oppose the return of feudality; to make war only for the defence and the glory of the republic; and to use his power only on behalf of the happiness of the people.

12. Can you speak here of an evolution—as in the US in 1787—whereby bills of rights seemed no longer necessary because the people were no longer in a state of nature and the constitution already protected civil rights? Furthermore, and as in France, a Bill of Rights is not binding if no control is exerted on the legislatures. So, even for Madison, a bill was seen as a parchment barrier. See J. N. Rakove, 'Parchment barriers and the politics of rights', in *A Culture of Rights*, eds M. J. Lacey and K. Haakonssen (Cambridge, 1991), 98–143.

13. *Oeuvres de Napoléon Bonaparte* (Paris, 1821–1822), vol. I, 284–285 (4 April 1814). On the 1st of June 1815, he proclaimed anew that his honour, his glory and happiness were 'l'honneur, la gloire et le bonheur de la France', ibid. 314.

14. Malcolm Crook, 'Confidence from Below? Collaboration and Resistance in the Napoleonic Plebiscites', in *Collaboration and Resistance in Napoleonic Europe. State-Formation in an Age of Upheaval, c. 1800–1815*, ed. Michael Rowe (London, 2003), 19–36.

15. In a way, Geoffrey Ellis is drawing the same conclusions, 'The Nature of Napoleonic Imperialism' in *Napoleon and Europe*, ed. Ph. Dwyer (London, 2001), 97–117. In spite of the title, Ellis does not describe the nature of Napoleonic Imperialism, but its different features.

16. Both notions are from J. G. A. Pocock, 'Between Gog and Magog: The Republican Thesis and the Ideologica Americana', *Journal of the History of Ideas* 48 (1987): 325–346 and from Gordon Wood, *The Radicalism of the American Revolution* (New York, 1991), 218.

17. See Annie Jourdan, *La Révolution batave entre la France et l'Amérique* (Rennes, 2008).

18. Annie Jourdan, *Napoléon. Héros, Imperator, Mécène* (Paris, 1998), 151–160.

19. Joël Félix, *Louis XVI et Marie-Antoinette, un couple en politique* (Paris, 2006).

20. Liberal-authoritarian is the term used by Howard Brown, but I would prefer to distinguish between a liberal–republican Directory and a liberal-authoritarian or dictatorial Consulate and Empire. During the Directory, indeed, the representatives were still chosen by the people and had a real representative and legislative power. Howard Brown, *Ending the Revolution. From the Terror to Napoleon* (Charlottesville & London, 2006).

21. Cf. Jourdan, *Napoléon. Héros*, 44–47. J.-P. Bertaud focused only on the military character of schools and neglected the curriculum.

22. To be sure, and despite Napoleon's orders, in the primary schools, which were often in the hands of the clergy, religion became more and more prominent. The same can be said of the *collèges*. In 1811, when the prefects investigated the imperial schools, they admitted that: 'in the places where the brothers of the Christian Doctrine and the Ursulines are teaching, the results are satisfactory. Elsewhere, one is faced with ignorance and indifference' (AN F17–9367). See also Charles Schmidt, *La réforme de l'Université en 1811* (Paris, 1905).

23. Jourdan, *Napoleon. Héros*, 225–227. The Museum Napoleon was part of this policy of French Grandeur and Civilization. Napoleon wanted to do more than Louis XIV. A.-F. Villemain, *Napoléon et l'Europe ou Napoléon expliqué par lui-même, 1812–1813* (Paris, 1947).

24. See my 'A National Tragedy: The Return of Works of Art in Their Country (1815)', in *Napoleon's Legacy: The Rise of National Museums in Europe, 1794–1830*, eds Ellinoor Bergvelt *et al* (Amsterdam & Berlin, 2009), 125–135.

25. These discussions can be found on the web site of the Fondation Napoléon: www.napoleonica.org. *Quarante-sept documents relatifs à la proclamation de l'Empire, 1802–1804*. Thierry Lentz has also published some of them in *La proclamation de l'Empire* (Paris, 2003). Lentz however did not analyse the texts as I do and did not draw the same conclusions.

26. Stéphane Rials, *Révolution et Contre-révolution au XIXe siècle* (Paris, 1987), 85. Rials seems not to understand that since 1789 the French had wanted the contract to be reciprocal and that is why he does not give enough attention to the subsequent pacts of 1804 and of 1814.

27. *Tribunat. Motion d'ordre du Tribun Curée. Séance extraordinaire du 10 floréal an 12*. http://www.napoleonica.org/proclamation/pro007.html.

28. Alphonse Aulard, *Histoire politique de la Révolution* (Paris, 1921), 772.

29. Worth noting is the shift from popular to national sovereignty. Since 1789, indeed, there was a contest between these two concepts. About this contest, Rials writes that national sovereignty expresses the transcendence of right/jurisprudence, and not the popular will, as it is proclaimed by the constitution of 1793. I would claim that national sovereignty was less dangerous to proclaim than the sovereignty of the people: the former could be seen as an abstraction, personified by the parliaments or the assembly; the latter could be interpreted as concrete, as the French people indeed did in the 1790s. Rials, *Révolution et contre-révolution* 140–142.

30. About the degenerated Bourbons, see the remarks of Fréville, Faure, Albisson and Duveyrier in *Documents relatifs à la proclamation de l'Empire*, www.napoleonica.org.

31. Tribunat. *Réplique improvisée de Carrion-Nisas au discours de Carnot. Séance extraordinaire du 11 floréal an 12*, http://www.napoleonica.org/proclamation/pro013.html. Concerning Poland see also, *Rapport fait par Jard-Panvillier au nom de la Commission chargée d'examiner la motion d'ordre du Tribun Curée*, http://www.napoleonica.org/proclamation/pro032.html and *Discours prononcé par Costaz, sur la motion d'ordre relative au Gouvernement héréditaire*, http://www.napoleonica.org/proclamation/pro010.html.

32. I do not distinguish here between republicans and constitutional monarchists. At that time the difference between both was a question of form, not of content. Both wanted a Bill of Rights, a written constitution, a national representation and a limited representative democracy.

33. *Réponse du Sénat au message du Premier Consul*, http://www.napoleonica.org/proclamation/pro001_03.html

34. *Le Moniteur Universel*, 1804, no. 71, 259–261. Neufchateau also said: 'it is not really a change we want to bring in the Republic, but it is the only way out to improve and to stabilize the regime'. Concerning Neufchateau, see James Livesey, *Democracy in the French Revolution* (Cambridge, Mass. & London, 2001). Neufchateau was a true republican.

35. *Le Moniteur Universel, ibid.* See also Thierry Lentz, *Nouvelle histoire du Premier Empire. Napoléon et la conquête de l'Europe, 1804–1810* (Paris, 2002), 19–28.

36. As Rials claimed, there are two sorts of contracts: one is reciprocal (Locke) and the other is not (Grotius; Pufendorf); it is a *pacte de société* (a society covenant). Neufchateau shows here that France was thinking of a reciprocal covenant.

37. The following Tribunes explain what they mean by emperor: Gillet; Grenier; Lahary; Leroy; Portalis; Chassiron and Koch. *Documents relatifs à la proclamation de l'Empire*, www.napoleonica.org.

38. *Discours prononcé par Son Excellence M. François de Neufchateau, président du Sénat Conservateur, le dimanche 7 prairial an XII, à l'occasion du serment prêté le même jour*

à Sa Majesté l'Empereur par les membres du Sénat, http://www.napoleonica.org/proclamation/pro002.html

39. Michael Sibalis, 'Arbitrary detention, human rights and the Napoleonic Senate', *Taking Liberties*, 166–184.

40. As does Rials, *Révolution et Contre-Révolution*, but also Jean Thiry, *Le Sénat de Napoléon* (Paris, 1949). Indeed, historians always emphasize the articles about the heredity of the Senate and its financial privileges and do not pay attention to all the constitutional articles. Pierre Rosanvallon gives a survey of the senatorial discussions in *La Monarchie impossible. Les Chartes de 1814 et de 1830* (Paris, 1994), 16–21, but does not mention the oath of 1804 and thus does not see the connection between the 1804 and 1814 discussions.

41. 'Napoleon had levied illegal taxes; he had violated people's rights when he had adjourned the legislative body without reason and destroyed a report of this body as criminal. As for wars, he did not respect article 50 of the Constitution, where it is stipulated that it had to be proposed, discussed and promulgated as a law; and he had enforced two constitutional decrees the previous March in which war was said to be a national matter instead of a proof of his overweening ambition. Furthermore, with his state prisons he had violated the constitutional laws; destroyed the independence of the judicial bodies; subjected the liberty of the press to the arbitrary of the police; etc...', *Le Moniteur*, no. 94, March 1814, 369. Twice the Senate tried to put the brakes on Napoleon's ambition but did not succeed in stopping him. Annie Jourdan, *L'empire de Napoléon* (Paris, 2000), 63–66.

42. The King of Holland, Louis Bonaparte, on the other hand, refused to violate the oath he had taken to the Dutch. He respected this oath very seriously and understood it to be a reciprocal pact between him and 'his' people. Félix Roquain, *Napoléon Ier et le roi Louis* (Paris, 1875), 239–251.

43. Beside all these rights and powers, the senatorial constitution asked for the abolition of confiscation of properties as a result of criminal judgement (it was reinstated by Napoleon in 1811) and the maintenance of the Civil Code. Once again, a proof that the Senate remained faithful to itself and to 1789. Thiry, *Le Sénat*, 309–311.

44. Louis XVIII said that the basis was good, but the whole text was 'not realistic'. The new king wanted to revive a monarchical tradition and not a popular one. In the Charter of 1814, there is no longer reference to the people—but to the 'subjects' or to the French—and it was granted by the King and not proposed to and accepted by the people, as were the revolutionary and imperial constitutions—including the *Acte additionnel* from April 1815. For the texts, see Godechot, *Les Constitutions*, 217–239 or Rosanvallon, *La monarchie impossible*, 183–278.

45. The same was true in 1815. In July 1815 once again, the legislators asked for national guaranties and a representative regime with the usual rights. Fouché spoke of a 'consented covenant' and of 'a representative system'. See A. Villemain, *Les Cent Jours. Souvenirs contemporains*, vol. II (Paris, 1855), 477–478 and 471.

46. To put it in Howard Brown's words, there was a shift 'from providing people with access to politics, to providing personal security and social stability', Brown, 'The Search for Stability', 30.

47. As noted by Steven Englund in *Napoleon. A political Life* (New York, 2004).

48. 'No taxation without representation' was a constant claim after the American Revolution, not only in the USA, but also in pre-revolutionary France, in the Netherlands or even in Italy.

49. This distinction is from Rials, *Révolution et Contre-Révolution*, 85–91. A limited (or temperate) monarchy is founded upon and limited by law, but always has the last word. An absolute monarchy does not have such constraints, whereas a parliamentary one possesses constitutional bodies with a real representative and legislative power. In 1804, in 1814 and even in 1815, the French wanted such a parliamentary monarchy, but got a limited one.
50. Like the Jacobins, in a way. About this assumption of Hobbes, see Lucien Jaume, *Le discours Jacobin de la démocratie* (Paris, 1989), 19.

Index

Abrassart, Pierre, 90, 94
Abrial, André Pierre Etienne, 92
Adams, John, 289
Affry, Ludwig August Philipp von, 136, 139
Albisson, Jean, 324 n. 30
Alexander I of Russia, 78
Almendingen, Ludwig Harscher von, 94
Alphonse, François Baron d', 107
Álvarez Junco, José, 265, 268, 269
Antonio Pascual, Infante of Spain (Antonio Pascual de Borbón y Wettin), 277
Aranda, 10th Count of, (Pedro Pablo Abarca de Bolea y Jiménez de Urrea), 268 n. 18, 286
Arbois (de Jubainville), Joseph Louis d', 44
Aron, Raymond, 31
Astorga, 15th Marquis of (Vicente Joaquín Osorio de Moscoso y Guzmán), 288
Augereau, Charles Pierre François, 28
Aymes, Jean-René, 13, 14, 280

Babut (Special Commissioner, Den Helder), 115
Baraguey d'Hilliers, Louis, 245
Barrocchio (Mayor of Alessandria), 224, 226
Beauharnais, Eugène de, 25, 201, 205, 245
Beauharnais, Hortense de, 25
Beauharnais, Josephine, see Bonaparte, Josephine
Bell, David, 322 n. 4
Belleville, Charles-Godefroy Redon de, 244
Benaiteau, Michèle, 235
Beneke, Ferdinand, 160, 164, 166, 169, 171
Beresford, William Lord, 258
Bernadotte, Jean Baptiste Jules, 28, 163

Bertaud, Jean-Paul, 322 n. 4
Berthier, Alexandre, 29, 36 n. 21
Bertrand, Henri-Gatien, 245, 246, 251
Beugnot, Jean Claude, 146
Beyts, François Joseph, 89, 90, 96, 98, 106
Bianchini, Lodovico, 228, 237
Bicker, Jan, 102
Blaufarb, Rafe, viii, ix
Bluche, Frédéric, 4
Bodin, Jean, 73
Bodinier, Gilbert, 27
Bonald, Louis Gabriel Ambroise de, 73
Bonaparte, Caroline, 202, 231, 232
Bonaparte, Elisa, 25, 202
Bonaparte, Jérôme, 25, 145, 146, 150, 152, 173, 177, 178, 179, 180, 183
Bonaparte, Joseph, 15, 25, 81 n. 39, 202, 227, 229, 231, 236, 240, 257, 258, 259, 261, 262, 264, 265, 270, 274, 279, 280, 290, 294, 298, 299, 301, 307
Bonaparte, Josephine, 23, 201
Bonaparte, Louis, 6, 25, 86, 104, 105, 109, 112, 113, 114, 115, 116, 117, 325 n. 42
Bonaparte, Lucien, 21, 322, 326
Bonaparte, Napoleon-Louis, 25, 145
Bonaparte, Napoleon passim
Bongars, Jean François, 182
Borghese, Camille, 25
Borgia, Cesare, 77, 79
Borrull, Francisco Xavier, 265, 266
Bourdonnaye, Anne François Augustin, comte de La, 278
Braunschweig, Duke of, see Brunswick, Duke of
Broers, Michael, 1, 21, 57, 94, 95, 97 n., 100, 129 n. 1, 184 n. 15, 205, 216, 251 n. 11, 252
Brouckere, Charles, 91, 96
Brown, Howard, 8, 12, 13, 15, 38, 55, 91, 323 n. 20, 325 n. 46

Bruix, Eustache, 28
Brune, Guillaume Marie Anne, 28
Brunswick, Duke of, Charles William
    Ferdinand, 145, 147, 149, 152, 174,
    181, 183, 311
Burke, Edmund, 2, 285
Busaall, Jean-Baptiste, 260, 267
Byerley, John Scott, 78

Cadoudal, Georges, 316
Caesar, Julius, 34, 268
Caffarelli, Augusto, 207
Camareno la Real, Marquis of, 276
Cambacérès, Jean Jacques Régis, 21,
    22, 74
Campomanes, Pedro Rodríguez de, 284
Caracciolo di Martina family, 235, 239
Caracciolo di Torchiarolo family, 234
Caracciolo di Torella family, 233
Carnot, Lazare Nicolas Marguerite, 36
    n. 21, 317
Carrion (de) Nisas, Marie Henri François
    Elisabeth, 317
Castellamonte, Ugo Vincenzo Botton di,
    224, 226
Caulaincourt, Armand Augustin, 36 n.
    21
Chabrol de Crouzol, André-Christophe
    Count, 244, 248, 251 n. 15
Chantre, Pierre Louis, 133
Chaptal, Jean-Antoine, 27, 33, 77
Charles Archduke of Austria, 243
Charles III of Spain, 284, 287
Charles IV of Spain, 257, 261, 262, 263,
    264, 265, 266, 284, 285, 287, 288,
    289, 290, 292 n. 18
Chassiron(-Lafosse), Pierre Charles
    Martin, 324 n. 37
Chuquet, Arthur, 71
Cincinnatus, Lucius Quinctius, 34
Clarke, Henri Jacques Guillaume, 36 n.
    21
Clausewitz, Carl Philipp Gottfried, 304
Clemens, Gabriele, 4, 5, 10, 11, 132, 169
    n. *
Cocaud, Martine, 62
Coffinhal-Dunoyer, Joseph, 244
Condove, Luigi Peyretti di, 224
Constant, Benjamin, 75
Costa, Fernando Dores, 8, 9, 10, 14, 304

Cuoco, Vincenzo, 227, 231
Curée, Jean François, 316, 317

D'Avalos, Tommaso, 235
D'Avalos family, 235
D'Azeglio family, 222
Dal Pozzo, Ferdinando, 224
Dauchy, Luc Jacques Éduard, 244
Daunou, Pierre Claude François, 314
Davey Wright, Hamish, 35 n. 1, 183 n. 1
Davies, Angela, 251 n. 1
Davis, John, 225, 235, 237
Davout, Louis Nicolas, 36 n. 21
Decrès, Denis, 36 n. 21, 79
Dejean, Jean François Aimé, 36 n. 21
Delbrel, Pierre, 48
De Marivault (General Commissioner,
    Rotterdam), 115
de Medici, Lorenzo, 78
Deponthière (Judge), 92
Desfourneaux, Edme Étienne Borne, 44
de Sousa Coutinho, Rodrigo Domingos,
    310
De Staël, Germaine, 59, 76
de Thomasis, Giuseppe, 232
Dicey, Albert Venn, 297, 301
Diderot, Denis, 285
Didier, Paul, 65
Dolfin, Gianpaolo, 208
Doria d'Angri family, 234
Dörnberg, Wilhelm von, 152, 153, 167
Drašković, Janko Count, 250
Drouot, Antoine, 28
Ducos, Roger, 21
Dumas, Alexandre (also known as
    Alexandre Davy de La Pailletterie),
    68 n. 37
Dupont de l'Etang, Pierre, 278
Duterrage, Paul-Etienne Devilliers, 114
Duverger, Maurice, 26, 36 n. 7
Duverger de Hauranne, Jean Marie, 296
Duveyrier, Honoré Marie Nicolas, 324
    n. 30

Ellul, Jacques, 26
Emmerich, Andreas, 152
Enghien, Duc d' (Louis Antoine Henri
    de Bourbon-Condé), 22
Englund, Steven, 2, 3
Escoiquiz, Juan, 264, 273, 280, 288

Esdaile, Charles, 13, 277
Espoz y Mina, Francisco, 277
Everaerts (Juge d'instruction, Bruges), 92
Eymard (Special Commissioner, The Hague), 115, 119

Falck, Anton Reinhardt, 105
Fargues, François-Marie, 244
Faure, Louis Joseph, 324 n. 30
Félix, Joël, 315
Ferdinand III, Grand Duke of Tuscany, 202, 223
Ferdinand IV of Naples, 236
Ferdinand VII of Spain, 257, 261, 263, 264, 265, 266, 267, 268, 269, 280, 283, 288, 292 n. 18, 294, 300
Fichte, Johann Gottlieb, 304
Filangieri, Gaetano, 227, 229, 285, 286
Flórez Estrada, Antonio, 265, 266, 268, 269
Fontanes, Louis de, 317
Forrest, Alan, viii, ix, 13, 49, 167
Fouché, Joseph, 21, 108, 242, 245, 248, 321, 325 n. 45
Franklin, Benjamin, 285
Franz (Sub-prefect, Halle district), 180
Fraser, Ronald, 274, 275, 276, 277
Frederick-Augustus I of Saxony, 145, 146
Frederick William III of Prussia, 189
Fréville, Jean Baptiste Maximilien Villot de, 324 n. 30

Gaj, Ljudevit, 250
Galiani, Ferdinando, 229
Gallego, Miguel Artola, 4, 6
Gálvez, José de, 284
Gasparin, Adrien Étienne Pierre de, 63
Gauchet, Marcel, 314
Genovesi, Antonio, 227, 229
Geyl, Pieter, 1
Gillet, Jean Claude Michel, 324 n. 327
Girardin, Stanislas de, 71, 80 n. 13
Gneisenau, August Neidhardt von, 151, 189, 191, 192, 195
Gobort, Charles, 91
Godechot, Jacques, 14, 26, 31
Godoy, Manuel de, 257, 262, 263, 264, 265, 286, 287, 288, 289, 305
Goethe, Johann Wolfgang von, 7
Gogel, Isaac, 103

Grab, Alexander, ix, 5, 10, 204
Grenier, Jean, 324 n. 37
Grondana, Stefano, 220
Guidal, Emmanuel Maximilien Joseph, 29
Guimera, Agustín, ix, 97 n.

Hagemann, Karen, viii, ix, 8, 169, 186
Hardenberg, Karl August von, 186, 191
Hatzfeld, Princesse de (Friederike Karoline Sophie von der Schulenburg-Kehnert), 77
Haussez, Baron d' (Charles Lemercier de Longpré), 61
Hazareesingh, Sudhir, 75
Healey, Francis George, 71, 72, 76, 79
Hegel, Georg Wilhelm Friedrich, 304
Hicks, Peter, 16, 70
Hitzeroth, Johann Caspar Philippe, 180
Hoche, Lazare, 42
Hocquellet, Richard, 275
Huerta, José, 266
Hughes, Victor, 44
Hugo, Leopoldo, 274, 277

Ibáñez de la Rentería, José A., 268 n. 17
Infantado, 13th Duke of the (Don Pedro Alcantara Álvarez de Toledo y Salm Salm), 264, 288
Ireland, Ruth, ix
Isabel II of Spain, 283

Jacob, Maximilien, 36 n. 19
Jerome of Westphalia, *see* Bonaparte, Jerome
João, Prince Regent of Portugal, 307
Joor, Johan, 112
Joseph I, *see* Bonaparte, Joseph
Joseph II of Austria, 85, 146, 201
Jourdan, Annie, 1, 14, 15, 16, 313
Jourdan, Jean-Baptiste, 22, 28, 49, 50, 51
Junco, Albierto, ix
Junot, Jean Andoche, 8, 36 n. 22, 223, 245, 248, 258, 304, 305, 306, 307, 308, 309, 311

Katt, Friedrich Wilhelm von, 168
Kemper, Joan Melchior, 103
King of Rome, (Napoleon Francois Charles Joseph Bonaparte), 23

Klespé, Reiner Josef Anton von, 128
Koch, Christophe Guillaume, 324 n. 37
Koepken, von (Prussian councillor), 180
Kopitar, Jernej, 246, 250

Laborda, Agustín, widow of, 271
Lacuée, Jean Gérard, 36 n. 21
Ladoucette, Jean Charles François de, 130 n. 2
Lafon, Jean-Marc, 275
la Harpe, Frédéric-César de, 134
Lahary, Jacques Thomas, 324 n. 37
Lahorie, Victor Claude Alexandre Fanneau de, 29
Lambertson, John, 169 n. *
Lambrechts, Charles Joseph Mathieu, 92, 98
Lannes, Jean, 28
La Parra Lopez, Emilio, 6, 9, 10, 12, 14, 260, 287
Lardizábal, Miguel de, 273
Latteur (President of the Brussels appeals court), 90, 98
Lebrun, Charles-François, 21, 86, 105, 107, 117, 118, 119
Leclerc, Victoire Emmanuel, 44
Lefebvre, Georges, 6, 14, 26, 306, 307
Lentz, Thierry, ix, 5, 14, 15, 24, 77, 79, 324 n. 25
Leroy, Pierre Thomas (also known as Leroy de Boisraumarié or Leroy de l'Orme), 324 n. 37
Levrero, Bruno, 220
le Yoncourt, Tiphaine, 63
Livy, Titus, 77, 78
Locke, John, 71, 324 n. 36
Lok, Mathijs, 4, 5, 6, 7, 9, 100
López Pelegrín, Ramón, 266
Lorente, Marta, 6, 9, 10, 12, 14, 293
Louis XIV of France, 223
Louis XVIII of France, 23, 108, 113, 320, 325 n. 44
Louis XVI of France, 23, 35, 257, 286, 315
Lucas, Colin, 91
Lyons, Martin, 322 n. 2

Mably, Gabriel Bonnot de, 285
Macdonald, Etienne Jacques Joseph Alexandre, 28
Machiavelli, Niccolò, 16, 70, 76, 77, 78

Malchus, Karl August, 180
Malet, Claude François, 28, 29
Malingré, Pierre Claude, 93
Malleval (special commissioner, Island of Texel), 115
Maresca di Serracapriola family, 234
Maria Christina of the Two Sicilies, 264
Mariandier (Special commissioner, Island of Goeree), 115
Maria Theresa of Austria, 245
Marie-Louise von Habsburg, 23, 33, 202, 225
Marmont, Auguste Frédéric Louis Viesse de, 79, 243, 244, 245, 246, 247, 248
Marquesa de Villafranca (María Tomasa Palafox y Portocarrero), 272
Martin, Siegmund Peter, 152
Martín Díez, Juan, 274
Martínez de la Rosa, Francisco, 283
Masséna, André, 28
Masson, Fédéric, 70, 71
Maximilian I of Bavaria, 146
McCall, Jenny, ix
Melzi d'Eril, Francesco, 201, 205, 207
Menou, Jacques François de Boussay, Baron de, 45
Metternich, Clemens Wenzel, Prince von, 76, 243, 245, 249, 250
Molé, Matthieu, 76
Moliner, Antonio, 275
Montesquieu, Charles-Louis de Secondat, Baron de La Brède et de, 34, 72, 73, 101, 284, 285
Montgelas, Maximilian von, 146
Moreau, Jean Victor, 28
Morla, Tomás de, 278
Mouton, Georges, 28
Murat, Joachim, 25, 29, 145, 202, 231, 232, 233, 236, 257, 263, 277, 288, 289, 290
Muscettola di Leporano family, 235

Necker, Jacques, 314
Neufchateau, François de, 318, 319, 324 nn. 34, 36
Nicolovius, Georg Heinrich Ludwig, 193
Nipperdey, Thomas, 186, 204

Ochs, Peter, 134, 136
Ortega y Gasset, José, 9
Orts, Auguste, 97

Pabón, Jesús, 4
Pagano, Mario, 231
Panietti, J.-G., 45, 48 n. 17
Paoli, Pasquale, 76
Pérez de Castro, Evaristo, 266
Pericles, 3, 7
Périer, Adolphe, 68
Peris, Martín, widow of, 271
Pestalozzi, Johann Heinrich, 136
Peter-Leopold II, Grand Duke of
    Tuscany, 217, 223
Philip V of Spain, 287
Pignatelli di Bisaccia family, 231, 235
Pirenne, Henri, 91
Pius VII (Barnaba Niccolò Maria Luigi
    Chiaramonti), 202, 222, 225
Planert, Ute, 148, 169 n.*
Plato, 71
Pocock, John Greville Agard, 315
Pondeville (Special commissioner,
    Petten), 115
Portalis, Jean Etienne Marie, 324 n. 37
Portillo Valdés, José Maria, 15, 282
Prina, Giuseppe, 210, 211, 212, 213, 214
Prince of Asturias, *see* Ferdinand VII of
    Spain

Quaglia, Siste, 219, 220
Quintana, Manuel José, 262

Rambaud, Jacques, 229
Rao, Anna-Maria, 227
Rapport, Michael, 5, 7, 9, 10, 88
Réal, Pierre-François, 115
Regnier, Etienne Joseph, 92
Reinhard, Charles Frédéric, 173
Reinhard, Hans von, 136, 139
Reitzenstein, Sigismund von, 146
Rials, Stéphane, 324 nn. 29, 36, 325 n.
    40, 326 n. 49
Riba, Mercader, 4, 6
Ricard, Gabriel-Joseph-Xavier, 61
Rivera Indarte, José, 283
Robespierre, Maximilien de, 126, 273,
    278, 280
Roederer, Pierre-Louis, 30, 72
Rosas, José Manuel, 283
Rosenvallon, Pierre, 325 n. 40
Rousseau, Jean-Jacques, 16, 70, 71, 72,
    73, 74, 75, 76, 286, 291, 317

Rowe, Michael, 5, 10, 11, 12, 109, 123,
    162, 167
Ruffo, Fabrizio, 201
Ruffo di Bagnara family, 234
Ruffo di Scilla family, 234

Sahlins, Marshal, 3
Saluzzo di Corigliano family, 234
San Carlos, 2nd Duke of (José Miguel
    de Carvajal-Vargas y Manrique de
    Lara), 264
Sarasola, Ignacio Fernández, 260, 261
Sardino, Fernández, 273
Sartoretti, Thierry, 133
Savary, Jean-Marie René, 36 n. 21, 119,
    122 n. 31
Schama, Simon, 100
Scharnhorst, Gerhard von, 189
Schill, Ferdinand von, 146, 160, 166,
    168, 170
Schimmelpenninck, Rutger Jan, 103, 109
Schneider, Anton, 154
Schuckmann, Friedrich von, 193
Schulenburg-Bodendorf, Comte de, 177,
    178, 184 n. 24
Scotti-Douglas family, 223
Selwyn, Pamela, 195 n.*
Sémonville, Charles louis Huguet,
    Marquis de, 101
Senbrant, Henri, 93
Serra di Gerace family, 234
Servan, Joseph, 28
Sieyès, Emmanuel Joseph, 21, 27, 31,
    32, 314
Siméon, Joseph Jérôme, 181
Soult, Jean de Dieu, 8, 305, 309, 312 n. 18
Speitkamp, Winfried, 168
Spiroux (President of the tribunal at
    Huy), 92
Stadion, Johann Philipp von, 151
Stauber, Reinhard, 241
Stein, Heinrich Friedrich Karl
    Reichsfreiherr vom und zum, 186,
    188, 189, 191, 195
Stendhal (Henri Beyle), 7, 59
Stoffa family, 222
Strang, Michael, ix
Strongoli, Prince (Francesco Pignatelli),
    231
Süssenberg, Janez Baselli von, 244

Taine, Hippolyte, 66
Talleyrand-Perigord, Charles Maurice
    de, 3, 21, 31, 33, 72, 101, 103, 139,
    257, 317
Thoral, Marie-Cécile, 8
Thucydides, 3
Tocco dei Montemiletto family, 235
Tocqueville, Alexis de, 2, 66, 296
Todorov, Nicola, 173
Toreno, 6th Count of (José Marcelino
    Queipo de Llano), 265
Toussaint-Louverture, Pierre
    Dominique, 44
Trifone, Romualdo, 232
Tulard, Jean, 6

Vadillo, José Manuel de, 282, 283
Van de Walle (Public prosecutor in the
    Lys), 97
van den Ende, Adriaan, 103
van der Burg, Martijn, 4, 5, 6, 7, 9
van der Linden, Joannes, 104
van Maanen, Cornelis Felix, 105, 106, 114
Varela Suanzes-Carpegna, Joaquín, 267
Vattel, Emmerich de, 289, 292 n. 15
Vázquez, widow of, 271
Vélez, priest, 279
Verhaegen, Paul, 91, 96, 97, 98, 99
Victor Amadeus III of Sardinia, 201
Vigneron, Philippe, 89, 97 n. 3

Viktor, Anton, 154
Villani, Pasquale, 232, 233
Visceglia, Maria Antonietta, 235
Vodnik, Valentin, 246, 247
Voltaire (François-Marie Arouet), 72
Vonck, Jean-François, 85

Walker, Mack, 124
Wattenwyl, Niklaus Rudolf von, 139
Weinmann, Barbara, 133
Wellesley, Arthur, *see* Wellington,
    Duke of
Wellesley-Pole, William, 311 n. 2
Wellington, Duke of, 23, 258, 259, 311
    n. 2
Westphalen, Ludwig von, 179
William I of Orange, 5, 87, 100, 102,
    108, 109
William V of Orange, 86, 102
Winspeare, Davide, 231
Wittgenstein, Ludwig, 128
Woloch, Isser, 3, 109, 207
Wood, Gordon, 315
Woolf, Stuart, 4, 5, 6, 108, 109, 161

Zavala, Lorenzo, 282
Zelli, Raffaele, 246, 247
Zimmer, Oliver, 133
Zois, Sigismund Baron von, 250
Zurlo, Giuseppe, 231, 232